P9-CNH-111
FORT WORTH PUBLIC
3 1668 01870 1471

The Southern League

Baseball in Dixie ❖ 1885-1994

By Bill O'Neal

EAKIN PRESS ★ Austin, Texas

FIRST EDITION

Copyright © 1994
By Bill O'Neal

Published in the United States of America
By Eakin Press
A Division of Sunbelt Media, Inc.
P.O. Box 90159 ★ Austin, Texas

ALL RIGHTS RESERVED. No part of this book may be
reproduced in any form without written permission from the publisher, except for brief passages included in a review appearing in
a newspaper or magazine.

ISBN 0-89015-952-1

Library of Congress Cataloging-in-Publication Data:

O'Neal, Bill, 1942–
    The Southern League : baseball in Dixie, 1885–1994 / by Bill O'Neal. —
1st ed.
        p.   cm.
    Includes bibliographical references (p.   ) and index.
    ISBN 0-89015-952-1 : $17.95
    1. Southern League — History. 2. Minor League baseball — South (U.S.) —
History. I. Title.
GV875.S675O53   1994
796.357'64'0975 — dc20
                                                        93-47554
                                                        CIP

For Karon,

with loving gratitude.

Contents

Foreword

During my boyhood in Birmingham I spent many happy hours at Rickwood Field, cheering for the Barons of the Southern Association. As a player in the 1950s, I wore the uniform of Columbia, Savannah and Macon in the SALLY League and of Mobile and Nashville of the Southern Association. In 1978 I managed Chattanooga of the Southern League, and since 1980 it has been my privilege to serve as president of the Southern League.

Because of my lifelong association with professional baseball in the South, I have been deeply grateful for the opportunity to serve as Southern League president. Indeed, when I played in SALLY and Southern ballparks during the 1950s, I never dreamed that one day I would preside over the successor to these historic leagues, and my duties have been a source of immense personal pleasure.

Throughout my tenure as Southern League president, my greatest thrill has been to witness the continual parade of players, managers, coaches, umpires, trainers, and club officials from the SL to the big leagues. Their success is a testimony to the high quality of Southern League operations. Furthermore, when I became president, Southern League franchises were selling for the approximate sum of $10,000. Today those same franchises are valued at $3.5 million, and the 1993 season witnessed the highest total attendance in Southern League history — more than 2.4 million. This marked the third consecutive year that SL attendance has surpassed two million. Fans throughout the South have discovered economical, professional, wholesome, family-oriented entertainment available at our stadiums.

Baseball historian Bill O'Neal has traced the roots of the Southern League back more than a century, and we are proud that his history of our circuit is available during the thirtieth anniversary of the modern SL. We were pleased to help him compile the official history of the Southern League, and we hope that you will visit a Southern League ballpark as often as possible.

JIMMY BRAGAN
Southern League President

Acknowledgments

My first Southern League contact was with President Jimmy Bragan, who had been a boyhood fan of the Birmingham Barons, a player in the SALLY and the Southern Association, a club official in the Southern League, and who has served as SL president for nearly a decade and a half. This knowledgeable gentleman responded enthusiastically to my proposed history of the Southern League, and for the past year he has offered me every cooperation. Jimmy and his lovely wife, Sarah, who serves as secretary at the SL headquarters in Trussville, patiently endured a long interview in their offices and loaned me invaluable materials. Jimmy plans to retire at the close of the 1994 season, and the loss of an old-time baseball man with his background and outlook will be irreplaceable to professional baseball in general and the Southern League in particular.

In Carthage I was assisted throughout this project by my wife, Karon, who computerized the manuscript from my handwritten copy and who offered useful tips on word selection. Karon has provided these services with other books of mine, and without her capable and selfless assistance I could not have met the deadline for this project. During the long months of writing, my youngest daughter, Causby, cheerfully performed numerous office chores that facilitated my tasks. Award-winning sportswriter Ted Leach, editor of the *Panola Watchman* and a valued friend, once again provided expert assistance in preparing photographs. Also in Carthage I met a recent veteran of the SL, Scott Bryant, who offered numerous insights about current playing conditions around the league. A former student of mine who pitched impressively for Birmingham in 1993, Robert Ellis, provided similar insights, and his charming bride, Jodi, also a former student, went to the trouble of digging up photos on short notice.

Red Underhill of Jacksonville took the initiative of contacting me by telephone and offering his assistance to a stranger. During the following months I learned that Red has a wealth of friends, and he willingly enlisted a great many of his acquaintances on my behalf. Red made countless long-distance phone calls and wrote detailed letters while arranging for photographs and other materials to be sent to me, and I am deeply grateful to this benevolent man.

The National Baseball Hall of Fame Library in Cooperstown provided a large amount of materials essential to this project, and I especially appreciate the efforts of Gary Van Allen. I also am grateful to Melissa Locke Roberts of Austin, who edited this book with her usual expertise and sensitivity to the author's goals.

During a long research trip to the cities of the Southern League I was aided by many gracious Southerners, as well as by equally gracious transplanted Yankees who are employees of the SL clubs. No one provided more help than Frank Buccieri, director of public relations of the Birmingham Barons, who opened his vast files to me, then permitted me to borrow more than a score of excellent photos. In Memphis Patty Haynes, receptionist in the Chicks' office, was friendly and cooperative. At the offices of the Huntsville Stars I was aided by Patrick Nichol, director of public relations, and by former big leaguer Don Mincher, who was Huntsville's first GM and currently is director of community relations.

When John Dittrich was GM of the Calgary Cannons, he provided exceptional courtesies to me during my research into the Pacific Coast League. Currently he is GM of the Columbus RedStixx, and once again he made available items I could not otherwise have obtained. At the Washington Memorial Library in Macon I was the beneficiary of the unusual resourcefulness of archivist Peer Ravnan. Mark Lee, Savannah's director of group sales, secured materials for me in the Cardinal front office.

I was overwhelmed with assistance at Five County Stadium, home of the Carolina Mudcats. Immensely proud of their new team, there was a group effort on my behalf from those present during my visit: Bob Licht, director of broadcasting; Jackie DiPrimo, office manager; Duke Sanders, director of sales and PA announcer; and Angel Branoff, director of community relations. Karl Lyles, Charlotte's director of media relations, offered various materials and conducted me on a tour of magnificent Knights Castle.

In Asheville I was aided by assistant GM Gary Saunders and concessions manager Jane Lentz, who took the trouble to open the souvenir shop so that I could purchase items useful to research. At Greenville I received helpful insights and materials from ticket manager Jimmy Moore and from Tracey Vandiver, director of food services. On a rainy morning in Knoxville Jennifer Jones was the only staff member on duty, but she courteously took time to deal with my requests. In the front office at Chattanooga, JoLynn Drake was equally courteous and helpful.

The late Carl Sawatski, longtime president of the Texas League, regaled me in Little Rock with tales of his days as a feared slugger in the Southern Association. In Nashville I was assisted by owner-president Larry Schmittou, executive vice-president George Dyce, director of publicity Jim Ballweg, secretary Jean Carney, and part owner Richard Sterban, the remarkable bass singer with the Oak Ridge Boys and a lifelong baseball enthusiast. In Evansville I encountered Carl M. Wallace, a former club owner who dropped everything to tour me around Bosse Field and to guide me through his scrapbooks and photo collections. Jerry Fortuna of Evington, Virginia, generously provided me with materials about baseball in Lynchburg. Billy Hitchcock, former major league player and manager who served as second president of the Southern League, was courteous and immensely informative during a lengthy telephone interview.

I received resourceful cooperation from staff members at public libraries I visited in the following Southern cities: Atlanta, Charlotte, Chattanooga, Columbus, Greenville, Huntsville, Knoxville, Memphis, Nashville, Orlando, Savannah, and Shreveport. Dedicated professionals in these libraries embraced my project and produced local history files, faded newspapers, microfilm, and miscellaneous other items that immeasurably enriched this book.

As I recall the numerous individuals who aided me throughout this project, I hope that my book will prove worthy in some degree of their efforts.

An editorial from
the Nashville *Daily Press & Times,*
October 22, 1867

Base Ball. — There is something a little won-
derful in the enthusiasm which our "national
game" has excited among all classes of people, in
all parts of our country. Beginning in our eastern
cities, it rapidly became popular, and organiza-
tions sprang up with the facility of mushrooms,
until no village or hamlet in the country, east or
west [or *south* — Author], was without its base ball
club . . . .
    Young men were fascinated with the sport;
older men encouraged it as promotion of hard
muscles and a good digestion. Teachers of morals
rejoiced that an amusement had been found which
broke none of the commandments and permitted
the spiritual sapling to pursue a perpendicular
growth. Merchants, bankers, and shopkeepers
closed their establishments, and gave their clerks
a holiday on Saturday afternoon, that they might
drive dyspepsia from their lank stomachs, and the
drowsy film from their cadaverous eyes. The ladies
lent the magnetism of the their presence to the
game, and through blistering hours exposed their
carefully nursed complexions to the bronzing sun
in their eagerness to witness the skill and prowess
of their brothers and lovers.

1885–1899

The Original Southern League

The Southern League originated during the outburst of athletic enthusiasm that surged across America late in the nineteenth century. Baseball in its primitive form was played in Southern communities prior to the Civil War, and Confederate soldiers learned the game in army camps throughout the long years of conflict. After the war, returning veterans brought baseball to every corner of Dixie (Union veterans similarly introduced the sport throughout the North). Southerners embraced the new game enthusiastically: young men organized amateur nines to take on rival clubs; boys played ceaselessly on cow pastures and vacant city lots; colleges and high schools established teams; and standout athletes began to be paid to play on semi-pro and professional squads.

As baseball became America's first team sport, nine teams formed the National Association of Professional Base-Ball Players, and five years later this organization was superseded by an eight-team National League. In 1882 a second "major league" was founded, the American Association, and the Union Association was organized two seasons later. Three "minor leagues" commenced play in 1877, and by 1884, when three major leagues were in operation, there were eight minor leagues.

Most of the junior professional franchises, like the major league clubs, were located in the industrialized, urbanized northeast. But in 1885 civic leaders and baseball enthusiasts in eight Southern cities formed the Southern League of Professional Clubs, and Alexander Proudfit of Macon agreed to serve as president. The Southern League was the first professional circuit to operate in the South, and the founders ambitiously planned a schedule of more than 100 games per club. Henry W. Grady, managing editor of the Atlanta *Constitution*, was elected league president. Grady ran the affairs of the Southern League from his newspaper office, and enthusiastically published SL news on the front page of the *Constitution*.

The Southern League of 1885 was the first minor league to launch a 100-game season, although last-place Birmingham (17–64) could not complete its schedule. Columbus (42–39) also played just 81 games, and next-to-last Chattanooga (30–59) staged 89 contests. But Atlanta, Nashville, and Memphis played over 90 games each, while Augusta and Macon played 104 and 106 games respectively.

Atlanta (60–31) edged Augusta (68–36) for the first Southern League pennant. Leading performers for the Atlantas included outfielder Walt Goldsby (.305 with 89 runs scored), shortstop John Cahill (.295 with 90 runs in 90 games), and catcher-outfielder George McVey (.290). Goldsby, Cahill and McVey, like most of their other teammates, had played or soon would play in the major leagues. All three Atlanta pitchers, all three catchers, and every position player except the center fielder (who hit a meager .177) and first baseman (.210) were past or future big leaguers.

The batting champ was Nashville first baseman Leonard Sowders (.309), who went up to Baltimore in 1886. Macon second baseman Reddy Mack led the SL in runs scored (.280 with 91 runs in 91 games), then went on to log six big league seasons, batting .410 for Louisville in 1887. Indeed, most of the leading Southern League players would see major league experience, and "kranks" (fans) in the SL cities quickly came to expect quality baseball in the wooden ballparks around the circuit. Salaries generally ranged between $50 and $60 per month, although top pitchers and catchers sometimes earned $75 monthly. (Of course, big league salaries also were unimpressive.)

Bill Hart

Bill Hart was a 19-year rookie with Chattanooga in 1885. The Lookouts' only other hurler, Toad Ramsey, sometimes disappeared, and Hart would have to pitch three or four days in a row. Once he pitched a four-game series and won each day. Hart worked 39 games (13–25) and, like other pitchers of the era, filled in as a right fielder or pinch hitter as needed in 20 other games. The next year he pitched for Memphis, then went up to the big leagues. He finished his career in the Southern Association, with Little Rock in 1907 (13–10), 1908 (13–16) and 1909 (15–11 at the age of 44), and with Chattanooga in 1910 (5–4).

The game witnessed from the plank grandstands of the Southern League resembled fast-pitch softball of contemporary times, since the pitching distance was just fifty feet and deliveries were underhanded. But the bases were 90 feet apart, although first and third were outside the foul lines (they were moved inside the playing field for 1886). Playing diamonds were not meticulously manicured and fielders' gloves were small and thin, which rendered fielding chances less than automatic and often treacherous. Catchers were not armored with protective equipment, and stationed themselves far behind the batters. The solitary umpire therefore called balls and strikes from a distance of 40 feet or more behind home plate, and when there were baserunners he moved behind the pitcher. Hitters had to take seven balls before being awarded first base, but could order pitch-

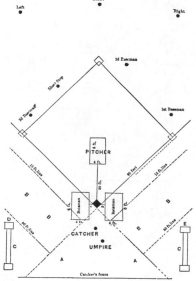

The "Correct Diagram of a Ball Ground" for 1885, the inaugural season of the Southern League. The pitcher's box was only 50 feet from the plate.

ers to throw high or low strikes. In 1885 hitters were allowed to use bats flattened on one side, but this experiment was abandoned after one season.

General enthusiasm demanded another year of Southern League baseball. Although Birmingham and Columbus did not return for 1886, the other six cities from 1885 fielded teams, along with Savannah and Charleston. Atlanta stormed to a second consecutive championship, although increasing competitiveness aroused widespread controversy: "The rather questionable tactics adopted by a few of the clubs towards the close [of the pennant race] made it not only a matter of much uncertainty, but also of doubted fairness."

Southern League Ballparks

ATLANTA

Peters Park. Built in 1885 at North Avenue and West Peachtree Street. There was a small wooden grandstand, bleachers, and a high wire fence.

Brisbane Park. Located in south Atlanta at Cumley, Glenn and Ira streets, Brisbane was used for SL play in 1892, 1893 and 1896.

Athletic Grounds. Consolidated Railway built the Athletic

Grounds adjacent to their tracks for the 1894 and 1895 seasons.

BIRMINGHAM

The Slag Pile. Built in the 1880s at 14th Street and First Avenue North. The grandstand could accommodate only 600 kranks, but beyond the plank outfield fence was the slag pile of the Alice Furnace, and many spectators perched on this handy mound.

CHATTANOOGA

Stanton Field. Built in the 1880s where the Stivers Lumber Company later was erected.

DALLAS

Gaston Park. Built in the 1890s on the Texas State Fair Grounds, about where the Music Hall is today.

MACON

Mulberry Park. The oldest grounds in town were located at the foot of Mulberry Street on the Central City side of Fifth. By the time Macon became a charter member of the SL, the grandstand was covered and a plank fence surrounded the park, although trees grew inside the fence.

Daisy Park. When SL play resumed in 1892 a new ballpark was erected at *Central City Park.* (The facility initially was named after Mayor S. B. "Daisy" Price, but soon became known as Central City Park.) The diamond was on the site of the old hippodrome, which was cut in half for use as an "immense" semicircular grandstand seating 4,000. Daisy Park was 350 feet wide by 450 feet long. The foul lines each were only 250 feet long, but the fence jutted sharply toward right center and left center, and center field was 400 feet away. A large blackboard served as scoreboard, and a wire screen went up in front of the grandstand. Grandstand seats cost 25¢, and bleacher space was 15¢ or 25¢ for two. The grandstand finally was destroyed by fire in 1926, and Luther Williams Field went up on the same site three years later.

MEMPHIS

Olympic Park. Built in the 1880s at the later site of the Memphis Area Transit Authority Bus Terminal.

NASHVILLE

Athletic Park. Built at the Sulphur Spring Bottom, where baseball had been played in Nashville since the 1860s, Athletic Park was bounded by 4th and 5th avenues and by Jackson and Summer streets. The plank grandstand for many years was located in the northeast corner of this block, and when the diamond was relocated to the southwest corner in 1926, the outline of the original diamond could be traced in the new center field.

NEW ORLEANS

Crescent City Base Ball Park. Built in 1880 at Banks and Carrollton streets (across from modern-day Jesuit High School). Renovated and enlarged to accommodate 5,000 kranks in 1887, and later was known as Sportsman's Park and Athletic Park.

The 1886 Atlantas (64–28, .695) were sparked by such future big leaguers as batting champ Mark Cline (.353 with 56 stolen bases), third baseman Dennis Lyons (.316), stolen base leader Blondy Purcell (.267 with 72 SB, and the best fielding percentage among SL left fielders), and pitchers John Schafer and Richard Conway, who won 22 and 20 games respectively. Savannah right-hander Henry O'Day led the SL with 26 victories, while righty Ed Knouff won 24 games for Memphis and struck out 390 batters. Again the Southern League had showcased talented players and helped to spread the swelling enthusiasm for baseball throughout the South.

As the 1887 season approached, two-time champ Atlanta dropped out of the Southern League, along with the bottom three clubs of 1886, Augusta, Macon, and Chattanooga. But Charleston, Memphis, Nashville, and Savannah again fielded teams, while Mobile and New Orleans joined the SL for the first time. Play began on Monday, April 18, but Mobile staggered to a 5–19 mark, then disbanded. Savannah's team was no better, halting operations after a 7–27 record. Although Nashville enjoyed a winning team (34–30), shaky finances forced club owners to drop out, leaving only New Orleans, Charleston, and Memphis with teams. But club backers in Birmingham were found, and the Southern League played on through October 11 with four teams.

During the 1887 season, batters no longer could order up high or low pitches. However, compensation was more than provided by two new rules: the number of strikes was raised to four, and bases on balls were counted as base hits. These experiments were dropped after one year, but, predictably, batting averages soared in 1887.

Charley "The Count" Campau, a 23-year-old rookie with Savannah and New Orleans, led the league in stolen bases and triples (.404, 18 3B, 17 HR, and 115 SB in 109 G), while the batting champ and run leader was Memphis first baseman Wally Andrews (.413, 135 R and 82 SB in 97 G). Other spectacular offensive performances were turned in by Charleston first baseman J. E. Powell (.390 with 84 SB); longtime major league outfielder Big Jim Clinton (.386), who roamed left field in 1887 for Nashville and Birmingham; New Orleans first baseman Jumbo Cartwright (.381 with 179 hits and 108 SB in 108 G); Charleston left fielder Mouse Glenn (.362 with 117 R and 98 SB in 96 G); and New Orleans manager-right fielder Abner Powell (.354 with 104 R and 89 SB in 98 G).

The Count

Charles Columbus "Count" Campau was a native of Detroit who did not enter professional baseball until the age of 23, but went on to play 19 seasons. His rookie year in the Southern League was spectacular. Playing 109 games for Savannah and New Orleans in 1887, he led the SL in stolen bases and triples (.404, 115 SB, 18 3B), while banging out 17 home runs. The next year the 5'11, 160-pound outfielder went up to Detroit of the National League, but resurfaced in New Orleans during the last half of the 1892 season (.331 in 40 games). Campau returned to the Pelicans in 1893 (.337), then played for New Orleans the next year (.299 in 65 games) before returning to the National League. He finished his career with Binghamton of the New York State League from 1901–1905, but he played nine games with New Orleans in 1903.

Count Campau became the first player to record 100 doubles, 100 triples and 100 homers in the minor leagues (he finished 368-172-136 and .293, including 79-28-40 in the SL). He made his home in the Crescent City, dying in New Orleans in 1938 at the age of 74.

Eleven players hit above .350, while over 30 athletes batted more than .300. Memphis first baseman Walter Andrews belted 28 home runs, the most in any professional league in 1887.

New Orleans charged to the championship in its first SL season and quickly became the bellwether franchise of the Southern League. Amateur baseball was hugely popular in the Crescent City by the 1870s, and in the 1880s the New Orleans Base Ball Park was built to attract barnstorming professional teams. The

Southern League Pelicans regularly drew crowds numbering in the thousands, even for weekday afternoon games. "Sportsman's Park" was renamed and expanded to seat 5,000, but on Sundays there was standing-room-only.

Ab Powell, who had spent two seasons in the majors as a pitcher-outfielder-infielder-catcher, was the Pelican player-manager. Because of frequent rains in New Orleans, Powell devised the rain check, by which kranks would keep their ticket stubs and be readmitted without charge to a future game following a rainout. Another Powell innovation was Ladies' Day, a designated weekday on which ladies would be admitted free to the ballpark. Women, too, began to become kranks in significant numbers, and Ladies' Day as well as the rain check began to catch on throughout the Southern League. Indeed, both innovations became standard with professional teams everywhere.

In 1888 only the four cities which had finished the previous season were willing to field Southern League teams. Birmingham, Charleston, Memphis, and New Orleans opened play on Saturday, April 7. Despite a miserable season in 1887, Birmingham put together a club in 1888 that was the class of the SL.

The inflated batting averages of 1887 plummeted in 1888 as the seven-ball walk was reduced to five, the number of strikes returned from four to three, and a walk no longer counted as a base hit. But nine players still hit above .300, and the top three offensive performances were impressive for any year: New Orleans center fielder John Sneed was the batting champ (.354 with 46 SB in 39 G); the run leader was Memphis right fielder Monk Cline (.339 with 46 R in 49 G); and close behind was Birmingham first baseman Tom Lynch (.331). New Orleans first sacker Moose Werden (.277) led the SL with 65 stolen bases, five homers and 56 games played.

Sneed, Cline, Lynch and Werden were former or future big leaguers, and so were many other SL players as the talent level remained high. But a four-team league does not offer enough variety to sustain fan interest through a long season. After three months of play in 1888 the clubs were in financial trouble, and early in July the Southern League halted play. Teams had played from 48 to 57 games apiece.

The Texas League staged its inaugural season in 1888, and

New Orleans had sent representatives to the organizational meetings. By the time the Southern League folded in July 1888,

Familiar Faces

During the first season of the Southern League George McVey played catcher and outfield for Atlanta and hit .290. In 1886 McVey wore the Nashville uniform, then moved to New Orleans for the next two years. During these same inaugural seasons Walt Goldsby roamed left field for the Atlantas in 1885 (.305), Nashville in 1886 (.277), and Birmingham in 1888 (.308). Leonard Sowders won the first Southern League batting title (.309) while holding down first base for the Atlantas, then moved to Nashville for 1886 (.284).

Baseball fans enjoy seeing familiar faces in their home uniforms and in opponents' lineups. Numerous players performed season after season in the Southern League, which allowed kranks to anticipate the performance possibilities of familiar athletes. Outfielder-infielder-pitcher Robert Gilks was a 17-year-old rookie with Chattanooga in 1885, then played for Mobile in 1892 and 1893 (.342). Dixie fans saw him again after the Southern Association was formed: he spent four seasons with Shreveport, 1903–1906, and ended his career with Savannah and Charleston in 1909 at the age of 42. Another versatile athlete, Sam LaRoque, played every position except pitcher and catcher for Nashville and Savannah in 1893 (.295) and 1894, and for Birmingham and Memphis of the SA in 1901 (.308) and 1902 (.288). Bill Hart pitched for Memphis and Chattanooga in 1885 and 1886, and for Little Rock in 1907, 1908 and 1909, before spending a final season with Chattanooga in 1910 at the age of 45. First sacker Moose Werden played for Memphis in 1885, New Orleans in 1888, where he was the stolen base and home run leader, then returned to Memphis for 1903. Piggy Ward played first, second and outfield for New Orleans in 1889 (.301) and 1893 (.336), while heavy hitting outfielder Joe Katz (.336 lifetime) played for Chattanooga in 1893 (.364) and Birmingham in 1896 (.359).

First baseman Lew Whistler played for New Orleans in 1894, then became a player-manager with the Chattanooga/Mobile club the next year, winning the batting title with a spectacular performance (.404). In the SA he was a player-manager with Chattanooga in 1901 (.344), Montgomery in 1903 (.305 with a league-leading 18 homers), and Memphis the next two seasons. Such men brought continuity to early pro ball in the South.

the Texas League also was in trouble. Two teams had disbanded by July, leaving only Dallas, Houston, Galveston, and San Antonio to sponsor clubs. New Orleans player-manager Ab Powell led his Pelicans to Texas to join the faltering Texas League. The Pelicans stayed in Texas for a month, compiling a 15–10 record—the second best winning percentage of the Texas League season. But by early September, Houston and Galveston had dropped out, and Dallas, San Antonio, and New Orleans decided to cease operations.

Macon's 1892 Opener

When the Southern League resumed play in 1892, backers in Macon decided to erect a new ballpark at Central City Park and field a team. The hippodrome was cut in half and used as a semicircular grandstand with a central entrance between the two halves. This cost-cutting device kept expenses for the new facility to "several hundred dollars." The "immense grand stand" seated 4,000 kranks. To the right of the entrance were dressing rooms, and "refreshment rooms" were "fitted up" under the grandstand. A separate entrance to the right of the grandstand admitted vehicles.

The contractor did not begin altering the hippodrome into a grandstand until early April, ten days before the season opener against Atlanta. But it was thought that the hippodrome transformation would take only "three or four days to do," whereupon a workforce would commence "grading the park" in time for the opening game.

Preparations were finished shortly before game time at 3:30 P.M. The third base grandstand was reserved for ladies and men who escorted ladies. The first base grandstand accommodated men, "and in this part only will smoking be allowed." The "Atlantians" marched onto the diamond for 15 minutes of pregame warmup. Then the blue and gray-clad Macon players filed out of their dressing room, paraded in front of the grandstand and reported to the umpire. A telegraph wire was run to the ballpark, permitting the progress of every SL game to be posted on the big blackboard/scoreboard, and at the same time telegraphed reports went onto a bulletin board for kranks in Atlanta. Such information stimulated constant betting throughout game afternoons.

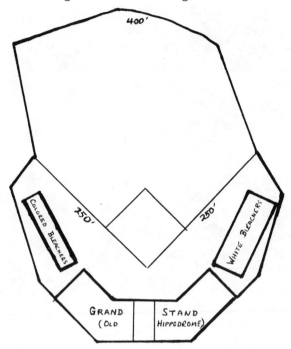

Diagram of Macon's Daisy Park, which opened with the Southern League season of 1892. The 4,000-seat grandstand was fashioned from the old hippodrome, and the foul lines extended only 250 feet from home to the fence.

Despite the dismal results of 1887 and 1888, in the spring of 1889 New Orleans, Atlanta, Chattanooga, and Mobile launched the sixth Southern League season. Ab Powell's Pelicans roared to a 9–2 start, and it quickly became clear that the four-team format again would lead to failure. The SL reorganized, adding clubs from Birmingham, Charleston, and Memphis. But New Orleans continued to dominate, carving up the other six teams at a 34–5 clip. Atlanta dropped out with a losing record, followed by Memphis. Birmingham, shaky with a miserable 4–17 mark, was dropped by the league. With New Orleans unchallenged (43–7 overall) atop a four-team circuit, the surviving clubs again disbanded in mid-season.

"The great Minor League failure of 1889" was the third consecutive early collapse by the Southern League, and the SL could not be revived in 1890 or in 1891. But by 1892 baseball enthu-

Future Hall of Fame outfielder Fred Clarke played for Montgomery in 1893 (.292) and Savannah in 1894 (.311).

siasts and civic leaders in eight Southern cities were prepared to resume SL competition (Montgomery was the sole entrant that had not previously backed an SL franchise). All eight clubs held steady as Chattanooga (52–30) and Montgomery (51–33) battled for first place. After more than 80 games it was decided that a second season would renew fan interest, and this time Birmingham (30–11) and New Orleans (29–12) outdistanced the pack. Birmingham closed play with the best overall record (73–50). Every team played 120 or more games, the longest schedule of any Southern League season to date.

Encouraged by their success, Southern League leaders added four cities for 1893: Augusta, Charleston, Nashville, and Savannah. The twelve-team schedule was drawn up by a young lady who had never seen a game of baseball, and the result was "a very clumsy schedule" which caused problems throughout the season. Another problem came from owners who sold off star players to National League teams during the year, which immediately damaged their teams and angered their fans. Furthermore, with twelve teams in the SL, losing clubs were impossibly far from first place.

A problem for pitchers was the extension of the distance to the plate to 60 feet, 6 inches. For a season or two pitchers had a difficult transition, especially with their curve balls, and hitters benefited accordingly. Memphis outfielder Charles Frank, for example, won the 1893 SL batting crown with a .390 average.

By early June, Birmingham, mired in eleventh place, suffered from demoralized players and fans. When the club disbanded on

---

Cities of the Old Southern League

Eighteen cities fielded franchises in the Southern League during the late nineteenth century. No city participated in every season. (* denotes league champion)

Atlanta (1885*, 1886*, 1889, 1892, 1893, 1894, 1895*, 1896)
Augusta (1885, 1886, 1893)
Birmingham (1885, 1887, 1888*, 1889, 1892*, 1893, 1896)
Charleston (1886, 1887, 1888, 1889, 1893*, 1894)
Chattanooga (1885, 1886, 1892, 1893)
Columbus (1885, 1896)
Dallas (1898, 1899)
Evansville (1895)
Little Rock (1895)
Macon (1885, 1886, 1892, 1893, 1894)
Memphis (1885, 1886, 1887, 1888, 1889, 1892, 1893, 1894*, 1895)
Mobile (1887, 1889, 1892, 1893, 1894, 1895, 1896, 1898, 1899*)
Montgomery (1892, 1893, 1895, 1896, 1898, 1899)
Nashville (1885, 1886, 1887, 1893, 1894, 1895)
New Orleans (1887*, 1888, 1889*, 1892, 1893, 1894, 1895, 1896*, 1898, 1899)
Pensacola (1893)
Savannah (1886, 1887, 1893, 1894)
Shreveport (1898, 1899)

June 10, the league agreed to carry the team through the season. But other problems materialized throughout the SL, and at a special league meeting on July 1, President Hart resigned, turning over $5,500 in league funds. During July three more meetings were called, but sparse attendance indicated a growing indifference among SL leaders.

A split season again had been planned, and Augusta (44–17) was awarded the first half title by the margin of a disputed victory

O1870 1441   FORT WORTH PUBLIC LIBRARY

Another future Hall of Famer, underhanded pitcher Joe McGinnity, broke into pro ball in 1893 with Montgomery (10–19).

over Charleston (the Augustas then nosedived into the cellar during the second half). Birmingham's club was transferred to Pensacola, Florida, but an outbreak of yellow fever quarantined the team for the rest of the season. At the same time Nashville and Chattanooga turned their teams over to the league. But J. B. Nicklin of Chattanooga had been elected SL president, and the league continued to operate both clubs. A spreading economic depression compounded the problems of the SL, and at another special meeting held in Atlanta on Friday, August 11, it was decided to end the season after the games of Saturday, August 12. Macon (21–7) won the second half crown, while Charleston (51–32) compiled the best record over the entire schedule.

On November 6, 1893, club owners from New Orleans, Atlanta, Memphis, Mobile, Nashville, and Savannah met in Chattanooga. J. B. Nicklin agreed to continue as president, and the unwieldy twelve-team format was scrapped. Clubs from Charleston and Augusta were admitted, and the eight teams agreed to pay $500 dues apiece and to guarantee $60 per game to a visiting team.

Connaughton's Catcher's Mitt

Frank Connaughton broke into professional baseball in 1891 as a 22-year-old catcher. He also saw duty at first base, where he used his catcher's mitt. In 1892 he played with Savannah of the Southern League as a catcher, outfielder, second baseman, and shortstop. Fielders' gloves of the era were small and thin with no webbing, so Connaughton wore his mitt into the field. Soon he switched almost exclusively to second and short (he played until the age of 44 in 1913), but he had to give up his catcher's mitt when oversized gloves were prohibited for fielders. Indeed, Connaughton's use of a mitt as an infielder apparently was a major factor in glove size restrictions.

The 1894 schedule was planned to last from Sunday, April 15, through the second week of September. But early in the season several teams began to be plagued by attendance and financial problems. A called meeting was held in Montgomery on June 26, and it was decided to split the season on June 29. After that date Charleston, Macon, Mobile, and Savannah dropped out of the league, while Atlanta, Memphis, Nashville, and New Orleans launched a second season. But a week later the remaining four clubs decided to halt play, and Memphis was awarded the pennant with the best overall record. Manager Frank Graves guided Memphis to victory in the first 12 games, and in 22 of the first 23 contests. The club also won the last eight games of the season, featuring outfielder Ollie Smith (.356) and the SL's best pitcher, ex-big leaguer Jack Wadsworth (16–6 with 110 strikeouts).

Soon baseball men optimistically began planning for 1895. Six veteran Southern League cities sponsored clubs, and new entries from Little Rock and Evansville rounded out an eight-team circuit. But the old instability recurred: "As usual the Southern League had a troublesome season, and practically went to pieces before [the end of the schedule]." In June, Memphis changed owners and Chattanooga turned its team over to the league. The league soon transferred Chattanooga's franchise to Mobile, and in July the new Memphis owners disbanded the club. The league then dropped Little Rock to keep the number of teams even. The six surviving clubs played on to the scheduled end of the season, but the pennant was disputed. Although Atlanta posted the best season record, Nashville protested a number of games, and when these protests were upheld Nashville claimed a controversial championship.

During the 1895 season Lew Whistler ripped out the second highest average (.404) ever posted by a Southern League batting champ. Almost 40 batters hit over .300, including New Orleans first baseman Robert Stafford (.384), Evansville shortstop Oliver Perry Beard (.376), and Nashville left fielder Frank Butler (.371). The run leader was Evansville center fielder C. McFarland (.340), who scored an incredible 149 runs in just 77 games. Atlanta righthander James Callahan led the SL with 23 victories in 28 games, closely followed by 22-game winners Fritz Clausen and Monte McFarland.

In 1896 only six teams opened the season, and Atlanta and Birmingham dropped out in June. Columbus, Mobile, Montgomery, and New Orleans struggled on for another month, but halted play before reaching 100 decisions. New Orleans won the pennant behind outfielder-manager Ab Powell (.318 with 94 R and

Chattanooga's 1895 club soon transferred to Mobile, but first baseman Lew Whistler (seated third from left with big mustache) hit .404 and won the batting title.

Team Nicknames

Team nicknames in the 1880s often were simple pluralizations: "Atlantas," "Birminghams," etc. Nineteenth-century clubs usually changed nicknames often, sometimes every year, although New Orleans settled on its traditional sobriquet, "Pelicans," by the 1880s. The best nickname of this era had to belong to the Memphis "Fever Germs," with the Mobile "Swamp Angels" claiming runner-up honors.

Atlanta
Atlantas (1885–86, 1889, 1894)
Firecrackers (1892)
Windjammers (1893)
Crackers (1896–97)

Augusta
Browns (1885–86)
Electricians/Dudes (1893)

Birmingham
Babies (1887)
Maroons (1888–89)
Grays (1892)
Pets (1893)
Rustlers (1896)

Charleston
Seagulls (1886–89, 1893–94)

Chattanooga
Lookouts (1885–86)
Chatts (1892)
Warriors (1893)

Columbus
Babies (1896)

Dallas
Scrappers (1898)

Evansville
Blackbirds (1895)

Little Rock
Travelers/Rose Buds (1895)

Macon
Central City (1892–93)
Hornets (1894)

Memphis
Grays (1885–86)
Reds (1887–89)
Giants (1892–95)
Fever Germs (1893)

Mobile
Swamp Angels (1887)
Bears (1889)
Blackbirds (1892–93, 1898–99)
Bluebirds (1894)

Montgomery
Lambs (1892)
Colts (1893)
Grays (1895–96)
Senators (1898–99)

Nashville
Americans (1885–86)
Blues (1887)
Tigers (1893–94)
Seraphs (1895)

New Orleans
Pelicans (1880s & 90s)

Savannah
Electrics (1893)
Modocs (1894)

Shreveport
Tigers (1899)

60 SB), who led the SL in runs and stolen bases; a shortstop-outfielder named Huston (.346); and a fine starting trio of pitchers that included victory and strikeout leader Tom Smith (22–12), a hurler named Carl (19–9), and Gus McGinnis (17–7).

The Southern League could not reorganize for 1897, but in 1898 club backers in several traditional SL cities attempted to launch a schedule. In April 1898, however, the United States entered into a war with Spain, and public preoccupation with the first foreign war in half a century dealt a hard blow to professional baseball. The Southern League sputtered to a quick halt in 1898, but the next season New Orleans, Mobile, Montgomery, and Shreveport tried again to revive the SL.

The 1899 schedule opened at Mobile as the visiting Montgomerys beat the home team, 8 to 1. The following Thursday New Orleans traveled to Mobile and won, 4 to 2, while at Montgomery the same day the Shreveports fell, 10 to 4. With this sporadic schedule the four clubs played for a month. But by May, Montgomery had the only losing record and dropped out. Dallas assumed the franchise and the SL limped along for another few weeks with a four-team format.

New Orleans boasted the tallest player in baseball, pitcher Arthur Switzer, who was called "The Giant" and "The Seven-Foot Hurler" (he was variously reported to be 6'10 to 7'4). Switzer was

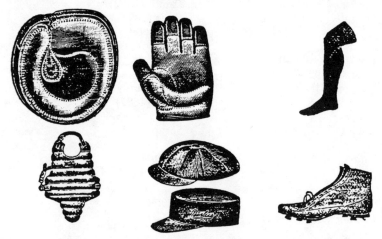

Equipment late in the 1890s included sturdy catchers' mitts. Fielders' gloves, however, were flimsy with no webbing. The "Boston" style of cap was popular, but some teams chose the flat-topped "Chicago" style. Shoes were high-tops, while colored stockings were pulled above the knees.

the leading pitcher in the SL, but Mobile ran away from the rest of the league. By early June, Mobile lost interest, and so did the fans of New Orleans. On June 4 these two clubs disbanded, which ended the season.

No support could be found to reorganize for 1900, so the Southern League did not play the last season of the nineteenth century. Despite failed franchises, abbreviated seasons, and no play at all in 1891, 1892, 1897, and 1900, during the last decade and a half of the nineteenth century the Southern League had created a keen appetite for quality baseball among the kranks of Dixie.

Although the Southern League ceased to exist after 1899, in 1901 the Southern Association was organized by backers in many of the old SL cities. Within the next few years other leagues were founded in smaller southern cities, but for more than six decades the finest baseball in the South was staged by the SA. When the historic Southern Association folded after the 1961 season, the gap soon was filled by another storied southern circuit, the South Atlantic Association — popularly known as the "SALLY."

The SALLY was a Class A circuit, and when the Class AA Southern Association disbanded, only two Double A leagues remained in operation. In 1963 the SALLY was elevated to Class AA status, and the following year the new Double A circuit was renamed the Southern League. During the ensuing three decades the modern Southern League expanded to ten clubs and brought quality baseball to a score of the leading cities of the South, thus carrying on the tradition established by the original Southern League in the late nineteenth century.

1901–1961

The Southern Association

1901–1909

Although the Southern League ceased to operate after 1899, baseball was more popular than ever by the turn of the century. The Southern League had so deeply implanted the attractions of quality professional baseball in the cities of the South that the creation of another circuit was inevitable.

In the fall of 1900 Abner Powell of New Orleans, Newt Fisher of Nashville, and Charley Frank of Memphis began to organize a league that would become known as the Southern Association (although for years fans often used the familiar "Southern League"). Powell, Fisher and Frank each had played big league ball and had played and managed in the Southern League, and now they tried to revive league play in Dixie by lining up clubs in traditional SL cities. New Orleans had logged ten seasons in the SL, and year in and year out had fielded the old league's cornerstone franchise. Memphis had spent nine seasons in the SL; Birmingham was a seven-year veteran of SL play; Nashville had participated for six seasons; Chattanooga for four. Little Rock had fielded a team in the SL only in 1895, but like Memphis, Birmingham, Nashville, Chattanooga and Little Rock, would go on to play Southern Association ball for half a century or more.

Shreveport had participated in the SL for two seasons but had gravitated to the nearby Texas League; the Texas League did not operate in 1900 and 1901, however, and Shreveport placed a team in the new circuit. The other charter member was Selma, which fielded a club only in the inaugural season. Powell, Fisher and Frank offered Atlanta a franchise for no charge, and only when no backers could be found in this key Southern city was a club placed in Selma. But fan reaction was so receptive to the new league that Atlanta joined up in 1902, maintaining a Southern Association franchise for the next 60 years.

The SA founders decreed that there would be 12 players on each roster, with a monthly salary cap of $1,200. No star earned as much as $100 per month; Doc Wiseman, for example, played right field for Nashville and hit .365, for which he was paid $85 monthly. Teams traveled by day coach or slept two per berth, while staying at the cheapest hotels.

Reed W. Kent was supposed to serve as league president in 1901, but he backed out shortly after the season opened (it was rumored that he "defaulted with all the available cash on hand") and was succeeded by W. J. Boles. By the end of the year Chattanooga's J. B. Nicklin, who had served as Southern League president, had agreed to preside over the new circuit, and he retained the Southern Association presidency during the 1902 season.

Birmingham opened the 1901 season before a crowd of more than 2,000, and Memphis attracted over 3,000 fans to its home opener. There was a tight pennant race, with Nashville edging Little Rock by a one-game margin. The first batting title was won by Jack Hulseman (.392) of Shreveport.

Southern Association Classifications

The original National Association classification system went into effect in 1902, organizing the minor leagues by the size of participating cities and regulating the maximum and minimum sizes of rosters and salaries. There were A, B, C and D leagues, with the largest cities in Class A leagues and the smallest in Class D circuits. In 1902 the Southern Association was designated as one of four Class B Leagues. In 1905 the

SA was elevated to Class A status, along with the American Association, Pacific Coast League, Eastern League (later renamed the International League), and Western League. By 1908 the proliferation of minor leagues caused the addition of a Class AA level, which included the American Association, PCL and Eastern League, leaving the SA and Western League as the only two Class A circuits.

In 1936 a Class A1 level was created; the SA and Texas League were the only two loops to operate under the 10 years of this classification. With the explosion of minor league baseball after World War II, the American Association, PCL and International League were promoted into a new Class AAA, while the SA and Texas League moved up into Class AA. The SA remained a Class AA league throughout the rest of its existence.

The 1901 season was a solid success with fans, and the Southern Association reorganized for another year, replacing Selma with one of the South's most important cities, Atlanta. Throughout 1901 the talk of baseball was the upstart American League. For a decade the National League had been the sole "major" circuit, but in 1901 the new American League challenged the senior league, luring numerous popular stars away from the established NL clubs by paying higher salaries. Minor leagues, caught in the middle of the turbulent conflict between the NL and AL, met in September and October 1901 and reorganized a National Association, which set regulations applicable throughout baseball. Although J. B. Nicklin was not one of the seven league presidents who attended the first organizational meeting in Chicago, he agreed for the Southern to be represented by proxy.

During the 1902 SA season catcher-manager Newt Fisher again guided Nashville to the championship. The best player in the league was Nashville pitcher-outfielder Hugh Hill, who set the all-time high Southern Association batting average with a spectacular hitting performance (.416). Hill also led the SA in runs (99 in 91 games) while posting the best record (21–11) on the pitching staff.

Following the 1902 season, Chattanooga owner Mims Hightower sold his franchise to Montgomery. In 1903 Judge William Kavanaugh became league president, providing stable leadership for the next 12 years. Memphis won the 1903 pennant by edging Little Rock, which finished a close second for the third

Atlanta's first Southern Association team was the "Firemen" of 1902. Former big league outfielder Ed Pabst (center, with mustache) served as manager, while 20-game winner Weldon Henley (standing third from right) went up to the Athletics the next year.

straight year. Memphis repeated as SA champion the next season, while Atlanta ace Frank Smith (31–10) became the league's first 30-game winner. The Atlanta manager was Ab Powell, who had purchased a half-interest in the club for $2,000 and left New Orleans.

Fire the Bums!

Early in the 1901 season New Orleans stumbled into last place. The resourceful owner-manager, Abner Powell, had no intention of remaining in the cellar of the new Southern Association. When a road trip took him to Memphis, Powell armed himself with $1,200 bonus money and ventured into the North Carolina League to assemble a fresh roster. He hired 12 new players, brought them to Memphis, and fired the old team before the next game. The discharged players sat together in the stands at Red Elm Park and booed the rookies. But the revamped lineup beat Memphis in 11 innings, won 18 games in a row, and sparked the Pelicans to a winning season.

New Orleans won the first of nine SA titles in 1905, despite an outbreak of yellow fever that sent the Pelicans on the road for the rest of the season. Shreveport, recognizing that other teams would not come to Louisiana during the epidemic, played the remainder of its home schedule in Chattanooga. During the late nineteenth century yellow fever epidemics had prematurely halted several Southern League seasons, but the willingness of New Orleans and Shreveport to play away from home allowed the Southern Association to complete its schedule.

The New Orleans pennant was produced by a superb three-man pitching rotation: percentage leader Sunny Jim Dygert (18–4), who finished the season in the American League with Philadelphia; southpaw Ted Breitenstein (21–5), an 11-year big league veteran; and Bill Phillips (21–8). The Montgomery Sleepers finished second behind batting champ Carleton Molesworth (.312), who would become manager at Birmingham in 1909 and guide the Barons for nearly 14 years.

The 1906 season featured a scintillating performance by 23-year-old Memphis righthander Glenn Liebhardt. Sporting "the

Chattanooga native Johnny Dobbs (seated second from left) played briefly with the 1902 Lookouts, but spent most of the season in the National League with Cincinnati and Chicago.

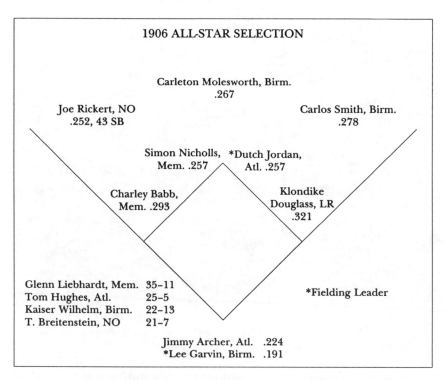

1906 ALL-STAR SELECTION

Carleton Molesworth, Birm.
.267

Joe Rickert, NO
.252, 43 SB

Carlos Smith, Birm.
.278

Simon Nicholls,   *Dutch Jordan,
Mem. .257   Atl. .257

Charley Babb,
Mem. .293

Klondike
Douglass, LR
.321

Glenn Liebhardt, Mem.   35–11
Tom Hughes, Atl.   25–5
Kaiser Wilhelm, Birm.   22–13
T. Breitenstein, NO   21–7

*Fielding Leader

Jimmy Archer, Atl.   .224
*Lee Garvin, Birm.   .191

greatest spitball in the circuit," Liebhardt set the all-time SA record for victories (35–11). He started 46 games (Memphis played 134 contests and won 79, good for second place behind Birmingham) and completed 45, being tossed out in the seventh inning of a May 5 game after protesting a ball call. "Prior to the start of the season," reminisced Liebhardt, "Manager Charley Babb told me to finish each and every game I started." Liebhardt pitched two 11-inning complete games and two 12-inning contests, and he hurled five doubleheaders, winning nine of the ten games. The Memphis iron man was sold to Cleveland at the end of the SA season, and he pitched and won two games for the big leaguers, giving him 37 victories for the season.

Liebhardt's mound heroics overshadowed other standout pitching performances. Birmingham's championship was produced by a steady trio of starters: Irving "Kaiser" Wilhelm (22–13), Ginger Clark (22–14), and Rip Reagan (20–8). Rosters were limited to 14 players, and managers still used the three-man rotation. Atlanta boasted two spectacular hurlers, Tom Hughes (25–5)

Ballparks in the late nineteenth and early twentieth centuries were built adjacent to trolley lines. Birmingham trolley motormen pose for a photograph while waiting for the end of a game at the Rickwood loop.

and Reid Zellars (24–12), while Shreveport's staff was led by Tom Fisher (24–12). During the first five seasons of SA play no one had pitched a no-hitter, but on July 9, 1906, Kaiser Wilhelm twirled a perfect game over Montgomery. The following September 1 Tom Fisher also fired a perfecto over Montgomery.

Double Shutouts

Successful ironman stints were commonplace for SA pitchers in 1907. Birmingham ace Kaiser Wilhelm (23–14) worked five doubleheaders, winning 9 of the 10 games, including a double shutout over Shreveport on the last day of the season. On June 15 Moxie Manuel (20–11) of New Orleans blanked Birmingham on both ends of a Saturday doubleheader. A Little Rock pitcher named Keith (14–8) shut out Shreveport twice on July 9, and Shreveport's William Becker (13–14) returned the favor with a double shutout over New Orleans on August 16.

The next year, on Saturday, July 25, 1908, Ruby Schwenk of Memphis allowed just seven hits in 18 innings while shutting out Montgomery twice. And on August 20, 1914, Jeff Clark of Chattanooga beat Birmingham, 1–0, then held the Barons scoreless for another nine innings before darkness ended the game in a 0–0 deadlock.

The next season Kaiser Wilhelm (also called "Little Eva") led the SA in victories (23–14) and set all-time league records with 56 consecutive scoreless innings and 11 shutouts. On September 1 he pitched two innings of scoreless relief, then hurled his sixth shutout the next day. Heading Birmingham's three-man rotation, on September 5, 8 and 11 he again pitched complete game shutouts, and he climaxed his performance on September 14, holding Shreveport scoreless in both ends of the season-ending doubleheader. After the first game against Shreveport he asked permission to pitch until he was scored upon, and the result was his sixth straight shutout in two weeks.

Atlanta won the 1907 pennant, but last-place Nashville vaulted from the cellar to win the 1908 flag with a 1–0 victory over New Orleans on the final day of the season. Tris Speaker, Little Rock's 20-year-old center fielder who had won the Texas League hitting crown in 1907, was the 1908 SA champ (.350). He also led the league in runs, doubles, and putouts and assists by an outfielder, before proceeding on to a 20-year American League career that would place him in the Hall of Fame. On May 3, 1908,

Baseball immortal Tris Speaker. In 1908 the 20-year-old Little Rock center fielder led the SA in batting (.350), runs and hits, as well as putouts (330) and assists (37) by an outfielder.

The 1909 Atlanta Crackers won the second of three SA pennants under manager Billy Smith (#13). The team's strength was pitching: Oliver Johns (#1, 20–7), Chic Fisher (#7, 20–8), and Tommy Atkins (#9, 19–11).

Mobile recorded the SA's first triple play when a Little Rock hitter lined out to the first baseman Warren Hart, who stepped on first for the second out, then threw to shortstop Paul Sentelle at second base to end the inning.

In 1908 Shreveport returned to the Texas League, replaced in the Southern Association by Mobile. Following the next season Little Rock sold its franchise, players and equipment for $12,000 to Chattanooga, which returned to the SA for the first time since 1902. Atlanta won the 1909 pennant behind Oliver Johns (20–7), Chic Fisher (20–8), and Tommy Atkins (19–11). The batting champ was Birmingham outfielder Bill McGilvray (.291) in the only SA season that produced no .300 hitters. Financially, the season was judged "quite successful," partially because of "the economic administration of President Kavanaugh." The Southern Association ended the first decade of the twentieth century as a solid component of the national pastime.

1910–1919

The most exciting player of 1910 was a Southerner, New Orleans outfielder Joe Jackson, who won his third batting title in his third season as a pro: Carolina League (.346) in 1908; SALLY

(.358) in 1909; and SA (.354). With Jackson triggering the offense, a trio of fine hurlers—Otto Hess (25–9), Pat Paige (24–14), and Ted Breitenstein (19–9)—pitched the Pelicans to the pennant. Southpaw Harry Coveleskie spent the first half of 1910 with Cincinnati, but was sold to Birmingham at mid-season and was spectacular during the remainder of the year (21–10).

Most games of this period were played late in the afternoon—3:30 was a common starting time—so that schoolchildren and businessmen could get to the ballpark. Since there were no lights, these games had to be played briskly so that they could be completed before darkness fell. Umpires kept the action moving, and small rosters dictated few substitutions to slow the game. But despite regular running times of approximately an hour and a half, there was still an impulse to tighten play. A speed-up experiment was conducted on September 19, as Mobile and Atlanta

Southern Association cities were popular spring training sites for big league and upper minor league teams. In the spring of 1911 the Toronto Maple Leafs of the International League trained at Macon's Daisy Park in the Central City Park. When a circus came to Central City Park, Maple Leaf players posed with elephants in front of the ballpark grandstand that had been constructed from the old hippodrome.

— Courtesy Middle Georgia Archives,
Washington Memorial Library, Macon, GA

played a full nine-inning game in just 32 minutes, an all-time professional record. The players hustled throughout the contest and swung at every good pitch. Only one batter walked and Mobile pulled off a triple play to edge the host Crackers, 2–1. That same afternoon in Nashville, another nine-inning game was reeled off in merely 42 minutes.

In 1911 New Orleans broke open a close race with a late surge, becoming the second team to win back-to-back SA pennants. Manager Charley Frank performed an extensive rebuilding job with the 1909 Pelicans, although Otto Hess returned to lead the league with victories (23–8) for the second year in a row. Doc Wiseman, Nashville's right fielder since the opening of the SA, retired after 11 seasons. His best performance was in 1901 (.333), and on Saturday, July 10, 1912, he was presented with a diamond ring, paid for by public subscription among Nashville fans. The 1912 pennant was won by Birmingham, which was led by righthander Ray Boyd (23–11), southpaw Bill Foxen (19–9), and stolen base champ John Johnston (.296 with 81 SB), who broke the record set by Joe Rickert of New Orleans in 1904 (.274

Jay Kirke, shown here in a Louisville uniform, hit .308 while playing second base for the pennant-winning New Orleans Pelicans in 1911.

— Courtesy Louisville Redbirds

with 77 SB). Mobile righthander Al Demaree led the SA in victories (24–10) and recorded 20 strikeouts while working an 18-inning game. Casey Stengel, a 23-year-old outfielder for Montgomery, hit with power and speed (.290, 34 SB), and moved up to Brooklyn at the close of the SA season.

Nashville outfielder Harry Welchonce won the 1912 batting title (.325). Last-place Atlanta acquired Welchonce and other quality players, and won the 1913 pennant on the final day of the season. Welchonce repeated as batting champ (.338), while Gil Price (21–9) and Eddie Dent (14–4) led a solid pitching staff. Southpaw Harry Coveleskie, who posted a brilliant half-season in 1910 (21–10), moved to Chattanooga with less success in 1911 (12–23) and 1912 (13–12). Coveleskie was back at Birmingham in 1913, led the SA in victories (28–9), and went on to win 22 or more games with Detroit in each of the next three seasons. Bill Prough of Birmingham was the 1913 percentage leader (23–6), and Mobile lefty Pug Cavet also was a big winner (23–12).

Casey Stengel managed the Toledo Mud Hens for six seasons, but early in his career he played in Southern Association outfields while hitting .290 for the 1912 Montgomery Rebels.

— Courtesy Louisville Redbirds

Johnny Dobbs

John Gordon Dobbs was born in 1876 in Chattanooga. He developed into a speedy outfielder, and on his way up he played in the Old Southern League in the 1890s. Johnny Dobbs saw National League action with three clubs from 1901 through 1905, but a .263 average in 574 games ended his big league playing career. Although he was named player-manager at Nashville in 1907, a last-place SA finish put him out of managing for a year.

In 1909 he took over his hometown team, leading Chattanooga to a SALLY pennant. The next season Dobbs and Chattanooga returned to the SA, and in 1911 Dobbs moved to Montgomery for three years. In 1914 he was hired by New Orleans, guiding the Pelicans for nine seasons and winning flags in 1915 and 1918. He led Memphis in 1923 and 1924, claiming another pennant in the latter season with his biggest winner, a 104–49 club. Next came five years with Birmingham, and back-to-back championships in 1928 and 1929, along with a Dixie Series title over Dallas in 1929. He spent 1930 and 1931 in Atlanta, then became co-owner of Charlotte in the Piedmont League. He filled in as manager of Charlotte for 19 games in 1933, but he died in 1934.

From 1907 through 1931 he spent 23 seasons managing Southern Association clubs, the second-longest managerial tenure in league history. Dobbs recorded a record of 1,841 wins against 1,452 losses for a .559 winning percentage in the SA (1,918–1,487, .563 overall), and he took five Southern Association pennants.

The Death of Johnny Dodge

A native of Tennessee, infielder Johnny Dodge played in the National League for Philadelphia and Cincinnati in 1912 and 1913 at the tender ages of 19 and 20. His batting average was anemic, however, and he went down to the minors, catching on with Nashville in 1914 (.199) and 1915 (.235). The light-hitting third baseman was dealt to Mobile, where his bat came alive in 1916 (.290 after 39 games).

On June 18 Dodge was at third when Mobile squared off against Nashville for a Sunday afternoon game. Nashville pitched the best hurler in the league, righthanded fastballer Tom "Shotgun" Rogers. When Dodge came to bat he leaned in on a Rogers offering, perhaps thinking it was a curve. But the pitch was a fastball that crashed into Dodge's head with tragic results. The 23-year-old Dodge died the next night.

No one blamed Rogers, but hitters were careful about digging in against him. Three weeks later he fired a perfect game over Chattanooga at the Sulphur Dell, then went on to lead the SL in victories (24–12) and pitch Nashville to the pennant.

In 1914 Chicago Cubs' outfielder Peter Knisely was released and arrived at Birmingham in time to spark the Barons to a pennant (.353 in 99 games), along with southpaw Curley Brown (21–7) and E. Hardgrove (20–9). New Orleans fireballer Roy Walker (15–11, 200 Ks), a 6'½, 185-pound righthander, won the first of four SA strikeout crowns. Last-place Montgomery had the dubious distinction of becoming the first SA team to lose 100 games. Montgomery dropped out of the league and Little Rock rejoined the SA.

William H. Kavanaugh, president of the SA since 1903, died after the season, and was replaced by another excellent executive, R. W. Baugh of Birmingham. New Orleans, led by Popboy Smith (20–12), stolen base and home run champ Fred Thomas (.265, 11 HR, 53 SB), and outfielder Tim Hendryx (.325), clinched the 1915 pennant a week before the season ended. SA hurlers fired four no-hitters in 1915, including one by Chattanooga righthander George Cunningham, who led the league in victories, winning percentage, and strikeouts (24–12, 167 Ks). Late in the season Chattanooga, managed by longtime big league shortstop Kid Elberfeld (who hit .288 at the age of 40 in 103 games), won seven consecutive shutouts.

The 1913 Chattanooga Lookouts were pictured on a postcard, which also included a schedule that listed games "At Home" and "Abroad."

In 1916 Chattanooga outfielder "Baby Doll" Bill Jacobson, who led the SA in homers and triples in 1914 (.319, 19 3B, 15 HR), won the batting title (.346) and moved up to the American League. But pitchers still dominated the league. There were three 24-game winners: Tom Rogers (24–12), who led Nashville to the pennant and hurled a perfect game against Chattanooga on July 11; Memphis southpaw Dickie Kerr (24–12); and Atlanta workhorse Scott Perry (24–20 in a league-leading 336 1P). Popboy Smith again was effective (23–13) for New Orleans, future Hall of Famer Burleigh Grimes enjoyed the best (20–11) of his four SA seasons with Birmingham, Rube Robinson made a spectacular debut (11–1) with Little Rock, and the Pelicans' Roy Walker won another strikeout crown (16–14, 173 Ks).

Walker repeated as strikeout king the next year and claimed the ERA title (19–11, 231 Ks, 1.64 ERA). Birmingham righty Carmen "Specs" Hill led the SA in victories (26–12 including a no-hitter), while southpaw Rube Bressler (25–15) sparked Atlanta's drive to the 1917 pennant, then resumed a 19-year big league career. On June 18 at Birmingham, Little Rock right-

The Birmingham Barons, 1914 champs, sporting their warmup sweaters early in the season. The pitching staff featured Brown (#12 – 21-7), Hardgrove (#9 – 20-6), Robertson (#17 – 20-18), and Johnston (#3 – 18-9). Player-manager Carleton Molesworth (#13 – .338 in 23 G) guided the Barons from 1909 until 1922, winning pennants in 1912 and 1914.

New Orleans owner Julius Heinemann (#16), who started as a vendor for the Pelicans, built a new ballpark for the 1915 season, and his team responded by winning the pennant. Roy Walker (#9 – 7-2 before going up to Cleveland) pitched all or part of nine seasons for the Pelicans and won four strikeout crowns. Heroes of 1915 included Popboy Smith (#7 – 20-12), Jim Bagley (#6 – 19-16), Harry Weaver (#8 – 17-11), outfielder Tim Hendryx (#3 – .325), and home run leader Fred Thomas (#13 – .265, 11 HR, 53 SB).

Hall of Fame pitcher Burleigh Grimes played for Chattanooga and Birmingham from 1913 through 1916. His best SA season was with the Barons in 1916 (20–11).

— Courtesy Minnesota Historical Society

hander Ben Tincup, a full-blooded Cherokee, pitched the fourth perfect game in SA history. Mobile lost 20 games in a row en route to the all-time SA record for futility (34–117).

The United States entered the Great War in April 1917, but the season was largely unaffected by wartime conditions. By 1918, however, transportation restrictions and conscription made minor league baseball a dubious prospect; just nine circuits opened the season, and only the International League would finish its schedule. Washington gave out assurances that professional baseball would be allowed to continue, but on May 23 it was announced that on July 1 all men not in a necessary occupation would be called to "work or fight." Many young players did not wait to be drafted, and, as these volunteers gave up their flannel uniforms for khakis (or signed up for "essential" work), numerous other players began to be drafted.

The Southern Association was one of the nine minor leagues which opened play in 1918, and despite the war SA clubs fared well at the gate. New Orleans righthanders Dick Robertson (10–1) and Hub Perdue (12–2) led the Pelicans to a big lead at mid-season, but on June 28 SA officials decided to shut down for the year. It was felt that after the "work or fight" order went into effect on July 1 operations would become more difficult, and there was a general sense that pro baseball was unpatriotic. New Orleans applied for admission to the Texas League as early as June 12, and the Pelicans' application was accepted. But on July 7 the Texas League also halted operations for the season.

The Southern Association rebounded strongly in 1919 under a new president, Judge John D. Martin of Memphis, who would head the league for nearly two decades. New Orleans outfielder Larry Gilbert led the SA in hitting and stolen bases (.349 with 42 SB), teammate Hub Perdue was the ERA champ (17–2, 1.56 ERA), and Rube Robinson of Little Rock posted the most victories (23–12). On Friday, June 13, at Andrews Field in Chattanooga, the last-place Lookouts hosted the first-place Atlanta Crackers. Chattanooga ace Rube Marshall (21–12) squared off against Ray Roberts (12–11), and both hurlers toiled for 23 innings in three hours and 40 minutes, until plate umpire Steamboat Johnson halted play because of darkness. The longest game in SA history ended in a 2–2 tie. Atlanta went on to win the pennant, its third of the decade, while New Orleans claimed four flags during the 'teens.

Early Southern Association Ballparks

ATLANTA

Piedmont Park. Built in 1896 at the Exposition Grounds of Atlanta. The seating capacity of 1,000 was doubled in 1904, but remained inadequate for weekend crowds. The Crackers rented Piedmont for $600 per year.

Ponce de Leon Park. Built in 1906 for "above $40,000" on Ponce de Leon Boulevard beside the Southern Railroad tracks. The seating capacity was 8,000, and a separate grandstand section was reserved for blacks. The left field boundary was a two-foot hedge.

BIRMINGHAM

Slag Pile Park. Built in the 1880s on First Avenue near 14th Street, close to the Southern Railroad tracks. The grandstand seated only 600, but many kranks watched from just beyond the plank outfield fence, perched on the slag pile of the Alice Furnace.

Rickwood Field with an overflow crowd behind ropes in the outfield.
— Courtesy Birmingham Barons

Rickwood Field. Built in 1910 by new owner Rick Woodward, this concrete-and-steel stadium was the finest facility in the minors, and over 10,000 fans attended the opening game. The right field foul line was a typical length of 334 feet, but the left field line stretched 405 feet and center was a distant 470 feet.

CHATTANOOGA
Stanton Field. Built in the 1880s where the Stivers Lumber Company was later erected.

Andrews Field. Built in 1910 at Third and O'Neal streets by new owner O. B. Andrews.

LITTLE ROCK
West End Park. Home of the Little Rock Travelers from 1901 through 1909.

Kavanaugh Field. When the Travelers returned to the SA in 1915, they played at Kavanaugh Field, later the site of Little Rock Central High School. On June 21, 1930, the first night game in SA history was played at Kavanaugh Field.

MEMPHIS
Red Elm Park. Built in 1896 at Edgeway and Dunlaps streets and Jefferson and Madison avenues. The seating capacity was 3,000, but overflow crowds could easily be placed behind ropes in left field. While right and center fields were cozy distances, 301 and 366 feet respectively, the left field line stretched 424 feet from the plate to the fence. In 1915 owner Russell Garner increased the seating to 6,500 and changed the name of the park to Russwood, and in 1921 the seating capacity was again increased (to 11,000).

NASHVILLE
Sulphur Dell. Baseball was first played at the Sulphur Spring Bottom north of the state capital in the 1860s. The ballpark, long called Athletic

Park and then Sulphur Spring Bottom, was located on a block bounded by 4th and 5th avenues and by Jackson and Summer streets. In 1907 Grantland Rice, destined to earn fame as a poetic sportswriter, became the first sports editor of Nashville's *Tennessean* and soon renamed the park Sulphur Dell, pointing out that it was easier to write rhyming with Dell than with Bottom. For decades the grandstand was in the northeast corner of the block, which gave the park a short right field fence. An open press box was built on the roof of the wooden grandstand. The old Sulphur Spring house stood in the left field corner on 4th, and the Cumberland River was only a quarter of a mile to the east, which meant that the ballpark was frequently flooded through the years. The proximity of Sulphur Dell to the city dump produced the odor-related nickname "The Dump." In 1926 a new grandstand was built at the southwest corner of the block. The new seating capacity was 7,000 and the new right field fence along 4th was just 262 feet down the line. Worse, right field moved up irregular hills to an elevated terrace where overflow crowds perched behind ropes only 235 feet from home. Lefthanded sluggers would flourish at Sulphur Dell, but pitchers and right fielders called the park "Suffer Hell."

NEW ORLEANS

Athletic Park. Built in 1880 as the Crescent City Base Ball Park, the facility was renovated and enlarged in 1887 to accommodate 5,000 — and a capacity crowd turned out for the first game, as well as for numerous weekend contests through the years. Located at Banks and Carrollton streets (across from modern-day Jesuit High School), the stadium also was known as Sprotsman's Park and, by the time of the Southern Association, Athletic Park.

Pelican Park. After the 1914 season owner Julius Heinemann, who had started as a vendor at Athletic Park, decided to relocate his ballpark. The old grandstand was dismantled and carried down Carrollton to Tulane Avenue and Gravier and Pierce streets, where it was rebuilt at a cost of nearly $50,000 in time for the 1915 opener. The outfield was vast — 427 feet to left, 405 in center, and 418 to right — in order to accommodate overflow crowds. At different times Pelican Stadium was called Julius Heinemann Stadium and Municipal Park.

1920–1929

The decade of the 1920s often is lauded as the Golden Age of Sports in America, and baseball reigned as the most popular professional game in the land. The Black Sox scandal over the

World Series of 1919 put the integrity of pro ball in question, but Babe Ruth suddenly lifted the sport into an exciting era of home run sluggers and high-scoring games. Batters began to swing from the heels, and the day of tight pitchers' duels, of games which featured hit-and-run, stolen bases and bunting to play for one run, was buried under a barrage of power hitting. Fans responded enthusiastically to a more exciting style of baseball that proved perfectly tailored to the accelerated pulse rate of the Roaring Twenties.

Rube Robinson

Born in 1889 in Floyd, Arkansas, John Henry Roberson signed with Newport News of the Arkansas State League in 1908. A lefthanded control artist, he studied hitters with unusual attention and was an extremely slow worker on the mound. By 1911 he had moved up to Fort Worth of the Texas League, and after leading the circuit in victories (28–7) he was purchased by Pittsburgh. A Pittsburgh writer called the Arkansas country boy Rube Robinson, and Rube permanently accepted the misspelling of his last name. Rube had two good seasons with the Pirates, then was sold to the Cardinals. The next two years were not as successful, and Rube came to detest St. Louis manager Miller Huggins. Big league salaries for marginal players often were less than the money paid to minor league stars, and Rube asked the Cardinals to sell his contract to Little Rock.

He was almost unbeatable in 1916 (11–1), his first Southern Association season. The next year he was a star for the seventh-place club (21–17), and after a fine start (8–2) in 1918, he was sold to the New York Yankees. But Miller Huggins now was managing the Yankees, and after the season Rube returned to Little Rock. He led the SA in wins in three of the next four seasons: 1919 (23–12), 1920 (26–12), and 1922 (26–11). He became the only SA hurler ever to win 25 or more games in two seasons, and he claimed the ERA title in 1922 (2.04) and 1925 (14–12, 2.73).

Rube spent part of 1923 with New Orleans, part of 1928 with Atlanta, and of course, part of 1918 with New York. Otherwise, he was with Little Rock continuously from 1916 through 1928, posting the all-time Southern Association victory mark (208–169) in 13 SA seasons. Rube retired at the age of 39 following the 1928 season (12–5), having compiled 311 victories during a 21-year career. He settled in North Little Rock, worked for the state highway department and the Missouri Pacific, and died at 75 in 1965.

During the 'teens, team batting avarages generally ranged from the .270s or .260s down to the .230s. But in 1921 New Orleans belted out a team average of .303. In 1925, 1926 and 1927 the highest team batting avarage was .308, and in 1928 Birmingham rode an explosive team average of .331 to the pennant. During most of the seasons of the 1920s the *lowest* team avarage was in the .270s or .280s — higher than the *best* team averages of the previous decade. From 1906 through 1919 there were 19 no-hitters, including four perfect games. There was one no-hitter in 1920, three in 1921 — and not another until 1932.

In 1920 SA President John Martin refused to permit Little Rock to use two pitchers expelled by the Pacific Coast League for collusion with gamblers. In the wake of the Black Sox embarrassment, SA officials strongly opposed "the extreme of an element which might have assailed the integrity of the league."

Six to *Eight* to Three?

In 1920 Little Rock outfielder Bing Miller (.322) was on the eve of an outstanding 16-year American League career. In a game against Nashville the Traveler center fielder participated in a unique double play. With a runner on first, the batter popped up to the shortstop, who backed up into the outfield grass while Miller hustled in as a backup. When the shortstop misjudged the ball, Miller was in position to make a diving catch. But when the runner saw the shortstop bobble the ball he dashed toward second. Miller scrambled up and threw to first for another out. It was recorded as a 6–8–3 double play — with the center fielder as the pivot man!

Little Rock went on to lead the SA in hitting, sparked by the batting champ and home run titlist, outfielders Harry Harper (.346) and Bing Miller (.322 with a record 19 homers). The best pitchers were Rube Robinson (26–12) and Moses "Chief" Yellowhorse (21–7), and Traveler manager Kid Elberfeld put a team together that produced Little Rock's first professional pennant. Pelican fastballer Roy Walker won his fourth SA strikeout title (26–11 with 237 Ks, the all-time league record), while Tom Sheehan of Atlanta worked more innings than any other hurler in SA history (26–17 with 375 IP in 48 G). Birmingham's pitching staff boasted a superb duo in righthanders Jughandle Johnny Morrison (26–13) and Charles Glazner (24–10).

The 1920 Barons boasted a number of SA standouts, including victory co-leader John Morrison (#9 – 26–13), Charles Glazner (24–10), third baseman Pooch Barnhart (#15 – .322), first sacker Tom Bernsen (#2 – .320), outfielder Rube Ellis (#4 – .316), and longtime manager Carleton Molesworth (#7).

A significant innovation of the 1920s was the Dixie Series, which became the most popular baseball event in the South for nearly four decades. As far back as the 1890s, Texas sportswriters had urged a post-season playoff series between the champions of the Texas League and the Southern League, and in 1909 the At-lanta Crackers, champions of the Southern Association, lost a seven-game series to the Chattanooga Lookouts, champs of the SALLY. For years SA officials declined overtures from the Texas League regarding post-season play, because the SA was more ad-vanced in classification than the Texas League and had nothing to gain and a great deal of prestige to lose by such a series. But in 1920, when Fort Worth won the first of six consecutive Texas League pennants, Paul LaGrave of the Cats contacted R. G. Allen, president of the Little Rock Travelers, and a seven-game series was arranged between the two league champions. Fort Worth won the first Dixie Series (four wins, two losses, one tie), but the seven games attracted 36,836 patrons and nearly $50,000 in gross re-ceipts. When the Texas League was elevated to Class A status

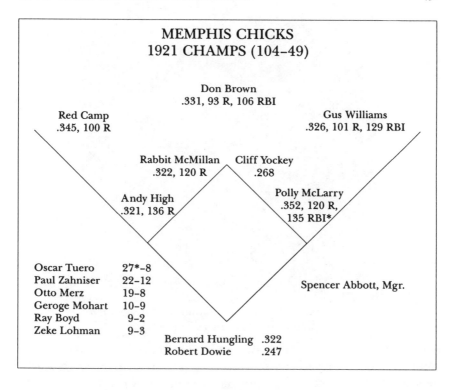

MEMPHIS CHICKS
1921 CHAMPS (104–49)

Don Brown
.331, 93 R, 106 RBI

Red Camp
.345, 100 R

Gus Williams
.326, 101 R, 129 RBI

Rabbit McMillan   Cliff Yockey
.322, 120 R   .268

Andy High
.321, 136 R

Polly McLarry
.352, 120 R,
135 RBI*

Oscar Tuero   27*–8
Paul Zahniser   22–12
Otto Merz   19–8
Geroge Mohart   10–9
Ray Boyd   9–2
Zeke Lohman   9–3

Spencer Abbott, Mgr.

Bernard Hungling   .322
Robert Dowie   .247

before the next season, the two now-equal circuits made formal arrangements for a best-four-of-seven Dixie Series. Although Fort Worth again downed the SA champs, the Memphis Chicks (four games to two), the additional revenue generated by the 1920 and 1921 Dixie Series made its continuance a certainty. The Southern Association determined that 25 percent of the league's half of the gate receipts would go to the SA champion club and players, while 65 percent would be split between the other seven club owners. The Dixie Series quickly became known as the "World Series of the South," and was avidly followed throughout the Southern states.

Before the start of the 1921 season, SA officials raised the roster limit from 15 to 16. Memphis won the 1921 flag behind victory leader Oscar Tuero (27–8), righthander Paul Zahniser (22–12), and an explosive offense led by RBI champ Polly McLarry (.352, 120 R, 135 RBI). Legendary hitter Ike Boone, who

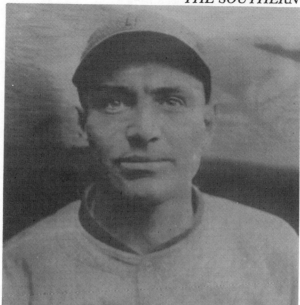

*Future Hall of Famer Pie Traynor played shortstop
for Birmingham in 1921 (.336).*

would become the all-time minor league batting leader (.370 career average), played his second pro season with New Orleans, leading the SA in average, doubles, triples and total bases (.389, 46 2B, 27 3B, 118 R, 126 RBI). Birmingham established the all-time SA record for stolen bases (278 thefts) as second baseman Stuffy Stewart won the first of a record five stolen bases titles (.323, 105 R, 66 SB). Dazzy Vance, a 30-year-old righthander with New Orleans, had the season (21–11) that elevated him to Brooklyn and a Hall of Fame career. Other fine pitching performances were turned in by percentage leader Tom Phillips of New Orleans (25–7 and a no-hitter) and ERA and strikeout champ Claude Jonnard of Little Rock (22–19, 234 K, 2.34 ERA, 58 G).

The 1922 ERA and victory leader was Little Rock's Rube Robinson (26–11, 2.01 ERA), while Roy Walker (12–1) and Oyster Joe Martina (22–6) pitched superbly for New Orleans, and Birmingham's Stuffy Stewart won another stolen base title (.300, 47 SB). Mobile edged Memphis for the pennant behind catcher John Schulte (.357) and hurlers Dutch Henry (19–4), Oscar Fuhr (22–14) and Charles Fulton (20–14). For the Dixie Series Fort Worth fans chartered a train, the "Dixie Special," and brought

Legendary minor league hitter Ike Boone (.370 career) led the SA in batting, doubles, and triples in 1921 (.389, 46 2B, 27 3B, 126 RBI) while playing for New Orleans.

The 1932 Mobile Bears won a close pennant race, then defeated Fort Worth for the SA's first Dixie Series victory. Note the emblem on the jerseys.

— Courtesy Erik Overby Collection
University of South Alabama Archives

along a Dixieland band, cowbells and raucous enthusiasm. But Mobile defeated Fort Worth for the Southern Association's first Dixie Series triumph. During the next three years, however, Jake Atz's Cats beat New Orleans, Memphis, and Atlanta in succession.

Oyster Joe

Joseph John Martina was born in 1889 in New Orleans, and by 1910 the 6'0 righthander had become a professional pitcher. At the end of the 1911 season "Oyster Joe" hurled two games for the Pelicans, and in 1916 he was effective in 14 games for Chattanooga (6–1). During the first half of his 22-year career he spent nine seasons in the Texas League, setting the all-time circuit record for innings pitched while leading the league in victories for Beaumont in 1919 (28–13, 378 IP).

In 1921 Oyster Joe donned the uniform of his home town Pelicans, and he was a 20-game winner in 1922 (22–6) and the pennant-winning season of 1923 (21–10 with a league-leading 149 Ks). He moved up to the Washington Senators in 1924, but was back with New Orleans in 1925, leading the SA in victories (23–13). Oyster Joe was a key figure in the Pelicans' back-to-back championships of 1926 (19–9) and 1927 (23–12), when he again led the league in victories and strikeouts.

In 1928 Oyster Joe, then 39, slipped a notch, and he spent the next three seasons knocking around in the Texas League and the Cotton States League. But the last game he pitched as a pro was for Knoxville of the SA in 1931. He had accumulated the second highest number of wins in minor league history (349–277, including 139–81 in the SA). Oyster Joe died in 1962 in New Orleans.

In 1923 outfielder Larry Gilbert was named player-manager at New Orleans, and he began the SA's longest managerial career by guiding the Pelicans to the pennant. New Orleans finished last in batting but first in fielding, and the pitching staff was led by Roy Walker (21–9) and Oyster Joe Martina (21–10). But the best pitching duo in the league was Mobile's Tommy Long (27–7) and Oscar Fuhr (23–14).

Johnny Dobbs guided Memphis to the 1924 championship behind RBI champ Roy Carlyle (.368, 117 R, 122 RBI) and percentage leader Otto Merz (20–6). Atlanta finished second despite the efforts of batting titlist Carlisle Smith (.385), victory leader Ray Francis (24–13), run leader Ben Paschal (.341, 136 R, 101 RBI), and first sacker Dick Burrus (.365). Birmingham second sacker Stuffy Stewart posted his third stolen base title (.326, 109 R, 67 SB), then won another in 1925 (.304, 108 R, 53 SB).

Jake Atz managed the Fort Worth Cats to six consecutive Texas League pennants, and Atz's Cats played in the first six Dixie Series, losing only in 1921 and 1924 to Memphis. Atz managed New Orleans in 1932. His real name was Zimmerman, which placed him last in the pay line when he was a player. More than once his team ran out of money before his turn came, and he had his name legally changed to Atz so that he could stand at the head of the line.

Action at Mobile in the 1920s.
— Courtesy Erik Overbey Collection
University of South Alabama Archives

Larry Gilbert

Born in New Orleans in 1891, Larry Gilbert would spend 32 consecutive seasons in the SA as a player, manager, and club president. At the age of 18 the lefthanded, 168-pound outfielder signed with Victoria of the Southwest Texas League, and by 1914 he had made it to Boston, playing with the "Miracle Braves." At mid-season of 1915 he was hitting just .151, however, and he resumed his minor league travels.

In 1917 he was purchased by New Orleans, hitting .269 and .282 before winning the 1919 batting championship and stolen base title with a .349 average and 42 thefts. During the next six years he hit .301, .326, .307, .312, .327, and .279, retiring as a player at the age of 33 following the 1925 season.

By that time Gilbert was a manager, taking over the reins of the Pelicans in 1923 and promptly leading his team to the SA pennant. He won back-to-back flags in 1926 and 1927, but in 1932 he became club president and hired Jake Atz as manager. A legend in the Texas League, where he won six consecutive pennants at Fort Worth, Atz could only direct a sixth-place finish in New Orleans.

Gilbert reassumed managerial control in 1933 and guided the Pelicans to another championship and a Dixie Series triumph over Dallas. The next season he again won the SA pennant and the Dixie Series, this time over Galveston.

In 1939, after five pennants and only one losing season (73–74 in 1928) in 15 years at New Orleans, Gilbert moved to Nashville, immediately guiding the Vols to the first of six consecutive playoff titles. He enjoyed his best SA season in 1940, carving out a 101–47 record en route to a first-place finish, victory in the playoffs, and the first of three straight Dixie Series championships. The Vols beat Houston in the 1940 Dixie Series, swept Dallas in four straight the next year, and downed Shreveport in 1942. In 1948 he brought the Vols into first place again, but after losing the playoffs Gilbert retired, having set the Southern Association standard for longevity and victories: 2,128–1,627 (.567) in 25 seasons.

Gilbert's son Charlie starred on the 1948 championship team, setting SA records with 178 runs and 155 walks, and the next year another son, "Tookie," led the league with 146 runs. Both boys were born in New Orleans, where Larry died at the age of 73 in 1965.

Atlanta finished second in 1924 with 99 victories, but took the 1925 pennant with just 87 wins. The Atlanta offense was sparked by batting champ Wilbur Good (.379, 130 R, 126 RBI), who set an all-time SA record with 236 hits, and by home run titlist Nick Cullop (.310, 30 HR, 139 RBI) and run leader Frank Zoeller (.311, 131 R). Nashville shortstop Harry Bates (.349) reeled off a 46-game hitting streak to establish another league record. Nashville first baseman Chick Tolson paced the SA in RBIs (.361, 19 HR, 143 RBI), while Pelican ace Joe Martina was the victory leader (23–13). More than $100,000 in gate receipts compensated for another Dixie Series loss to Fort Worth.

Larry Gilbert guided New Orleans to consecutive championships in 1926 and 1927. Gilbert always stressed defense, feeling that a run saved was as good as a run scored, and the Pelicans led the league in fielding both seasons. Reliable Oyster Joe Martina anchored both championship pitching staffs (19–9 and 23–12); veteran Sam Vick operated in center field both years (.348 and .350); Ray Gardner held down shortstop each season; and the catching was split both seasons by journeymen named Lingle and Dowie. Starting alongside Martina in 1926 were victory leader Lute Roy (24–10), Mike Cvengros (18–5 and .352 as a hitter) and Earl Hilton (16–3); Oyster Joe's principal help in 1927 came from ERA champ Dave Danforth (16–3, 2.25). The 1926 run leader was Pelican first baseman Gink Hendrick (.371, 137 R), who went up to Brooklyn and was replaced at first by the equally productive Wilbur Davis (.376, 107 R, 121 RBI), who won the 1927 batting championship.

Birmingham set a league record in 1927 by reeling off 19 consecutive victories, but Johnny Dobbs' Barons could only finish second to New Orleans. The next two years, however, Dobbs led his club to back-to-back pennants. There was a split-season experiment in 1928, and Birmingham beat Memphis in a playoff for the flag. The experiment was dropped after one year and the Barons won the 1929 title outright. The 1928 Barons led the SA with an incredible team batting average (.331), and also posted the best fielding percentage. Right fielder Babe Bigelow won the hitting title (.395), catcher Yam Yaryan was right behind (.389), and first sacker Mule Shirley was the RBI champ (.342, 113 R, 133 RBI). Second baseman Stuffy Stewart won his fifth SA stolen base crown (.318, 61 SB, and a league-leading 138 R) as the Barons led the circuit with 185 thefts. The pitching staff featured victory leader Eddie Wells (25–7) and percentage winner Lute Roy (19–5). The 1929 mound corps featured ERA and percentage champ Dick Ludolph (21–8) and Bob Hasty (22–11). Left fielder Butch Weis took the batting crown (.345), while catcher Yam Yaryan again hit well (.335). Only once in nine years had the

---

Babe Bigelow

Elliott Allardice Bigelow was born in Florida in October 1898. A lefthander, he began a professional career as a slugging first baseman at the age of 21. Babe spent his first five seasons in the Florida State League, twice winning the batting title and leading the circuit in numerous other offensive categories.

In 1925 he was purchased by Chattanooga and led the SA in triples (.349, 27 3B, 111 RBI). After another fine year in 1926 (.370, 118 RBI), Babe was sold to Birmingham. In 1927 he paced the league in homers, RBIs and runs (.361, 19 HR, 137 R, 143 RBI). The next season Babe won the batting championship (.395, 115 R, 123 RBI) and led the Barons to the 1928 pennant.

He went up to the Red Sox in 1929 (.284), but started 1930 in the Pacific Coast League. Babe spent the last half of the season with Chattanooga (.331), then returned to the Lookouts in 1931 and led the SA in doubles and RBIs (.337, 48 2B, 125 RBI). Dealt to Knoxville for 1932, he was still a formidable hitter (.327, 120 RBI) at the age of 31. But after the season his health failed, and he died in Tampa the next year. He had compiled a .349 career average, and over half of his career had been spent pounding Southern Association pitchers.

Southern Association champ (Memphis in 1922) defeated the Texas League in the Dixie Series, but the 1929 Barons downed Dallas, four games to two.

1930–1939

The 1930 season was the first baseball year affected by the Great Depression. Minor leagues adjusted by introducing night games to boost attendance, which proved to be an especially effective attraction in the South, where fans could cool off at the ballpark. Colonel Bob Allen, president of the Little Rock Travelers, rigged lights at Kavanaugh Field, and on Saturday, June 21, 1930, the Southern Association staged its first night game (the Travelers beat Birmingham in 10 innings). SA attendance in 1931 exceeded one million, in great part because of crowds at night games, as owners began to install lights at stadiums around the league.

Jim Poole, a former American League first baseman, had led the SA in home runs and RBIs (.340, 33 HR, 127 RBI) while playing for Atlanta and Nashville in 1929. In 1930 Poole wore a Nashville uniform all season, becoming the first of a procession of left-handed sluggers to pile up impressive numbers because of the short right field fence at Sulphur Dell. On Saturday, June 14, Poole blasted three home runs and added a double and a single. For the 1930 season Poole repeated as RBI-home run champ (.364, 50 HR, 167 RBI), and his left-handed-hitting teammate, second baseman Jay Partridge, was almost as deadly (.361, 40 HR, 127 RBI, and a league-leading 153 R). Batting titlist Joe Hutcheson (.380, 20 HR, 113 RBI) led Memphis to the 1930 pennant.

Zeke Bonura, a lumbering first baseman who would split almost 2,000 professional games between the minor leagues (.349 career average) and majors (.307), spent his first three seasons with his native New Orleans team: 1929 (.322), 1930 (.352), and 1931 (.375). Another fabled minor league slugger, Moose Clabaugh (.339 lifetime), won the 1931 batting and home run titles (.378, 23 HR, 104 RBI) while playing for Nashville, and he repeated as hitting champ in 1932 (.382, 32 HR, 107 RBI).

The Baron of Ballyhoo

In 1918 Joe Engel, a 25-year-old southpaw with five years' experience in the big leagues (17–22), received $4,000 and a contract for $800 per month to pitch for the Atlanta Crackers. He twirled a 1–0 victory over Mobile, but worked only one other game before being called into the army. After the war he returned briefly to Atlanta, pitched his final major league game for Washington in 1920, then accepted an offer from Clark Griffith to become head of scouting for the Senators (a native of Washington, Engel had been batboy for the Senators from 1907 through 1909).

After the 1929 season Griffith sent Engel to take over his newly-acquired Chattanooga franchise. Engel supervised construction of a 12,000-seat ballpark, which was called the "Finest in the South" when it opened in April 1930. Over 15,000 fans came to the new park, which was only the first of numerous Engel crowds to win the Opening Day Trophy. On May 1, 1936, almost 25,000 fans jammed into Engel Stadium when Joe gave away a *house*, and in 1948 and 1949 Engel set SA attendance records for last-place teams.

Joe Engel proved to be an energetic, innovative club executive who retained a keen eye for talented players and who possessed such a flair for promotion that he became known as the "Baron of Ballyhoo," the "Baron of Baloney," and the "Barnum of Baseball." He installed the SA's first pressroom in Engel Stadium, and after trading shortstop Johnny Jones to Charlotte for a 25-pound turkey, he invited 25 SA sportswriters to a turkey dinner. Engel reflected that he got the worst end of the deal: "That was a mighty tough turkey."

During the 1931 exhibition season, Engel hired a lefthanded girl pitcher, Jackie Mitchell, to play against the New York Yankees, and in a brief — and supposedly honest — appearance, she struck out Babe Ruth and Lou Gehrig. Following a wrangle with Dizzy Dean in 1935, Engel offered Diz $10,000 to fight him at home plate in Chattanooga, but spoilsport Commissioner Kenesaw Mountain Landis nixed the charity bout. During World War II Engel was selling war bonds over the radio, and a caller offered to buy a $50,000 bond "if you get off the air."

"If you buy a $50,000 bond, I'll do even better than that," replied the irrepressible Baron of Ballyhoo. "I'll jump into the Tennessee River." But this time it was Mrs. Engel, concerned about winter temperatures, who spoiled the fun. When Joe arrived at the river's edge, she had the Coast Guard waiting to restrain him.

Engel's favorite stunt was staged on Opening Day of 1938, when more than 14,000 fans crowded into Engel Stadium to witness a "wild elephant hunt." Braying was magnified over the loudspeakers, and only when shots began to explode did the spectators realize that each falling "elephant" was two men inside an animal suit. But the elephant hunt was such a big hit that the Barnum of Baseball took his safari on the road.

Birmingham charged to the 1931 pennant, winning 36 one-run games behind the SA's best pitching staff: lefthanded control artist Jimmy Walkup (20–5), victory leader Bob Hasty (21–13), and Ray Caldwell (19–7). The offense was led by outfielder Butch Weis (.369, 20 HR, 122 RBI, and a league-leading 102 walks). The Barons went on to beat Houston in the Dixie Series, the first of four consecutive SA triumphs in the postseason classic. In the Series opener before 20,000 at Rickwood, 43-year-old Ray Caldwell outdueled Texas League MVP Dizzy Dean, 1–0, and singled in the only run in the eighth. The Buffs rebounded with three straight shutouts, but the Barons rallied to win Game Five, then returned to Birmingham and took the final two games at Rickwood.

Colonel Bob Allen sold his successful Little Rock franchise in 1931, but soon re-entered the league with another club. After a disastrous season in 1930 (40–112), Mobile owners attempted to move the team to Knoxville. A depressed economy in Knoxville thwarted the move, but a year later Allen purchased Mobile's Bears and shifted to Knoxville's brand-new ballpark on July 22,

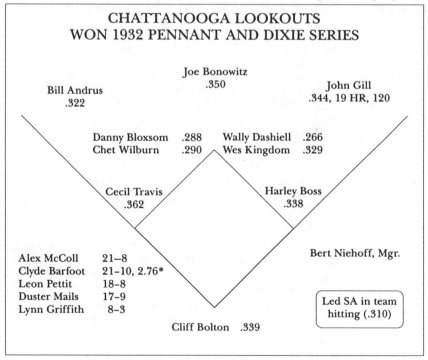

CHATTANOOGA LOOKOUTS
WON 1932 PENNANT AND DIXIE SERIES

Joe Bonowitz
.350

Bill Andrus
.322

John Gill
.344, 19 HR, 120

Danny Bloxsom   .288   Wally Dashiell   .266
Chet Wilburn   .290   Wes Kingdom   .329

Cecil Travis
.362

Harley Boss
.338

Alex McColl   21–8
Clyde Barfoot   21–10, 2.76*
Leon Pettit   18–8
Duster Mails   17–9
Lynn Griffith   8–3

Bert Niehoff, Mgr.

Led SA in team hitting (.310)

Cliff Bolton   .339

1931. The Knoxville Smokies continued to be perennial losers, though, prompting their patient fans to chant, "S.O.S—same old Smokies."

The Chattanooga Lookouts started 1932 with a nine-game winning streak and went on to finish first by an eyelash (98–51, .658), even though Memphis won three more games (101–53, .656). It was Chattanooga's first SA pennant, although manager Bert Niehoff previously had won with Mobile in 1922 and Atlanta in 1925. The Vols boasted the league's best offense (.310), sparked by third baseman Cecil Travis (.356), center fielder Peck Hamel (.352), and stolen base leader Andy Reese (.336, 33 SB, 121 RBI). The pitching staff featured a trio of reliable starters: Alex McColl (21–8), Clyde Barfoot (21–10), and Leon Pettit (18–8). But the best pitcher in the league was Memphis righty Walter "Boom-Boom" Beck (27–6), while teammate George Granger (11–8) worked a seven-inning no-hitter, the first since 1921.

For 1933 the SA decided to try a split-season format with a championship playoff between the two half-season winners, a device to stimulate attendance that had been utilized in 1928. Doc Prothro, who had managed Memphis to the 1928 playoff

---

You Can't Strike Him Out

Lee Head was a native of Birmingham who became a professional catcher. A fine hitter (.304 average in 2,179 minor league games), Head always got the bat on the ball, and with a catcher's eye for the strike zone he never took close pitches for a third strike. By the time he reached the Southern Association, at the age of 33 with Knoxville late in the 1932 season, he was almost impossible to strike out. In 43 games with the Smokies (.323) he fanned just four times in 164 at-bats.

The next year he was even better, catching 131 games for the Smokies (.331) but striking out only three times in 469 at-bats. In 1934 he played in 124 Knoxville games (.313), whiffing six times in 437 at-bats. The following season, his second as player-manager, was his masterpiece: in 122 games (.281) and 402 at-bats he struck out merely once!

In 1936 Head moved to Little Rock, not fanning a single time in 28 games and 85 at-bats, before moving up to Sacramento of the Pacific Coast League. He made one final appearance in the SA, with Memphis in 1937, whiffing twice in 12 games and 39 at-bats. During all or part of six seasons in the 1930s, Lee Head played in 460 SA games, but struck out only 16 times in 1,595 at-bats.

and to the 1930 pennant, guided the Chicks to the first half title. For the second year in a row Memphis registered the most victories in the SA (95–58), but Larry Gilbert brought New Orleans (88–65) in ahead of Memphis in the second half, then went on to win the playoff and the Dixie Series.

Gilbert repeated this success the next year, winning the second half, downing Nashville in the playoff, then repeating as Dixie Series champion. It was the ninth SA pennant for New Orleans, but there would not be another championship in the remaining quarter century of the Pelican tenure in the Southern Association. Gilbert's Pelicans registered the best fielding percentage in both championship seasons, and his 1934 pitching corps was led by percentage leader Fred Johnson (20–5) and ERA titlist Al Milnar (22–13, 2,61). Victory leader Harry Kelley (23–11), who moved from Memphis to Atlanta during the season, was a 20-game winner for the second year in a row, and Nashville right-hander Byron Speece (22–8) also pitched well. But the best performance of 1934 was turned in by a hitter, Nashville outfielder

The New Orleans Pelicans finished first in 1934, won the playoffs, and, for the second year in a row, claimed the Dixie Series championship. Al Milnar (back row, third from right) was the ERA champ (22–13, 2.61) and Fred Johnson (back row, fourth from left) was the percentage leader (20–5).

Phil Weintraub (.401), who became only the second SA batting champ to hit over .400.

For 1935 SA officials decided to adopt the Shaughnessy Plan, which was spreading rapidly through the minor leagues as a means of sustaining fan interest throughout the season. Frank "Shag" Shaughnessy, general manager of the Montreal Royals of the International League, persuaded the IL to begin utilizing the plan in 1933. According to the Shaughnessy Plan, the top four teams would square off in a post-season playoff series. It seemed fair for the pennant winner to play the fourth-place team in the opening round of playoffs, while the second- and third-place finishers squared off. At first in the SA the opening round would feature a best-three-of-five series, and the two winning clubs would play for the right to advance to the Dixie Series in a best-three-of-five playoff. Later a best-four-of-seven format was used in the semifinals and finals. Even late in the season, a second-division team might surge into fourth place, then win the semifinals and finals, and perhaps the Dixie Series. The Shaughnessy Plan would prove to be almost as effective an antidote to Depression attendance problems as night games, and in time almost all minor leagues adopted some form of the playoff system. The SA decided to award the first-place finisher $1,000, an amount increased to $2,500 a year later.

"It's a Bird — It's a Ball — It's a Hit!"

On August 11, 1935, during a Sunday afternoon game at Rickwood Field against New Orleans, Pelican left fielder Eddie Rose stepped into the batter's box against Birmingham righthander Legrant Scott. Rose lined a fastball toward left — but the ball thumped into a low-flying pigeon! The bird fluttered to the diamond with a broken neck, and the ball dropped nearby as Rose scampered to first. Rose retrieved the unfortunate pigeon and proudly had him mounted.

Atlanta marched to the 1935 pennant behind ERA champ Harry Kelley (23–13), L. B. Thomas (20–16), and first sacker Alex Hooks (.341). New Orleans lefty Al Milnar (24–5) set a league record with 17 consecutive victories, boosting the Pelicans into second place and a three-game sweep over third-place Memphis in the playoff opener. Nashville showcased batting and home run

The 1935 Atlanta Crackers finished first and won the playoffs. Harry Kelley (23–13) and first baseman Alex Hooks (.341) were among the Cracker stars.

leader Poco Tait (.355, 17 HR) and righthander Tiny Chaplin (24–11), but the fourth-place Vols were swept by Atlanta in the opening round of playoffs. The Crackers then executed a three-game sweep over New Orleans in the finals. Atlanta set an SA attendance record with 330,000 fans, over one-third of the league total. Although the Crackers lost to Oklahoma City in the Dixie Series, four games to two, 26,000 fans turned out for the three games staged in Atlanta's Ponce de Leon Park, as opposed to only 17,000 for the three games in Oklahoma City. At the end of the season both the Southern Association and the Texas League were elevated to a new classification, A1.

In This Corner . . . Dizzy Dean!

In 1935 Dizzy Dean won 28 games and Paul Dean recorded 19 victories for the St. Louis Cardinals (the brothers won 30 and 19 decisions respectively in 1934). Capitalizing on their fame, the Deans and Cardinal catcher Mike Ryba barnstormed as soon as the season ended, and peerless promoter Joe Engel signed them to pitch three innings apiece in a Peerless-Dixie charity exhibition (clubs by those names had recently played for the Chattanooga amateur crown).

The game was scheduled for 3:00, but when the three big leaguers arrived at 2:00 only a few hundred fans had filed into the stadium. Although Engel pointed out that there would be a large crowd when school was dismissed and when people could leave work, Dizzy walked out in a huff and refused to play. Angrily, Engel threatened to punch Diz in the nose, and Dean replied that if he ever tried it he would hang Joe off a crag on Lookout Mountain.

Sensing a unique promotion, Engel offered Dean $10,000 to fight him at Engel Stadium. Although the profits were to go to charity, Commissioner Kenesaw Mountain Landis forbade a boxing match involving baseball's most famous pitcher. But the following spring Dizzy got into a fight with a New York sportswriter in the lobby of a Tampa hotel. The irrepressible Engel promptly telegraphed Diz: "You're just as dumb as I thought, fighting for nothing. I offered you $10,000 to fight me at home plate at Chattanooga."

Manager Eddie Moore's Crackers had never been out of first place in 1935, and in 1936 Moore again brought the pennant to Atlanta. The defending champs bolted to a 26–4 start and never looked back. The Crackers won with pitching and defense, leading the league in fielding, again enjoying the services of L. B. Thomas (18–8), and receiving a special charge when Brooklyn optioned Dutch Leonard at mid-season (13–3 the rest of the way). More than 301,000 fans came to Ponce de Leon Park, while overall league attendance (1,164,265) was the best since 1927. The Shaughnessy playoffs brought in 115,000 fans. Each of the two opening series went the full five games, with Atlanta losing to New Orleans and Birmingham defeating Nashville. Third-place Birmingham swept New Orleans in the finals, but suffered a Dixie Series sweep at the hands of Tulsa. Chattanooga outfielder Freddie Sington (.384, 22 3B, 107 RBI) led the league in triples and won the batting title by a single point over Nashville outfielder Joe Dwyer (.383, 65 2B, 127 R, 117 RBI), who led the SA in runs and established the circuit's record for doubles.

Men's Night

By the 1930s Ladies' Night was a staple of professional baseball, introduced by Ab Powell in New Orleans in 1887 and providing free or half admission to females who accompanied paying men customers to the ballpark. But one of the many innovations of Earl Mann, Atlanta's energetic young president, was Men's Night, suggested in 1936 by a woman "who wanted to see the opposite sex get a break, instead of going broke." Over 18,000 men jammed Ponce de Leon Park as guests of the management, while just 1,500 ladies responded to the role of paying customers.

In 1937 ace manager Doc Prothro, who had left Memphis after seven seasons because of a salary dispute, brought the SA pennant to Little Rock with a franchise-high 97 victories. Outfielders Lindsey Deal (.340) and Lee Nonnenkamp (.332 with a league-leading 145 runs) headed the championship drive. Little Rock downed New Orleans and, in a seven-game title series, Atlanta, to claim playoff honors. In their only other pennant season, 1920, the Travelers fell to Fort Worth in the Dixie Series, and the Texas League Cats put a similar ending on Little Rock in 1937.

After 19 highly successful years as league president, federal judge John D. Martin of Memphis resigned with two years remaining on his contract, citing the pressure of his legal and judicial responsibilities. The owners split, four to four, on a successor, and finally settled on Major Trammell Scott of Atlanta as the new president.

To welcome Atlanta as the new headquarters of the Southern Association, the Crackers dominated the 1938 season behind catcher Paul Richards (.316), who made a spectacular managerial debut. "Richards' Rifles" spent the year in first place, entitling them to take on the SA's best players in the league's first All-Star Game. Under the lights at Ponce de Leon Park the SA's best team slaughtered the All-Stars, 16–6, then went on to finish first, win the Shaughnessy playoffs, and dismantle Beaumont in the Dixie Series without a defeat. Third baseman Johnny Hill was the batting champ (.338), Lefty Sunkel posted a rare pitcher's triple crown (21–5, 178 K, 2.33 ERA), and righthander Bill Beckman added prowess from the other side of the mound (20–13).

The next year belonged to the hitters. For the first time in league history, except for the abbreviated war season of 1918, no pitcher won 20 games. But 34 regulars hit over .300, and 10 batted over .350, including batting champ Bert Haas of Nashville (.365), RBI leader Babe Young of Knoxville (.364, 21 HR, 137 RBI), and, in his only SA season and the next-to-last year of a legendary career (.367 lifetime), Memphis outfielder Ox Eckhardt (.361).

The 1939 pennant race was a wild scramble that was not decided until the last day of the schedule, when Memphis clinched first place. The Chicks won the All-Star Game, 3–0, but were swept by Nashville in the playoff opener. Although player-

FORT WORTH DIXIE SERIES PENNANT PLAYERS · 1939 NASHVILLE

The 1939 Dixie Series pitted Nashville against Fort Worth. The two teams are shown here in Fort Worth, and the Cats prevailed over the SA champs, four games to three.

— Courtesy Jess Cummings

In 1939 famed minor league hitter Ox Eckhardt (.367 career) pounded SA pitching (.361) as a Memphis outfielder.

Hall of Fame pitcher Bob Lemon started his career as a position player, and in 1939 he was an outfielder and third baseman for New Orleans (.309).

manager Paul Richards (.300) again led the Crackers to the finals, Nashville prevailed in a seven-game championship series.

The Southern Association finished the Depression decade with an exciting season of hard-hitting baseball. During the 1930s, when many minor leagues disbanded and others suffered frequent franchise transfers, the SA had only one franchise move (Mobile to Knoxville in 1931). The SA rapidly equipped itself for night baseball, postseason playoffs further stimulated attendance, fans listened avidly to radio broadcasts of SA games, and the Dixie Series became entrenched as the greatest baseball event of the South. The Southern Association successfully met the challenges of the Great Depression, but the outbreak of war in Europe late in the 1939 season suggested that a new decade would bring serious new problems.

1940–1949

While the Nazi *blitzkrieg* was unleashed upon Europe in the spring and summer of 1940, a Nashville *blitzkrieg* swept through the Southern Association. After 15 years and five championships at New Orleans, Larry Gilbert moved to Nashville in 1939, finished third, and won the first of six consecutive playoff championships. In 1940 he managed the Vols to the highest winning percentage in the 40-year history of the Southern Association (101–47, .682), with a roster so satisfactory that Gilbert made just one player change the entire season. Nashville led the league in team hitting (.311) and, as usual for a Gilbert club, team fielding (including 208 double plays). The pitching staff featured a brilliant performance by Boots Poffenberger (26–9), along with strong support from strikeout leader Ace Adams (13–5), starter-reliever Leo Twardy (17–11 in 53 games), and rising star Johnny Sain (8–4, and .395 in 38 games). The offense was a wrecking crew powered by outfielders Oris Hockett (.363), Arnold Moser (.347 with a league-leading 216 hits), and Gus Dugas (.336 with a league-leading 22 HR and 118 RBI), third baseman Robert Bohen (.302, 118 RBI), second sacker John Mihalic (.317 with a league-leading 127 walks), first baseman Mike Rocco (.305, 21 HR, 101 RBI), and catcher Charles George (.335). Although Nashville lost the All-Star Game, 6–1, the Vols swept Chattanooga in the playoff opener, downed Atlanta in the finals, and beat Houston for the first of three consecutive Dixie Series triumphs. In the Chattanooga series George Jeffcoat (14–6) set an all-time SA record by fanning 18 Lookout batters.

Oddities of 1940

On August 20 at Little Rock, Memphis first baseman Frank Piet had four assists — but not a single putout! In a 20-inning night game at Chattanooga, Little Rock left fielder Willie Duke (.361, including a 26-game hitting streak) played the entire 20 innings without ever having a fielding chance.

The most spectacular performance of 1941 — or almost any other SA season — was turned in by Nashville first baseman Les Fleming. The lefthanded slugger blasted 10 homers in his first 13 games. Fleming played in 106 games before going up to Cleveland and became only the third SA hitter to bat .400 (.414, 29

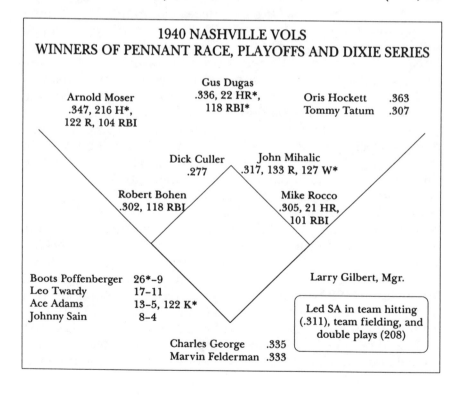

1940 NASHVILLE VOLS
WINNERS OF PENNANT RACE, PLAYOFFS AND DIXIE SERIES

Gus Dugas
.336, 22 HR*,
118 RBI*

Arnold Moser
.347, 216 H*,
122 R, 104 RBI

Oris Hockett   .363
Tommy Tatum   .307

Dick Culler
.277

John Mihalic
.317, 133 R, 127 W*

Robert Bohen
.302, 118 RBI

Mike Rocco
.305, 21 HR,
101 RBI

Boots Poffenberger   26*–9
Leo Twardy   17–11
Ace Adams   13–5, 122 K*
Johnny Sain   8–4

Larry Gilbert, Mgr.

Led SA in team hitting
(.311), team fielding, and
double plays (208)

Charles George   .335
Marvin Felderman   .333

HR, 103 RBI). Nashville teammates Oris Hockett (.359, 32 HR), Tommy Tatum (.347) and Charles Workman (.334) helped produce the league's top team batting mark (.303), while southpaw Russ Meers led the SA in winning percentage and strikeouts (16–5, 161 Ks).

Atlanta player-manager Paul Richards again guided the Crackers into first place, behind outfielder Bud Bates (.324), home run champ Les Burge (.311 with 38 homers), and righthander Ed Heusser (20–8). The pennant-bound Crackers roared to a spectacular 30–5 start and stayed in first place. But Larry Gilbert's heavy-hitting Vols won the playoffs, including a seven-game classic with Atlanta in the finals, then beat Dallas in the Dixie Series.

By the time the 1942 season opened, Pearl Harbor was four months in the past and baseball faced another world war. But the Southern Association had become a remarkably stable league, and 1942 proved to be a season relatively unaffected by the war, even though gasoline and tire rationing began to hurt attendance. Little Rock pitcher-manager Willis Hudlin, a 15-year big league veteran, guided the Travelers to their third pennant with a late-season surge that included a 13-game winning streak. Third sacker Buck Fausett (.334) and center fielder Tommy McBride (.329) led a potent attack, and MVP Roy Schalk (.288) turned more double plays than any other second baseman in the league.

But Larry Gilbert again worked his magic in Nashville. Once more the Vols led the SA in team hitting behind third baseman Charles English, who paced the league in batting, hits, doubles and RBIs (.341, 50 2B, 139 RBI). Other potent bats were added by home run champ Charles Workman (.326 with 29 homers), outfielders Calvin Chapman (.332) and Gus Dugas (.309), and run leader John Mihalic (.301 with 124 runs). The Vols' pitching staff was led by southpaw Vito Tamulis (20–8), while another lefthander, New Orleans workhorse Bill Seinsoth (24–10 in 50 games) was the victory leader. Second-place Nashville again won the playoffs, executing a four-game-sweep over Atlanta in the finals, then dumped Shreveport for a third consecutive Dixie Series championship. Fort Worth of the Texas League was the only team that had previously won three straight Dixie Series, in 1923–1925, and the feat would never again be repeated.

After the season Major Trammel Scott, who had guided the

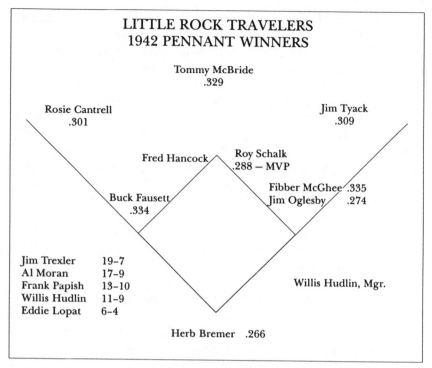

LITTLE ROCK TRAVELERS
1942 PENNANT WINNERS

Tommy McBride
.329

Rosie Cantrell
.301

Jim Tyack
.309

Fred Hancock

Roy Schalk
.288 — MVP

Buck Fausett
.334

Fibber McGhee .335
Jim Oglesby   .274

Jim Trexler   19–7
Al Moran   17–9
Frank Papish   13–10
Willis Hudlin   11–9
Eddie Lopat   6–4

Willis Hudlin, Mgr.

Herb Bremer   .266

league for five years, resigned as league president. Billy Evans, a future Hall of Famer who had been a superb American League umpire from 1906 through 1927 before becoming a major league executive, was elected SA president at the National Association meeting in Chicago in December 1942. Evans moved the league office back to Memphis, and launched a year-long project that involved the study of 50,000 box scores and that resulted in a richly detailed record book of the Southern Association.

The primary responsibility of President Evans was to keep the Southern Association operating. President Franklin D. Roosevelt expressed the hope early in the war that professional baseball would carry on as a boost to public morale. But wartime travel restrictions and a rapidly declining manpower pool caused most clubs, particularly in the lower minors, to cease operations. There were 43 minor leagues in 1940, with a total paid attendance of almost 20 million. But by the next year attendance dropped to 16 million as the country became distracted by the threatening international situation, and during the 1942 season

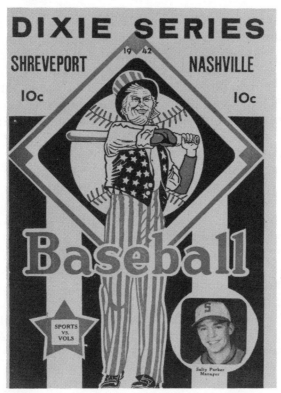

Cover of Shreveport's game program for the 1942 Dixie Series, won by Nashville, four games to two.

the number of minor leagues dropped to 31. For 1943 just 10 minor leagues decided to operate; the number remained the same in 1944, then increased to 12 in 1945 as Germany and Italy collapsed. The Texas League was one of the circuits that suspended play in 1943–44–45, which meant there would be no Dixie Series.

But there would be baseball in Dixie. SA owners intended to protect their investments, and the Southern Association was one of the 10 minor leagues which continued to play in 1943. As healthy young men joined the military by the millions, baseball rosters soon bulged with players past their prime, raw youngsters, and 4-Fs. The most famous 4-F of them all joined the Memphis Chicks in 1943. Pete Gray (born Peter Wyshner in 1917) lost his right arm in a boyhood accident, but he was speedy and quick, and he learned to field and throw a baseball with a rapid transfer of the glove to his right underarm. He played 42 games in the Canadian-American League in 1942 (.381), and the next year he held down a regular outfield position with the Chicks (.289), even legging out a few extra-base hits. Gray was a sensation the next year (.333), leading the league with 68 stolen bases, the highest total in the SA in more than two decades. He was purchased by the St. Louis Browns for 1945 (.218 in 77 games), and he was a magnificent inspiration for disabled vets. After the war Gray spent a season each in the American Association, Eastern League, and Texas League, compiling a minor league batting average of .307.

Along with the quality of athletes, the quality of baseballs declined as manufacturers took shortcuts. It was suspected that the yarn was not wound as tightly around the core, and for a time balata (a substance used in golf balls) was substituted for rubber, which was in short supply during the war. With balata at the core, baseballs had little carry, and while the "balata ball" was in use, home run and RBI totals dropped accordingly. Home run numbers were reminiscent of the dead ball era: Cecil Dunn was the home run champ of 1943 (19 homers), followed by Melvin Hicks in 1944 (16) and Gil Coan in 1945 (16). Little Rock compiled a .306 team batting average in 1943 but totaled only 16 homers, and the Memphis Chicks managed 11, Little Rock 18, and four other teams were in the 20s. In 1945 Little Rock hit just 14, New Orleans 16, and Birmingham 18.

For 1943 the Southern Association trimmed its schedule from a standard 154 to 140 games, and the league stayed with the reduced travel of a 140-game schedule in 1944 and 1945. The SA dropped the Shaughnessy Plan for 1943 and reverted to a split-season format, with a best-four-of-seven playoff between the two first-place teams. The same scheme was utilized in 1944, but in 1945 the SA returned to the Shaughnessy Plan.

In 1943 Larry Gilbert brought Nashville to the first-half title behind batting and stolen base champ Hank Sauer (.368, 30 SB), percentage leader Bill Stewart (18–5), and the league's best offense (.309). Sparked by victory leader Jess Danna (22–7), New Orleans won the second half, but Nashville took four of five play-off games to post a fourth consecutive championship. Little Rock lefty Ed Lopat won the ERA crown (19–10) and hit impressively (.325 in 67 games), then moved up to the big leagues. Knoxville, constant losers (42–111 in 1937) since acquiring Mobile's fran-

Lefthanded knuckleballer Eddie Lopat pitched for Little Rock in 1942 (6–4) and 1943 (19–10 with a league-leading 3.05 ERA), before going up to the American League.

Future Hall of Fame umpire Billy Evans was Southern Association president from 1942 through 1946, and he was instrumental in keeping the SA operational throughout World War II.

chise in 1931, moved back to Mobile during the season; the night-time transfer was so abrupt that Knoxville fans found out only when they came to the ballpark the next day.

Inspired by one-armed stolen base champ Pete Gray (.333, 68 SB) and by fiery righthander Ellis Kinder (19–6), Memphis won the first half of 1944. Nashville had a losing record, but Larry Gilbert rallied the Vols to the top spot in the second half. Southpaw Boyd Tepler was spectacular in half of the season (12–2), third baseman Pete Elko starred for two-thirds of the schedule (.351), and Nashville outlasted Memphis in a seven-game finals series to win a fifth straight title. Atlanta finished second in both halves, but enjoyed no honors or postseason play.

In 1945 future Hall of Famer Kiki Cuyler returned to the SA as manager of Atlanta. Cuyler starred for Nashville in 1923, managed Chattanooga to the 1939 pennant, and led the Lookouts to the playoffs the next two years. He guided the 1945 Crackers to the flag behind the hitting of RBI and run leader Ted Cieslak (.364, 127 R, 120 RBI) and the brilliant performance of bespectacled southpaw Lew Carpenter, who paced the SA in victories and ERA (22–2, 1.82).

In 1945 Chattanooga outfielder Gil Coan led the SA in batting, doubles, triples, homers, and stolen bases (.372, 40 2B, 28 3B, 16 HR, 37 SB, 117 RBI).

Incredibly, Carpenter was not the percentage leader. Chattanooga lefty Larry Brunke not only pitched superbly (15–1), but hit well enough (.275 in 72 games) to see extra duty as an outfielder and pinch-hitter. The year's best offensive player was Chattanooga outfielder Gil Coan, who led the league in hitting, doubles, homers and stolen bases, and who set the all-time record for triples (.372, 40 2B, 28 3B, 16 HR, 126 R, 117 RBI). Mobile catcher Harry Chozen (.353) broke Johnny Bates' 20-year-old record of batting safely in 46 straight games. Even though he twice had to deliver as a pinch hitter and twice more entered a contest late with just one at-bat, Chozen put together a 49-game hitting streak.

Chozen helped put Mobile into the Shaughnessy playoffs, with each series a best-four-of-seven. The Bears beat Chattanooga in the opener, while fourth-place New Orleans upset first-place Atlanta, then Mobile downed the Pelicans in the finals. Mobile's pitching staff was led by 40-year-old righthander Bill Thomas (20–

Atlanta righthander Lew Carpenter headed the Crackers' 1945 pennant drive with a brilliant performance, leading the league in victories, ERA, and winning percentage (22–2, 1.82).

13 with a league-leading 274 IP). Thomas had pitched for Knoxville in 1932, then led the SA in games pitched with 51 for New Orleans in 1935 (19–15) and 1936 (18–18) and with 44 for Mobile in 1944 (17–9). In 1946 he was winless for the Bears after three games, but went to Houma of the Evangeline League and performed brilliantly (35–7). Thomas won 26 games in 1950, and when he finally retired at 47 he set the all-time record with 383 career victories in the minors.

By the end of the 1945 season World War II was over, and for the next few years professional baseball would enjoy a heyday. Postwar fans, starved for baseball and in a festive mood, flocked to ballparks across the country in unprecedented numbers. As new leagues proliferated everywhere a new AAA classification was created for the largest circuits, which elevated the Southern Association to AA status.

In 1946 SA players put on a show for their crowds. Birmingham outfielder Tom Neill won the hitting and RBI titles (.374, 116 R, 124 RBI), and Chattanooga infielder Hillis Layne was right behind (.369, 117 R). On July 21 in a game against Memphis, Little Rock outfielder Lew Flick (.346) banged out nine consecutive base hits, while Traveler first baseman Kerby Farrell (.294) added eight hits.

The best hitting show was put on by Atlanta, which led the league in batting behind outfielders Billy Goodman (.389 in 86 games), Lloyd Gearhart (.332 with a league-leading 139 runs) and Ralph Ellis (.319, 14 HR, 122 RBI), third sacker Ted Cieslak (.354, 106 RBI), and second baseman Charles Glock (.334). The pitching staff was spectacular, producing—for only the second time in league history (Birmingham in 1906 was the first)—three 20-game winners: lefthander and victory leader Earl McGowan (22–10), ERA champ Bill Ayers (21–10, 1.95), and Shelby Kinney (20–9). This talented aggregation put Atlanta in first place for the second consecutive season, and that year manager Kiki Cuyler won the playoffs. With the Texas League back in operation the Dixie Series was resumed, but the Crackers were swept by Dallas.

Billy Evans accepted a position as general manager of the Detroit Tigers, and Charles Hurth of New Orleans was selected as league president. Hurth would lead the SA until 1960, a tenure second only to Judge John D. Martin. Attendance was spectacular during the season, soaring past the 2.1 million mark around the league, with another 94,000 at the playoffs. Despite fielding a second-division team, Atlanta led the league in attendance with 404,584 fans, and second-place New Orleans also attracted crowds exceeding 400,000 into Pelican Stadium.

Out at Home

Chattanooga's irrepressible president, Joe Engel, had a long-running — and usually good-natured — feud with SA umpires. On one occasion, however, his jibes launched from atop the roof of Engel Stadium so aroused the ire of one ump that the official pointed up at Engel and angrily ordered him off the roof.

One afternoon the umps called a game because of darkness, even though considerable daylight remained. Engel stuck his tongue into his cheek and wired the league president: "Suggest a rule be passed no umpires can have dates until 9 p.m."

Engel, of course, made the telegram public, and for months one umpire tried in vain to convince his wife that Joe's telegram was another bad joke.

SA fans enjoyed an air-tight pennant race in 1947 with Mobile finishing first over New Orleans by half a game. Bolstered by ERA champ Bob Hall (18–8, 2.80), run and walk leader Cal Abrams (.345, 134 R, 124 W), and SA veteran Lindsey Deal (.327), the Bears swept Chattanooga in the opener, then beat Nashville for the playoff title.

Muscular Ted Kluszewski, first baseman at Memphis, was the 1947 batting champ (.377), while New Orleans first baseman Al Flair led the league in homers and RBIs (.308, 24 HR, 128 RBI). Gil Coan, the offensive star of 1945, returned to Chattanooga with another fine performance (.340, 22 HR, 126 R, and a league-leading 17 triples).

Steamboat Johnson

Harry "Steamboat" Johnson began his umpiring career in 1909, and by 1914 he had worked his way up to the National League. After just one season, however, he was back in the minors, gravitating to the Southern Association in 1919. Johnson umpired for two years in the SA, spent 1921 in the SALLY, then returned to the Southern Association for good.

The colorful arbiter would boom out his decisions in SA ballparks for more than three decades. During his first SA season Steamboat was the plate umpire for the league's longest game, a 2–2 tie at Chattanooga that lasted 23 innings. Twenty years later, Steamboat again was behind the plate for the longest night game in SA history when Little Rock beat Chattanooga in 20 innings.

At New Orleans on August 27, 1927, Steamboat officiated what he termed the longest nine-inning game on record. A bean-ball started a brawl between the Pelicans and the visiting Birmingham Barons. When Joe Sonnenberg, a New Orleans police captain, charged out of the stands, Birmingham second baseman Max Rosenfield thought he was a fan mixing into the players' fight. Rosenfield punched Sonnenberg, and the two men squared off. When the melee ended Sonnenberg had Rosenfield sent to jail, but Steamboat insisted that Max be released because he had not been aware that his opponent was an officer. After a two-hour delay Rosenfield was returned to Pelican Stadium. The game finally resumed, and New Orleans marched on to a 25–16 win.

In 1935 Steamboat published an autobiography, *Standing the Gaff,* and he estimated that 4,000 bottles had been thrown at him since 1909, although he had only been hit by about 20. "That does not speak very well for the accuracy of the fans' throwing," he wrote.

When he retired after the 1946 season (he accepted an appointment as supervisor of SA umpires), he had spent 27 years in the Southern Association, an all-time longevity record for any minor league. Honored with a "night" in New Orleans in 1949, he died two years later in Memphis at the age of 66.

Muscular Ted Kluszewski won the SALLY hitting title while with Columbia during his rookie season of 1946 (.352), then went to Memphis in 1947 and won the SA batting championship (.377).

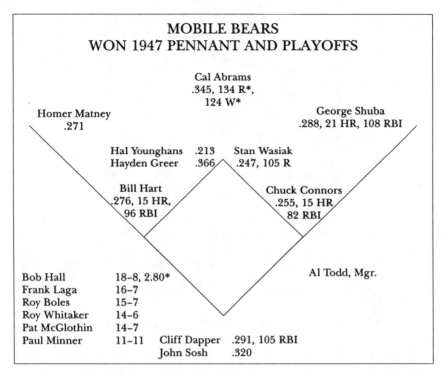

MOBILE BEARS
WON 1947 PENNANT AND PLAYOFFS

Cal Abrams
.345, 134 R*,
124 W*

Homer Matney
.271

George Shuba
.288, 21 HR, 108 RBI

Hal Younghans   .213   Stan Wasiak
Hayden Greer   .366   .247, 105 R

Bill Hart
.276, 15 HR,
96 RBI

Chuck Connors
.255, 15 HR
82 RBI

Bob Hall   18–8, 2.80*
Frank Laga   16–7
Roy Boles   15–7
Roy Whitaker   14–6
Pat McGlothin   14–7
Paul Minner   11–11

Al Todd, Mgr.

Cliff Dapper   .291, 105 RBI
John Sosh   .320

In 1948 the SA again exceeded two million in total attendance, with another 137,000 fans attending the playoffs, and a crowd of 9,174 at the All-Star Game. Rickwood Field in Birmingham hosted a league-leading 445,926 fans. In Nashville Larry Gilbert concluded 25 years as a manager by assembling a heavy-hitting roster that led the league in batting (.307) and walloped an unprecedented 183 home runs (the old record of 157 was set in Nashville in 1930). Gilbert signed three left-handed sluggers who took deadly aim at the Sulphur Dell's short right field porch: his son Charley, who set the all-time SA mark for runs and walks (.362, 42 HR, 178 R, 155 W, 110 RBI); batting champ Smokey Burgess (.386, 22 HR, 102 RBI); and outfielder Charles Workman (.353, 137 R, 52 HR, 181 RBI), who broke Jim Poole's records, also set in Nashville in 1930, of 50 homers and 167 RBI.

The offense-minded Vols pounded their way to first place and to the playoff finals, but they were bushwhacked for the Shaughnessy title by third-place Birmingham. Led by outfielder Tom O'Brien (.359, 19 HR, 137 RBI), first sacker Walt Dropo

The Mobile Bears won the 1947 pennant and playoffs. Future television star (The Rifleman) Chuck Connors was the first baseman (rear, third from left), outfielder Cal Abrams (front, third from left) led the SA in runs and walks (.345, 134 R, 124 W), and outfielder George Shuba (rear, second from right – .288, 21 HR) added power. The pitching staff featured southpaw Roy Whitaker (front, second from right – 14-6), ERA champ Bob Hall (front, second from left – 18-8, 2.80), and fellow righthanders Frank Laga (rear, second from left – 16-7) and Pat McGlothin (middle, far right – 14-7). The manager was Al Todd (middle, third from right).

—Courtesy Erik Overbey Collection
University of South Alabama Archives

(.359, 14 HR, 102 RBI), and ERA champ Mike Palm (14–8, 2.20), the Barons rode their momentum to a Dixie Series triumph over Fort Worth.

In 1949 another trio of left-handed home run hitters again helped lift Nashville to first place: catcher Carl Sawatski (.360, 45 HR, 153 RBI), who led the SA in homers and RBIs; outfielder Babe Barna (.341, 42 HR, 138 RBI); and run leader Harold "Tookie" Gilbert (.334, 33 HR, 146 R, 122 RBI), another son of Larry Gilbert. The Vols also boasted batting champ Bob Borkowski (.376) and three standout pitchers: victory and percentage leader Garman Mallory (20–4); Frank Marino (19–7); and Ben Wade (18–8). This talented aggregation roared through the playoffs, then outlasted Tulsa in a seven-game Dixie Series.

Catcher Smokey Burgess was the 1948 batting champ (.386) while leading Nashville to the SA pennant.

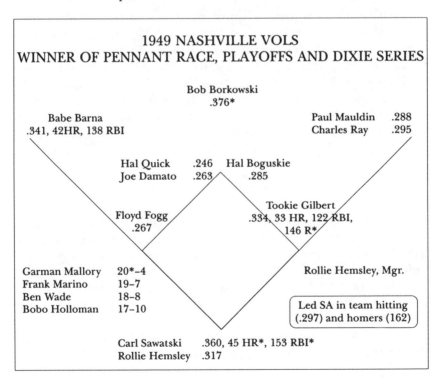

1949 NASHVILLE VOLS
WINNER OF PENNANT RACE, PLAYOFFS AND DIXIE SERIES

Bob Borkowski
.376*

Babe Barna
.341, 42HR, 138 RBI

Paul Mauldin   .288
Charles Ray   .295

Hal Quick   .246   Hal Boguskie
Joe Damato   .263   .285

Tookie Gilbert
.334, 33 HR, 122 RBI,
146 R*

Floyd Fogg
.267

Garman Mallory	20*–4
Frank Marino	19–7
Ben Wade	18–8
Bobo Holloman	17–10

Rollie Hemsley, Mgr.

Led SA in team hitting
(.297) and homers (162)

Carl Sawatski   .360, 45 HR*, 153 RBI*
Rollie Hemsley   .317

A full house at Rickwood Field, viewed from right field. Big crowds were common during the first few seasons after World War II.

— Courtesy Birmingham Barons

Although attendance dipped for the second year in a row, the total was nearly two million. Almost 90,000 attended the play-offs, and over 11,000 fans came to the All-Star Game. Second-place Birmingham again drew well over 400,000 fans into Rickwood, and Atlanta pulled more than 370,000 fans into Ponce de Leon Park with a losing team. For the Southern Association, which began the decade under the threat of war, the 1940s ended on a high note of strong attendance and impressive play.

1950–1961

The 50th pennant race of the Southern Association was won by Atlanta, winners of the first Southern League flag in 1885. The 1950 Crackers were managed by longtime big league out-fielder Dixie Walker, and featured Art Fowler (19–12), outfielder Ben Thorpe (.324), and third baseman Eddie Mathews (.286, 32 HR, 106 RBI), an 18-year-old slugger who would go on to blast 512 major league home runs.

Little Rock started the season with three road losses, won their home opener, then set an all-time SA record with 21 con-

Future Hall of Fame slugger Eddie Mathews starred for the Atlanta Crackers (.286, 32 HR, 106 RBI) at the age of 18 in 1950.

secutive defeats en route to a cellar finish. In compensation, the batting title was won by a fraction of a point by Little Rock outfielder Pat Haggerty (.3464) over Nashville outfielder Tom Neill (.3460). The home run and RBI crowns were claimed by Memphis outfielder Bill Wilson (.311, 36 HR, 125 RBI), who would tie for the 1953 home run title (.311, 34 HR, 101 RBI). In 1950 Wilson was closely pursued by Birmingham first baseman Norb Zauchin (.287, 35 HR, 104 RBI). Although catcher Carl Sawatski spent part of the year with the Cubs, he played 80 games with Nashville and continued to display a powerful left-handed stroke (.308 with 24 homers).

A pair of southpaws were the pitching stars of 1950. Marv Rotblatt of Memphis (22–9, 253 IP, 203 K, 2.67 ERA) led the league in ERA, strikeouts, and innings pitched. Robert Schultz of Nashville led the SA in victories, percentage, games pitched and shutouts (25–6, 51 G, 5 ShO, 202 K, 2.68 ERA), and barely missed a pitcher's Triple Crown. Schultz helped Nashville win a second consecutive playoff title, although the Vols fell to San Antonio in the seventh game of the Dixie Series.

Despite an All-Star crowd of 15,293, playoff attendance sagged to 80,000 and overall attendance fell to 1,730,047, a one-

Bobo

One of the most colorful players in baseball history was a big righthanded pitcher from South Carolina, Louis "Bobo" Newsom. Bobo played for Macon of the SALLY League in 1929 (19-18), his second season as a pro. He spent part of 1929 and 1930 with Brooklyn, but finished the latter season back at Macon (6-3). Bobo pitched for Little Rock in 1931 (16-14 in 51 games, with 152 Ks and 150 walks), leading the SA in games, strikeouts and walks.

Following a long big league career, Bobo signed with Chattanooga for 1949. On August 9 — two days before he turned 42 — Bobo won an iron-man doubleheader triumph over Little Rock, 10-6 and 9-6. Later in the month Bobo was given a "day" by Chattanooga fans, but he wrangled with an umpire and was tossed out of "his" game in the seventh inning! He finished the season with another SA strikeout crown (17-12, 141 Ks) and the distinction of being the league's oldest strikeout king.

The next season Bobo led the SA in losses (13-17). He moved to Birmingham for 1951, and at the venerable age of 44 became the leader in innings pitched (16-11, 237 IP). Incredibly, this performance put him back in the big leagues, and during the next two seasons he pitched winning ball for losing clubs (6-5) before finally retiring at the ripe old age of 46.

Memphis lefhander Marv Rotblatt led the 1950 SA in ERA, strikeouts and innings (22-9, 253 IP, 203 Ks, 2.67 ERA).

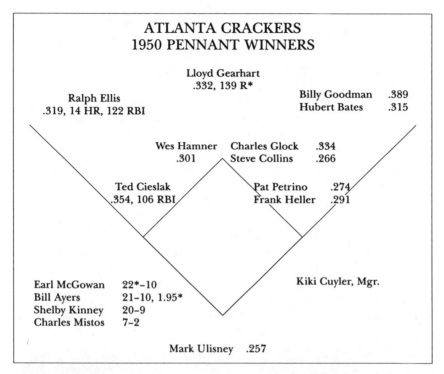

ATLANTA CRACKERS
1950 PENNANT WINNERS

Lloyd Gearhart
.332, 139 R*

Ralph Ellis
.319, 14 HR, 122 RBI

Billy Goodman   .389
Hubert Bates   .315

Wes Hamner   Charles Glock   .334
        .301   Steve Collins   .266

Ted Cieslak
.354, 106 RBI

Pat Petrino   .274
Frank Heller   .291

Earl McGowan   22*–10
Bill Ayers   21–10, 1.95*
Shelby Kinney   20–9
Charles Mistos   7–2

Kiki Cuyler, Mgr.

Mark Ulisney   .257

fifth decline since 1947. Overall attendance dropped again in 1951, to 1,534,111, and the attendance decline would continue annually. After a postwar boom of four seasons, the minors began to suffer a steady and precipitous dropoff in interest. In 1949 there were 59 minor leagues with an all-time record attendance of 41,872,762, but by 1963 there were merely 18 junior circuits, with a total paid attendance of just 9,963,174.

What caused the disastrous conditions that forced scores of franchises and entire leagues to disband? For years Southern Association fans habitually listened to radio sportscasts (on warm evenings it was possible to stroll down a neighborhood sidewalk and keep up with a game from porchside radios), and by 1950 there were experiments with televised games. But a major league Game of the Day began to be broadcast coast to coast in 1950, and soon a televised Game of the Week increased the availability of the big leagues. Televised games proved less of a problem than network programming, as former fans chose to stay at home in front of a TV set. And with the simultaneous advent of home air conditioning, an evening at the ballpark no longer was the best way for Southerners to cool off on a hot summer night. Little League baseball also exploded in popularity, and with two or three games per week and frequent practices, families stayed away from minor league stadiums in droves.

Little Rock finished in the cellar in 1950 with 21 consecutive losses, and attendance dropped to less than 83,000. But in 1951 the Travelers vaulted to a first-place finish with a 10 1/2-game margin, and more than 225,000 fans came out to Travelers Field. Left fielder Hal Simpson put in an MVP year (.311, 23 HR, 128 RBI), and he was strongly supported by third baseman Dave Jaska (.309), center fielder John Grice (.308), right fielder Ken Humphrey (.304), and second baseman R. C. Otey (.305), who enjoyed his best season in 10 years as a Traveler.

Birmingham stayed a close second until Verne Williamson (12–5) no-hit the Barons in a crucial series in Little Rock in August. The Barons enjoyed revenge a month later, sweeping Little Rock in the playoff finals, then defeating Houston in the Dixie Series. Birmingham was sparked by flashy center fielder Jimmy Piersall (.346) and fellow outfielders Marvin Rackley (.351) and

Colorful outfielder Jimmy Piersall (left) hit .346 and helped Birmingham win the 1951 playoffs and Dixie Series.

— Courtesy Birmingham Barons

George Wilson (.325, 29 HR, 112 RBI). Nashville failed to make the playoffs but provided crowd-pleasing fireworks, leading the league in team average and home runs. Nashville's best two left-handed sluggers of 1951 were batting champ Babe Barna (.358 with 19 homers) and HR king John Harshman (.251, 47 HR, 141 RBI). Mobile outfielder Walt Moryn won the RBI crown (.299, 24 HR, 148 RBI).

In 1952 Nashville again led the SA in hitting and home runs and provided the batting champ, third baseman Rance Pless (.364). En route to big league stardom, New Orleans outfielder Frank Thomas won the home run and RBI titles (.303, 35 HR, 131 RBI). The best pitcher of the year was Chattanooga left-hander Al Sima (24–9).

The Cinderella team of 1952 was Memphis, managed by future Hall of Famer Luke Appling (who started his career in 1930 with Atlanta). The Chicks barely made postseason play, defeating New Orleans, 3–2, in a September 8 playoff game to determine the fourth-place team. Memphis then stunned first-place Chattanooga with a four-game sweep in the opening series. The Chicks beat Mobile in the finals, and dumped Shreveport, 4 games to 2, to win the Dixie Series.

Appling brought the Chicks in first the next year, but Memphis was defeated in the playoff opener by Birmingham. Nashville beat Atlanta in the opener and the Barons in the finals to win the playoff title. Nashville's championship drive was led by lefthanded John Harshman, the 1951 home run champ, who turned to the mound and led the SA in victories and winning percentage (23–7, plus .315 with 12 homers in 86 games at the plate). Other key Vols included batting champ Bill Taylor (.350 with 22 homers in 107 games), strikeout king Jim Constable (19–13, 183 K), run leader Bob Boring (.315, 21 HR, 111 RBI, 108 R), and lefthanded sluggers Gail Harris (.281 with 25 homers) and Bob Lennon (.266 with 25 homers).

Lennon made Southern Association history in 1954. The Nashville outfielder became the first SA hitter to win a Triple Crown, leading the league in average, homers and RBIs, as well as runs and hits (.345, 64 HR, 161 RBI, 139 R, 210 H). Taking aim at the inviting right field fence at Sulphur Dell, he set the all-time SA record for homers with the fourth-highest total in baseball history. (Also in 1954, Joe Bauman walloped 72 homers for Roswell; Joe Hauser and Bob Crues each blasted 69, Hauser

Outfielder Bob Lennon hit well for Nashville in 1952 and 1953, then in 1954 set the all-time league record for homers and became the first SA hitter to win a Triple Crown (.345, 64 HR, 161 RBI).

for Minneapolis in 1933 and Crues for Amarillo in 1948; and in 1956 Dick Stuart passed Lennon by stroking 66 for Lincoln.)

Despite Lennon's eye-popping performance, Nashville finished next-to-last in 1954, drawing only 89,000 fans (attendance in Mobile and Little Rock was even worse). Atlanta dominated the season, placing first in the standings, winning the playoffs, and defeating Houston in a seven-game Dixie Series. Manager Whitlow Wyatt's pitching staff was led by victory and percentage leader Leo Cristante (24–7) and fellow righthander Dick Donovan (18–8 and .307 in 70 games). The hitting attack was powered by walk leader Robert Montag (.305, 39 HR, 105 RBI, 122 W), catcher James Solt (.321), second sacker Frank Di Prima (.316), and outfielder Chuck Tanner (.323, 20 HR, 101 RBI), who had logged several solid seasons with the Crackers and who would return to Atlanta as manager of the major league Braves.

Atlanta dropped to seventh place in 1955, but led the SA in attendance (239,037). Little Rock was in the cellar (52–102), and attendance was so low (51,514) that the franchise became endangered. Across the league total paid admissions were only about half (1,127,112) of the 1947 totals, even though six teams enjoyed winning records. But a record All-Star crowd (19,830) jammed Rickwood Field on July 19, as first-place Birmingham took on the Stars. The fans were treated to four home runs by Chattanooga outfielder-third baseman Jim Lemon (.278, 24 HR, 109 RBI). The righthanded slugger lofted two homers over the left field fence and two more over right, becoming the only hitter in any Southern Association contest to blast four homers in a single game.

SA Segregation

The Southern Association, like every other institution in the South, was segregated. Outstanding Negro League baseball was played in the ballparks of the Southern Association. When SA teams were on the road, local Negro League clubs—the Atlanta Black Crackers, Birmingham Black Barons, Memphis Red Sox, and Nashville Elite Giants—moved into the stadiums, and whites were among the appreciative fans.

But even after Jackie Robinson broke the big league "color line" in 1947, the Southern Association ignored integration. The majority of white fans adamantly opposed integration, and the problem was compounded by the segregation of restaurants and hotels used by SA teams.

In 1954, however, Atlanta opened the season with a black power hitter, Nat Peoples, on the roster. But Peoples was harshly treated everywhere, and he could not eat or sleep with his team. He appeared in only two games, and did not collect a hit in four at-bats. He was sent down to Jacksonville of the SALLY League as a replacement for another black slugger who had been promoted to the Milwaukee Braves—Hank Aaron. The Southern Association disbanded after the 1961 season and before the great acceleration of the civil rights movement, and Nat Peoples remained the only member of his race to play in the SA.

Nashville outfielder Bob Hazle was the home run champ for the season (.314 with 29 homers), while infielder Charles Williams (.368) became the fifth Vol in as many years to win the batting championship. Indeed, from 1948 through 1958 Nashville players won 9 of 11 hitting titles.

Memphis player-manager Jack Cassini (.305 in 82 G) was badly beaned in an August 2 game against Nashville and was lost for the season. The parent White Sox sent future Hall of Fame pitcher Ted Lyons to manage the Chicks. Lyons, who already had managed the White Sox, put together a charge which placed Memphis atop the final standings. Slick-fielding shortstop Luis Aparicio led the league in stolen bases (.273 with 48 steals) and hard-hitting Ed White (.342, 17 HR, 107 RBI) led all outfielders in fielding. Reliever Joe Dahlke (44 G with 2 starts) only pitched 117 innings but paced the league in victories (19-5, 1.85 ERA). Fellow righthanders Paul Stuffel (12-3) and Dick Strahs (10-2) also were high percentage winners.

Memphis fell to Mobile in the playoff opener. The Bears, sparked by ERA champ Ralph Mauriello (18-8, 2.76) and RBI co-leader Jim Gentile (.290, 28 HR, 109 RBI), then beat Birmingham in the finals and swept Shreveport in the Dixie Series.

Atlanta dominated the next two seasons, finishing first in 1956 and 1957, then winning the playoffs both years. Opposing Atlanta in the finals each season was Memphis: the Chicks did not fall until the seventh game in 1956, but the Crackers pulled off a four-game sweep the next year. In both seasons Clarence Riddle held down first base, Frank Di Prima was on second (.298 and .281), and Sam Meeks was a utilityman. In 1956 most of the power was supplied by outfielder Jack Daniels (.257 with 34 homers). A solid one-two-three punch was provided in 1957 by a trio of starter-relievers, righthander Don Nottebart (18-10, 46 G, 25 GS), southpaw Ken MacKenzie (14-6, 43 G, 27 GS), and lefthander Jack O'Donnell (16-10, 59 G, 13 GS), who won four decisions in four days against Mobile.

Elsewhere around the league in 1956, New Orleans outfielder John Powers won the home run crown (.312, 39 HR, 116 RBI) and Memphis righthander Al Papai was the victory leader (20-10). Robert Kelly of Nashville fired the most victories in 1957 (24-11), while home run champ Harmon Killibrew of Chattanooga demonstrated the power (.279, 28 HR, 101 RBI) that would propel him into the Hall of Fame.

Southern Association Cities and Nicknames

Thirteen cities fielded franchises in the Southern Association from 1901 through 1961. Birmingham and Nashville were the only cities to participate in all 61 seasons.

Atlanta (1902–61). Firemen (1902), Crackers (1903–61).
Birmingham (1901–61). Barons.
Chattanooga (1901–02, 1910–61). Lookouts.
Knoxville (1932–43). Smokies.
Little Rock (1901–10, 1915–58, 1960–61). Travelers.
Macon (1961). Peaches.
Memphis (1901–60). Egyptians (1901–08), Turtles (1909–10), Chickasaws or Chicks (1911–60).
Mobile (1908–31, 1944–61). Sea Gulls (1908–17), Bears (1918–30, 1944–61), Marines (1931).
Montgomery (1903–14, 1943, 1956). Black Sox (1903), Senators (1904–08), Sleepers (1905), Climbers (1909–10), Billikens (1911), Rebels (1912–14, 1943, 1956).
Nashville (1901–61). Volunteers or Vols.
New Orleans (1901–59). Pelicans.
Selma (1901). Christians.
Shreveport (1901–07, 1959–61). Giants (1901–03), Pirates (1904–07), Sports (1959–61).

On July 14, 1956, Little Rock, with few fans attracted to another cellar dweller, transferred to Montgomery. It was the first franchise move since 1931, but owner Ray Winder brought his club back home to Little Rock for 1957. The franchise began to label itself the "Arkansas" Travelers, in an effort to generate broader fan appeal. But attendance remained poor (75,181) in Little Rock and worse in Mobile (71,522). The worst attendance of all was at last-place New Orleans (67,287), long a bellwether franchise of the SA. Attendance at the 1957 playoffs was a meager 22,943. New Orleans again finished last in 1958 and attendance in the Crescent City continued to drop (50,369). Total SA attendance in 1958 nosedived below the million mark (804,175), then bottomed out in 1959 (614,214).

The diehard fans who kept coming to the aging ballparks of the SA continued to enjoy quality play. On May 21, 1958, Nashville first baseman Chuck Coles (.307, 29 HR, 107 RBI) slammed three home runs in a seven-inning game at Birmingham. Coles' teammate, Jim Fridley, won the batting title (.348, 20

HR, 101 RBI), and Little Rock catcher-manager Les Peden finished second (.334 with 26 homers). There were three 20-game winners: Birmingham starter-reliever Bill Harrington (20–7 with 17 GS in 53 G); Nashville strikeout leader Jim O'Toole (20–8 with 189 Ks); and Atlanta lefty Bob Hartman (20–10).

Birmingham finished first in 1958, then won the playoffs and downed Corpus Christi in the Dixie Series. By this time the Texas League was suffering as badly as the SA at the gate. The Texas League could muster only six clubs for 1959, necessitating a schedule reduction. With the two leagues ending their seasons at different times, and with a severe decline in interest in the Dixie Series, the famous old sporting event was suspended.

After the close of the 1958 season Ray Winder and his partners sold their Little Rock franchise to Shreveport, which had dropped out of the Texas League a year earlier. Shreveport returned to the SA for the first time since 1907 and led the league in team hitting and homers, but fans at SPAR Stadium did not respond (47,636).

Nashville outfielder Stan Palys led the SA in batting and runs in 1957 (.359, 24 HR, 116 R, 112 RBI). He won another batting championship with Birmingham in 1960, and also posted the most hits, doubles, and triples (.370, 28 HR, 116 RBI). The next season Palys again played for the Barons and won the RBI crown (.333, 114 RBI).

With poor fan turnout for recent Shaughnessy playoffs, it was decided to play a split season in 1959 with a best-four-of-seven series between the two winners. Birmingham won the first half and, for the second consecutive season, finished with the league's best record. But Mobile took the second half and dumped Birmingham in the playoff.

Mobile manager Mel McGaha enjoyed the services of the best pitching staff in the league, including ERA champ Bill Dailey (11–5, 2.41) and strikeout king Carl Mathias (17–9 with 183 Ks). The biggest star of the season was Mobile first baseman Gordon Coleman, the 1956 RBI titlist (.316, 27 HR, 118 RBI). In 1959 Coleman became only the second player in SA history to win a Triple Crown (.353, 30 HR, 110 RBI).

After years of poor attendance, New Orleans — a key franchise of the Southern since the nineteenth century — dropped out of the league. A public stock drive in Little Rock purchased the bankrupt franchise and resurrected the Travelers. Charles Hurth of New Orleans, SA president since 1947, resigned and was replaced by Hal Totten of Birmingham.

An additional problem came on Easter Sunday, April 17, 1960, two days before the Memphis home opener. Historic Russwood Park was destroyed by fire, forcing the Chicks to move to Hodges Field, a concrete high school football stadium. The right field foul line was only 204 feet from home plate. A 40-foot screen was erected in right field, but Memphis and Birmingham blasted a record 11 home runs in the first game, necessitating a ground rule limiting balls that cleared the screen to doubles. In mid-July the Chicks transferred to Toby Park, another municipal field with larger dimensions. Memphis played five "home" games at Columbus, Georgia, and Mobile also staged two games there.

For 1960 the league decided to return to the Shaughnessy Plan, with each series a best-three-of-five format. Atlanta, which finished last the previous year, vaulted all the way to first place in a race that was not decided until the last inning of the final game. Manager Rube Walker's Crackers held a commanding lead in August but went into a tailspin, which climaxed with doubleheader losses to Mobile on the last two days of the season, September 10 and 11. In the meantime Shreveport became almost unbeatable under catcher-manager Les Peden (.327). The Sports ended the season on September 11 with a doubleheader in

Catcher Les Peden played for Little Rock in 1957, (.297), then was player-manager of the Travelers the next year (.334 with 26 homers). He served as player-manager of Shreveport in 1959 (.300), 1960 (.327), and 1961 (.283).
— Courtesy Bill McIntyre, *Shreveport Times*

Nashville, winning the opening game for their 25th victory in 28 games. A win in the nightcap would give Shreveport the pennant, and the Sports led, 1–0, into the eighth inning. But the Vols rallied to tie the contest, then won in the ninth, 2–1, to hand Atlanta its 17th Southern Association title by half a game.

Atlanta was upset by fourth-place Birmingham in the playoff opener, while Shreveport fell to Little Rock. The Travelers, led by player-manager Fred Hatfield (.277), went on to edge the Barons in the finals. With no big league working agreement, 75-year-old Ray Winder had pieced together a championship roster which attracted the SA's highest attendance (179,471).

Birmingham outfielder Stan Palys, who had won the 1957 hitting title while playing for Nashville (.359, 24 HR, 112 RBI), repeated as batting champ in 1960 (.370, 28 HR, 116 RBI). Shreveport outfielder Leo Posada (.314, 18 HR, 112 RBI) was the RBI leader, while teammate Jim McManus (.304, 32 HR, 117 RBI) was the home run king. The best pitcher in the league was Atlanta's fireballing lefty Pete Richert, who led the SA in victories, strikeouts, complete games and shutouts (19–9, 251 Ks in 225 IP, 18 CG, 6 ShO).

Memphis, with no professional ballpark and a seventh-place team, mustered the league's smallest attendance (48,487), and the franchise moved to Macon for 1961. The 1960 playoffs had attracted barely 20,000 fans, and it was decided that there would be no post-season play in 1961. The pennant race was between Chattanooga and Birmingham, with the Lookouts under manager Frank Lucchesi edging the Barons by a one-game margin. But Chattanooga and Birmingham each attracted only a little more than 100,000 fans, while Little Rock was the attendance leader with just 136,316 admissions. All of the other clubs were well under 100,000, and Shreveport managed just 28,349, an average of only 368 fans per game. Overall SA attendance was a meager 647,831.

Chattanooga's pennant drive was led by third baseman Wayne Graham (.331, with a league-leading 199 hits and 51 doubles) and righthander John Boozer (19–9). Birmingham boasted RBI champ Stan Palys (.333, 13 HR, 114 RBI), run and walk leader Legrant Scott (.314, 129 R, 123 W), and brilliant lefthander Howard Koplitz (23–2, 2.11 ERA, and the league's final nine-inning no-hitter on June 30), who led the SA in victories and percentage, and barely missed the ERA title. The ERA champ was Atlanta reliever Jack Smith (12–7, 2.09 in 70 G and 155 IP), while colorful Little Rock southpaw Bo Belinsky won the final strikeout crown (9–10, 182 K in 174 IP).

Despite these fine performances and a tight pennant race, fan interest was indifferent and everyone was losing money. No improvement in the discouraging state of minor league baseball was in sight, and leagues were folding everywhere. For decades the Southern Association was a model of minor league stability, but in recent seasons the SA had scrambled to field eight teams. The loss of franchises in New Orleans and Memphis was especially painful, and other key cities were on the verge of collapse. After 61 seasons of play, the historic Southern Association suspended operations.

Classic SA Stadiums

ATLANTA

Ponce de Leon Park. Wooden Ponce de Leon Park, built in 1906 on Ponce de Leon Boulevard, was consumed in a spectacular blaze on September 9, 1923. The Crackers finished the season at Grant Field on the campus of Georgia Tech. A new $250,000 concrete-and-steel facility was built on the 23-acre stadium site, providing seating for 15,000 fans (21,812 were admitted on opening day of 1948). Christened Spiller Park after the club president, the name was changed back to Ponce de Leon Park in 1932. Right field was 321 feet down the line, but left was 365 feet and center was a distant 462 feet. A magnolia tree was in deep right center, and the scoreboard was in left center. A slope in right eventually sported four ascending rows of billboards. When Earl Mann brought in the fences in 1949, a two-foot hedge was planted from left to center. But outfielders caught deep flies on the run and tumbled over the hedge, creating a ground rule homer. A four-foot chain link fence soon removed this eccentricity. Atlanta-Fulton County Stadium opened in 1965, and Ponce de Leon, once called "the most magnificent park in the minors," was torn down in 1967.

BIRMINGHAM

Rickwood Field. Built in 1910 for $75,000 along the lines of Pittsburgh's new Forbes Field, Rickwood was the first concrete-and-steel stadium in the SA. Located at 1137 West Second Avenue, Rickwood seated 14,500, and over 20,000 crowded in for opening game of the 1931 Dixie Series. The original outfield was vast (405 in left, 470 in center), and the big hand-operated scoreboard stood in left center. A 1921 cyclone wrecked the outfield fence and bleachers, and repairs cost $30,000. When the playing fence was brought in to facilitate home runs, the original walls were left standing, and light poles were erected between the old and new fences in 1938. Within a few years the grandstand roof was extended to the right field corner, and bleachers curved behind the wall in right. Utilized by the Barons through 1987,

Rickwood still hosts high school baseball and is a magnificent example of early ballpark architecture, having been placed on the National Register of Historic Places.

CHATTANOOGA

Joe Engel Stadium. In 1929 Clark Griffith purchased the Chattanooga Lookouts as a farm club for his Washington Senators. Griffith sent Joe Engel to run the club, and his first assignment was to erect a 12,000-seat brick-and-steel stadium to replace 20-year-old Andrews Field at Third and O'Neal streets. Right field was 318 feet down the line and left was 368 feet away, while center field was an overnight hike — 471 feet from the plate. The hand-operated scoreboard was in left, and in deep center a five-foot incline led to a terrace that was an adventure for outfielders. Joe Engel proved to be a promotional genius, and when he raffled off a house in 1936 almost 25,000 jammed the stadium.

KNOXVILLE

Smithson Stadium. Until 1930 professional baseball in Knoxville was played at wooden Caswell Park, located at Jessamine Street off Magnolia Avenue. But city councilman W. N. Smithson persuaded the council to dismantle Caswell Park and erect a new stadium, which was named in his honor (although most fans continued to call the facility Caswell Park). When the Mobile Club transferred to Knoxville on July 22, 1931, the new Smokies occupied new Smithson Stadium. But the Smokies proved to be chronic losers, and club owners felt that they could not afford to install lights, even though other SA stadiums invested in lighting systems during the 1930s to stimulate attendance. The franchise moved back to Mobile in 1944, and Smithson Stadium burned in 1953. It was rebuilt as Knoxville Municipal Stadium, and renamed Bill Meyer Stadium in 1957.

LITTLE ROCK

Travelers Field. In 1932 the Little Rock Travelers left old Kavanaugh Field for a new stadium in Fair Park, now known as War Memorial Park. Travelers Field seated 7,000 and had a hill in left that was not as irregular or steep as right in the Sulphur Dell. Left field was 345 feet down the line, right was a distant 395 feet, and center was a more distant 450 feet. After World War II these distances were considerably reduced when home plate was moved almost 30 feet closer to the fences, so that the grandstand could be extended for additional reserved seating.

MACON

Luther Williams Field. Built in 1929 just north of the burned grandstand of Central City Park, which had been erected in the namesake park in 1892. Projected expenses were $40,000, but the stadium finally cost $60,000. There was a covered grandstand, with a large bleacher section for whites down the right field line and "colored bleachers" along the left field line. The seating capacity totaled 6,000, but had been reduced by 1,000 when Macon joined the SA for the league's final season in 1961. "Operation Face Lift" in 1956 replaced the old wooden bleachers with steel bleachers, and moved the light poles out of the outfield.

MEMPHIS

Russwood Park. A major renovation of Russwood in 1921 modernized the stadium and increased seating from 6,500 to 11,000. The first night game was played on May 13, 1936. Following an exhibition game between the White Sox and Indians on April 17, 1960, a massive conflagration consumed Russwood and destroyed surrounding buildings.

MOBILE

League Park. Located at Ann and Tennessee streets, the 11,000-seat stadium also was known as Monroe Park and Hartwell Field. A 1964 hurricane swept away the big scoreboard in left field.

MONTGOMERY

Cramton Bowl. Located on the south side of Madison Avenue at Hillard street, the Cramton Bowl was used for many years for football and baseball, including Montgomery's 1943 Southern Association club. The football field was laid out north to south, while a covered baseball grandstand was in the northwest corner. The football visitors' stands along the east sideline provided left field bleacher seating for baseball, while across the field larger bleachers stretched down the right field line. Roofed stands also extended from the grandstand across the north end zone, which offered baseball fans seating down the third base-left field line. Left field was extremely short, but the right field line was more than 600 feet long.

Paterson Field. In 1949 Paterson Field was built above Madison Avenue across from the Cramton Bowl. The symmetrical grandstand and bleachers seated 6,000, and accommodated Montgomery's 1956 SA entry, as well as the later Southern League teams. The foul lines are 330 feet deep and center field is 380 feet from the plate.

NASHVILLE

Sulphur Dell. Baseball had been played at the Sulphur Spring Bottom since the 1860s, and in time an enclosed park covered the block bounded by 4th and 5th avenues and by Jackson and Summer streets. The wooden grandstand of the Sulphur Dell park stood in the northeast corner of the block. In 1926 a new grandstand was erected at the southwest corner, creating a 262-foot right field with a steep hill angling sharply upward at 224 feet from the plate. Left fielders used a path up the hill to a 25-foot-high shelf, where most outfielders positioned themselves. The wooden outfield fence was 16 feet high, but a 30-foot screen was added in 1931, stretching from the right field foul line pole to a point 186 feet into right center. Lefthanded sluggers still feasted on the short right field porch, and pitchers called the stadium "Suffer Hell." Sulphur Dell also was termed "The Dump," because of odors that wafted from a nearby city dump. Also nearby was the Cumberland River, and Sulphur Dell suffered considerable flooding through the years. Sulphur Dell was even more intimate than most minor league parks: third base was just 26 feet from the seats, and first base was only 42 feet from the fans. Lights were added in 1938, when seating was increased from 7,000 to 8,500.

NEW ORLEANS

Pelican Stadium was built in 1915 at a cost of nearly $50,000, utilizing materials from old Athletic Park. Also known as Julius Heinemann Stadium and Municipal Park, the facility was bounded by Tulane Avenue and by Carrollton, Gravier and Pierce streets. The spacious outfield stretched 427 feet down the left field line, 418 in right, and 405 in center. Pelican Stadium was torn down after the 1957 season.

City Park Stadium. A horseshoe-shaped football stadium in City Park, the facility was used for Pelican baseball in 1958 and 1959. Both foul lines were short, but center field was spacious. A 440-yard track extended into fair territory, coming into play most commonly down the lines.

SHREVEPORT

SPAR Stadium. Built as Texas League Park in 1938 on the Park Avenue site of Gasser Park, which burned during the 1932 season. The groundskeeper was Al Gaedke, a crusty bachelor who lived year round in a little house in the far right field corner. During the off-season he transformed the outfield into a small golf course, and his well-tended domain was informally known as "Gaedke's Gardens." Shreveport left the Texas League after the 1956 season, and when the Sports played SA ball in 1959–61, the aging facility was called SPAR Stadium. Shreveport reentered the Texas League in 1968 and played in decaying SPAR Stadium through 1985, after which the team moved into beautiful new Fair Grounds Field.

SPAR Stadium still stands as of this writing, badly deteriorated but a tangible reminder of the last three seasons of the Southern Association.

Many historic SA ballparks burned or were razed, but others have been beautifully refurbished. Ray Winder Field, christened Travelers Field when it opened in 1932, hosted SA baseball for 30 seasons, and has since been handsomely maintained as a Texas League stadium. Montgomery's Paterson Field was built in 1949 and accepted the Little Rock franchise for part of the 1956 season. Unused by pros since Montgomery left the Southern League in 1980, Paterson Field appears ready to resume play on short notice. Macon's Luther Williams Field, erected in 1929 on the site of a burned ballpark built in 1892, was used during the last season of the Southern Association, as well as for three years of SL ball during the 1960s and for SALLY play through the 1987 season. Also built in 1929 and the home of SA baseball for more than three decades is Chattanooga's magnificently renovated Joe Engel Stadium.

The richest repository of Southern Association memories is Rickwood Field, which opened in Birmingham in 1910 and for more than half a century paraded minor league stars and future Hall of Famers from across one of the nation's most historic baseball circuits. At Rickwood in 1917 the fourth — and final — nine-inning perfect game was pitched in the SA; at Rickwood venerable Ray Caldwell beat Dizzy Dean 1–0 in the 1931 Dixie Series opener before an overflow crowd of 20,000; at Rickwood in 1935 Eddie Rose killed a pigeon with a line-drive single. At Rickwood and at Joe Engel Stadium, at Luther Williams Field and at Paterson Field, at SPAR Stadium and at Ray Winder Field, the baseball buff can happily indulge himself in a nostalgic reverie of vanished heroes in baggy, sweat-soaked flannel uniforms.

1904–1963

The SALLY League

1904–1917

The growth of minor league baseball during the early years of the twentieth century may be traced by the number of leagues in the National Association. During 1902, the first season of the National Association, there were 15 member leagues. In 1903, 21 leagues began the season. The number increased to 27 in 1904, and in 1905 there was another jump to 34 member leagues. In 1903 there were only two Class C leagues, but in 1904 there were five Class C circuits, including the new South Atlantic League, soon to be known throughout baseball as the "SALLY."

In 1903, with the Southern Association in its third season and the popularity of professional baseball spreading rapidly, Charles W. Boyer, secretary-treasurer (equivalent to the modern GM) of the Atlanta Crackers, received a letter from Jacksonville businessman J. B. Lucy. Lucy suggested "the formation of a Coast League," and he and Boyer began to correspond with potential backers in promising cities. An organizational meeting was held in Savannah's DeSoto Hotel on Tuesday, November 24, 1903, and Boyer agreed to serve as league president at a salary of $1,500 per year. Umpires were to be paid $150 monthly, but they had to provide their own travel expenses, and there would be just one ump per game. Teams would have a $1,000 monthly salary cap for players, with a 12-player limit per club.

The Georgia Peach

In 1904, at the age of 17, Georgia native Ty Cobb played his first 37 games as a professional with the Augusta Tourists. He did not hit well (.237) and was farmed out to Anniston of the outlaw Tennessee-Alabama League (.302 in another 37 games). The next year Cobb was back with Augusta, where the Detroit Tigers held their 1905 spring training. Cobb played 103 games with Augusta, enough to qualify for the SALLY batting title (.326). In August Detroit loaned Augusta rookie pitcher Ed Cicotte and paid $700 for Cobb, who played in 40 games for the Tigers (.240) and went on to collect 12 American League batting championships.

While in the SALLY, Cobb would buy two bags of popcorn prior to the start of the game and secure the sacks inside his loose flannel uniform shirt. Then he would munch on popcorn while he was in the outfield. On the basepaths he was speedy and aggressive, and Augusta manager Con Struthers observed that "the only way you could hold Cobb on a base was to tie him there."

After another meeting in January 1904, an April 26 starting date was set with six clubs: the Columbia Skyscrapers; the Augusta Tourists; the Charleston Sea Gulls, who would play at a new ballpark; J. B. Lucy's Jacksonville Jays, who also had a new park; the Macon Highlanders, who would play on a diamond at the

State Fairgrounds; and the Savannah Pathfinders, who leased an old ballpark. The original Savannah backer withdrew, and Boyer agreed to operate the Pathfinders. Boyer moved to Savannah and, since he would serve as league president for five years, the first SALLY headquarters was in Savannah (he sold the Pathfinders after two seasons).

First Sally League Box Scores

TUESDAY, APRIL 26, 1904

CHARLESTON	AB	R	H	PO	A	E
Hayes, lf	4	0	0	1	0	0
Ashenbach, cf	4	1	1	1	0	0
Smith, 3b	5	1	2	0	1	0
Doyle(rf	5	0	0	1	0	0
Mitchell, ss	5	0	2	2	3	1
McKernan, 1b	5	0	1	12	1	0
Hempleman, 2b	4	0	1	3	1	0
Lehman, c	4	1	2	7	1	0
Childs, p	3	0	0	0	1	0
TOTALS	39	3	9	27	8	2

SAVANNAH	AB	R	H	PO	A	E
Bratton, 2b	4	0	1	1	2	0
Ray, cf	4	0	0	3	1	1
Burt, lf	4	0	0	2	0	0
LaRocque, 1b	4	0	1	10	1	0
Eggert, ss	4	0	0	3	3	2
Webster, rf	3	0	0	1	0	1
Kinsky, c	3	0	0	3	1	0
Oyler, 3b	3	0	1	3	3	0
Welch, p	2	0	0	1	2	1
TOTALS	31	0	3	27	13	5

```
Charleston ..........0   0   1   0   1   0   0   1   0——3
Savannah   ..........0   0   0   0   0   0   0   0   0——0
```

Earned runs: Charleston 3. Home run: Smith. Left on bases: Charleston 6, Savannah 5. Double plays: Mitchell to McKernan, Hempleman to McKernan. Struck out: by Childs 7, Welch 1. Bases on balls: off Childs 1, Welch 2. Time of game 1:37. Umpire: Thomas Connors. Attendance: 3,200.

COLUMBIA	AB	R	H	PO	A	E
Reardon, ss	5	1	1	1	3	1
Kuhn, 2b	5	0	0	1	3	1
Miller, 3b	4	0	1	2	3	0
Jacobs, 1b	1	1	0	13	0	0
Gunter, rf	4	2	1	0	0	0
Stewart, cf	4	1	0	2	0	0
Wilson, lf	5	1	1	3	0	0
Shea, c	4	1	2	5	2	0
Engle, p	5	1	2	0	3	0
TOTALS	37	8	8	27	14	2

AUGUSTA	AB	R	H	PO	A	E
Spratt, 3b	4	2	0	3	4	0
Butler, lf	5	1	1	0	0	1
McMillin, rf	4	1	0	1	0	0
Truby, 2b	4	0	1	1	1	0
Bussey, 1b	4	0	1	8	1	0
Edmonds, c	4	0	0	11	1	0
Cobb, cf	4	2	2	0	0	0
Thornton, ss	3	1	0	2	1	2
Durham, p	4	0	2	1	2	0
TOTALS	36	7	7	27	10	3

```
Columbia ..........1   0   3   0   0   0   0   1   3——8
Augusta  ..........1   0   0   0   0   0   5   1——7
```

Earned runs: Columbia 2, Augusta 1. Two-base hits: Shea, Cobb. Three-base hit: Gunter. Home runs: Cobb, Engle. Left on bases: Columbia 10, Augusta 4. Stolen bases: Augusta 6. Struck out: by Engle 4, Durham 8. Bases on balls: off Engle 2, Durham 5. Hit by pitcher: by Durham 3. Passed ball: Edmonds. Time of game 2:05. Umpire: Mace.

JACKSONVILLE	AB	R	H	PO	A	E
Springs, 3b	4	0	0	1	0	0
Dingle, ss	4	0	0	1	2	1
Nichols, lf	4	0	1	1	0	1
Persons, p	4	0	1	0	2	0
Wynne, 2b	3	1	1	4	1	1
Chappell, rf	4	1	0	2	0	0
Reed, 1b	4	0	2	10	0	2
Womble, cf	3	0	0	2	4	3
Robinson, c	3	0	0	3	1	1
TOTALS	33	2	5	24	10	9

MACON	AB	R	H	PO	A	E
Lipe, 3b	4	1	1	3	1	2
Smith, cf	4	1	0	0	0	0
Duplane, lf	4	2	0	0	0	1
Harnish, c	5	2	3	6	0	1
Sentell, ss	4	0	1	4	2	0
Sens, 2b	4	1	2	1	0	0
Hays, 2b	4	1	1	2	2	1
Hoffman, 1b	4	2	4	10	0	2
Bayne, p	4	0	1	1	4	0
TOTALS	37	10	13	27	9	7

```
Jacksonville ..........0   1   0   0   0   1   0   0   0——2
Macon        ..........3   0   2   1   2   1   1   0   x——10
```

Two-base hits: Sentell, Hoffman, Harnish. Three-base hits: Harnish 2, Hoffman. Double plays: Wynne to Reed, Womble to Reed. Struck out: by Bayne 6, Persons 2. Bases on balls: off Bayne 2. Hit by pitcher: Womble. Attendance: 2,500. Time of game 1:50. Umpire: McNamara.

The first SALLY box scores, April 26, 1904.

"The season was successful financially," observed the *Reach Guide* at the end of 1904, "the conduct of the players and managers was good, and the administration of President Boyer so just and tactful that there was never any serious clash." Macon won the first two SALLY pennants behind manager-outfielder Billy Smith. The Highlanders were led to the 1904 flag by victory and strikeout leader Brindle Bayne (30–13 with 288 Ks) and right fielder George Stinson, the league's second highest hitter (.297). In 1905 there were five Highlanders among the league's top eight batters, including Stinson (.270), Billy Smith (.285), and two-year shortstop Paul Sentell (.315), who led the SALLY in runs and hits. Rob Spade led the league in victories (25–8) and also played 28 games in the outfield, while S. D. Loucks was the percentage leader (16–3).

Savannah edged Augusta for the 1906 flag behind batting champ Ed Sabrie (.290), run leader F. J. King, and percentage leader Walt Deaver (18–4). Augusta aces Nap Rucker (27–9) and Ducky Holmes (26–16) were sold to the big leagues. In 1907 it was Charleston's turn to claim the pennant. Outfielder Tom Raftery led the league in batting, stolen bases, runs and hits (.301 with 80 steals), while righthander Bugs Raymond set all-time SALLY records for victories and strikeouts (35–11 with 355 Ks).

Phil's Finish

In 1908, a season in which SALLY teams played only 104 to 116 games, Augusta hurler Phil Sitton led the league in victories (19–9) and became invincible during the last part of the year. On July 27 he shut out Columbia, 7–0, then beat Charleston, 5–1, four days later. He twirled a no-hitter against Columbia on August 4, matching the hitless game produced against Columbia three days earlier by his brother, Carl, a Jacksonville righthander who led the SALLY in winning percentage (17–5).

Two days after his no-hit shutout over Columbia, Phil blanked Jacksonville in both ends of a doubleheader, 3–0 and 6–0. On August 12 he fired his second no-hitter in nine days, dumping Charleston, 3–0. Four days later he ended the season with a 13–0 romp over Savannah.

Phil Sitton won his last seven games in the SALLY, with six shutouts and two no-hitters, and only one run in his final 65 innings. He ended the SALLY season with merely 14 hits in 46 consecutive scoreless innings, and pumped out five shutouts and two no-nos in 13 days.

With the early end of the SALLY schedule, Phil and Carl went up to

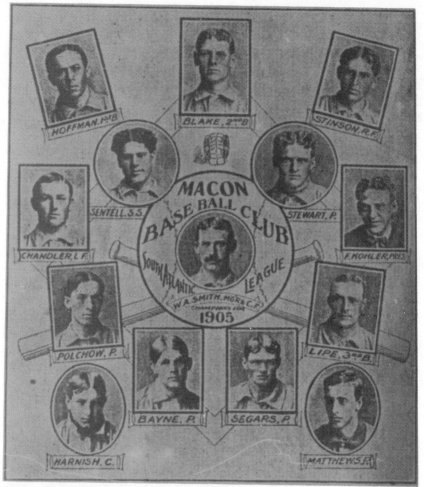

Player-manager Billy Smith (center) led Macon to the first two SALLY pennants. Despite the label, this is the 1904 club. The 1904 champs boasted victory and strikeout leader Brindle Bayne (30–13, 288 Ks), who recorded nearly half of the team's wins. Playing for both pennant-winners were Sentell at shortstop, Lipe at third, Harnish behind the plate, Stinson in right, and Smith in center.

the Southern Association. Phil pitched seven games for Atlanta, but had little luck with a losing team (1–6). Carl, however, advanced to New Orleans, working 10 games (6–4) and pitching a dramatic 1–0 triumph over Nashville that gave the Pelicans the 1908 pennant on the final day of the season.

After the 1908 season, which was won by the Jacksonville Jays, Charles Boyer resigned as SALLY president and was replaced by W. R. Joyner of Atlanta. The SALLY expanded to eight teams, adding Chattanooga and Columbus. The two newcomers fielded the best clubs in the league, and Chattanooga outdistanced the competition behind percentage leader Prince Gaskill (21–4) and third baseman Scotty Alcock (.349). Columbus showcased victory leader Roy Radabaugh (25–9), while the batting champ was Savannah outfielder Shoeless Joe Jackson (.358).

Charleston, the cellar team of 1908, fell out of the 1909 race early, and the club folded on July 1. The franchise was transferred to Knoxville, and it was decided to split the season to restore fan interest throughout the league. Augusta finished ahead of Chattanooga in the second half, and in a best-four-of-seven playoff, the Lookouts won the seventh game and the pennant.

Chattanooga returned to the Southern Association, and Knoxville was dropped from the league, cutting the SALLY back to six teams for 1910. Columbus edged Macon for the pennant, while pitchers were the star performers of the season. Roy Radabaugh again sparked Columbus (22–15); Sam Weems of Macon was the victory leader (25–14); Bill Pope of Jacksonville was right behind (24–11); and Rufus Nolley was almost unbeatable (19–3) for Savannah.

Savannah won the 1906 pennant behind batting champ Ed Sabrie (standing at far right – .290), run leader F. J. King (bottom, far right), and pitchers Walt Deaver (standing, third from right – 18–4), Bugs Raymond (middle, far right – 19–8) and Klondike Kane (standing, third from left – 17–9).

Shoeless Joe Jackson (middle, second from right) won the 1909 SALLY hitting title (.358) while playing for Savannah. The next season Shoeless Joe was the SA batting champ (.354) with New Orleans.

Player-manager Jim Fox (far right) gave his name to his team when the Columbus Foxes joined the SALLY in 1909. Righthander Roy Radabaugh (front, fifth from left) starred in 1909 (25–9) and for the pennant-winners of 1910 (22–15) and 1911 (27–6).

No-hit Parade

On April 12, 1909, three days before the start of the SALLY season, the Macon Peaches won a 1–0 exhibition over Mercer University. The winning pitcher, Sam Weems, allowed no hits or walks and fanned 14 en route to a perfect game. Weems' performance set the stage for seven no-hitters in 1909, the most of any SALLY season.

Percentage leader Prince Gaskill (21–4 for Chattanooga) fired the first no-hitter, on May 13, and there were two more no-nos before the month was over. On July 19 Al Demaree (18–11 for Savannah) no-hit Knoxville, a victim of three of the 1909 no-hitters, including the last one, tossed on September 1 by H. D. Clark (17–10 for Chattanooga).

The other two no-hitters were registered by strikeout leader L. R. Wagner (13–22, 202 Ks) on July 5 and August 31. On July 14, 1911, Wagner, now pitching for Columbia (22–10), twirled his third SALLY no-hitter, the all-time league standard.

In 1911 Charleston returned to the league and Albany, Georgia, was added, again making the SALLY an eight-team circuit. Columbus promptly marched back into first place, and in June the SALLY owners once more resorted to a split season. But in July Augusta disbanded, although the team was maintained by the league as the "S.A.L. Club." Then Charleston's ballpark was wrecked by an August 29 storm, causing the Sea Gulls to cease operations. The S.A.L. Club then was disbanded as the league finished the season with six teams. Columbia won the second half but fell to Columbus in the playoffs, four games to two, as the Foxes claimed their second consecutive pennant.

Albany third-sacker Scotty Alcock was the 1911 batting champ (.333), but pitchers again dominated play. Roy Radabaugh again won big (27–6), becoming the only pitcher in SALLY history to win 20 games in three seasons. There were nine 20-game winners, including Fullenwider (26–9), Clark (23–13) and Wagner (22–10) of Columbia, Ed Porray (27–13) of Albany, and victory leader Phil Douglas (28–11) of Macon. There also were three 20-game *losers*, including Savannah workhorse Dick Robertson, who set the all-time SALLY record for defeats (16–26). Fie Fullenwider tossed one of four no-hitters during the season.

Following three consecutive shaky seasons, the league hired a new president, N. P. Corish of Savannah, dropped Augusta and Charleston in order to have a tight six-team circuit, "and rid itself of a lot of high-salaried veteran players by the adoption of stringent salary-limit and team-limit rules." Jacksonville won the first half, Columbus took the second half, then the Tarpons downed the Foxes in the playoff series to claim the flag. The star of 1912 was Savannah ace Albert Schultz, who led the league in victories, strikeouts, and games and innings pitched (25–12, 318 Ks, and only 243 hits in 371 IP), working in 43 of his team's 116 contests.

In 1913 Charleston returned to the SALLY as a replacement for Columbia. A split season again was planned, but Savannah won both halves to take the pennant without a playoff. Savannah was sparked by batting champ Coalyard Mike Handiboe (.314), victory, strikeout and percentage leader Dick Robertson (28–8 with 235 Ks), and Rebel Adams (20–12).

The next season the SALLY once more tried an eight-team format by readmitting Augusta and Columbia. Savannah successfully defended their championship by winning the first half, then defeating second-half winner Albany in the playoffs, four games to two. Coalyard Mike Handiboe again was an offensive standout for Savannah (.305), leading the SALLY in runs, while hit leader Sam Mayer (.314) and longtime big league catcher Harry Smith (.332) were major factors in the league's best attack.

In 1915 a split season was planned, with the first half scheduled to end on June 19 and the second half on August 29. But bad weather severely affected attendance, and the first half was halted on June 9. Conditions remained shaky during the second half, and the league shut down five weeks early, on July 20. Teams had played only 86 to 88 games apiece. Macon won the first half, but Columbus won the second half and the playoff. Macon was led by batting champ C. M. Chancey (.359), while Columbus ace Phil Redding, who had won the strikeout title in 1914, was the victory and percentage leader in 1915 (19–6).

Last-place Savannah dropped out of the league, replaced by Montgomery. Augusta won the first half, but during the second half Albany folded. The league then voted to drop Montgomery and finish the season with six teams. Columbia won the second half, but lost four straight games to Augusta in the playoffs. Roy Radabaugh returned to the SALLY, resuming his winning ways (19–9) with Columbus. Macon ace Reid Zellars led the league in victories, strikeouts, innings and games (22–15, 237 Ks, 376 IP,

Team Nicknames

Albany
Babies (1911–16)
Asheville
Skylanders (1924)
Tourists (1925–30, 1959–63)
Augusta
Tourists (1904–11, 1914–17)
Dollies (1919)
Georgians (1920–21)
Tygers (1922, 1924–29)
Tigers (1923, 1936–42, 1946–52,
1955–58)
Rams (1953–54)
Wolves (1930)
Confederate Yankees (1962–63)
Charleston
Sea Gulls (1904–09, 1913–17)
Gulls (1919)
Palmettos (1920)
Pals (1921)
Rebels (1940–42, 1946–53)
Chisox (1959)
White Sox (1960)
Charlotte
Hornets (1919–30, 1954–63)
Chattanooga
Lookouts (1909, 1963)
Columbia
Skyscrapers (1904)
Gamecocks (1905–10)
Commies (1911)
Comers (1912, 1914–17,
1919–23, 1925–30)
Senators (1936–37)
Reds (1938–42, 1946–55,
1960–61)
Gems (1956–57)
Columbus
Foxes (1909–17, 1956–57)
Red Birds (1936–42)
Cardinals 1946–55)
Pirates (1959)

Gastonia
Comers (1923)
Pirates (1959)
Greenville
Spinners (1919–30, 1938–42,
1946–50, 1961–62)
Jacksonville
Jays (1904–10)
Tarpons (1911–16)
Roses (1917)
Tars (1936–42, 1946–52)
Braves (1953–60)
Jets (1961)
Knoxville
Appalachians (1909)
Smokies (1956–63)
Lynchburg
White Sox (1962–63)
Macon
Highlanders (1904)
Brigands (1905)
Tigers (1917)
Peaches (1904–16, 1923–30,
1936–42, 1946–56, 1961–63)
Dodgers (1956–60)
Montgomery
Rebels (1916–17, 1951, 1954–56)
Grays (1952–53)
Nashville
Vols (1963)
Norfolk-Portsmouth
Tides (1961–62)
Savannah
Pathfinders (1904–10)
Scouts (1911–12)
Colts (1913–15)
Indians (1936–42, 1946–54)
Athletics (1955)
Redlegs (1956–58)
Reds (1960)
White Sox (1962)
Spartanburg
Pioneers (1919–21)
Spartans (1922–29, 1938–40)

and 50 of 122 games), while the percentage leader was a Columbia pitcher with the intimidating name of Jesse James (15–5).

The United States entered the Great War in the spring of 1917, and the public preoccupation with the war effort resulted in severe difficulties for the minor leagues. Only 21 leagues opened play in 1917, down from 43 in 1914, and many clubs and circuits folded during the season. The SALLY opened with six teams, but on May 19 Macon (7–19) and Columbus (8–19) dropped out. Although the remaining four teams started a second season on June 4, a month later Jacksonville and Augusta disbanded. The two surviving clubs, Columbia and Charleston, each had won a half season, and Columbia took the pennant play-off series in mid-July, four games to two.

The SALLY did not attempt to operate in 1918 (only nine minor leagues opened play, and the International League was the sole circuit to complete its schedule). During its first few seasons the SALLY was noted as a "fast and prosperous" league. But several wobbly years followed, with franchise transfers between cities, clubs disbanding, and shortened seasons. The SALLY ceased operations in 1918, although it was hoped that the league could be revived after the war.

1919–1930

The postwar years witnessed a comeback for professional baseball that developed into a minor league heyday during the Golden Age of Sports. The SALLY was reorganized in 1919 by six cities: Augusta, Charleston and Columbia were league veterans, while Charlotte, Greenville and Spartanburg were new to the circuit. The new president was W. H. Walsh of Charleston.

Columbia player-manager Tom Clarke, who had just concluded a 10-year career as a National League catcher, led the Comers to the pennant behind batting champ Walter Johnson (.362). At the end of the season Columbia of the Class C SALLY challenged Atlanta, champion of the Class A Southern Association, and the Crackers fell to the Comers, four games to one.

Columbia repeated as champions in 1920 with a lineup that

bristled with future or former big leaguers: outfiedler Goose Goslin (.316, and 5–4 as a pitcher), player-manager Zinn Beck (.313), first-sacker Swats Swacina (.315), catcher Lew Wendell (.306), righthander Lawrence Cheney (23–6), and southpaw Earl Whitehill (20–10). The victory leader was another future big leaguer, Greenville righty Jess Doyle (25–8), and the stolen base champ was speedy Charleston outfielder Maurice "Flash" Archdeacon (.310, 44 SB).

The next year Goose Goslin sparked Columbia to a third consecutive pennant. Before finishing the season with Washington, the future Hall of Famer led the SALLY in batting, hits, runs and RBIs (.390, 214 H, 124 R, 131 RBI). Player-manager Zinn Beck (.383) was second to Goslin in the hitting race, and his pitching staff boasted a formidable one-two punch in victory leader Lee Johnson (24–13) and percentage and ERA champ Roy Jordan (21–2, 2.10).

In 1921 the SALLY was advanced back into Class B from Class C, and the schedule was expanded from 120 to 148 games, although it was cut back to 132 games in 1922. In 1922 Charleston broke Columbia's stranglehold on the SALLY throne room, winning the pennant behind strikeout king George Pipgras (19–9, 175 Ks) and ERA champ Godfrey Brogan (18–9, 2.90, and .346 at the plate). The star of the season was Charlotte outfielder Ben Paschal, who played in only 98 games but led the league in runs, hits, RBIs, triples and homers (.326, 131 R, 174 H, 114 RBI, 19 3B, 18 HR). Future Hall of Famer Kiki Cuyler brought the stolen base title to Charleston (.309, 35 SB).

Ben Paschal again was a standout in 1923, leading the SALLY in runs, RBIs and homers (.361, 26 HR, 147 R, 122 RBIs). No one had ever hit as many as 26 homers in SALLY play, and during the next four seasons the home run champion blasted 28, 29, 35 and 39 roundtrippers. Furthermore, in 1923 no fewer than 24 regulars batted over .300, and four players hit above .360. Such numbers proved that the slugging explosion of the 1920s, triggered by New York Yankee star Babe Ruth, had reached the SALLY.

Zinn Beck, the player-manager who had guided Columbia to back-to-back pennants, was hired away by Greenville. Beck won the batting crown (.370) by a fraction of a point over teammate George Rhinehardt (.370, 212 H, 44 2B, 28 3B, 101 RBI), who did lead the league in hits, doubles, and triples.

Five of the six SALLY teams posted winning records in 1923. But Columbia's three-time champions plunged into the cellar and disbanded in June. The team was transferred to Gastonia, while Charleston's club was moved to Macon. Revitalized, the Macon Peaches won the second half of a split season, but fell in the play-offs to first-half winner Charlotte. Charlotte's championship club was led by Ben Paschal and a deep pitching staff headed by victory and strikeout leader Lee Bolt (20–10).

Greenville outfielder George Rhinehardt became the only hitter in SALLY history to bat .400 in 1924, also leading the league in runs, hits, and doubles (.404, 110 R, 200 H, 45 2B). Asheville replaced Gastonia in the six-team SALLY, and W. G. Bramham also was president of the Class C Piedmont League. Augusta won a tight race over defending champion Charlotte by the margin of a single game. Augusta's championship drive was led by victory and ERA titlist Charles Fulton (24–8, 3.07) and outfielder Odie Strain (.352).

The SALLY tried the eight-team format again in 1925, read-mitting Columbia and Knoxville, but the new teams finished last and next-to-last during the next two seasons. Spartanburg won the pennant behind victory leader Jack Killeen (27–9), run titlist Mike Kelly (.365, 23 HR, 134 R), outfielder John Jones (.352, 25 HR, 112 R, 105 R), and righthander John Berly (21–8, and .331 with 5 homers as a hitter). The batting champ was Columbia out-fielder Everett Bankston (.388).

On September 5, with only a week remaining in the 1925 season, a car carrying several Augusta Tygers home from Char-lotte turned over into a ditch with tragic results to two of the league's best players. Manager-first baseman Emil Huhn (.361) and catcher Frank Reiger (.350 with 23 homers) were instantly killed. ERA champ Harry Smythe (16–9, 2.83) suffered a broken collarbone, and four other Tygers sustained minor injuries. Hard-hitting center fielder Odie Strain (.353 with 115 runs in 129 games) managed the battered club to the end of the schedule.

The next two seasons were dominated by Greenville. The 1926 Spinners roared to the pennant by a 17-game margin, over-whelming the competition behind batting champ Bill Rhiel (.386), run, hit and doubles leader Russell Scarritt (.377, 243 H, 57 2B, 150 R), home run and RBI champ Roy Moore (.371, 35 HR, 134 RBI), victory leader Wilcy Moore (30–4), player-manager Frank

In 1927 Greenville won the second of two consecutive pennants. Starring for the Spinners were RBI king Mule Shirley (#3 – .331, 32 HR, 128 RBI), victory and ERA champ Bill Bayne (#13 – 26–10, 2.87), catcher Doc Leggett (#2 – .334 with 24 homers), outfielder Charles Fitzberger (#4 – .332 with 21 homers), righthander Grapefruit Yeargin (#6 – 19–7), and player-manager Frank Walker (#11 – .335).

Walker (.332), and strikeout titlist Lee Ormand (22–12, 160 Ks). Greenville led the SALLY in team hitting (.318–22 points higher than any other club) and home runs (168–66 more). The 1927 Spinners won the flag by an 11-game margin, featuring the play of victory and ERA titlist Bill Bayne (26–10, 2.87), RBI champ Mule Shirley (.331, 32 HR, 128 RBI), third baseman Pat Crawford (.334 with 24 homers), catcher Doc Leggett (.311 with 24 homers), player-manager Frank Walker (.335) and outfielder Charles Fitzberger (.332 with 21 homers).

Elsewhere around the SALLY, future Hall of Famer Paul Waner starred for Columbia in 1926 (.345), while eight-year American League veteran Elmer Myers was a pitching standout for Knoxville both in 1926 (26–11) and in 1927 (23–11). Knoxville catcher Bill Barrett was the 1927 batting and home run champ (.360, 39 HR, 100 RBI), while more than 30 regulars hit .300 or better. Despite this onslaught from lively ball sluggers, however, Elmer Myers was just one of several SALLY pitchers to put up impressive numbers in 1927: Climax Blethen (25–11) of Macon; John Berly (22–13) and strikeout leader John Walker (21–16, 139 Ks) of Spartanburg; and J. LeRoy (22–12) of Charlotte.

Gimme a Bat!

Righthander Clise Dudley was on the mound for Greenville on May 7, 1926, as the eventual pennant-winner trounced Columbia, 17–1. A native North Carolinian, Dudley pitched well, but he was a terror at the plate. Batting from the left side, Dudley went five-for-five and belted two home runs. Curiously, he batted only .240 for the season and stroked just one other homer, but he put on a hitting clinic against Columbia.

Asheville won its first SALLY pennant in 1928, outdistancing second place Macon by 18 games. The Tourists led the league in team hitting (.304) with the bats of player-manager Ray Kennedy (.366), triples leader Dusty Cooke (.362, 30 3B, 112 R), 19-year-old shortstop Ben Chapman (.336), and right fielder

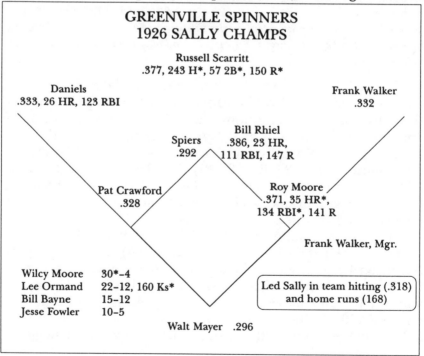

GREENVILLE SPINNERS
1926 SALLY CHAMPS

Russell Scarritt
.377, 243 H*, 57 2B*, 150 R*

Daniels
.333, 26 HR, 123 RBI

Frank Walker
.332

Spiers
.292

Bill Rhiel
.386, 23 HR,
111 RBI, 147 R

Pat Crawford
.328

Roy Moore
.371, 35 HR*,
134 RBI*, 141 R

Frank Walker, Mgr.

Wilcy Moore   30*–4
Lee Ormand   22–12, 160 Ks*
Bill Bayne   15–12
Jesse Fowler   10–5

Led Sally in team hitting (.318)
and home runs (168)

Walt Mayer   .296

Asheville won its first SALLY pennant in 1928 by an 18-game margin. The Tourists featured right fielder Stanley Keyes (#2 – .330), ERA champ Joe Heving (#5 – 13-5, 2.46), triples leader Dusty Cooke (#6 – .362 with 30 3B), Bill Harris (#7 – 25-9), 19-year-old shortstop Ben Chapman (#9 – .336), Bud Chaney (#12 – 21-11) and player-manager Ray Kennedy (#19 – .366).

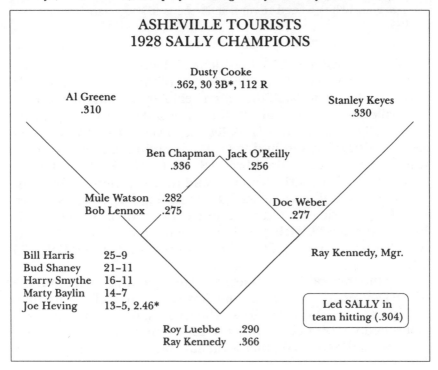

ASHEVILLE TOURISTS
1928 SALLY CHAMPIONS

Dusty Cooke
.362, 30 3B*, 112 R

Al Greene
.310

Stanley Keyes
.330

Ben Chapman   Jack O'Reilly
.336   .256

Mule Watson   .282
Bob Lennox   .275

Doc Weber
.277

Bill Harris   25–9
Bud Shaney   21–11
Harry Smythe 16–11
Marty Baylin   14–7
Joe Heving   13–5, 2.46*

Ray Kennedy, Mgr.

Led SALLY in
team hitting (.304)

Roy Luebbe   .290
Ray Kennedy   .366

Stanley Keyes (.330). The pitching staff featured Bill Harris (25–9), Bud Shaney (21–11), and ERA titlist Joe Heving (13–5, 2.46).

Macon ace Norman Rauch paced the SALLY in victories (26–10), while Popeye Mahaffey was the league workhorse, leading the circuit in games and innings pitched (21–19, 329 IP), toiling in 57 of his team's 147 contests. The batting champ was Knoxville outfielder Oscar Felber (.366), Greenville outfielder Clarence Walker hit the most home runs (.344 with 33 homers), and the RBI leader was Augusta outfielder Stormy Davis (.315, 27 HR, 125 RBI).

Asheville continued to win in 1929 behind right fielder Stanley Keyes (.377, 17 HR, 108 RBI), who won the batting crown, strikeout king John Allen (20–11, 173 Ks), and percentage leader Harry Smythe (15–5).

Big Inning

On Wednesday, June 11, 1930, Asheville exploded in the third inning of a game with Columbia. Batting around more than twice, the Tourists ripped out 12 hits, scored 15 runs, and went on to slaughter the Comers, 20–4.

At mid-season SALLY President William G. Bramham called a special meeting and it was decided to split the season. Knoxville surged to the second-half title, then beat Asheville in the playoffs. Knoxville's pennant-winning effort was sparked by victory leader John Walker (25–9) and L. Bates (23–11), and by the league's best team fielding and hitting (.301), including outfielder Frank Waddey (.354), run leader Elwood Smith (.322, 119 R), and shortstop Eric McNair (.391), who was sold to the Athletics after playing 90 games and commenced a 14-year big league career. Veteran Augusta slugger Odie Strain led the SALLY in hits (.361, 202 H, 106 R, 113 RBI), while Greenville outfielder Murray Howell pounded his way to the RBI crown (.341, 21 HR, 135 RBI).

By the start of the 1930 season, America was sinking into the Great Depression. Knoxville did not return to defend its title, and Spartanburg also withdrew. The six remaining clubs played a split schedule, with Greenville and Macon finishing first and second during the first half, then switching places during the second half. Macon finished with the best season record, but Greenville led the league in team hitting (.310), homers (128), and fielding, and defeated Macon in the playoffs. Greenville's pitching staff boasted victory leader Hugh Harmon (25–9), Frank Pearce (22–13), and a heavy-hitting hurler named Anderson (17–8, and .344 with 6 homers in 53 games). The Spinners' offense was triggered by young Dixie Walker (.401 in 73 games before a promotion to the International League), veteran slugger George Rhinehardt (.353), outfielder Murray Howell, who repeated as RBI champ and also led the SALLY in runs and hits (.340, 25 HR, 123 R, 147 RBI), and home run king Jim Hudgens (.305, 39 HR, 114 RBI).

Despite a tight race attendance lagged, and Augusta and Asheville joined other minor league clubs in resorting to night baseball. It was argued that the poor quality of early lighting systems gave power pitchers a considerable advantage over hitters, a point seemingly proved during the first SALLY night game on July 19, 1930. Charlotte southpaw Jim Mooney, a fireballer who fanned 185 batters in 189 innings to win the strikeout crown, mowed down 23 Augusta hitters in nine innings under the lights. Charlotte won, 7–3, and Mooney's 23 strikeouts still stand as the all-time SALLY record.

In 1931, with the Depression worsening and minor league clubs and leagues folding everywhere, the SALLY did not attempt to operate. Several of the old SALLY cities placed teams in other leagues, but the total number of minor circuits dropped to just 14 in 1933. Five years passed with no serious attempt to reorganize the SALLY.

1936–1942

Judge William G. Bramham, president of the defunct SALLY and of other minor leagues, was elected president of the National Association in 1932 and began to revive the minors with energy and resourcefulness. In 1935, 21 leagues were organized. On December 15, 1935, a group of sportsmen met in Savannah, the birthplace of the SALLY. Roy William of Macon, Bob Lamotte of Charleston, Theo Reeves of Columbus, Troy Agnew of Augusta, and Bob Fisher and Harry Hatcher of Jacksonville each contributed $1,000 to the coffers of a revised SALLY. Dr. E. M.

Wilder of Augusta agreed to serve as league president, a position
he held until illness forced his retirement 10 years later.

The reorganized SALLY would enter the 1936 season as a
Class B league with six teams: Augusta, Columbia, Columbus,
Jacksonville, Macon and Savannah. Every city in the league except Columbus had a lighted ballpark. The Jacksonville Tars won
the first half, but the Columbus Red Birds, members of the vast
St. Louis Cardinal farm system, edged Macon for the second half
title, then beat the Tars in the playoff.

The Red Bird pennant drive was headed by run, hit and walk
leader Jim Gruzdis (.330, 147 R, 108 W), third-sacker Stan Tutaj
(.329), hustling triples leader Enos Slaughter (.325, 20 3B, 118
RBI), victory leader Art Evans (21–11), and ERA champ Joe Sims
(14–7, 2.44). Jacksonville's club featured a pair of 20-game winners, Henry Bazner (20–7), and Gene Walker (20–8), and
strikeout titlist Ralph Braun (16–9, 172 Ks). Macon missed the
second-half title by half a game, despite the efforts of batting
champ Bill Prout (.342), victory leader Arthur Evans (21–11), stolen base king Lee Gamble (.340, 51 SB), and versatile home run
champ Dee Moore (.335, 18 HR, 107 RBI), who played catcher,
outfield, first and third, and went 4–2 as a pitcher.

*Enos "Country" Slaughter played with the Yankees while in his forties. When
he was 20 he wore a Columbus Red Birds uniform and led the SALLY in
triples (.325, 20 3B, 118 RBI).*

The Southern Championship

The success of the annual Dixie Series between the Southern Association and Texas League champions encouraged the SALLY to engage in a postseason "Southern Championship" series with the Virginia League. Local fans were proud to be part of their own version of the World Series, owners profited from well-attended postseason games, and underpaid minor league players fought hard for playoff money. The Junior World Series between the International League and the American Association was older than the Dixie Series, and through the years many lower minor leagues staged postseason inter-league playoffs. In 1922 SALLY champion Charleston defeated Wilson of the Virginia League, four games to two, and in 1923 Wilson fell to Charlotte by the same margin.

There was no playoff the next two years, but in 1926 Greenville dumped Richmond, four games to one. The Spinners were back in 1927, and the Southern Championship was expanded. Greenville beat Portsmouth, four games to one, then faced off against Jacksonville, champions of the Southeastern League. Greenville won the opening game, 1–0, then lost a 1–0 decision in the second contest. Greenville took the third game, then Jacksonville won two in a row. The Spinners evened the series at three apiece, but lost the finale, 3–0.

For 1928 the Southern Championship was set up as a single series between the SALLY and Southeastern League winners, and Asheville lost to Montgomery, four games to two. There was no series in 1929, but in 1930 Greenville lost to Selma of the Southeastern League, four games to one.

The SALLY disbanded after the 1930 season, but reorganized in 1936, and in 1937 rejoined the Southern Championship series. Savannah of the SALLY fell to the Southeastern League champs, Mobile, four games to two. Mobile was back the next year to engage in a classic series against Macon. The first three games were played in Macon, and the Peaches won the opener. But Mobile took the next two games, then needed to win only two of four at home to claim the championship. Macon evened the series with a victory against the home team, but Mobile won the fifth game and needed just one more to win. Macon battled back with a 4–2 victory in 12 innings, then the seventh game also went 12 innings before Macon triumphed, 2–1.

In 1939 Pensacola defeated Augusta of the SALLY, four games to two, but in 1940 the Columbus Red Birds dropped Jackson in five games. There were no further postseason playoffs involving the SALLY champions after 1940. From 1922 through 1940 SALLY champs had engaged in 11 series against the winners of other leagues, winning six and losing five. Greenville represented the SALLY four times, winning twice. Seven other cities carried the SALLY colors once: Charleston, Charlotte, Columbus and Macon were Southern Championship winners, while Asheville, Augusta and Savannah lost to their opponents from other leagues.

For 1937 the SALLY changed from the split-season format to the Shaughnessy Plan, which would involve four of the six teams in postseason playoffs. Columbus, the 1936 champion, finished first, but the Red Birds were swept in three straight games in the playoff opener by Savannah. Second-place Macon defeated Jacksonville in the opener, but lost the finals to Savannah. The Indians advanced to the championship behind outfielder Harry Stratton (.340), righthander Ed Levy (20–8), home run champ Nick Etten (.304 with 21 homers), and stolen base titlist Cecil Garriott (.295, 30 SB, 105 R). Macon featured batting champ Jack Bolling (.343) and victory leader Art Evans (23–8, 27 CG), who also led the SALLY in complete games for the second year in a row.

Greenville and Spartanburg returned to the league for 1939, bringing the SALLY up to eight teams for the first time since 1929. Savannah edged Macon for first place by half a game, but both clubs advanced to the playoff finals, which Macon won, four games to three. Savannah drew almost 200,000 fans into Municipal Stadium in 1937 and in 1938, and over 9,000 spectators attended the pennant-winning game on the last day of the 1938 season.

Savannah fans enjoyed the performance of the league's best pitcher, southpaw John "Pretzels" Pezzullo, who led the SALLY in victories, strikeouts, and games and innings pitched (26–9, 47 G, 288 IP, 218 Ks). The batting champ was infielder Doug Dean (.385), who split the season between Savannah and Greenville. The 1936 batting champ, Bill Prout, was the 1938 RBI and hit leader (.354, 196 H, 110 RBI) while holding down first base for Columbus. Jacksonville first-sacker Nick Etten, the 1937 home run king, stroked the most doubles in 1938 (.370 with 40 2B). Macon southpaw Jake Baker (10–8, 1.97 ERA) broke a 1908 record by hurling 49 consecutive scoreless innings, firing five straight shutouts in the process.

In 1939, for the third time in the four seasons since the revival of the SALLY, Columbus posted the league's best record. The Red Bird strength was a pitching staff that featured ERA champ Bill Seinsoth (17–10, 2.41), fellow lefthander Ed Wissmann (21–9), and strikeout titlist Rollie VanSlate (17–12, 170 Ks), while first baseman Walt Alston (.323) played 63 consecutive games without an error.

Columbus won the pennant by half a game over Augusta and ran out of gas in the playoffs, losing a seven-game opener to Savannah. In the finals Augusta swept Savannah in four straight. Augusta lefty Leo Twardy (21–12), the 1938 ERA champ, tied Ed Wissmann for most victories, while Tiger second baseman Jim Adlam led the league in runs, walks and stolen bases (.273, 130 R, 115 W, 30 SB).

Sally All-Stars

The first official SALLY All-Star Team was not designated until 1936, and the first All-Star Game did not take place until 1939. The same format would be followed for more than two decades; the club in first place at a specified date would host a team of All-Stars. On Wednesday, August 9, 1939, the first SALLY All-Star Game was played at Columbus, with the Stars downing the Red Birds, 3–0.

Future games would be played about a month earlier, during the first or second week of July. On July 8, 1940, the Stars won at Savannah, 4–1 in 10 innings. The next two years resulted in victory for the Macon Peaches over the Stars, 3–2 and 11–10. The Stars took the first three games after the war again the next year, giving Macon the only three victories registered by a first-place team in the initial nine All-Star contests.

No All-Star Game was played in 1952, but 1953 was celebrated as the 50th anniversary of the SALLY, and Savannah hosted a game between teams of East and West All-Stars. The SALLY returned to its customary format, and for the next three seasons Jacksonville hosted the Stars, with the Braves recording back-to-back wins in 1955 and 1956.

In 1960 there were *two* All-Star games, on Monday and Tuesday, July 18 and 19. Before 3,442 home fans at Clark Griffith Park, Charlotte rallied for three runs to tie the game in the bottom of the ninth, then beat the Stars in the eleventh inning, 6–5. The next day the two teams shifted to Portsmouth, where efforts were being made to attract a SALLY franchise. At Lawrence Stadium an overflow crowd estimated at 8,500 watched the Stars defeat the Hornets, 8–3, and Portsmouth, having produced a far larger crowd than the first-place club, entered the SALLY the following season.

Columbus roared back in 1940 with the "Junior Gashouse Gang," an aggressive but inexperienced aggregation that was patiently tutored by manager Clay Hopper (.412 as a pinch hitter). The scrappy Red Birds jelled late in the season, winning 19 of 24 games to finish second behind Savannah. Momentum carried the

Red Birds to a four-game sweep of Greenville in the playoff opener, while Savannah fell to Macon. Columbus then beat Macon for the playoff title and trounced Jackson for the Southern Championship.

The Red Birds featured batting champ Hooper Triplett (.369, 133 R, 108 RBI), MVP first baseman Ray Sanders (.349, 108 R, and a league-leading 152 RBIs), run leader Eddie Knoblauch (.345, 135 R), strikeout champ Freddie Martin (17–12, 208 Ks), and veteran pitchers Bill Seinsoth (16–10) and Rollie VanSlate (10–1). Other fine performances were turned in by victory leader Jim Davis of Augusta (23–9), Greenville righthander Alex Zukowski (22–14), doubles leader Alec Rebel of Augusta (.346, 47 2B, 123 RBI), and Augusta first-sacker Harry Ashworth (.328), who set a record with 11 consecutive base hits.

During the season Spartanburg, with a team that would lose 106 games, moved to Charleston. Charleston remained in the SALLY for 1941, a year in which six clubs registered losing records. Macon and Columbia battled for the pennant all season, with the Peaches finally winning by one game. But Macon and Columbia were the only two teams involved in the playoffs, and the Reds prevailed, four games to two. Macon's pennant-winners featured ERA champ Frank Marino, who set the all-time SALLY standard for winning percentage (19–1, 2.16), victory leader Stan

The "Junior Gashouse Gang" of 1940. The Columbus Red Birds won the 1940 playoffs behind player-manager Clay Hopper (rear, far right – .412 as a pinch hitter), batting champ Hooper Triplett (beside Hopper – .369), run leader Eddie Knoblauch (rear, far left – .345), MVP RBI champ Ray Sanders (beside Knoblauch – .349 with 152 RBIs), strikeout leader Freddie Martin (beside Sanders – 17–12, 208 Ks) and Bill Seinsoth (beside Martin – 16–10).

West (23–7), hitting and RBI titlist Cy Block (.357, 112 RBI), and scrappy shortstop Eddie Stanky (.315, 112 R). For the second year in a row Columbus outfielder Eddie Knoblauch led the SALLY in runs (.336, 114 R).

By the time the 1942 season began, the Japanese were sweeping victoriously through U.S. forces in the Pacific, and professional baseball faced another world war. In 1941, 41 minor leagues had finished the season; the next year, however, only 31 circuits began play and five disbanded early. Travel restrictions and manpower needs rendered minor league ball extremely difficult, and only nine leagues would finish the 1943 season.

The SALLY began 1942 with plans to resume a full Shaughnessy playoff. The annual All-Star Game was conducted in Macon, and the Peaches beat the Stars in 10 innings. Charleston later surged past Macon into first place, but after the playoff openers the Rebels and Peaches met in the finals, and Macon won the series. The offensive star of 1942 was Jacksonville outfielder Vic Bradford, who led the league in batting, runs, homers, RBIs and hits (.342, 12 HR, 113 R, 107 RBI), while victory leader Mack Stewart of Savannah was the year's best pitcher (24–8).

As the 1943 season approached, the player pool began to dry up, bus and rail transportation became increasingly restrictive, and the feeling grew that it was unpatriotic to employ able-bodied men in a sport. The majority of minor leagues did not reorganize for 1943, and the SALLY was one of many circuits that halted operations for the duration of the war.

1946–1963

The end of the war brought an enormous demand for recreation, and for a few years minor league baseball enjoyed unprecedented popularity. From 12 leagues in 1945, the minors jumped to 41 circuits the next year and to 59 in 1949.

The SALLY reorganized for 1946 under the leadership of longtime president Dr. E. M. Wilder. (Health difficulties forced Dr. Wilder to resign within the year, and he was succeeded by Earl Blue of Columbia.) The same eight cities that participated in 1942 fielded teams in 1946, and the SALLY was rated a Class A league.

At the end of the 140-game schedule, three games separated the top four teams. Columbus squeaked past Columbia for the pennant by half a game, but fourth-place Augusta knocked off Columbus in the playoff opener, then swept four games from Columbia in the finals. Augusta righthander Richard Starr won a pitcher's Triple Crown, leading the SALLY in victories, ERA, strikeouts, walks, innings and complete games (19–10, 2.07, 233 K, 136 W, 287 IP, 24 CG), although Sheldon Jones of Jacksonville stayed neck-and-neck in wins and strikeouts (19–9, 232 K). Columbia had the league's best offense, boasting the top three hitters: rookie first baseman Ted Kluszewski (.352), outfielder Frank Baumholtz (.343), and catcher Jack Warren (.343).

In 1947 there was another pitcher's Triple Crown, as Savannah southpaw Lou Brissie overcame severe wounds suffered in combat to lead the SALLY in victories, ERA, strikeouts and complete games (23–5, 1.91, 278 Ks in 254 IP, 25 CG). Augusta outfielder Ralph Brown paced the league in batting, hits, and runs (.356, 228 H, 117 R). On July 21 Columbus first-sacker Don Bollweg (.293, a league-leading 18 triples, 115 RBI) set an all-time SALLY record by driving in nine runs on two homers, a double and a single during a 21–3 trouncing of Augusta.

Augusta righthander Richard Starr won a pitcher's Triple Crown in 1946 (19–10, 233 Ks, 2.07 ERA).

Although badly wounded in combat, Savannah southpaw Lou Brissie recorded a Triple Crown in 1947 (23–5, 278 Ks, 1.91 ERA) and went up to the big leagues.

The schedule was expanded for the first time to 154 games in 1947, and fans responded with a record attendance exceeding 1.1 million. Another 66,192 turned out for the playoffs. Columbus finished the schedule in first place, but second-place Savannah won the Shaughnessy playoffs.

Tough Day for Frenchy

On July 14, 1947, Greenville player-manager Frenchy Bordagaray (.342) exploded at umpire Dallas Blackiston during a game at Augusta. Frenchy furiously hit and spat upon the ump, and he was fined $50 and suspended for 60 days. Since the suspensions would last for the remainder of the season, former Cardinal star Pepper Martin was brought in to manage Greenville. (In 1949 Martin was manager of the Miami Sun Sox of the Florida International League; on September 1 he was fined $100 and suspended for the rest of the season for choking an umpire during a game at Havana.)

On the same day that Frenchy was suspended and fined, he was notified that the house he was renting for his family had been sold and would have to be vacated. As a consolation prize, however, three days later he was presented with the 1946 MVP trophy of the Canadian-American League, where he had been the batting champ (.363) and manager of Three Rivers.

Attendance again exceeded one million in 1948. Charleston won the pennant but fell to Columbia in the playoff opener, while the Reds lost to Greenville in the finals. Augusta outfielder Hal Summers ripped SALLY pitching for a Triple Crown, leading the league in hitting, homers and RBIs (.331, 28 HR, 115 RBI). Columbia righthander Frank Smith was the year's most impressive pitcher (21–6).

Macon ran away with the 1949 pennant and won the playoffs, drawing more than 212,000 fans to Luther Williams Field. But total attendance sagged below one million, and the playoffs attracted merely 31,102. Pitchers dominated the season. For the first time since 1938 (and the last time, period) there were four 20-game winners: Robert Spicer (20–6) and James Atchley (20–7) of Macon, Al Burch (20–6) of Savannah, and John Faszholz (20–14) of Columbus. Greenville righthander Ray Moore fanned 229 batters in 204 innings to cop the strikeout title.

In 1950 Macon again won the pennant and the playoffs, sweeping second-place Columbia in the finals. Peaches manager Ivy Griffin relied on RBI champ Lew Davis (.305, 14 HR, 119 RBI), run and hit leader Gus Gregory (.295, 116 R), and a pitching staff that included victory leader Stan Karpinski (20–10), fel-

Augusta outfielder Hal Summers banged out a Triple Crown in 1948 (.331, 28 HR, 115 RBI).

Columbia southpaw Al Boresh was the 1948 ERA champ (15–10, 2.13), while Macon righty Don Osborn was the percentage leader (17–3).

low righthander Fred Woolpart (19–9), and SALLY veteran Bill Seinsoth (18–11).

Kill the Umpire!

During a single luckless week in 1950, umpire Charley Harris was kayoed by a ball three times in three different cities. In Macon he took a ball in the forehead and was knocked unconscious. Three days later, in Columbia, a wild pitch bounded up into the pit of his stomach. In Savannah three days later, Charley was flattened by a foul tip. But the rugged ump shook it off all three times and did not miss a single inning of work.

Montgomery won the 1951 pennant, then took the playoffs with a four-game sweep over second-place Jacksonville in the finals. Jacksonville boasted the best pitcher of the year, southpaw Vince DiLorenzo (22–8). Montgomery won with an offense that featured home run king Dick Greco (.310, 33 HR, 103 RBI in just 110 G), run and walk leader Banks McDowell (.299, 121 R, 148 W), and RBI champ Bill Johnson (.274, 12 HR, 107 RBI).

In 1952 the personable Dick Butler of Columbia succeeded

Earl Blue as SALLY president. Columbia (100–54) outdistanced the rest of the league behind victory and strikeout titlist Barney Martin (23–7, 174 Ks) and run leader Robert Wilson (.303, 40 2B, 112 R). Player-manager Charlie Metro again led Montgomery to the playoff crown, as outfielder Dick Greco repeated as home run champ and also won the RBI title (.298, 24 HR, 135 RBI). Augusta suffered through a hapless season (38–116), changing managers four times to no avail.

Although the official integration of professional baseball dates from 1946, when Montreal second baseman Jackie Robinson led the International League in hitting, runs and fielding, the South remained segregated for years. In 1953, when "Aunt Sally" celebrated her 50th anniversary, the historic old league brought integrated baseball to the Deep South. The five young pioneers were Henry Aaron, Horace Garner and Felix Mantilla of Jacksonville, and Al Israel and Fleming Reedy of Savannah. All five of these players were regulars, and they endured bitter racial taunts from fans and opposing players.

"You were never sure what was going to happen," recounted SALLY president Dick Butler. "Those people had awfully strong feelings about what was going on. I knew, because they would call me all hours of the night to tell me."

Jim Crow laws forbade the black players from donning their uniforms at the ballparks with white athletes, so they came to the stadiums in their flannels. The black players had to eat on the team bus while their white teammates went to a restaurant, and except for Montgomery, where there was a second-class hotel available, black players on the road stayed in private homes. But these men who were breaking the color line were welcomed into black neighborhoods, and black fans flocked to SALLY ballparks. Jacksonville opened the season in Savannah before a crowd of 5,500, and Jacksonville would lead the league with a total attendance of 143,000.

Israel (.304) and Reedy (.240) played solid ball for Savannah, but Aaron (.362, 22 HR, 125 RBI, 115 R, 208 H, 36 2B), Garner (.305), and Mantilla (.278, 110 R) sparked Jacksonville to the 1953 pennant. Aaron, a 19-year-old second baseman, led the league in hitting, runs, RBIs, doubles, hits, putouts and assists, and was voted Most Valuable Player. Jacksonville outhit every team in the circuit by 22 points, while southpaw Larry Lassalle (19–5 with a

In 1953 19-year-old Henry Aaron helped break the color line in Southern baseball with a spectacular performance for the Jacksonville Braves. Aaron played second base, and he led the SALLY in batting, runs, RBIs, hits, doubles, putouts, assists and errors (.362, 22 HR, 125 RBI).

league-leading 185 Ks) and righthander Ray Crone (19–11) were the victory leaders. During the season Charleston starter-reliever Paul Almonte set an all-time SALLY record with 64 consecutive scoreless innings.

Jacksonville and Columbia made a shambles of the race (third-place Columbus was 26 games back). The Braves and the Reds were the only two teams in the SALLY to register winning records, and disposed of their opposition in the opening round of playoffs. In the finals Jacksonville won three of the first four, but Columbia stormed back with three consecutive victories and an upset. Aaron jumped from the Class A SALLY to the parent Milwaukee Braves the next year, launching a Hall of Fame career that would see him break Babe Ruth's record for total home runs.

"We had shown the people of Georgia and Alabama and South Carolina and Florida that we were good ballplayers and decent human beings," reflected Aaron, "and that all it took to get along together was to get a little more used to each other."

In 1954, the same year he was named to the Hall of Fame, former New York Giant slugger Bill Terry assumed the SALLY presidency. Charleston's last-place 1953 club was transferred to Charlotte.

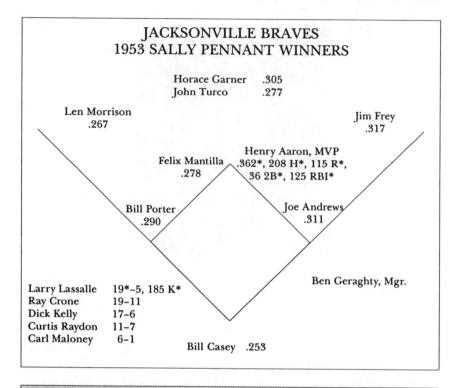

JACKSONVILLE BRAVES
1953 SALLY PENNANT WINNERS

Horace Garner   .305
John Turco   .277

Len Morrison   Jim Frey
.267   .317

                              Henry Aaron, MVP
            Felix Mantilla   .362*, 208 H*, 115 R*,
                 .278   36 2B*, 125 RBI*

            Bill Porter   Joe Andrews
               .290   .311

                                           Ben Geraghty, Mgr.

Larry Lassalle   19*-5, 185 K*
Ray Crone   19-11
Dick Kelly   17-6
Curtis Raydon   11-7
Carl Maloney   6-1
                            Bill Casey   .253

Bought a Ticket to Hit a Grand Slam

On April 24, 1954, Joe Carolan, a 21-year-old outfielder from Detroit, arrived by bus in Columbus. An hour before game time he paid his way into Golden Park and bought a scorecard to learn the name of the Cardinals' GM Jim Grieves, so that he could ask for a tryout. Manager George Kissell watched the 230-pounder clout three drives over the fence and promptly signed him to a contract.

Carolan was immediately inserted into the lineup, and he first came to bat in the second inning, with the Cardinals trailing Macon, 3-0. The bases were loaded, and Carolan blasted a grand slam home run to give his team the lead. Macon came back to win the game in 13 innings, and Carolan quickly was shipped to another club, but not before he executed the most dramatic debut in SALLY history.

Manager Ben Geraghty brought another pennant to Jacksonville behind returnees Horace Garner (.323), Jim Frey (.317 and .316 for the two flag winners) and Joe Andrews (.296), home run

The Jacksonville Braves repeated as pennant-winners in 1954.
— Courtesy Red Underhill

and RBI titlist Clarence Riddle (.318, 28 HR, 112 RBI), and a superb mound corps: Triple Crown winner Humberto Robinson (23–8, 243 K, 2.41 ERA), and fellow righthanders Paul Cave (18–6) and Bob Trowbridge (18–8). But the playoffs were won by second-place Savannah. Led by batting champ Al Pinkston (.360, 27 HR, 102 RBI), the Indians swept Macon in the playoff opener, then outlasted Jacksonville in a seven-game final series. During the season SALLY fans watched a 19-year-old future Hall of Famer, Columbia run leader Frank Robinson (.336, 112 R, 25 HR, 110 RBI).

Another pitcher's Triple Crown was recorded in 1955, by Columbia southpaw Charley Rabe (21–7, 219 K, 2.01 ERA). Rabe, lefthander Gerald Davis (18–12), third baseman Marvin Williams (.328), second-sacker Jimmy Bragan (.308), and run leader Ultus Alvarez (.301, 102 R) led Columbia to the pennant by a 10-game margin over second-place Jacksonville. Columbia and Jacksonville were knocked off in the playoff opener, which had been reduced to a sudden-death single game, and Augusta defeated Montgomery two games to one, in the abbreviated finals.

Lean righthander Humberto Robinson won a pitcher's Triple Crown for the 1954 Jacksonville pennant-winners (23–8, 243 Ks, 2.41 ERA).

The batting champ was Jacksonville outfielder Wes Covington (.326), while Albie Pearson, diminutive (5'5) Montgomery outfielder, established a remarkable record as walk leader (.305, with 132 Ws in just 128 G). Montgomery was visiting Augusta on May 24 when a sudden windstorm toppled a concrete wall at Jennings Stadium, killing a man and two boys outside the ballpark. The next year Montgomery sagged into the cellar, and on June 18, 1956, the club moved to Knoxville.

Veteran field general Ben Geraghty guided Jacksonville to the 1956 pennant and playoff title. The Braves' offense was triggered by home run and RBI champ Ed Barbarito (.310, 27 HR, 99 RBI), while 19-year-old southpaw Juan Pizarro dominated SALLY batters (23–6, 1.77 ERA, 318 Ks in 274 IP). The Puerto Rican fireballer fanned 21 Charlotte Hornets in 12 innings on April 21, and on June 26 he struck out 20 Macon Dodgers in nine innings. Pizarro completed 27 of 31 starts, leading the league in both categories. Another fine performance was turned in by Charlotte righthander Evelio Hernandez (18–4), who led the league in winning percentage and matched Pizarro's six shutouts.

In 1957, for the first time since 1952, the SALLY returned to a 154-game schedule. But Augusta ran away with the pennant,

Southpaw Charles Rabe led Columbia to the 1955 pennant with a Triple Crown performance (21–7, 219 Ks, 2.01 ERA).

Hall of Fame first baseman Bill Terry, who made his home in Jacksonville, served as SALLY president from 1954 through 1956.

finishing the season with an 11½-game margin over second-place Charlotte. Despite a longer schedule, total attendance dropped from 650,000 in 1956 to 564,000 in 1957, and merely 7,000 fans turned out for three short playoff series (seven games total, with Charlotte defeating Augusta in the finals). The SALLY went back to a 140-game schedule the next season, and Bill Terry resigned the presidency in favor of Jacksonville owner Sam Wolfson. Manager Bill Adair's 1958 Augusta champs were sparked by right-hander Ron Rozman (15–1, 1.64), who led the SALLY in winning percentage and ERA.

Plagued by weak attendance, Columbia (39,536) and Columbus (68,193) dropped out of the league, and the SALLY entered 1958 with just six teams. The SALLY also had a new president, Sam Smith, who would serve until his death in 1971. Augusta repeated as pennant-winners, edging Jacksonville by one game. In the playoffs, Augusta lost the opening game to Macon, while Jacksonville beat Charlotte. Macon won the finals with a two-game sweep over Jacksonville. With only six clubs playing a 140-game schedule, attendance dropped to 419,958.

The Longest Games

During the first half-century of SALLY play, no tie game had lasted as long as 20 innings. Finally, on August 1, 1952, Jackson and Columbia played for 20 stanzas. Another 20-inning contest, on April 24, 1954, lasted five hours and 13 minutes, the all-time league record by the clock. There were other 20-inning games on July 7, 1954, and April 22, 1959, when Jacksonville defeated Knoxville, 3–2, in 21 innings.

Sam Smith became SALLY president in 1959, then served as first president of the Southern League.

Augusta, despite two consecutive pennants, drew only 62,000 fans in 1958 and pulled out of the league. But Asheville, Charleston and Columbus rejoined the circuit, and in 1959, with only 21 minor leagues in operation (there were 59 leagues 10 years earlier), the SALLY expanded to eight clubs. Columbus quickly experienced problems, but the franchise was transferred on July 6 to Gastonia.

It was decided to enlarge postseason play, so that each of the three playoff matchups would be a best-three-of-five series. Knoxville won the pennant race, but lost to Charleston in a five-game opener. Fourth-place Gastonia beat Charlotte in the opening round, then executed a three-game sweep over Charleston in the finals.

Knoxville righthander Jim Proctor led the league in winning percentage and ERA (15–5, 2.19). Savannah third-sacker Cliff Cook was the home run and RBI king (.255, 32 HR, 100 RBI), while Asheville third baseman Nate Dickerson won the batting crown (.362). Savannah outfielder-infielder Tom St. John, the 1957 batting champ (.326), was the 1959 hit leader (.283, 148 H).

Although there were eight teams in 1959, attendance totaled only 491,194. The Columbus-Gastonia franchise moved to Columbia, and the Columbia Reds marched to the 1960 pennant behind victory, strikeout and percentage leader Ken Hunt (16–6 with 221 Ks in 211 IP) and ERA champ Charley Rabe (13–8, 2.39), who was Columbia's pitching hero in 1955.

Savannah knocked off Columbia in the playoff opener, then swept Knoxville in the finals. Knoxville had the best offensive club in the league, featuring batting champ Purnal Goldy (.342, 20 HR, 106 RBI), RBI titlist Leo Smith (.301, 16 HR, 111 RBI) and run and triples leader Dick McAuliffe (.301, 21 3B, 109 R). Savannah's title run was led by home run king Donn Clendenon (.335, 28 HR, 109 RBI). In the opening round of playoffs, Knoxville southpaw Doug Gallagher twirled a no-hitter over Charlotte.

In 1960 two All-Star games were staged, one on July 18 at Charlotte, where the first-place Hornets fell to the All-Stars, 6–5, in 11 innings before 3,442 fans. The next day the Hornets and Stars moved to Lawrence Stadium in Portsmouth, Virginia, where another contest was played before an estimated crowd of 8,500. Bill McDonald, millionaire owner of the Miami Marlins, was heading a movement to place a Portsmouth-Norfolk club into the

SALLY, and in 1961 the Tidewater Tides, along with the Greenville Spinners, replaced Savannah and Macon.

No-Nos and a Perfecto

During the 1961 season SALLY pitchers hurled a record 20 1-0 shutouts, seven one-hitters, and four no-hitters, including the first perfect game in league history. Two hard-luck no-hitters were pitched on Saturday, May 27. Jacksonville righthander Benny Griggs hurled nine hitless innings against Greenville, but in the 10th he gave up three safeties and lost, 1-0. On the same date Columbia righty Jim Duckworth also worked nine hitless innings over Charleston, but he was removed for a pinch-hitter, and in the 10th his reliever allowed a homer for another 1-0 heart-breaker.

On August 27 Greenville lefty Larry Miller, pitching the first half of a doubleheader against Jacksonville, won a 1-0 seven-inning no-hitter. A few days later, on September 2, Charleston righthander Ron Woods also started the seven-inning opener of a twin bill, against ERA, strikeout and shutout champ Nick Wilhite. Woods (14-8) outdueled Wilhite (16-9, 1.80, 6 ShO), 7-0, and put the first perfect game in the SALLY record book.

Asheville ran away with the 1961 pennant, outdistancing second-place Knoxville by 13 games. Playoff attendance in recent years had been poor, and there was no postseason play. Asheville led the SALLY in team hitting and home runs (155 in 137 G) behind homer and RBI champ Gary Rushing (.311, 25 HR, 99 RBI) and young outfielder Willie Stargell (.289, 22 HR, 89 RBI), a future slugging star of the Pirates. Righthander Jim Hardison won his first 11 decisions and finished as the league's percentage leader (16–2). Greenville southpaw Nick Wilhite led the league in ERA, strikeouts, innings and shutouts (16–9, 1.80, 161 K, 230 IP, 6 ShO), and Columbia outfielder Teo Acosta won the hitting and stolen base crowns (.343, 40 SB).

Jacksonville finished in last place with miserable attendance (25,000) and dropped out for 1962, along with Columbia (26,000) and Charleston (40,000). Returning to the SALLY as replacement cities were Augusta, Macon and Savannah, and Savannah won the pennant. Playoffs had been reinstated for 1962, and Savannah fell to Macon in the opener. Macon beat Knoxville for the playoff title, and the Peaches were the only club to draw 100,000 fans.

Asheville outfielder-first baseman Elmo Plaskett (.3498, 27

HR, 96 RBI) edged Charlotte outfielder Pedro Oliva (.3497) for the batting title by an eyelash. Outfielder Dick Means, who played for Charlotte and Asheville, was the home run king (.235, 36 HR, 95 RBI), and Savannah first baseman Grover Jones won the RBI crown (.319, 26 HR, 101 RBI). Greenville righthander Camilio Estevis led the SALLY in victories and complete games (18–9, 23 CG in 25 starts). Macon's champs were paced by percentage titlist Marv Fodor (15–4), hit and doubles leader Tommy Helms (.340, 38 2B, 195 H), and second baseman Pete Rose (.330, 17 3B, 136 R), who led the league in triples and runs, and moved up from Class A to Cincinnati the next year.

The Southern Association had disbanded following the 1961 season, leaving only the Texas League and the Mexican League with Double-A clubs for 1962. Each league had just six teams, providing 12 Double-A franchises for 20 big league clubs, while the Triple-A American Association suspended operations for 1963. The major leagues were instrumental in a 1963 overhaul of the minors which, among other significant developments, eliminated Class B, C and D leagues. President Sam Smith led the SALLY to Double-A status for 1963, which added eight teams to the higher classification.

Late in the 1962 season Savannah's final home games were played in Lynchburg because of racial difficulties, and the Lynchburg White Sox became members of the Double-A SALLY in 1963. The Tidewater Tides remained in Class A with the Carolina League, and so did Greenville, with the Western Carolinas League. But these clubs were replaced by two former Southern Association cities, Chattanooga and Nashville.

The Double-A SALLY stayed with a 140-game schedule, but split the season. The Augusta Yankees won the first half, and Lynchburg took the second half. Macon finished with the best overall record of the year, but failed to make the playoffs. Augusta defeated Lynchburg in the playoff series, three games to two.

Despite the championship, the Yankees moved their Double-A farm club to Columbus for 1964. Last-place Nashville dropped out of pro ball, replaced in the SALLY by former Southern Association stalwart Birmingham. With the SALLY so long identified with lower classification baseball, it was decided to rename the Double-A circuit. The minors were still struggling, and the league

In 1963 the SALLY was elevated to Double-A, and the Augusta Yankees won the championship. The leading hitter was second baseman Ike Futch (middle, third from left – .317), the key pitcher was righthanded reliever Pete Mikkelson (front, fourth from left – 11–6 and a 1.47 ERA in 49 G), and the manager was Rube Walker (standing, far left).

did not want to be identified with the failed Southern Association. The name of the South's first professional league was resurrected, and beginning in 1964 the circuit would be called the Southern League.

The SALLY had been reorganized after both world wars and the Great Depression, and following a 16-year absence from organized baseball the historic league again reappeared in 1980 with eight cities, six of which were former SALLY members. In 1994 the Class A South Atlantic League, stronger then ever, prepares to celebrate its 80th anniversary with 14 clubs in two divisions, including eight in old-time SALLY cities.

Sally Ballparks

ASHEVILLE

McCormick Field. Built at a cost of $200,000 in 1924, the year the Asheville Skylanders entered the SALLY, McCormick Field was placed on a hill above Valley Street. In addition to the wooden

Asheville's McCormick Field opened in 1924. For years it was known as the oldest wooden ballpark still in use, but following the 1991 season it was razed and replaced with a beautiful new version of McCormick Field.

grandstand from first to third, bleachers extended down the foul lines, and another roofed grandstand stood in left field. The hand-operated scoreboard was in center field. There was a low rail fence around the outfield, and "railbirds" regularly viewed the action while leaning on the rails. But the fence soon was removed, and outfielders chased deep flies up the hill beyond the original outfield. When a permanent fence finally was erected after World War II, center field was 404 feet from the plate, left field was 328 feet down the line, but right was only 301 feet away. Lights were installed in 1930 but the system soon was removed, although permanent lighting was in place by 1940. A 1935 fire destroyed the central grandstand, but the seating and pressbox were replaced by the end of the season. The left field grandstand disappeared during this period, perhaps dismantled for replacement materials in 1935.

AUGUSTA

Heaton Park. Built beside Lake Olmstead on Milledge Avenue, with a seating capacity of 4,000.

CHARLESTON

College Park. A wooden ballpark was built early in the century for college athletics. Located on Rutledge Avenue between Grove and Cleveland streets, by the 1940s (when SALLY baseball came to College Park) there were steel bleachers and grandstand, both 14 rows high.

CHARLOTTE

Hayman Park. A compact wooden facility with left field only 286 feet down the line, right field 309 down the line, and center 410 from the plate. Lights were installed during the 1930s.

Clark Griffith Park. Clark Griffith, owner of the Charlotte Hornets as well as the Washington Senators, built a new $40,000 park for the 1941 season at 400 Magnolia Avenue. The wooden grandstand seated 4,000, with 600 box seats. A bleacher for whites accommodated another 1,000, and there was a 500-seat "colored bleacher." The foul lines were 340 feet and center was 430 feet, and there was a good lighting system. Later the fences were moved in (320 down the lines and 390 to center) and 1,000 additional seats were added.

CHATTANOOGA

Chamberlain Field. Home of the 1909 Lookouts.

Joe Engel Stadium. Built by Clark Griffith in 1930 for his Southern Association farm club. Located at Third and O'Neal streets, in 1963 center field still was 471 feet from the plate, with a sharp incline to a terrace in deep center. During the 1963 SALLY season the seating capacity remained at 10,000, but crowds were sparse.

COLUMBIA

Capital City Park. Home of the SALLY Reds, 1946–57 and 1960–61, the 3,500-seat Capital City Park was (and is) located at 300 South Assembly Street.

COLUMBUS

Golden Park. When Columbus joined the reorganized Southeastern League in 1926, there was a bitter disagreement over whether newly completed Memorial Stadium was suitable for professional baseball. Finally, just two weeks before the start of the season, a wooden ballpark named after T. E. Golden was erected beside the Chattahooche River. Golden Park was rebuilt in steel and concrete at a cost of $195,000 after the 1950 season, with a new seating capacity of 6,600.

GASTONIA

Sims Legion Park.

GREENVILLE

Meadowbrook Park. Early professional clubs in Greenville played at a ballpark bounded by Memminger, Calhoun and Dunbar streets and Arlington Avenue. Later another wooden park, Furman Park on Furman University property off Augusta Street, was home to SALLY baseball in the 1920s. In 1938 the Greenville Spinners reentered the SALLY and moved into Meadowbrook Park, also sometimes called Cambria Park after owner Joe Cambria. Cambria erected the $25,000 facility in the swampy flats of Mayberry pasture off Hudson Street. Construction included a lighting system, giving Greenville its first night baseball. The grandstand was badly damaged by fire after the 1948 season, but repairs were made within a few months. Meadowbrook was devastated by fire in 1972, and even though temporary seating was set up, the park was abandoned after the season.

JACKSONVILLE

Barr's Field/Douglas Field/Durkee Field. This wooden ballpark at 1701 Myrtle Avenue hosted SALLY League baseball during 1936–42 and 1946–54. Also the home of Negro League teams whose players also worked as depot red caps, the facility became known as *Red Cap Stadium.*

Jacksonville Baseball Park/Sam W. Wolfson Baseball Park. Built in 1955 at 1201 East Duval Street, this 10,264-seat stadium has an old-fashioned grandstand with roof support beams, and a brick outfield fence.

KNOXVILLE

Chilhowee Park. The 1909 Knoxville Appalachians of the SALLY played on a diamond at Chilhowee Park.

Caswell Park. The Knoxville Smokies of 1925–29 played at

wooden Caswell Park, located at Jessamine Street off Magnolia Avenue.

Knoxville Municipal Stadium. In 1931 Smithson Stadium was built on the site of old Caswell Park. In 1953 Smithson Stadium burned, but was rebuilt and renamed Knoxville Municipal Stadium. The 6,700-seat facility again was renamed in 1957, and *Bill Meyer Stadium* continued to host SALLY baseball under a new label.

LYNCHBURG

City Stadium. Built in 1940 at Fort Avenue and Wythe Road, City Stadium has been the home of pro baseball in Lynchburg for more than half a century.

MACON

Central City Park. Built in 1892 in Macon's Central City Park, the ballpark was 12 years old when the SALLY opened play. The 4,000-seat grandstand was semicircular with a wide central entrance, fashioned from an old hippodrome which had been sawed in two and converted to baseball seating. The foul lines were just 250 feet long, but the fence deepened sharply, and center field was 400 feet from the plate. The big wooden grandstand burned in 1926.

Luther Williams Field was completed in 1929 at a cost of $60,000 and located just north of old Central City Park. The seating totaled 6,000, with a grandstand, a long bleacher section for whites down the right field line and smaller "colored bleachers" along the left field line. In 1956 "Operation Face Lift" replaced the old wooden bleachers with steel bleachers, and moved the light poles out of the outfield. The fences were so deep (360 feet down the lines and 450 in center) that only 11 homers were hit in two decades, and the distances were reduced in 1949.

MONTGOMERY

Paterson Field. Built for $200,000 just north of Madison Avenue in 1949, in time to accommodate Montgomery's SALLY teams of the 1950s. The 6,000-seat symmetrical stadium measures 330 feet down the foul lines and 380 feet in center.

NASHVILLE

Sulphur Dell. The final season for the famous old stadium was 1963, Nashville's only year in the SALLY. The sunken ballpark seated 8,000 and was not sunken in right field, notorious for its steep hill and 262-foot depth, although a 30-foot screen was perched above the 16-foot fence. After the Vols disbanded, the historic facility was razed. The Sulphur Dell, site of Nashville baseball for a century, subsequently became a parking lot.

PORTSMOUTH

Lawrence Stadium. Baseball executive Frank Lawrence was the driving force behind the construction of the stadium that bore his name. Built in 1941 on Queens Street at Williamsburg Avenue, the 7,500-seat ballpark was the home of the Tidewater Tides of the SALLY League in 1961 and 1962, and was the site of the 1960 All-Star Game. The grandstand seated 6,000, and in left center there was a large set of football bleachers (Lawrence Stadium was also used for high school football).

SAVANNAH

Bolton Street Park. A wooden ballpark located east of the Atlantic Coast Line Railroad tracks behind the later site of the Bright-Brooks Lumber Company. Young Ty Cobb and Shoeless Joe Jackson played at Bolton Street Park, which was the earliest pro diamond in Savannah.

Fairview Park. Built in southwest Savannah near the State Fair Grounds, Fairview Park could seat more than 5,000 fans in the grandstand and bleachers.

Municipal Stadium/Grayson Stadium. When a 3,500-seat grandstand and a set of bleachers was completed in 1927, the Savannah Indians moved to the new Municipal Stadium located in Daffin Park. Savannah high schools soon began to play football in Municipal Stadium, and the WPA renovated and expanded the facility. By 1940 there was a covered concrete grandstand which seated 3,000, plus two sets of large concrete football bleachers which expanded the seating capacity to 10,000. The north bleachers are adjacent to the grandstand on the first base side, while the south bleachers are in left field. Renamed Grayson Stadium, the facility long has been the center of Savannah athletics.

SPARTANBURG

Duncan Park. Located on Duncan Park Drive at South Converse Street, Duncan Park has hosted professional baseball in Spartanburg for six decades. The first lighting system was installed in 1936, but, like the old wooden fence, it has been replaced and modernized.

1964–1969

Southern League Beginnings

The SALLY changed its name to the Southern League for the 1964 season. The Yankees moved their Double-A farm club from Augusta to Columbus for 1964, while Nashville, the last-place SALLY team of 1963, dropped out of organized baseball, replaced in the new SL by Birmingham. Asheville, Charlotte, Chattanooga, Knoxville, Lynchburg and Macon returned from 1963, and so did President Sam Smith, who maintained league headquarters at Knoxville. Each city except Birmingham had participated in the SALLY; Birmingham, Chattanooga, Knoxville and Macon had fielded Southern Association clubs; and Birmingham, Chattanooga, Columbus and Macon had held franchises in the nineteenth-century Southern League. The roots of the charter members of the new Southern League ran deep, through the richest traditions of baseball in Dixie.

It was decided to play a 140-game schedule to a pennant with no postseason playoffs. There was an All-Star Game, held in Birmingham, and 7,458 fans came out to Rickwood. Overall, however, attendance in 1964 was poor (484,180), despite a scintillating flag chase between Birmingham and Lynchburg. Finalists in the 1963 SALLY, the 1964 White Sox (81–59) edged the Barons (80–60) by a single game.

The Lynchburg White Sox won the first Southern League pennant. Home run champ Dick Kenworthy (front, third from right – .312, 24 HR, 97 RBI) sparked the offense. Shot Johnston (rear, third from left – 20–7, 2.46 ERA) won the ERA title and set the all-time SL record for victories. Other quality pitching came from fellow righthander Jose Lizondro (rear, second from right – 15–9) and fireballing reliever Dennis Higgins (rear, second from left – 7–5, 58 G, 100 Ks in 87 IP).

Lynchburg won the first Southern League championship behind third-sacker Dick Kenworthy (.312, 29 HR, 97 RBI, 99 R), who led the SL in homers, runs, hits, at-bats and total bases, and righthander Manly Johnston (20–7, 2.46 ERA, 5 ShO, 15 CG, 227 IP), the league leader in victories, ERA, shutouts, winning percentage, complete games and innings pitched. The first SL batting title was won by Macon infielder Len Boehmer (.329), Macon first baseman Lee May was the first RBI champ (.303, 25 HR, 110 RBI), Macon righthander Dave Galligan was the first strikeout king (17–8, 168 K), and Asheville outfielder George Spriggs claimed the first stolen base crown (.322, 33 SB). On May 3 Knoxville lefty Doug Gallagher made his only start of the season (there were two brief relief appearances) in the seven-inning opener of a doubleheader against Asheville, and pitched the first no-hitter in SL history.

Despite fielding a fine club, Macon's attendance was only 60,000, and for 1965 the franchise was shifted to Montgomery. There was another white-hot pennant race, this time between the

Columbus Confederate Yankees (79–59) and the Asheville Tourists (80–60). Columbus, a New York Yankee farm club, claimed the flag by a fraction of a percentage point (.572 to .571). Columbus won with the most effective pitching staff in the league, led by righthanders Richard Beck (13–7) and Tom Shafer (10–2), and an offense sparked by run, hit, triples and total base leader Roy White (.300, 14 3B, 103 R). The ERA and strikeout champ was Asheville southpaw Luke Walker (12–7, 2.26, 197 K in 183 IP), while Asheville righthanders Tom Frondorf (16–7) and Darrell Osteen (16–9) paced the SL in victories.

One Win, No Pitches

One of the most unusual victories in baseball history was credited to Charlotte southpaw Hal Stowe, who picked up a win without throwing a pitch. In a game with Asheville on July 11, 1964, the Tourists erupted for four runs in the top of the ninth inning to tie the game at 5–5. With a runner on first and two out in the ninth, Stowe was brought in from the bullpen.

Completing his warmup tosses, Stowe took a stretch — then picked the runner off first base to end the inning. Charlotte pushed a run across in the bottom of the ninth to win the game, and Stowe, who had not made a single delivery to a batter, was credited with one of his eight victories for 1964.

Columbus hosted the All-Star Game, but fewer than 4,000 fans attended. Total attendance across the league dropped to a meager 380,000, with Chattanooga (25,707) and Birmingham (28,001) at the bottom. Chattanooga and Birmingham dropped out of organized baseball, while Lynchburg moved into the Class A Carolina League. But the SL reorganized for 1965, placing teams back into Macon and Mobile and into Evansville, Indiana, an old Three-I League city that had been out of organized baseball since 1957.

The Mobile Athletics roared to the 1966 pennant, finishing 9½ games ahead of second-place Asheville, while the other six teams in the league posted losing records. With no suspense and so many losers, SL attendance sagged to 362,180. The fans who turned out saw exciting offense from home run and RBI king Bob Robertson of Asheville (.287, 32 HR, 99 RBI), stolen base, run and hit leader Sam Thompson of Knoxville (.307, 60 SB, 114

The Columbus Confederate Yankees won the second SL pennant by a fraction of a percentage point behind outfielder Roy White (middle, fourth from left – .300) and righthander Richard Beck (rear, fourth from left – 13-7).

R), batting champ and triples leader John Fenderson of Knoxville (.324, 15 3B), and speedy Charlotte outfielder Pat Kelly, who finished second in steals and batting average (.321, 52 SB). But Mobile manager John McNamara won the flag with the SL's best mound corps, including victory and percentage leader Bill

Team Nicknames During the 1960s	
Asheville 　Tourists (1964–66) *Birmingham* 　Barons (1964–65) 　Athletics (1967–69) *Charlotte* 　Hornets (1964–69) *Chattanooga* 　Lookouts (1964–69) *Columbus* 　Confederate Yankees (1964–68) 　White Sox (1969) *Evansville* 　White Sox (1966–68)	*Knoxville* 　Smokies (1964–67) *Lynchburg* 　White Sox (1964–65) *Macon* 　Peaches (1964, 1966–67) *Mobile* 　Athletics (1966) *Montgomery* 　Rebels (1965–69) *Savannah* 　Senators (1968–69)

Manager John McNamara (middle, fourth from right) led the Mobile Athletics to the 1966 pennant. Future managerial standout Tony LaRussa (middle, far right – .294) played second base, and third-sacker Sal Bando (beside LaRussa – .277) soon became a big league star. Southpaw Bill Edgerton (middle, far left – 17-4) led the SL in victories and winning percentage.

Luther Williams Field, built in 1929 and the home of the Macon Peaches of the Southern League in 1964, 1966, and 1967.

Edgerton (17–4, including 12 in a row), and future Oakland star Blue Moon Odom (12–5).

Despite the championship, dismal attendance forced Mobile out of the Southern League, along with Montgomery and Asheville (Asheville moved down to the Carolina League, but the other two cities dropped out of Organized Baseball). The Athletics moved John McNamara and their Double-A club to Birmingham, but President Sam Smith could find no other replacement cities, and the SL would operate as a six-team circuit in 1967. In order to keep the SL and other minor circuits in operation, major league teams had to provide player salaries, transportation expenses, uniforms, equipment, and other subsidies to their farm clubs.

The Athletics put another championship roster in the SL for 1967, and Birmingham beat out Montgomery for McNamara's second straight pennant. Future Hall of Famer Reggie Jackson led the league in runs, triples and total bases (.293, 17 3B, 17 HR, 84 R). Other budding Athletic stars included first-sacker Joe Rudi (.288) and righthander Rollie Fingers (6–5, 2.21 ERA). Righty George Lauzerique pitched a seven-inning perfect game and led the SL in ERA and winning percentage (13–4, 2.30). Charlotte shortstop Minnie Mendoza (.297) became the only SL batting champ to hit below .300.

With only six teams, total attendance for 1967 plummeted to 240,566, and Knoxville (21,390) and Macon (30,658) again dropped out. But Savannah and Asheville fielded teams, and Manager Sparky Anderson guided the Asheville Tourists to the 1968 pennant. Tourist outfielder Arlie Burge won the batting crown (.317), southpaw Grover Powell led the league in victories

The Athletics moved from Mobile to Birmingham for 1967, and John McNamara (middle in light cap) produced another pennant. Outfielder Reggie Jackson (middle, far left – .293) led the SL in runs and triples. Joe Rudi (rear, fifth from left – .288) played first base and Rollie Fingers (rear, fifth from right – 6–5, 2.21 ERA) pitched half the season. George Lauzerique (middle, fourth from left – 13–4, 2.30 ERA) led the league in ERA and winning percentage, and pitched a perfect game.

and ERA (16–6, 2.54), and offensive spark was provided by outfielder Bernie Carbo (.281 with 20 homers), switch-hitting second-sacker Darrel Chaney (.231 with 23 homers), first baseman Archie Moore (.281 with 20 homers), and catcher Fred Kendall (.291).

Lauzerique vs. 100-Pitch Rule

When George Lauzerique opened the 1967 season with the Birmingham Athletics, he was 19 years old. The farm director of the A's applied a 100-pitch-per-game limit to Lauzerique, as well as to other young pitchers throughout the system. On May 11 the 6'1 righthander no-hit Montgomery through seven innings, but he had thrown 97 pitches and a reliever took over for the last two innings. The reliever allowed two hits, and sportswriters throughout the SL decried the 100-pitch rule that cost him a chance at a no-hitter.

"They put in the rule to protect us," shrugged Lauzerique philosophically, "and I'm all for it."

On June 8 the parent Athletics played an exhibition at Birmingham, and after seven innings Lauzerique held a 1–0 lead over the big leaguers. He had allowed only one single, but again he had thrown 97 pitches, and again he was pulled. Kansas City jumped on the relievers, and won, 7–2.

Lauzerique started the seven-inning opener of a doubleheader against Asheville on July 6. No batter reached base during the first six innings. In the seventh the leadoff hitter worked the count to 3–2 before grounding out. The next batter rolled out, but the next man up, a good hitter named Gary Johnson (.280), took the first three pitches for a 3–0 edge in the count. The next offering was a called strike, then Johnson fouled off the next pitch. The 3–2 pitch was bounced back to Lauzerique, who threw to first for the final out. Lauzerique had thrown 85 pitches and the first perfect game in SL history.

Lauzerique went on to lead the SL in ERA and winning percentage (13–4, 2.30), and he was called up to Kansas City late in the year. But his four big league seasons were disappointing (4–8), and he never lived up to the promise he demonstrated in the Southern League.

The Montgomery Rebels won 16 straight games in July and finished second. Montgomery righthander George Korince was the strikeout king (13–7, 146 Ks in 161 IP), a title he had also won in 1966 (9–8, 183 Ks in 182 IP). Charlotte shortstop Minnie Mendoza, the 1967 batting and hit leader, paced the 1968 SL in hits, doubles, and at-bats (.303, 35 2B, 165 H). For the third year

Manager Sparky Anderson (front, fourth from right) led the Asheville Tourists to the 1968 pennant. Outfielder Arlie Burge (front, fourth from left – .317) was the batting champ. Also providing offense were outfielder Bernie Carbo (front, fifth from left – .281, 20 HR), catcher Fred Kendall (rear, third from left – .291), and first sacker Archie Moore (rear, far right – .281, 20 HR). Southpaw Grover Powell (front, third from right – 16-6, 2.54 ERA) was the ERA and victory titlist. Outfielder Don Anderson (rear, second from left) won the batting crown in 1969 (.324).

in a row, Charlotte righthander Garland "Duck" Shifflett led the league in appearances (12–6 in 77 G). Shifflett had pitched for the Hornets since the inaugural season of the SL, primarily as a starter in 1964 (7–7) and 1965 (10–8), then as the circuit's hardest-working reliever in 1966 (9–8, 1.98 ERA in 63 G), 1967 (12–7, 1.45 ERA in 69 G), and 1968.

Encouragingly, attendance in 1968 jumped by more than a third, to 324,487. Although last-place Evansville drew only 35,000 and dropped out, Columbus rejoined the league. Attendance rose again in 1969, to 333,516, and a crowd of more than 14,000 turned out for the All-Star Game at Birmingham's Rickwood Field. Charlotte won the 1969 pennant and drew 146,141 fans, becoming the first Southern League club to break 100,000 in season attendance.

Charlotte's championship club was sparked by victory leader Bill Zepp (15–3), who tied a 1966 record with 12 consecutive wins, righthanded reliever Robert Gebhard (13–3, 1,23 ERA in 50 G), and All-Star second baseman Danny Thompson (.302). Birmingham finished second with another strong team that featured All-Star catcher Gene Tenace (.319, 20 HR, 74 RBI in 89 G),

Montgomery outfielder Wayne Redmond was the 1968 home run champ (.260 with homers).

fireballing southpaw Vida Blue (10–3, 112 K in 104 IP), ERA champ LaDon Boyd (13–5, 2.19) and home run, RBI and run titlist Robert Brooks (.292, 23 HR, 100 RBI, 102 R).

Asheville first-sacker Don Anderson won the batting crown, tied Brooks for the RBI title, and led the league in triples and total bases (.324, 9 3B, 100 RBI). On July 1 Montgomery first baseman George Kalafatis (.254, 21 HR, 86 RBI) set an SL record by blasting four home runs in a single game. Late in the season Hub Kittle, 53-year-old manager of the last-place Savannah Senators, reinforced his hard-pressed pitching staff by working six innings of relief, thereby becoming the oldest pitcher in Southern League history.

The Southern League was christened in 1964 during a low point in minor league operations. For the first few seasons attendance steadily declined, franchises were transferred from city to city, and the league dropped from eight to six clubs. But the Southern League persistently drew upon cities and fans with the traditions and background of the old Southern Association and SALLY. By the end of the 1960s SL attendance commenced a slow improvement as families and club executives began to recognize the immense potential of minor league baseball as wholesome, inexpensive entertainment, and it was indicative of an optimistic future that the Southern League entered a new decade by expanding to eight teams.

1970–1979

Southern League
Upsurge

In 1970, for the first time in its seven-year existence, the Southern League returned every city from the previous season. Jacksonville and Mobile were added, returning the SL to eight teams. In 1969 the major leagues expanded from 20 to 24 clubs, but there were only 20 Double-A franchises: six in the SL, eight in the Texas League, and six in the Eastern League. The Southern League expansion for 1970 brought the number of Double-A clubs to 22.

The 1970 pennant race came down to a fraction of a percentage point between Columbus (78–59, .569) and Montgomery (79–60, .568). The Columbus Astros were led to the pennant by a pair of All-Star infielders, first baseman John Dolinsek (.296) and shortstop Ray Busse (.264), victory leader Ken Forsch (13–8), and righthanded reliever Ray Strable (11–5 in 56 G). The Montgomery Rebels kept up the pace with co-victory leader and strikeout champ Bill Gilbreth (13–11, 192 Ks) and percentage leader Lerrin LaGrow (11–4). Batting and triples titlist Steve Brye (.307, 10 3B) was the only SL hitting qualifier to reach .300. Montgomery righthander Charles Swanson (12–5, 1.88 ERA) fired a nine-inning perfect game on August 14 against Savannah.

A New President

On April 19, 1971, Sam Smith, who had become president of the SALLY in 1959 and had been the only head of the Southern League, died of a heart attack in Knoxville at the age of 50. His widow, Louise, had assisted in league operations, and she continued to administer SL business from the office in Knoxville until mid-season.

In the meantime, Montgomery general manager Woody Parks asked Billy Hitchcock if he would be interested in the SL presidency. Hitchcock replied affirmatively, then departed with his wife on a planned trip to Scandinavia. Bright and amiable, Hitchcock had been an American League infielder during the 1940s and 1950s, and a big league manager during the 1960s. SL owners selected him as Smith's replacement while he was still abroad, and he assumed control in July. A native of Alabama, Hitchcock established league headquarters in his hometown of Opelika, and he would preside effectively over the SL for the next decade.

Mobile finished next-to-last in the standings and last in attendance with a paltry 28,720. Mobile dropped out of organized baseball, and a replacement city could not be enlisted. Like the Southern League, the Texas League also could field only seven clubs for 1971, so the two circuits merged into an unusual three-division arrangement called the "Dixie Association." The Eastern Division was made up of six Southern League teams: Asheville, Charlotte, Columbus, Jacksonville, Montgomery, and Savannah. Birmingham joined the Texas League clubs Arkansas, Memphis and Shreveport in the Central Division, while the other four Texas League teams comprised the Western Division. Central Division clubs would play each other and members of both the Eastern and Western divisions, but clubs from the East and the West would not meet during the regular schedule because of the immense distances involved. A postseason playoff involving four teams — the three division winners and a "wild card" — was planned.

Birmingham finished last in the Western Division with the worst record of any team in the Dixie Association, although fireballer Chris Floethe was the strikeout king (225 K in 174 IP) of the association. The Eastern Division race between six SL clubs turned into a dogfight between Charlotte and Asheville. Asheville led the division in team fielding, hitting and homers behind home run and RBI champ Ken Hottman (.302, 37 HR, 116 RBI), first baseman Don Anderson (.305), and catcher Vic Correll (.273 with 22 homers). Southpaw Jim MacDowell paced the division in victories and shutouts (17–7, 5 ShO), while righty Dennis O'Toole was the percentage leader (13–3). This fine aggregation was edged for the Eastern Division title by Charlotte, but with a better record (90–51) than any club from the other two divisions, the Tourists made the playoffs as the wild card team.

Minnie Mendoza

A throwback to the career minor leaguer, Minnie Mendoza spent 20 seasons in the minors and became a fixture at Charlotte of the SALLY and SL. Born Christobal Rigoberto Carreras Aizpuru in Cuba in 1933 or 1936, the six-foot infielder batted righthanded and broke into pro ball in

1954 in the Florida International League.

Mendoza played with eight clubs in eight minor leagues during the 1950s, before signing with Charlotte of the SALLY for 1960. He was the Hornet second baseman in 1960 (.295), then played second, third and short in 1961 (.282). Mendoza moved up to the Pacific Coast League for 1962, before returning to Charlotte for the next six years.

During the 1963 SALLY season as a Double-A circuit, Mendoza (.285) held down third base for the Hornets. In future seasons he would play predominantly at third, but he filled in at second, short and outfield whenever needed. The 1964 season was the first year of the Southern League, and Mendoza responded with one of his best performances (.302).

Mendoza was a solid favorite of Hornet fans in 1965 (.275) and 1966 (.279 with 29 steals). In 1967 he won the batting title (.297), and in 1968 he led the SL in hits and doubles (.303, 35 2B, 30 SB).

He moved up to Denver in 1969, and led the American Association in base hits (.333, 194 H). He was promoted to Minnesota the next year, but his only major league appearance was a disappointment (.188).

Mendoza signed with Charlotte for 1971, and he celebrated his return by claiming another SL hitting crown (.316). In 1972 Mendoza tailed off (.248), and he finished his 20-year career the next season in the Mexican League. Minnie Mendoza spent 10 full seasons with Charlotte, and he was the only two-time batting champ in Southern League history until Jim Bowie matched the feat in 1991 and 1993.

Charlotte won the Eastern crown behind the division's stingiest pitching staff: southpaw Dick Rusteck was the ERA champ and co-victory leader (17–8, 2.40), lefthanded reliever Vic Albury made the most appearances (12–7, 1.73 ERA in 66 G), and Greg Jaycox provided quality from the right side (15–5). The Hornet offense centered around veteran third baseman Minnie Mendoza, who won his second batting championship (.316).

In the Dixie Association playoffs Charlotte manager Harry Warner led his Hornets over wild card Asheville, two games to one. The other postseason opener saw the Arkansas Travelers of the Central Division down the Amarillo Giants of the Western Division. Charlotte and Arkansas squared off for the Dixie Association Championship, and the fine Hornet pitching staff executed a three-game sweep over the Travelers.

The next season both the Southern League and the Texas League added a team, and the Dixie Association was discontinued after one year. The return of Knoxville to the SL brought the league back up to eight teams, and the circuit was aligned into

Eastern and Western Divisions. The divisional alignment would prove permanent, and division champions would stage a post-season playoff for the annual SL crown.

During the first season of division play, Montgomery manager Fred Hatfield guided Montgomery to the title in the West, while Asheville field general Cal Ripken led the Orioles to the Eastern Division crown with the best SL record of 1972. In the first playoff between SL division champions, Montgomery dumped Asheville in three straight games.

Thou Shalt Not Kill the Ump

On June 15, 1972, southpaw reliever Pablo Torrealba (3-3, 2.08 ERA) took the mound for Savannah against Knoxville. Torrealba took exception to several ball and strike calls by plate umpire Fred Spenn. When Torrealba came up as a batter, another disputed call by Spenn ignited a tirade by the pitcher. When Spenn turned to walk away, Torrealba furiously swung his bat at the ump's back. The bat was broken across the small of Spenn's back and he was out of action for several days. SL President Billy Hitchcock promptly issued a $250 fine and suspended Torrealba for the rest of the season.

Asheville outfielder Mike Reinbach was the dominant hitter of 1972, claiming a Triple Crown (.346, 30 HR, 109 RBI) while leading the SL in hitting, homers, RBIs, runs (123), hits, doubles, walks and total bases. On June 12 Reinbach went six-for-six during a 17–1 rout of Columbus. He blasted two homers, a double and a triple, and registered nine RBIs. Reinbach deservedly won the SL's first Most Valuable Player Award.

Asheville's best pitchers were victory leader Paul Mitchell (16–8), percentage titlist Herb Hutson (14–3), and relievers Dave Johnson (7–4 in a league-leading 50 G) and Sam Weems (4–2 and a league-leading 22 saves). But Charlotte's staff was even better, featuring ERA champ Danny Vossler (8–5, 2.11), strikeout king Bill Campbell (13–10 with 204 Ks), righthanders Steve Grilli (11–3) and Danny Fife (14–7), and southpaw Dan Bootchack (12–6).

On July 21 the Savannah Braves established a league record during a game against Jacksonville. The Braves ran uncontrolled on the basepaths against a rookie catcher for the Suns, stealing 10 bases en route to a 7–2 victory.

For the first time since the SL's inaugural season, total attendance climbed above 400,000 (434,274), and it was even better in 1973 (443,812). But in 1972 Charlotte — in anticipation of Nashville in 1993 — hosted *two* Minnesota affiliates: the SL Hornets and the Twins of the Class A Western Carolinas League. The Hornets, however, drew only 30,789, while the Twins pulled in merely 13,835 fans, and after the season Charlotte dropped out of Organized Baseball. Minnesota moved their Double A club to Orlando, which provided a good SL rivalry for Jacksonville.

Jacksonville won the Eastern Division by a comfortable margin, while the Montgomery Rebels claimed the Western title by an even larger gap. The Rebels beat the Suns in the playoff series, three games to one. It was not a good year for hitters: Bob Andrews of Asheville was an unspectacular batting champ (.309), and only one other hitter, MVP outfielder Jason Moxey (.301) of Columbus, broke .300. Terry Clapp of Asheville led the SL in homers and RBIs (.259, 35 HR, 98 RBI). Knoxville righthander Joe Henderson led the SL in victories and percentage (17–4), and Columbus fastballer Doug Konieczny was the strikeout king (12–12, 222 Ks in 213 IP).

On April 14 Columbus and Savannah squared off for a Saturday doubleheader. But the opener went on — and on and on —

Jacksonville's Sam W. Wolfson Park, built in 1955. The Suns won back-to-back Eastern Division crowns in 1973 and 1974.

for a record 23 innings, and when it ended at 1:00 A.M. the nightcap was canceled.

Tommie Aaron had played seven seasons with his older
brother Hank on the Milwaukee and Atlanta Braves, but 1972
found the 32-year-old first baseman with the Savannah Braves
(.262). On June 15 he replaced Clint Courtney as manager, thus
becoming the first black field general in any Double A league and
of any pro team in the deep South. Of course, the SALLY had
been integrated for two decades, every pro roster in the South
now sported numerous black athletes, and the managerial appointment of the outgoing, universally popular Aaron proclaimed
the end of racial problems in Southern sports.

There were no franchise changes for 1974, an indication of
the increasing stability and success of minor league baseball in
general and the Southern League in particular. The Columbus
Astros finished last in the Eastern Division but drew over 106,000
fans into Golden Park, and total attendance was nearly half a
million (491,580).

Jacksonville again won the Eastern Division — and again lost
the playoff series. The Suns were defeated, three games to two,
by the Knoxville White Sox. The Knoxville championship charge
was led by MVP outfielder Nyls Nyman (.325), who led the SL in
batting, runs, hits and triples. Orlando sluggers Bob Gorinski
(.278, 23 HR, 100 RBI) and Mike Poepping (.262, 23 HR, 75 RBI)
were the home run co-leaders, and Gorinski added the RBI
crown. Jacksonville reliever Norman Angelini led the SL in appearances (9–7 in 56 G), and fellow southpaws Domingo Figueroa
(15–4 for the highest winning percentage) of Savannah and Paul
Siebert (15–7) of Columbus were the co-victory leaders.

In 1975, for the third consecutive year, the Southern League
roster of cities remained the same. Neither divisional race was
close: Orlando won the East by nine games, and Montgomery
took the West with the only winning record in the division. Orlando was led by home run and RBI king Jim Obradovich (.229,
27 HR, 74 RBI), first baseman Jack Maloof (.317), co-victory
leader Bob Maneely (14–8), and starter-reliever Mike Seberger
(13–7).

Montgomery swept Orlando in three games for the SL championship. The Rebel offense was sparked by total base leader John
Valle (.283 with 23 homers) and third baseman Phil Mankowski

Team Nicknames During the 1970s	
Asheville	*Knoxville*
Tourists (1970–71)	White Sox (1972)
Orioles (1972–75)	Sox (1973)
Birmingham	Knox Sox (1974–79)
Barons (1970–75)	*Memphis*
Charlotte	Chicks (1978–79)
Hornets (1970–72)	*Mobile*
O's (1976–79)	White Sox (1970)
Chattanooga	*Montgomery*
Lookouts (1976–79)	Rebels (1970–79)
Columbus	*Nashville* Sounds (1978–79)
Astros (1970–79)	*Orlando* Twins (1973–79)
Jacksonville	*Savannah* Indians (1970)
Suns (1970–79)	Braves (1971–79)

(.283), and the pitching staff featured co-victory leader Bob Sykes (14–10) and lefthander Ed Glynn (10–5). Asheville switch-hitter Chuck Heil won the batting crown (.322), while teammate Eddie Murray tuned up for a long big league career (.264 with 17 homers).

Perhaps because there was no suspense in the title races, SL attendance nosedived almost 20 percent to 398,802. Just 1,910 fans turned out for the All-Star Game, and the three playoff games attracted a meager total of 1,337. Birmingham, with the worst attendance in the league (30,483), again dropped out of the SL, but the Athletics relocated in Chattanooga for 1976. The Orioles moved their SL club from Asheville to Charlotte, although the Tourists found a Class A home in the Western Carolinas League. The two new SL cities each drew well over 100,000 fans in 1976, triggering a total attendance jump to 566,329.

One reason for the increased fan interest was a split schedule device that doubled the number of teams in postseason play. Charlotte won the first half in the East, but fell to second-half winner Orlando in the single-game playoff opener. First-half champ Chattanooga lost to second-half victor Montgomery in the opening round. For the second year in a row, therefore, the division titlists were Orlando and Montgomery, and also for the second year in a row manager Les Moss guided the Rebels to the SL championship.

Montgomery's pennant chase was fueled by ERA champ Dave Rozema (12–4, 1.57), lefthanded reliever Dennis DeBarr (11–2), and outfielder-first baseman Tim Corcoran (.309). For the second consecutive season Orlando's offense was triggered by first baseman Jim Obradovich, who repeated as home run and RBI champ, and also led the SL in runs and total bases (.265, 21 HR, 68 RBI, 84 R). Charlotte righthander Dave Ford paced all pitchers in victories and strikeouts (17–7, 121 Ks).

Charlotte first-sacker Eddie Murray again performed well (.298), and the next year began an illustrious big league career with Baltimore. Another future superstar, Dale Murphy, spent most of the season catching for Savannah (.267), but he would win back-to-back MVP awards with Atlanta as a home-run-hitting outfielder.

The two most notable future big leaguers of 1977 were second baseman Lou Whitaker and shortstop Alan Trammell of Montgomery. Whitaker made the All-Star Team, led the SL in runs (.280, 81 R), and was promoted to Detroit late in the year. Trammell also was named to the All-Star team, led the league in triples (.291, 19 3B), was voted Most Valuable Player, and like Whitaker donned a Detroit uniform by the end of the season.

There were no franchise changes for 1977. Savannah won the first half behind such future Atlanta Braves as All-Star catcher Bruce Benedict (.273), slick-fielding second-sacker Glenn Hubbard, and outfielder Terry Harper. But Jacksonville bolted from last-place in the first half to the second-half title, then beat the Braves in the playoff opener, two games to one.

The dominant team of 1977, however, was Montgomery. The Rebels posted the best record of the season, won both halves in the West, then dumped Jacksonville in two straight to keep the SL pennant in Montgomery for the third consecutive year. Alan Trammell and Lou Whitaker gave manager Ed Brinkman a superb double-play combination and solid offense, and outfielder Dave Stegman put in a torrid half-season (.345, 11 HR, 59 RBI in 67 G). Key pitchers were percentage leader Gary Christensen (13–4), righthander Mike Burns (11–5), and lefthanded reliever Julio Alonso (6–2, 1.58 ERA).

In 1977 the American League added two franchises, bringing the number of major league clubs to 26. Each of the three Double-A leagues had eight teams, and the Southern League was awarded two expansion franchises for 1978. Memphis made its inaugural appearance in the SL with a Chicks teams that drew 153,686 fans. The other expansion team also was awarded to another old Southern Association stalwart. Nashville, out of Organized Baseball for 15 years, moved into a new stadium built at the instigation of dynamic club president Larry Schmittou. Schmittou involved country-western music stars in the operation of the Nashville Sounds, and clever promotions and an exciting atmosphere produced an unprecedented attendance of 380,159 for a losing team. The addition of two teams with such spectacular gate results pushed Southern League total attendance to more than one million.

No-Hit Debut

On April 14 Darrell Jackson took the mound for the Orlando Twins against Jacksonville. The 22-year-old lefty from Arizona State was nonplussed by his professional debut. For nine innings Jackson shut down the Suns with no hits and five strikeouts. But at the end of regulation play neither team had scored, and Orlando manager Johnny Goryl refused to risk Jackson's arm for the sake of a no-hitter. Jackson gave away to reliever Jeff Holly, who yielded a hit in the 10th inning but hung on to win a 1–0 decision in the 12th.

After 10 starts Jackson was 4–3 with a 1.80 ERA, and he was called up to Minnesota. Holly, incidentally, went 6–0 with a sparkling 0.77 ERA in 25 relief appearances, and he too won promotion to the parent club.

Columbus moved into the Eastern Division, while the two new clubs joined the Western Division. Orlando easily won the first half in the East, then Savannah survived an airtight race in the second half. Knoxville piled up the best record of 1978 and won both halves in the West. Savannah beat Orlando in the opening series of the playoffs, then fell to Knoxville in the finals.

Knoxville boasted the league's best attack, as SL veteran Joe Gates won the batting crown (.332) and also led the circuit in runs and hits. More punch was provided by outfielder Tom Spencer (.331 in 81 G), All-Star third-sacker Mark Naehring (.302), and future big league star Harold Baines (.275). The home run champ was Memphis outfielder Eddie Gates (.315 with 25 homers), who was named Most Valuable Player, while Chatta-

Tim McCarver stadium, home of SL baseball in Memphis since 1978.

nooga first baseman Sal Rende led the SL in doubles and RBIs (.273, 29 2B, 87 RBI).

Orlando righthander Terry Sheehan (17–8) paced the league in victories and winning percentage, and twirled a nine-inning no-hitter against Savannah on May 26. Savannah righty Roger Alexander won the ERA crown (10–6, 1.84), Nashville reliever Geoffrey Combe made the most appearances (12–6, 1.89 ERA in 66 G), and the strikeout king was Nashville righthander Jay Howell (173 Ks in 166 IP). Jim Bouton, a 39-year-old righthander who had pitched his last big league game in 1970, persuaded Ted Turner to let him attempt a comeback with the Savannah Braves. The author of the controversial *Ball Four* had developed a knuckleball, and he was effective enough with Savannah (11–9, 2.82 ERA) to pitch five games with Atlanta late in the season (1–3).

All 10 clubs returned to the Southern League for 1979. Knoxville outfielder Joe Charboneau won the batting crown with the highest mark yet attained in the SL (.352 with 21 homers). Home run king Alan Knicely of Columbus (.289 with 33 homers) and teammate Danny Heep, who led the league in hits (.327, 21 HR, 171 H), were named co-MVPs. Also impressive were Memphis

Chattanooga outfielder Joe Charboneau was the 1979 batting champ (.352 with 21 homers).

teammates: first baseman Dave Hostetler, who set a new SL record for RBIs (.270, 20 HR, 114 RBI), and second-sacker Tim Raines, a 19-year-old future superstar who led the league in runs (.290, 104 R). Jacksonville outfielder LaMart Harris won his second straight stolen base title (.263 with 68 thefts — he stole 45 bases for Memphis in 1978).

Charlotte won the first half in the East, but Columbus finished on top in the second half, then claimed the division title with victory in the playoff opener. Memphis and Montgomery finished the first half deadlocked for first in the West, and the Chicks won the single-game playoff. The Nashville Sounds, enjoying phenomenal fan support, won the second half, beat Memphis for the division crown, then downed Columbus in the finals.

In Nashville more than half a million fans thronged into Hershel Greer Stadium, and attendance exceeded 100,000 in Charlotte, Jacksonville, Columbus and Chattanooga. Counting the playoffs, total attendance for 1979 was more than one and a half million.

Throughout the 1970s, President Billy Hitchcock and the club owners had worked to increase the attractiveness of SL baseball. Stadiums were painted and refurbished, clean restrooms were provided, and a concentrated effort was exerted to appeal to families. By the end of the decade, for the first time in circuit history, the Southern League enjoyed growing popularity, extraordinary attendance, and financial stability. Billy Hitchcock, who had led the SL toward these goals throughout the 1970s, announced his retirement. The Southern League would march into the 1980s with new leadership and an exciting sense of opportunity.

1980–1989

Southern League Prosperity

The Southern League opened the 1980s hoping to capitalize on the promise of escalating attendance and a general upsurge of interest. The first order of business was to find a replacement for longtime President Billy Hitchcock. After the 1979 season numerous applicants were screened, then the top candidates were assembled at an Atlanta hotel and interviewed by Hitchcock and the league directors. Hitchcock recommended Jimmy Bragan, and the directors concurred, appointing him in October 1979.

The new president proclaimed himself "an old-fashioned baseball man." His father, Bobby Bragan, was a former big league catcher and manager who also had played and managed in the minors, served as president of the Texas League, and later presided over the National Association. Jimmy Bragan played for Mississippi State University, and spent several seasons as a minor league infielder after graduation. He coached at his alma mater, and his minor league managerial stints included Savannah of the SALLY and Chattanooga of the SL. Bragan brought a compatible personality and a wealth of experience to the Southern League presidency, and his tenure would prove so effective that he would serve through the 1994 season.

During his first year, Bragan saw SL attendance soar past the

1.7 million mark, while 31,000 fans came to the playoffs. By this time motion pictures had become filled with violence, profanity and nudity, and were almost as prohibitively expensive as amusement parks. Minor league baseball, with cheap admission prices and nightly promotions, increasingly became a center of wholesome and affordable family entertainment.

The quality of minor league play also exerted a growing appeal. During the 1980s the image of professional as well as amateur sports became tarnished by drugs, player strikes, astronomical salaries, greedy agents, recruiting violations, under-the-table payments, doctored transcripts, and other shabby practices. Many major leaguers, lionized by the media and paid fortunes through long-term contracts, pampered their injuries and became guilty of lackadaisical play. But hustle and a reckless zest for the game continued to rule Southern League diamonds, as young athletes risked life and limb to make plays which might bring promotion to Triple A or the parent club.

In 1980 Nashville first baseman Steve Balboni blasted his way to Triple A and then on to the majors, leading the SL in homers, RBIs and runs (.301, 34 HR, 122 RBI, 101 R), while earning MVP designation. Similar promotion came to three other All-Stars: Chattanooga batting champ Chris Bando (.345), Nashville second baseman Pat Tabler (.296 with 16 homers), and Charlotte shortstop Cal Ripken, Jr. (.276 with 25 homers), who had played Little League ball for three summers when his father managed Knoxville of the SL in the 1970s. Nashville righthander Andy

Team Nicknames During the 1980s	
Birmingham Barons (1981–89) *Charlotte* O's (1980–86) Knights (1987–89) *Chattanooga* Lookouts (1980–89) *Columbus* Astros (1980–89) Mudcats (1989) *Greenville* Braves (1984–89) *Huntsville* Stars (1985–89)	*Jacksonville* Suns (1980–84) Expos (1985–89) *Memphis* Chicks (1980–89) *Montgomery* Rebels (1980) *Nashville* Sounds (1980–84) *Orlando* Twins (1980–89) *Savannah* Braves (1980–83)

McGaffigan moved up after winning the ERA crown (15–5, 2.38) and tying a league record with 12 consecutive victories, and Savannah righty Steve Bedrosian also was promoted after claiming the strikeout title (14–10 with 161 Ks).

Nashville recorded nearly 600,000 paid admissions while posting the best record in the league (97–46). Manager Stump Merrill enjoyed the SL's stingiest pitching staff and the most productive offensive lineup, including MVP slugger Steve Balboni, Pat Tabler, outfielders Buck Showalter (.324) and Willie McGee (.283), and third baseman Dan Schmitz (.296). But the Sounds lost the playoff opener to first-half winner, Memphis. The Chicks won the Western Division behind stolen base king Anthony Johnson (.299, 60 SB) and outfielder Pat Rooney (.280, 28 HR, 102 RBI). Southpaw Charlie Lea started nine games for the Chicks with brilliant success (9–0, 0.84 ERA, 7 CG, 3 ShO, and in his final game fanned the last nine batters), then was called up to Montreal for the rest of the season (7–5).

In the East, Charlotte won the first half then sagged to a .500 season record, while Savannah took the second half. But Charlotte manager Jimmy Williams rallied shortstop Cal Ripken, slugging outfielder Drungo Hazewood (.261 with 28 homers), and the other O's for postseason play. Charlotte executed a three-game sweep over Savannah to win the Eastern Division, then beat Memphis, three games to one, for the SL championship.

During this period Jimmy Bragan approached Texas League President Carl Sawatski regarding the revival of the Dixie Series. The postseason classic had been staged between the Southern Association and Texas League champs from 1920 through 1958. In 1967 a Dixie Series was held between Birmingham of the Southern League and the Texas League champion, Albuquerque. Birmingham won, four games to two, but attendance averaged only a little more than 2,000 per contest, and the Series again was dropped. By the 1980s the major leagues wanted minor league schedules to end as early as possible so that promising prospects could be called up, and the Texas League had a shorter schedule than the Southern League. The Texas League declined to participate, and minor league fans can only hope that one day the Dixie Series might be resumed.

Montgomery left Organized Baseball after the 1980 season. Jimmy Bragan had established SL headquarters in Trussville, a

Rickwood Field. By the time Birmingham rejoined the SL in 1981, large crowds were common at minor league ballparks.

— Courtesy Birmingham Barons

suburb of his hometown, Birmingham. Bragan lined up backers in Birmingham, historic Rickwood Field was refurbished, and the Barons returned to the Southern League.

After a six-year absence, more than 220,000 fans flocked to Rickwood. For the third consecutive year Nashville enjoyed well over half a million paid admissions. For the second consecutive season Memphis brought in more than 300,000, Charlotte exceeded 200,000, and four other clubs went over 100,000. Total attendance again broke all records: 1,911,436.

Birmingham failed to make the playoffs but entertained fans with the best team offense of 1981, provided by outfielder Glenn Wilson (.306), DH-outfielder Jedd Kenaga (.301), All-Star first baseman Mike Laga (.289 with 31 homers), and future Met star Howard Johnson (.266 with 22 homers). Chattanooga outfielder Kevin Rhomberg won the batting championship with the highest average ever compiled in the Southern League, and he also stole more bases than any previous theft champ (.366, 74 SB, 104 R). Jacksonville catcher Don Slaught finished second in the hitting race (.335), taking a long step toward the big leagues.

Nashville satisfied the vast crowds at Herschel Greer Stadium by compiling the best record in the SL and seizing the Western Division title with a three-game sweep of first-half winner Memphis. The Sounds showcased doubles leader Don Mattingly (.316, 35 2B, 98 RBI), fleet Willie McGee (.322), run leader Thad Wilborn (.295, 43 SB, 106 R), strikeout king Jamie Werly (13–11 with 193 Ks in 184 IP), and, for half a season, southpaw Pete Filson (10–2, 1.82 ERA).

Orlando won the first half in the East, then beat Savannah in the opener and powerful Nashville in the finals. The SL champs led the league in homers behind MVP catcher Tim Laudner, who established the all-time record for four-baggers (.284, 42 HR, 104 RBI), third-sacker Gary Gaetti (.277, 30 HR, 93 RBI), and outfielder Randy Bush (.290, 22 HR, 94 RBI).

In 1982 Nashville again accumulated over half a million paid admissions, again won the Western Division, and claimed another SL championship. Managed by Johnny Oates, the Sounds defeated Knoxville in the playoff opener and Jacksonville in the finals by margins of three games to one. Righthander Stefan Wever won a pitcher's Triple Crown (16–6, 2.78 ERA, 191 K), although teammate Clay Christiansen (16–8) was co-victory leader. The offense was fueled by MVP outfielder Brian Dayett (.280, 39 HR, 96 RBI), third baseman Erik Peterson (.301), outfielder Buck Showalter (.294), and speedy switch-hitter Otis Nixon (.283), who stole 61 bases in just 72 games before being promoted to Triple A.

Memphis outfielder Mike Fuentes led the SL in homers, RBIs and runs (.267, 37 HR, 115 RBI, 104 R), while Birmingham outfielder Kenneth Baker claimed the batting crown (.342). Jacksonville won both halves of the schedule in the East with the best record of 1982, then beat the second-best Eastern team, Columbus, in the playoff opener, before losing the finals. Jacksonville was one of eight clubs to draw over 100,000. In addition to Nashville's 508,000, Memphis attracted 316,000 and Birmingham drew 231,000 *with losing teams*. Total league attendance again exceeded 1.9 million.

Birmingham did not lose in 1983. The Barons won the first half in the West, posted the best season record of any team, beat second-half winner Nashville, three games to two, for the division title, then won three out of four games from Jacksonville. The

Barons boasted a standout pitching staff that featured victory leader Don Heinkel (19–6), ERA champ Roger Mason (7–4, 2.06), and percentage titlist Keith Comstock (12–3). Offense was provided by run leader George Foussaines (.270, 22 HR, 106 R), outfielder Stanley Younger (.309), and first baseman Greg Norman (.300).

Stolen base champ Michael Cole (.285, 75 SB) and RBI leader Miguel Sosa (.245, 17 HR, 93 RBI) helped Savannah win the first half in the East. Jacksonville beat the Braves for the Eastern Division crown behind strikeout king Mark Gubicza (14–12, 146 Ks) and 19-year-old rookie Bret Saberhagen (6–2 after a 10–5 start in Class A), who both vaulted into the Kansas City rotation the next year, and MVP outfielder John Morris (.288, 23 HR, 92 RBI). Columbus outfielder Glenn Davis (.299, 25 HR, 85 RBI) was called up to Tucson before the season ended, which caused him to share the home run title with Charlotte outfielder Larry Sheets (.288, 25 HR, 87 RBI).

Despite success on the field, Savannah finished last in attendance (66,000). The Braves moved their SL franchise to Greenville for 1984, while Savannah returned to the Class A SALLY as a Cardinal affiliate. The Greenville Braves promptly posted the best record of 1984 and finished behind only Nashville in attendance (217,000). Greenville outfielder Doc Estes won the batting title (.341), outfielder Michael Cole led the league in runs and walks, (.308, 105 R, 110 W), and righthander David Clay provided outstanding relief (10–3 and a 1.80 ERA in 51 appearances).

Nashville righthander Stefan Wever pitched his way to a Triple Crown in 1982 (16–6, 191 Ks, 2.78 ERA).

Alvin Davis, Chattanooga's All-Star first baseman in 1983 (.296), was the 1984 American League Rookie of the Year.

Greenville edged Jacksonville by half a game for the first half title in the East, while Knoxville finished atop the West. Both divisions had airtight races during the second half. Charlotte and Orlando finished in a deadlock in the East (with Greenville right behind), and Nashville and Birmingham had identical records in the West. Single game tiebreakers were played: Charlotte won, 4–3, and Nashville prevailed, 3–2. Nashville then lost the division playoff to Knoxville. But Charlotte, seizing momentum from its victory over Birmingham, defeated Greenville for the Eastern crown, then swept Knoxville in three games to win the SL championship.

Charlotte righthander Ken Dixon paced the league in victories, strikeouts, and innings pitched (16–8, 211 Ks in 240 IP, the most worked by any pitcher in SL history), although southpaw Bryan Oelkers (16–11) matched his win total. Knoxville's division winners were led by All-Star second baseman Mike Sharperson (.304), while Nashville's playoff club was sparked by home run champ Dan Pasqua (.243, 33 HR, 91 RBI). Orlando DH-third baseman Stan Holmes won the RBI title (.280, 25 HR, 101 RBI), and Jacksonville first-sacker Andres Galarraga (.289, 27 HR, 87 RBI) was voted MVP after hitting for the most total bases.

Southern League family photo in 1983. Left to right: Emmo Hein, Memphis, GM; Gary McCune, Knoxville GM; Carrington Montague, Chattanooga owner; Bruce Baldrin, Savannah GM; Mike Mondina, Jacksonville GM; Frances Crockett, Charlotte owner-GM; Art Clarkson, Birmingham owner-GM; Bob Willis, Orlando GM; Jimmy Bragan, league president; George Dyce, Nashville GM; Dayton Preston, Columbus GM.

From Ballparks to Stadiums

When the Southern League opened play in 1964, the ballparks were aging facilities that reflected not only the tradition and history of minor league baseball in the South, but also the depressed state of the minors in general. The oldest SL ballpark was Birmingham's Rickwood Field, with a rich heritage that had begun in 1910. McCormick Field in Asheville was a charming wooden park that dated from 1924.

Golden Park was built in Columbus in 1926 and Luther Williams Field was erected in Macon in 1929, although the old wooden grandstands were replaced with concrete and steel at Golden Park in 1950, and at Luther Williams six years later. Chattanooga's Engel Stadium was erected in 1930, and Knoxville Municipal Stadium was built in 1931, then rebuilt following a 1953 fire. City Stadium in Lynchburg was constructed in 1940 and Charlotte's Crockett Park opened the following season. And in 1966 Evansville joined the league, bringing into the SL one of the nation's oldest ballparks, Bosse Field, built in 1915.

The ballparks of the early SL, therefore, dated from 1910 to 1941, and were decades old when the league was founded. Three of these old parks had been extensively rebuilt during the 1950s, but by the 1960s there was little money available to refurbish minor league facilities. Around the nation, ballparks in the minors were unpainted, not very clean, and in various stages of deterioration.

But by the 1980s minor league baseball had become a popular and profitable activity, housed in streamlined new stadiums that boasted luxury boxes, sparkling restrooms, handsome concourses, and clean, symmetrical architectural lines. Greenville Municipal Stadium opened in 1984 and Huntsville's Joe W. Davis Stadium welcomed fans the next year. The Birmingham Barons abandoned historic but dilapidated Rickwood for magnificent Hoover Metropolitan Stadium in 1988, and in 1990 Charlotte fans began to enjoy the splendid surroundings of Knights Castle.

During its early years the Southern League was a treasury of historical —but decaying—ballparks. Indicative of the newfound prosperity of minor league baseball, the modern Southern League now has become a treasury of comfortable, state-of-the-art sports architecture.

Greenville run leader Michael Cole stole more bases (85) than any player in previous SL history. But he could not even claim the 1984 theft title, because Chattanooga outfielder Donnell Nixon set the all-time SL record for stolen bases (102).

Since reviving pro baseball in Nashville and joining the Southern League in 1978, Larry Schmittou's Sounds had produced more attendance then any other Double A club and more than most Triple A franchises. It was inevitable that Nashville would move up to Triple A, and after the 1984 season the Sounds joined the American Association. But Huntsville, an affluent Alabama city that was home to a division of NASA, proved to be an excellent replacement. Although there had been no professional baseball in Huntsville in 55 years, the Stars moved into new Joe W. Davis Stadium and led the 1985 SL in attendance (301,000).

Huntsville fans were treated to a league championship in the Stars' first season. Talented outfielder Jose Canseco performed brilliantly, winning the MVP award even though he was promoted after only 58 games (.318, 25 HR, 80 RBI). All-Star first baseman Rob Nelson provided power all season (.232, 32 HR, 98 RBI). The Stars won the first half in the West, beat Knoxville for the division title in the playoff opener, then downed defending champion Charlotte, three games to two, in the finals.

Orlando had the best offense in the league, fueled by run, hit and stolen base leader Alexis Marte (.320, 64 SB, 117 R), home run and RBI champ Mark Funderburk (.283, 34 HR, 116 RBI), and All-Star outfielder Mark Davidson (.302, 25 HR, 106 RBI). Slugging first baseman Cecil Fielder showcased his skills in Columbus (.294, 18 HR, 81 RBI in 96 G) before earning promotion to Toronto. Other impressive power hitting was turned in by All-Star outfielder Bill Moore (.259, 33 HR, 104 RBI) and first

Jose Canseco played only 58 games for Huntsville in 1985 before winning promotion, but his performance was impressive enough to bring him MVP honors (.318, 25 HR, 80 RBI).

— Courtesy Huntsville Stars

baseman Mike Hocutt (.259, 28 HR, 92 RBI) of Jacksonville, Birmingham outfielder Rondal Rollin (.259, 30 HR, 108 RBI), and Chattanooga first-sacker Randall Braun (.314, 22 HR, 100 RBI).

Knoxville Southpaw Steve Davis led the SL in victories and ERA (17–6, 2.45). The league's best righthanders were Les Straker of Orlando (16–6), and percentage leader Mike Skinner (11–1) and John Habyan (13–5 with a no-hitter) of Charlotte. Charlotte's Crockett Park burned before the season started, and Skinner, Habyan and the other O's played in a patchwork facility at the old park, somehow drawing over 104,000 fans.

Like 1985, 1986 was a hitters' year. Team batting averages and home run totals rose noticeably, and every club except Chattanooga launched more than 100 homers. Chattanooga first baseman Brick Smith won the batting title (.344, 23 HR, 101 RBI), and more regulars hit .300 than in any previous SL season. Terry Steinbach, who had played catcher, pitcher, third, first and outfield for Huntsville in 1985 (.272), won the 1986 MVP award while setting the all-time SL record for RBIs (.325, 24 HR, 132 RBI in 138 G).

The home run champ was Knoxville outfielder Glenallen Hill (.279, 31 HR, 96 RBI). Huntsville second baseman Gary Jones led the league in runs and walks (.311, 166 R, 128 W in 130 G).

Luis Polonia (left) was the 1985 triples leader (.289, 18 3B), while fellow Huntsville outfielder Stan Javier led the SL in walks (.284, 112 W, 105 R).

Productive sluggers included Jacksonville third-sacker Jeff Reynolds (.268, 29 HR, 113 RBI), Columbus DH-outfielder Larry Ray (.275, 24 HR, 108 RBI), and Charlotte DH-third baseman Tom Dodd (.323, 28 HR, 100 RBI). All-Stars Gary Thurman (.312 as a Memphis outfielder) and Billy Ripken (.268 as the Charlotte second baseman) were among the future big leaguers honing their skills in the '86 SL. Despite the offensive onslaught, there was strong pitching from Columbus victory leader Anthony Kelly (14–4) and Greenville southpaw Tom Glavine (11–6).

Huntsville won the first half in the West, then went on to post the best season record and defeat Knoxville for the Western Division crown. Jacksonville claimed the first half in the East and finished with the season's second-best mark. But Columbus, which changed managers in June and compiled only a .500 season record, rallied to win the second half, then beat Jacksonville for the Eastern title and downed Huntsville to seize the 1986 SL championship.

The next year Jacksonville carved out the best record of 1987, but again lost the Eastern championship, this time to first-half winner Charlotte. Birmingham, playing the final season at Rickwood Field, brought a championship to the historic ballpark. Manager Rico Petrocelli guided the Barons to first place in the West during the first half, but Birmingham slumped to a 68–75

Huntsville catcher Terry Steinbach played well in 1985 (.272), then led the Stars to the best record of 1986. Steinbach was named MVP after setting the all-time SL RBI record (.325, 24 HR, 132 RBI).

mark by the end of the season. The Barons came to life in the playoffs, however, sweeping Huntsville in three straight for the Western title, then winning three of four against Huntsville for the SL flag.

Home run champ Rondal Rollin (.244, 39 HR, 106 RBI) powered Birmingham's pennant drive. Charlotte DH Tom Dodd, an All-Star in 1986, was named MVP for 1987 after leading the SL in RBIs (.289, 37 HR, 127 RBI). The 1985 RBI/home run champ, Mark Funderburk, blasted 28 homers for Orlando in 1987, while Knoxville slugger Geronimo Berroa (.287, 36 HR, 108 RBI) led the SL in total bases. Jacksonville boasted the league's best pitching staff, which featured 6'10 strikeout king Randy Johnson (11–8 with 163 Ks in 140 IP), ERA champ Brian Holman (14–5, 2.50), victory leader John Trautwein (15–4), and All-Star reliever Kevin Price (9–4 in 57 appearances).

Pitchers dominated the hitters of 1988, as only batting champ Butch Davis (.301) of Charlotte reached .300. Chattanooga won the team batting title with a .254 average, while Huntsville finished on top in 1986 with a .289 mark, and the *lowest* team average of 1986 was .261, set by Memphis. Memphis outfielder-first baseman Matt Winters won the home run and RBI titles (.275, 25 HR, 91 RBI), but both totals were the lowest in several seasons.

A pickoff attempt at first.
— Courtesy Birmingham Barons

Stealing second.
— Courtesy Birmingham Barons

*Historic Rickwood Field was replaced by state-of-the-art Hoover Metropolitan
Stadium in 1988. Although Birmingham suffered a losing record, "The Met"
hosted the SL's largest attendance.*

— Courtesy Birmingham Barons

All-Star Mark Lemke, Greenville's second baseman (.279 and the
league leader in hits and total bases), and Francisco Cabrera,
Knoxville's catcher (.284 with 20 homers), were among the future big leaguers on parade for SL fans.

Chattanooga righthander Chris Hammond was the victory
and ERA champ (16–5, 1.72), and teammate Kevin Brown was
dazzling in a brief stint with the Lookouts (9–1 with a 1.42 ERA
in 10 starts). Knoxville righty Alex Sanchez won the strikeout
crown (12–5 with 166 Ks in 149 IP). The league's premier
relievers were Charlotte games leader Paul Thorpe (6–5 in 64 G),
Orlando saves titlist German Gonzalez (31 saves and a 1.02 ERA
in 50 G), and Greenville righthander Ed Mathews (10–4 with a
1.72 ERA in 57 G).

Greenville won both season halves in the East with the best
record of 1988. But Chattanooga led the league in team hitting,
ERA and fielding. The Lookouts won the first half in the West,
beat second-half winner Memphis for the division title, then executed a three-game sweep over Greenville in the finals.

The Chicken entertains another big crowd at The Met.
— Courtesy Birmingham Barons

Birmingham posted the top record the next season, and attracted the best season attendance of 1989 (281,754). The Barons' offense boasted All-Star third baseman Robin Ventura (.278), run leader Richie Amaral (.285, 90 R, 57 SB), hit titlist Craig Grebeck (.287), and stolen base champ Charles Penigar (64 thefts). A deep mound corps included righthander Antonio Menendez (10–4) and southpaw Wedsel Groom (13–8), Gardner Hall (12–8) and Wayne Edwards (12–8). This solid club won the first half in the East, defeated Huntsville for the division crown, and swept Greenville for the 1989 championship.

Huntsville's finalists were led by slugging outfielder Dann Howitt (.281, 26 HR, 111 RBI) and southpaw reliever Joe Klink (a league-leading 26 saves in 57 G). Orlando won the first half in the East behind RBI king Paul Sorrento (.255, 27 HR, 112 RBI), batting titlist Scott Leius (.303), and righthander Paul Abbott (9–3).

Two remarkable pitching performances were turned in by relievers. Orlando righthander Pete Delkus qualified for the ERA title (1.87) while working 76 relief appearances. Although he

Crowd-pleasing antics in Birmingham.
— Courtesy Birmingham Barons

started only twice in 78 appearances, Charlotte righty Laddie Renfroe led the league in victories (19–7). The Most Valuable Player of 1989 was Columbus home run champ Eric Anthony (.300 with 28 homers).

The Southern League ended the 1980s as the only Double A circuit with 10 teams. There was solid attendance throughout the circuit as families and fans found wholesome entertainment at new or refurbished ballparks. Club executives had become masters of promotion, President Jimmy Bragan had provided firm leadership during the entire decade, and franchise values had escalated into the millions. Following ten seasons of consistent success, the Southern League approached the 1990s with confident expectations.

1990–1994

"The Major Minor League"

Southern League prosperity continued in the 1990s, as performance and profits soared along with attendance. The SL talent pool reached an all-time high during the 1990s, when Double-A farm clubs became the most direct route to the big leagues for top prospects. Instead of the time-honored progression from Class A to AA to AAA, by the 1990s Triple-A teams had become taxi squads stocked with seasoned but unexceptional players who served as temporary replacements, going up for brief periods of time to fill in for injured players. The most gifted athletes were primed at the Double-A level, then jumped to the parent club. Southern League fans literally watched the stars of tomorrow. Within a few seasons, baseball's largest Double-A circuit was dubbed "The Major Minor League" by *The Sporting News*.

The 1990 roster of SL cities remained unchanged for the fifth season in a row; previously the league had never gone for more than two years without a franchise change. Two months before the opening of the 1990 season, the Birmingham Barons were sold for an estimated $3.6 million to the Suntory Corporation, the largest privately owned company in Japan.

The Barons won the second half in the West for their new bosses, showcasing RBI champ Matt Stark (.309, 14 HR, 109 RBI),

Team Nicknames During the 1990s	
Birmingham	*Jacksonville*
Barons (1990–94)	Expos (1990)
Carolina	Suns (1991–94)
Mudcats (1991–94)	*Knoxville*
Charlotte	Blue Jays (1990–94)
Knights (1990–92)	*Memphis*
Chattanooga	Chicks (1990–94)
Lookouts (1990–94)	*Nashville*
Columbus	Xpress (1993–94)
Mudcats (1990)	*Orlando*
Greenville	SunRays (1990–94)
Braves (1990–94)	
Huntsville	
Stars (1990–94)	

slugging first-sacker Frank Thomas (.323, 18 HR, and league-leading 112 W), and other members of the best-hitting lineup of 1990.

The most efficient pitching staff was at Jacksonville, where the Expos featured southpaw stikeout king Brian Barnes (13–7 with 213 Ks in 201 IP) and ERA champ Jeff Carter (8–3, 1.84 in 52 games, mostly in relief). With hitting from home run co-leader Terrell Hansen (.260 with 24 homers) and All-Star catcher Greg Colbrunn (.301), the Expos surged to the second-half title in the West.

The 1990 Greenville Braves.
— Courtesy Greenville Braves

Orlando won the first half in the East behind victory leader Doug Simons (15–12), fellow lefthander Dennis Neagle (12–3), and run titlist Jarvis Brown (.260, 33 SB, 104 R). The SunRays compiled the season's top record and beat Jacksonville for the division championship, but lost the finals to Memphis. The Chicks were led by MVP righthander Hector Wagner (12–4), infielder Stewart Cole (.308), All-Star outfielder Bobby Moore (.303), and All-Star third baseman Sean Berry (.292).

In 1989 Raleigh businessman Steve Bryant bought the Columbus franchise, with the eventual goal of bringing professional baseball back to his home area. The club nickname was changed from "Astros" to "Mudcats." Although the affiliation with Houston remained in effect, Columbus management wanted to establish a team identity with commercial possibilities, and the Mudcat logo proved lucratively popular. On opening night the entire *season's* supply of Mudcat caps was sold out!

According to plan, Steve Bryant moved Mudcat Mania to North Carolina for the 1991 season. Territorial rules required that the team had to be located more than 35 miles from the nearest professional franchise, the Class A Durham Bulls. Determining the exact distance from Durham, Bryant purchased a tobacco field just north of the small town of Zebulon. The Carolina Mudcats would play at Five County Stadium, but weather

Chattanooga outfielder Scott Bryant hit well in 1990 (.313 in 44 G) and 1991 (.304 in 91 G).

The Carolina Mudcat at Five County Stadium.
— Courtesy Carolina Mudcats

delays forced the club to open the 1991 schedule at an old pro park at nearby Wilson. When Five County Stadium opened on July 3, auto headlights were visible for miles, not only from the cars of latecomers but from vehicles of those just driving past "the real field of dreams" to view the revival of baseball in the area.

Despite a losing record Carolina drew over 218,000 fans, who cheered knuckleballer Tim Wakefield (15–8). Jacksonville boasted batting champ Jim Bowie (.310) and a total attendance exceeding 231,000. Greenville won the most games of 1991 behind MVP Ryan Klesko (.291), victory leader Napoleon Robinson (16–6), fireballing reliever Mark Wohlers (0.57 ERA and 44 Ks in 31 IP), and All-Star outfielder Keith Mitchell (.327 in 60 G). The Braves pulled in 222,000 fans, while last-place Huntsville attracted 224,000. Charlotte moved into Knights Castle in 1990 and proceeded to lead all Double-A clubs in attendance for three consecutive seasons. In 1991 Charlotte paced the SL in at-

The 1991 Carolina Mudcats. The first game in team history was started by knuckleballing righthander Tim Wakefield (second row, third from right), who compiled an excellent record (15–8) for a losing club.

— Courtesy Carolina Mudcats

tendance with 313,791, and Western Division winner Birmingham was right behind with 313,412.

When Jimmy Bragan became SL president in 1980, total attendance was over 1.9 million, a number reached again the next year. Bragan set an attendance goal of two million, but there were slight declines for the succeeding several seasons. At last, in 1991, SL attendance went over the 2.1 million mark, and in 1992 total attendance was more than 2.3 million.

Former big league slugger Chris Chambilss managed the Braves to the first half title in the East, but Greenville lost the division to second-half winner Orlando. In the West, Birmingham took the first half behind southpaw Wilson Alvarez (10–6, 1.83 ERA, 165 Ks in 152 IP), then beat Knoxville in the playoff opener before losing to Orlando in the finals. The champion SunRays won with ERA leader Pat Mahomes (8–5, 1.78), strikeout champ Mike Trombley (12–7, 175 Ks), and All-Star third baseman Cheo Garcia (.282).

Highly touted righthander Todd Van Poppel struggled for Huntsville and led the SL in losses (6–13). But another fine prospect, All-Star outfielder Reggie Sanders, was impressive in 86 games for Chattanooga (.315), and Charlotte first baseman Elvin

Tim Wakefield was a position player who picked up a knuckleball, pitched well for the 1991 Mudcats (15–8), then was a rookie sensation with Pittsburgh.
— Courtesy Carolina Mudcats

The 1991 Huntsville Stars showcased All-Star DH Troy Neel (standing, sixth from right) and the top draft pick of 1990, Todd Van Poppel (middle, far right).

— Courtesy Huntsville Stars

Paulino paced the league in homers and RBIs (.257, 24 HR, 81 RBI).

The SL lineup was unchanged for 1992, although Charlotte, along with Ottawa, had been named a Triple-A expansion franchise for 1993. Birmingham finished third in the expansion com-

Righthander Todd Van Poppel was drafted number one in 1990, and the next year he pitched for the Huntsville Stars (6–13).
— Courtesy Huntsville Stars

Greenville first-sacker Ryan Klesko was the 1991 MVP (.291).
— Courtesy Greenville Braves

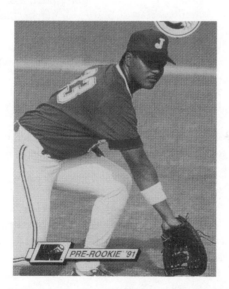

Jacksonville first baseman Jim Bowie was the 1991 batting champ (.310). In 1993, now playing for Huntsville, Bowie became only the second player in SL history to win two batting crowns (.333).
— Courtesy Jacksonville Suns

petition, then attempted unsuccessfully to purchase Denver's Triple-A franchise.

Greenville, with one of the finest minor league teams in recent history, won the first half (49–23, .681) by an 11-game margin.

The Double-A All-Star Game

In 1988 the Pacific Coast League, American Association and International League staged the first annual Triple-A All-Star Game at Buffalo's magnificent Pilot Field. Stars from all 26 Triple-A teams divided into National League and American League squads, and an overflow crowd of more than 18,000 encouraged the leagues to make the game permanent, but at a different site each year.

The three Double-A leagues followed the Triple-A example in 1991. Joe Davis Stadium in Huntsville was the site of the first Double-A All-Star Game. Over 4,000 fans watched the American League squad defeat the National Leaguers, 8–2. The next year the Texas League and Eastern League were skipped over so that the All-Stars could be showcased in Charlotte's gleaming Knights Castle, and Huntsville first baseman Marcos Armas was selected as the "Star of Stars" winner because of his fine performance before another crowd of 4,000.

In 1993, for the third year in a row, an SL city hosted the Double-A All-Star Game. Among the 6,335 fans at Tim McCarver Stadium in Memphis were Larry King and Bob Costas in the broadcast booth, and historian Shelby Foote, who won national television attention as a drawling commentator on Ken Burns' documentary series on the Civil War. The National League Stars won, 12–7, and Memphis outfielder Les Norman, who cracked a home run for the losing team, was named Southern League MVP. Birmingham of the Eastern League was awarded the 1994 All-Star Game, breaking a three-year SL stranglehold on the mid-season event.

Usually mid-season promotions dictated a slide during the latter half of the schedule, but the Braves improved (51–20, .718) and won the second half by 16½ games. Greenville became the first Southern League team ever to win 100 games (100–43, .699). The Braves then faced Charlotte, which had the second-best record in the East (70–73), in the opening round of playoffs. Greenville swept the Knights in three straight to clinch the division title. In the meantime Chattanooga defeated Huntsville for the Western crown. The finals went the full five games, but the Braves prevailed, capping a magnificent season with the league

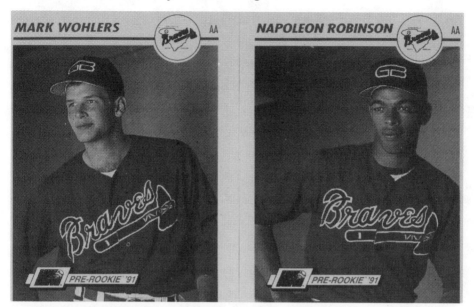

Greenville fireballer Mark Wohlers was voted 1991 Outstanding Pitcher (0.57 ERA in 28 relief appearances), while righthander Napoleon Robinson led the SL in victories (16–6).

— Courtesy Greenville Braves

championship. Grady Little was named Manager of the Year, among many other honors.

Greenville led the SL in team hitting, home runs, ERA, and fielding. The Braves executed 24 shutouts while being blanked merely six times all season. A brilliant home record of 50–20 was only slightly better than the road mark of 50–23. The offensive leaders were catcher Javy Lopez (.321 with 16 homers), shortstop Chipper Jones (.346 in 67 G), and outfielders Melvin Nieves (.283 with 18 homers), Anthony Tarasco (.286 with 33 steals) and Mike Kelly (.229 with 25 homers). The pitching staff performed superbly, led by Nathan Minchey (13–6), Patrick Gomez (7–0, 1.13 ERA), Kevin Coffman (6–0, 2.13 ERA), Lloyd Johnson (6–0, 1.71 ERA), Brian Bark (5–0, 1.15 ERA), Don Elliott (7–2, 2.08 ERA), Andy Nezelek (9–2, 2.26 ERA), and Pedro Borbon (8–2).

The strikeout leader was Jacksonville righthander James Converse (12–7, 157 Ks in 159 IP). Chattanooga was propelled to the finals by hitting and run titlist Scott Pose (.342), home run champ Tim Costas (.241 with 28 homers), victory co-leader Mike Anderson (13–7), and the league's top reliever, righthander Jerry

*Charlotte first baseman Elvin Paulino was the 1991 home run and RBI champ
(.267, 24 HR, 81 RBI), while Orlando righty Mike Trombley led the SL in
strikeouts and innings (12–7, 175 Ks in 191 IP).*
— Courtesy Charlotte Knights and Orlando SunRays

Spradlin (1.38 ERA and 34 saves in 59 G). Huntsville made the
playoffs behind victory co-leader Bronswell Patrick (13–7), first-
sacker Marcos Armas (.283, 17 HR, 84 RBI), and infielder Darryl
Vice (.295).

Charlotte moved up to Triple-A for 1993, and the Southern
League planned to place a franchise in New Orleans. Since 1959,
when the historic baseball city dropped out of the Southern Association, New Orleans had held a professional franchise only one
season (1977, in the American Association). Tom Benson, owner
of the New Orleans Saints, purchased Charlotte's SL franchise
for $3.6 million in October 1992 and leased 3,500-seat Privateer
Park from the University of New Orleans.

But the revival of the Pelicans was placed in jeopardy in November, when the Triple-A Zephyrs of the American Association
announced plans to relocate to the Crescent City. Denver would
begin major league play in 1993, and New Orleans, the largest
city in the United States without a professional franchise, was a
natural site for the American Association club. Benson and the

The 1992 Greenville Braves became the only team in SL history to win 100 games. Manager Grady Little (standing second from right) then led the Braves to the Eatern Division title and the SL championship in the playoffs. Key players included All-Star catcher Javy Lopez (standing sixth from right – .321), Nate Minchey (standing eighth from right – 13-6), Pedro Borbon (standing third from left – 8-2), Tony Tarasco (front, second from left – .286), Judd Johnson (front, third from left – 6-0), and Brian Bark (standing seventh from left – 5-0, 1.15 ERA).

— Courtesy Greenville Braves

The 1993 Jacksonville Suns. Ruben Santana (front, second from right – .301 with 21 homers) was the All-Star second baseman, and third-sacker Craig Clayton (front, fourth from right – .298) also hit well.

— Courtesy Jacksonville Suns

Southern League protested, but under National Association rules the Triple-A claim had precedence.

This decision was reached at the Winter Meeting in December, leaving the SL with a homeless franchise. Tom Benson canceled the sale and turned the franchise back to Charlotte owner

Righthander Robert Ellis, shown outside the Citrus Bowl, which is adjacent to Orlando's Tinker Field, came up to Birmingham late in 1993 (6–3).
— Courtesy Robert Ellis

George Shinn. But Shinn was rescued by Larry Schmittou, who boldly announced plans for the Nashville "Xpress" of the SL to share Herschel Greer Stadium with Schmittou's Triple-A Nashville Sounds. It was the first time two minor league clubs had tried to operate in the same city since 1972, when the Minnesota Twins placed their Double-A SL team and their Single-A Western Carolinas League franchise in Charlotte. The two Charlotte teams combined for a total attendance of merely 44,000, but the Sounds drew 438,745 in 1993, along with 178,387 for the Xpress. Schmittou was so pleased with the success and publicity from his experiment that he and Shinn kept the Xpress in Nashville for 1994, while the SL searched for a permanent franchise site for 1995.

The first half of 1993 was won by Nashville in the West and Greenville in the East. But player promotions sent both the Xpress and the Braves staggering into last place during the second half. Knoxville and Birmingham finished first in their division in the second half of the schedule, as the Barons fashioned the league's best record.

The playoffs began spectacularly when Greenville right-

SL President Jimmy Bragan at his office in Trussville, outside Birmingham.
— Courtesy Jimmy Bragan

hander Mike Hostetler (8–5) fired the first no-hitter ever recorded in SL postseason play. But Knoxville recovered to win the series, three games to two. At the same time, Birmingham won the Western Division with a three-game sweep over Nashville. The Barons then won the 1993 SL championship, three games to one. Birmingham field general Terry Francona was named Manager of the Year.

Birmingham's lineup bristled with talented players, including ERA titlist Jim Baldwin (8–5, 2.25), strikeout champ Scott Ruffcorn (9–4 with 141 Ks in 135 IP), stolen base leader Brandon Wilson (.270 with 43 thefts), outfielder Jerry Wolak (.305), and third basemen Olmedo Saenz (.347) and Ron Coomer (.324). Three pitchers performed impressively in brief stints with the Barons: Steve Schrenk (5–1 with a 1.17 ERA in 8 G); towering fastballer Robert Ellis (6–3 in 12 G); and reliever Jeff Carter (1.02 ERA and 8 saves in 13 G).

Knoxville reached the finals behind MVP catcher Carlos Delgado, who led the SL in homers and RBIs (.303, 25 HR, 102 RBI), victory co-leader Huck Flener (13–6), and first-sacker Tim Hyers (.306). Greenville and Nashville both rode good pitching to the playoffs: percentage leader Oscar Munoz (11–4) for the

Hoover Metropolitan Stadium opened in 1988 south of Birmingham. "The Met" cost $14 million and seats 10,000.

— Courtesy Birmingham Barons

Xpress, along with short-timers Sean Gavaghan (4–0 with a 0.49 ERA in 20 appearances), Jon Henry (4–2 in 6 starts), and southpaw Eddie Guardado (4–0 with a 1.24 ERA in 10 starts); Mike Hostetler was the Braves' best starter, while sterling relief work was turned in by righty Carlos Reyes (8–1 in 33 G) and lefty Dale Polley (8–1 in 42 G).

Huntsville first baseman Jim Bowie (.333, 14 HR, 101 RBI) won his second hitting crown (he was .310 with Jacksonville in 1991); Minnie Mendoza was the only other two-time SL batting champ (in 1967 and 1971 with Charlotte). Carolina righthander Bobby Hunter (5–3 with a 1.01 ERA in 46 relief appearances) set an all-time SL record by twirling 40⅓ consecutive innings without allowing a run. Carolina was the attendance leader with more than 328,000 admissions, as total paid admission exceeded 2,400,000, the highest attendance in Southern League history.

During the 1993 season SL president Jimmy Bragan announced his retirement. Bragan intends to serve throughout the 1994 season, and his 15-year tenure will span half of the 30-year

Greenville Municipal Stadium has been the home of the Braves since 1984.
— Courtesy Greenville Braves

history of the Southern League. A search committee to find Bragan's successor was appointed: Peter Bragan, Jr. GM of the Jacksonville Suns; Dan Rajkowski, GM of the Knoxville Smokies; and Larry Schmittou, president of the Huntsville Stars and GM of the Nashville Xpress.

The Major Minor League Owners

The primary reason that the Southern League currently is regarded as "The Major Minor League" is the quality of club leadership. Minor league owners always have had to be enterprising, resourceful and community-minded, and no band of owners has been more progressive than the men who have invested their money and time in the teams of the Southern League. The principal owners are:

Birmingham Barons	Shiro Yasuno
Carolina Mudcats	Steve Bryant
Chattanooga Lookouts	Richard M. Holtzman
Greenville Braves	Stan Kasten
Huntsville Stars	Larry Schmittou

Jacksonville Suns	Peter Bragan, Jr.
Knoxville Blue Jays	Pat Gillick
Memphis Chicks	David Hersh
Nashville Xpress	George Shinn
Orlando SunRays	Richard M. DeVos

Perhaps the most significant duty of President Bragan during his final season will be to lead the selection of a permanent home for the Nashville Xpress. As this book goes to press, the leading candidates were Mobile and Lexington, although neither city had yet constructed a suitable stadium. But whatever city is selected, there certainly will be another fine ballpark available for SL baseball. The Southern League again will exceed two million in attendance, families across the South will continue to view big league stars of the future, and once more the SL will affirm its label as "The Major Minor League."

Southern League Stadiums

ASHEVILLE

McCormick Field. When the Southern League was christened in 1964, McCormick Field was 40 years old. Located on a hill above Valley Street, the wooden ballpark was built at a cost of $200,000 in 1924. The outfield walls were covered with thick vines, and the seating capacity was 3,200 in 1964, expanded to 3,500 before Asheville left the SL 11 years later. Eventually known as the oldest wooden ballpark still in use, picturesque McCormick Field was used as a backdrop in the 1988 movie *Bull Durham*. But following the 1991 season, the venerable structure was razed, except for a concession stand, and McCormick Field was beautifully rebuilt as a brick stadium reminiscent of the historic old facility.

BIRMINGHAM

Rickwood Field. Erected in 1910, the concrete and steel facility was modeled on Pittsburgh's recently-completed Forbes Field. When the Southern League commenced play, Rickwood still seated 14,500, an excessive capacity for the 1960s. Birmingham was out of baseball for six years following the 1975 season, and

195

when the Barons returned to Rickwood, seating was reduced by 4,000. The old hand-operated scoreboard in left field was replaced in 1981 by a computerized board. The Barons' final season at Rickwood was 1987, and by that time Rickwood was the oldest stadium in the minor leagues.

Hoover Metropolitan Stadium. Constructed at a cost of $14 million, Hoover Metropolitan Stadium is located at the junction of Highways 150 and 459 south of Birmingham. The streamlined facility seats 10,000, and there are plans to increase the seating by stages to 23,000.

CAROLINA

Fleming Stadium. When the Mudcats were moved from Columbus to North Carolina, Five County Stadium was erected just outside the 35-mile territorial limit from Durham. But the new facility was not ready for the start of the 1991 season, and for more than two months the Mudcats played at Fleming Stadium, a former Class D ballpark located at nearby Wilson. Built in 1939 and originally named Municipal Stadium, the ballpark seated 3,000 and was jammed (crowds averaged 4,000 with temporary bleachers) during the months Fleming Stadium hosted Southern League baseball.

Five County Stadium was built in 1991 on a "field of dreams," 55 acres from a former tobacco farm located north of Zebulon. Indeed, dirt was sprinkled on the infield that had been brought from the Iowa farm used in the popular movie *Field of Dreams.* And like the final scene of that film, automobile lights were bumper to bumper for miles on opening night of Five County Stadium. The stadium seats 6,000, and major steps are taken each season to upgrade the facility.

CHARLOTTE

Crockett Park/Knights Park. Clark Griffith, owner of the Washington Senators, also owned Charlotte's minor league club, and in 1941 he built a $40,000 wooden ballpark at 400 Magnolia Avenue. Griffith named the 6,500-seat facility after himself, and when the SALLY moved up to Double A the Hornets still were at home at Clark Griffith Park. In 1972 the Hornets shared the aging stadium with the Class A Charlotte Twins, and when attendance nosedived both franchises were moved. But Charlotte business-man Jim Crockett brought another Southern League club back to the ballpark in 1976. Crockett Park was badly damaged by fire in March 1985, and when it was repaired the seating capacity was reduced. Dubbed Knights Park during the final season of use in 1988, the old ballpark was abandoned when the Knights moved to a site just outside the city for 1989.

Knights Castle. When Knights Castle was under construction during the 1989 season, a temporary facility was utilized in an area that later would be converted for parking. Knights Castle was ready for the 1990 opener, a 10,000-seat state-of-the-art stadium that was planned with a potential expansion to 70,000, if a major league or NFL franchise could be attracted. Indeed, Knights Castle hosted the largest Double A attendance the next year, and in 1993 the Knights moved up to Triple A.

CHATTANOOGA

Joe Engel Stadium. Constructed in 1930 by Clark Griffith for his Southern Association farm team, the 10,000-seat stadium was built at Third and O'Neal streets. The outfield was ranch size (368 feet down the left field line, 471 feet in center), and a sharp incline in center led upward to a terrace far from home plate (the fences finally were moved in closer in recent years). A $2.2 million renovation in 1989–90 transformed Engel Stadium into a jewel of a facility, a nostalgic blend of a traditional ballpark with a streamlined modern stadium.

COLUMBUS

Golden Park. Originally a wooden ballpark erected in 1926 beside the Chattahoochee River, Golden Park was rebuilt in steel and concrete after the 1950 season. Reconstructed at a cost of $195,000, Golden Park was a symmetrical field (315 feet down the lines and 415 feet to center) with a seating capacity of 6,600. Today it remains a beautiful park in which to view a game.

EVANSVILLE

Bosse Field. Named after Mayor Benjamin Bosse, who helped design and implement construction of the park, Bosse Field was the first municipally-owned stadium in the history of Organized

Baseball. Built in 1915 at a cost of $100,000 by the Evansville school board, Bosse Field was intended as an all-sports facility (indeed, after the opening baseball game of 1915 was played before a capacity crowd, that night 1,500 fans watched a wrestling match under improved lighting). The 8,000-seat stadium was located just north of Evansville's downtown area in Garvin Park. The covered grandstand and outfield fences were built of brick, and even today Bosse Field is an evocatively handsome ballpark that was used in the hit movie *A League of Their Own*. The outfield was extremely deep until an interior wire fence was built in 1951, and there never has been a ball hit over the 477-foot center field fence.

GREENVILLE

Greenville Municipal Stadium. Opened in 1984 for the return of professional baseball, Greenville Municipal Stadium was erected on the outskirts of town off Maudlin Road at One Braves Drive. The concrete grandstand is roofless and provides 7,027 seats. Outfield dimensions are 335 feet down the lines and 405 feet in center. Scattered throughout the ballpark are Greenville Baseball Hall of Fame plaques, which offer a fascinating history of local stars, from Shoeless Joe Jackson to Textile League standouts.

HUNTSVILLE

Joe W. Davis Stadium. Named after Huntsville's longtime mayor, Joe W. Davis Stadium was constructed in 32 weeks from September 1984 through April 1985. Located on 30 acres of the old airport grounds adjacent to Highway 231, the 10,260-seat ballpark features a large pressbox and VIP rooms atop the grandstand. A multi-purpose municipal stadium, the facility is utilized for high school and college football during the fall. Portable bleachers down the right field line are moved onto the field during football season to provide visitors' seating.

JACKSONVILLE

Sam W. Wolfson Baseball Park. Built in 1955 as Jacksonville Baseball Park, the facility was renamed for local sportsman Sam Wolfson, who brought an International League franchise to the city in 1962, but died the following year. The 10,000-seat ballpark was constructed at 1201 East Duval Street near Gator Bowl Stadium. The covered grandstand sports traditional support beams and the outfield is surrounded by a brick fence. Renovations have reduced the current seating capacity to 8,200.

KNOXVILLE

Knoxville Municipal Stadium. In 1931 City Councilman W. N. Smithson persuaded the Knoxville Council to raze old Caswell Park and build a new facility at the familiar site at 633 Jessamine Street. Smithson Stadium was rebuilt after a 1953 fire and renamed Knoxville Municipal Stadium. The 6,700-seat facility again was renamed, Bill Meyer Stadium, in 1957 after the death of a Knoxville native who played and managed in the big leagues.

LYNCHBURG

City Stadium. Erected in 1938 by the WPA, Lynchburg City Stadium was located on the old fairgrounds. City Stadium had back-to-back football and baseball fields. The baseball park had 5,000 seats, 2,500 under a covered grandstand.

MACON

Luther Williams Field. Central City Park was built in 1892 and burned in 1926. Luther Williams Field replaced the old park in 1929 at a cost of $60,000. In 1949 the fences were pulled in, reducing the cavernous outfield distances — 360 feet down the lines and 450 feet in center — to 330, 405, and 330 feet. "Operation Face Lift" in 1956 moved the light poles out of the outfield and replaced the old wooden bleachers with steel bleachers.

MEMPHIS

Tim McCarver Stadium. In 1968 the Memphis Blues of the Texas League moved into a ballpark originally intended for high school play. Located on the State Fairgrounds near the Liberty Bowl, Blues' Stadium became Chicks Stadium when the Memphis Chicks joined the Southern League in 1978. By 1985 the seating capacity had been expanded to 10,000, and the park is now named for the Memphis native who became a standout catcher and a noted sportscaster. Tim McCarver Stadium has the only artificial turf infield in the Southern League.

MOBILE

Hartwell Field. Also known as Monroe Park and League Park, the 11,000-seat stadium at Ann and Tennessee streets was the home of Mobile's SL teams in 1966 and 1970. Outfield distances were 335 feet down the lines and 406 feet in center.

MONTGOMERY

Paterson Field. Built in 1949 for $200,000, Paterson Field was placed just north of Madison Avenue (the Cramton Bowl, a fine football stadium, and, for many years, the home of pro baseball in Montgomery, stands just south of Madison Avenue). Paterson Field seats 6,000 and is only 380 feet to dead center, although the foul lines are 330 feet long.

NASHVILLE

Herschel Greer Stadium. When Larry Schmittou organized the Nashville Sounds for the 1978 SL season, Herschel Greer Stadium was built on a 26-acre tract south of downtown at the foot of St. Cloud Hill in Fort Negley Park. During Nashville's seven seasons in the SL, Herschel Greer Stadium annually recorded the league's largest attendance. Nashville moved up to the American Association in 1985, but in 1993 Schmittou offered 18,000-seat Herschel Greer Stadium as the temporary home of a homeless SL franchise. When the Triple A Sounds were on the road, the Nashville Xpress would host their SL opponents at Herschel Greer Stadium.

ORLANDO

Tinker Field. Originally constructed in 1914, Tinker Field was named after Hall of Fame shortstop Joe Tinker ("Tinker to Evers to Chance"), who became the owner-manager of Orlando's Florida State club, and who lived the rest of his life in The City Beautiful. In 1936 Clark Griffith began to send his Washington Senators to Tinker Field for spring training, an association which continued when the franchise became the Minnesota Twins in 1961. After the 1972 season the Twins moved their SL club from Charlotte to Orlando. By this time a 1963 renovation had replaced the old wooden grandstand with a concrete structure. Another renovation in 1990 gave Tinker Field a new facade, and the historic ballpark was landscaped with palm trees. Tinker Field currently seats 5,104, including 500 wooden seats from Griffith Stadium which were installed at the top of the grandstand. Located southwest of downtown Orlando, Tinker Field stands in the shadow of the Citrus Bowl, which looms just to the east.

SAVANNAH

Municipal Stadium/Grayson Stadium. In 1927 a 3,500-seat concrete grandstand was built in Daffin Park, and Municipal Stadium became the home of professional baseball in Savannah. Football also was played in Municipal Stadium, which was renovated and expanded by the WPA. By 1940 there was a covered concrete grandstand which seated 3,000, plus two sets of large concrete football bleachers which expanded the seating capacity to 10,000. The north bleachers are adjacent to the grandstand on the first base side, while the south bleachers are in left field. The left field foul line was only 290 feet from home plate, and a 90-foot light tower was in play all the way to the top. Renamed Grayson Stadium, the venerable facility was a home of SL baseball from 1968 through 1973, and today the Savannah Cardinals of the SALLY play there.

Nicknames

Joseph Jefferson Wofford Jackson was an illiterate South Carolina millboy who starred for Textile League teams, then turned pro and won three consecutive minor league batting crowns, including the 1909 SALLY title and the 1910 Southern Association championship. Jackson dubbed his carefully-crafted bat "Black Betsy," and because the country boy sometimes played barefooted (he later said that he went without shoes during a game just once, when a new pair had rubbed blisters on his feet) he acquired one of baseball's most famous nicknames, "Shoeless Joe."

A great many country boys played during the early years of the Southern and SALLY, and callow youths straight off the farm inevitably were called "Rube." Rube Eldridge, Rube Ellis, Rube Kissinger, Rube Marshall, Rube Pressler, and Rube Robinson were among those branded by their teammates as farm boys, and so were Country Davis and Country Slaughter. Other fresh-faced types included Babe Barna and Babe Bigelow, Kid Elberfeld and Kid Nichols, Baby Doll Jacobson, and Schoolboy Hoyt.

Native Southerners included Dixie Walker (from Georgia), Dixie Carroll (Kentucky), Dixie Upright (North Carolina), and Rebel Adams (Georgia). Travis Jackson inescapably acquired the sobriquet "Stonewall" when he ventured into Southern Association ballparks. Tex Covington, Tex Hoffman, Tex Jeanes, and Tex McDonald hailed from the Lone Star State. Cactus Johnson and Klondike Douglas brought an air of remote frontier locales to the Old South.

Charles Dillon Stengel was branded "Casey" because he was from K. C. (Kansas City), while "Poco" Tait learned the game in his hometown of Pocatello. Irish Meusel received one of the unsubtle ethnic monikers of his time, and so did Fritz Clausen and Heinie Berger. Berger also was called Dutch, an all-purpose appellation that was applied to Dutch Leonard, Dutch Meyer, Dutch Henry, Dutch Schliebner, Dutch Prather, Dutch Bernsen, Dutch Beck, Dutch Mele, and Dutch Yaryan. Irving Wilhelm was entitled "Kaiser," joining such other nobility as Prince Gaskill, Prince Kenna, and Charles "The Count" Campau.

"Luckless" Ernie Palmieri pitched 16 shutout innings against Savannah in 1957, only to lose, 2–0, in the 17th. Jinx Poindexter and Gloomy Gus Williams also felt the sting of misfortune on Southern diamonds. Sunny Jim Blakesley enjoyed a brighter existence, and so did Shine Cortazzo and Sparky Olson. Free spirits included Dazzy Vance, Dizzy Carlyle, Bobo Newsom, and Boob McNair. Players with more maturity were awarded respectful appellations such as Pop Eyler and Pop Hixon, or Doc Leggett and Doc Wiseman.

"Gentleman" Jake Daubert was labeled because of his meticulous and immaculate appearance. Less immaculate in appearance was Burleigh "Old Stubblebeard" Grimes. Physical appearance also branded Big Jim Clinton, Jumbo Cartwright, Tiny Chaplin, and muscular Popeye Mahaffey. Specs Hill wore glasses, Jughandle Johnny Morrison had big ears, and Satchelfoot Wells had big feet. Scores of carrot-topped ballplayers included Reddy Mack, Red Barrett, Red Bittman, Red Davis, Red Durrett, Red Evans, Red Howell, Red Lucas, and Red McColl. Hair color also nicknamed Blondy Purcell and Whitey Glazner.

Eating habits produced nicknames for Pretzels Pezzullo, Buttermilk Meek, Oyster Joe Martina, Noodles Hahn, Spud Krist, and Grapefruit Yeargin. Lefty Mailho and Lefty Sigman are only two of the legions of Southern players who threw the ball from portside, and fastball pitchers such as Cy Warmoth were nicknamed after cyclones. Men who played with abandon or hit the ball hard included Rip Repulski, Rip Dunbar, Rip Radcliff, and Rip Reagan.

On-field fights were not uncommon during any period of Southern baseball history. Welcome teammates in altercations were such dangerous-sounding men as Pug Bennett and Pug Cavet, Punch Knoll, Slug Hutcheson, Coalyard Mike Handiboe, Tacks Latimer, Scrappy Moore, and Stormy Davis, while boxing fans would have flocked to see a card matching Dynamite Dunn versus Boom-Boom Beck.

Other rugged-sounding athletes were Bull Ellis, Moose Clabaugh, Moose McCormick, Moose Werden, and Ox Eckhardt. The Southern menagerie also included Chicken Hawks, Chick Autry, Chick Fullis, Chick Tolson, Duck Shifflett, Ducky Holmes, Goose Goslin, Horse Leven, Mule Shirley, Mule Watson, Goat Walker, Piggy Ward, Kitty Wickman, Snake Henry, Monk Cline, Mouse Glenn, Hippo Vaughn, and Toad Ramsey.

Righthander Philip Douglas was such a slow worker on the mound that he was known as "Fiddlin' Phil" and "Shufflin' Phil." Among other Southern players and managers with intriguing nicknames were Hootman McKenzie, Patcheye Gill, Peek-A-Boo Veach, Gee Gee Gleeson, Hobo Carson, Shovel Hodge, Boots Poffenberger, Climax Blethen, Moon Ducote, Pooch Barnhart, Popboy Smith, and Mudball Grant. There were many more, of course, all adding to the color and enjoyment of baseball in Dixie.

Southern League Cities

During three decades of SL play, nineteen cities in eight states have placed teams in the Southern League. Alabama and Tennessee have had four cities each; there have been three apiece in Georgia and North Carolina; two cities are in Florida; and Indiana, South Carolina, and Virginia have hosted one franchise each. Eight of these cities participated in the old Southern League during the late nineteenth century. Eight cities fielded teams in the Southern Association, and twelve cities belonged to the SALLY at one time or another. Macon, Montgomery, and Nashville have the distinction of participating in the old Southern League, the SALLY, the Southern Association, and the modern SL.

Asheville
(Tourists, Orioles)

Baseball became popular in Asheville, as in countless other American communities, during the Civil War. Games were first played in an Asheville prisoner-of-war camp. After the war an unfenced diamond frequently was in use at the Barn Field, a large lot between Aston Park and Grove Street where political gatherings, picnics, and military musters were held. By the turn of the century, Asheville nines played at a field near the end of Charlotte Street.

In 1910 Asheville became a charter member of the Class B Southeastern League, playing at newly-constructed Riverside Park, located beside the French Broad River at the foot of Montford Avenue. The next year Asheville helped organize another Class D circuit, the Appalachian League. After two seasons in the Appalachian League, Asheville became a charter member of yet another Class D loop, the North Carolina State League. The following year, 1914, Asheville moved into Oates Park, a wooden ballpark bounded by Choctaw, McDowell and Southside streets.

Asheville finished in the cellar in 1914, then rebounded to the 1915 pennant behind player-manager Jack Corbett and slugger Jim Hickman, who went on to win the 1916 batting championship (.350). But wartime conditions forced Asheville to drop out of the North Carolina State League early in the 1917 season, and seven years passed before the city re-enlisted in organized baseball.

The Golden Age of Sports lured Asheville and many other cities into the minor leagues during the 1920s. McCormick Field was completed in 1924 at a cost of $200,000. A wooden ballpark built on a hillside near the downtown area, McCormick Field was named after Dr. Lewis McCormick, a bacteriologist known as "The Fly Man." Early in the century Dr. McCormick had conducted a campaign to rid Asheville of a plague of house flies. Financed by the city as an all-purpose facility, McCormick Field also was the site of football games, and for a time there was a cinder running track, an area for "barnyard golf," and a shooting range. At first there was only a low rail fence around the outfield, and railbirds could watch the games without visiting the ticket booth. McCormick Field boasted an electric scoreboard, a maid and attendant in the ladies' room, and plumbing considered "the most sanitary, being of the class used at the best hotels in the country." The ballpark was lighted in 1930.

The Asheville "Skylanders" joined the Class B SALLY League in 1924 (the team nickame soon would revert to the more traditional "Tourists"). In 1928 the Tourists won Asheville's first SALLY pennant behind player-manager Ray Kennedy (.366), triples leader Dusty Cooke (.362, 30 3B), 19-year-old shortstop Ben Chapman (.336), outfielders Stan Keyes (.330) and Al Green (.310), ERA champ Joe Heving (2.46), Bill Harris (25–7), and Struttin' Bud Shaney (21–11). Six members of this magnificent Class B club were sold to the big leagues, with Chapman becoming the most successful star.

Keyes won the batting crown in 1929, (.377), and the next year Hal Sullivan (.374) kept the title in Asheville. When the SALLY halted operations after the 1930 season, the Tourists moved to the Class C Piedmont League. The Tourists dropped out in July of the Depression-ravaged 1932 season, but Asheville rejoined the Piedmont League (now a Class B circuit) as a mid-season replacement for Columbia.

The grandstand and pressbox at McCormick Field were ravaged by fire a month before the start of the 1935 season, but a left field grandstand was dismantled and the ballpark was quickly repaired. That year Asheville became a Cardinal farm club, and manager Bobby Southworth led the Tourists to the 1935 pennant. The Tourisis plummeted into the cellar the next year (40–103), then charged to another flag in 1937 and won it all again in 1939.

After the 1942 season, Asheville dropped out of professional baseball for the duration of the war. In 1946, with a surge of postwar popularity in minor league baseball, Asheville helped form the Class B Tri-State League as a Brooklyn Dodger affiliate. The Tourists made the playoffs behind batting champ Dick Bouknight (.367) and player-manager Bill Sayles (.338 with a league-leading 105 RBIs).

Manager Clay Bryant directed the Tourists to the 1948 pennant with a standout team of Dodger farmhands: run leader Norm Koney (.335, 39 SB, 145 R), outfielder Joe Belcastro (.342), second baseman Spook Jacobs (.328, 47 SB, 92 RBI), ERA champ Joe Landrum (17–4, 2.77), and Tom Lakos (21–8). Asheville returned to the playoffs the next three years, reaching the finals in 1950 and 1951.

Under Manager Ray Hathaway, the 1954 Tourists outdistanced the rest of the league by 13 games. Shortstop Jackie Spears led the circuit in runs and hits (.329, 24 3B, 120 R) and Les Fessette paced the pitching staff (22–8). The Tri-State League expired a year later, and McCormick Field was utilized as a motor speedway. But pro ball returned in 1959, when local businessmen formed Community Baseball, Inc., and placed an Asheville club in the Class A SALLY.

First baseman Nate Dickerson won the 1959 batting title (.362), and in 1961 the Tourists won the SALLY pennant. Ray Hathaway again was at the helm, and again his team outdistanced the rest of the circuit by 13 games. First baseman Gary Rushing led the SALLY in homers, RBIs and runs (.311, 25 HR, 99 RBI, 108 R), outfielder Willie Stargell (.289 with 22 homers) demonstrated Hall of Fame talent, and Jim Hardison (16–2) headed a deep pitching staff.

The next year Elmo Plaskett (.349) brought another hitting crown to Asheville, and in 1963 the SALLY moved up to Double-A status. The following year the circuit became the Southern League, but the Tourists finished in the cellar, a fate which cost longtime manager Ray Hathaway his job at mid-season. Outfielder George Spriggs was the stolen base titlist and finished second in the batting race (.322 with 33 thefts).

The 1965 Tourists (80–60, .571) lost the SL pennant to Columbus (79–59, .572) by a fraction of a percentage point. Southpaw Luke Walker was the strikeout and ERA king (12–7, 2.26, and 197 Ks in 183 IP), first baseman Charles Leonard was the RBI leader (.270, 14 HR, 78 RBI), and catcher/third-sacker Orlando McFarlane won the home run crown despite playing in only 86 games (.292 with 22 homers).

Manager Pete Peterson again guided the Tourists to second place in 1966. First-sacker Charles Leonard once more hit well (.308), third baseman Bob Robertson led the SL in homers and RBIs (.287, 32 HR, 99 RBI), and lefty Dave Roberts was the ERA champ (14–5, 2.61). After the season a long affiliation with Pittsburgh ended, and Asheville moved to the Class A Carolina League as a Houston farm club.

For 1968 Asheville affiliated with Cincinnati and returned to the Southern League. With talented Sparky Anderson at the helm, the Tourists won the pennant by 4½ games. Outfielder Arlie Burge was the batting champ (.317), future big leaguers Bernie Carbo (.281 with 20 HR) and Darrel Chaney (.231 with 23 HR) added power to the hitting order, first baseman Archie Moore (.279) and catcher Fred Kendall (.291) made the All-Star Team, and southpaw Grover Powell led the league in ERA, victories, starts and innings (16–6, 2.54).

The Tourists dropped to .500 the next year, although first baseman Don Anderson led the SL in batting, triples, total bases and RBIs (.324, 18 HR, 100 RBI) and third-sacker Kurt Bevaqua finished second in the hitting race (.316, 16 HR, 91 RBI). In 1970 the Tourists sank to the cellar, in attendance (28,720) as well as the standings.

The next season the SL and the Texas League, each limited to only seven teams, formed the three-division Dixie Association. Manager Larry Sherry led Asheville to second place in the six-team Eastern Division and the wild-card playoff slot, although the Tourists were defeated in the opening round. Asheville led all seven SL clubs in team hitting and home runs (131). Outfielder Ken Hottman was the SL home run, RBI and run champ (.302, 37 HR, 116 RBI), catcher Vic Correll provided more power (.273 with 22 homers), and Charles Miller was named All-Star shortstop (.287 with 14 homers). The Tourists boasted the best one-two, lefty-righty combination in southpaw victory leader Jim MacDowell (17–7) and percentage titlist Dennis O'Toole (13–3).

The next year the SL returned to an eight-team two-division format, and Asheville became part of the Baltimore farm system. The Orioles sent Cal Ripken to manage their new club, and for the next three summers his sons, future big leaguers Cal, Jr., and Billy, played Little League ball in Asheville. Ripken, Sr., guided the Asheville Orioles to the best record of 1972, as Asheville again led the SL in team hitting and home runs (126). MVP outfielder Mike Reinbach won a Triple Crown, leading the league in batting, homers, RBIs, runs, hits, total bases, doubles and walks (.346, 32 2B, 39 HR, 123 R, 109 RBI). The pitching staff featured victory leader Paul Mitchell (16–8), fellow righthander Herb Hutson

(14–3), and saves leader Mark Weems (4–2 and 22 saves in 48 G). Royle Stillman (.297 with 23 homers) was an All-Star outfielder, and third base was manned by future big leaguer Doug DeCinces (.263).

In 1973 second baseman Rob Andrews won the batting title and led the SL in runs and hits (.309, 98 R), catcher Terry Clapp was the home run and RBI champ (.259, 35 HR, 98 RBI), fellow catcher Don Hickey (.291) and shortstop Bob Bailer (.293) were named to the All-Star team, and righthander Randy Stein (14–6) anchored the pitching staff. The next year the All-Star squad included second baseman Kim Andrew (.317) and shortstop Alfonse Garcia (.274), and promising infielder Rich Dauer played impressively in 53 games (.328).

The 1975 Orioles led the SL in team hitting for the fifth consecutive season, and for the sixth time in seven years. Outfielder Charles Hall was the batting champ (.322), outfielder Creighton Tevlin also hit well (.296), and first base was manned by future major league star Eddie Murray (.264 with 17 homers). But the team finished last in their division, and Baltimore moved their SL franchise to Charlotte for the 1976 season.

The beautiful new version of McCormick Field opened in 1992, a splendid replacement for the historic old ballpark that had been built in 1924.

Asheville placed a club in the Class A Western Carolinas League and won the 1976 pennant, behind Triple Crown winner Pat Putnam (.361, 24 HR, 142 RBI). David Rivera produced another Triple Crown for the Tourists in 1977 (.346, 26 HR, 118 RBI). In 1980 the Tourists moved into the reorganized SALLY League, and the next season Danny Murphy was the batting champ (.369). Asheville won the 1984 SALLY playoffs, and ran away with the Northern Division crown in 1986. The 1987 Tourists posted the best record in the league behind hitting and RBI titlists Ed Whited (.323, 126 RBI) and home run king Mike Simms, who blasted 39 roundtrippers — the most ever hit by an Asheville slugger. Season after season McCormick Field has hosted well over 100,000 fans annually, and in 1992 the venerable ballpark was beautifully rebuilt, virtually assuring continued large crowds for the Tourists.

Year	Record	Pcg.	Finish
1964	52–86	.377	Eighth
1965	80–60	.571	Second
1966	78–61	.561	Second
1968	86–54	.614	First
1969	69–69	.500	Third
1970	59–80	.424	Eighth
1971	90–51	.638	Second
1972	81–58	.583	First (lost finals)
1973	71–69	.507	Fourth
1974	70–67	.511	Fifth
1975	63–75	.457	Seventh

Birmingham
(Barons, Athletics)

Baseball already was a popular recreation when Birmingham was founded in 1871 as a coal mining center. The game was first played at a vacant block at the corner of Lower Highland Avenue and 33rd Street. A small grandstand was built at the corner of the block, while "Bleacherites" stood near the baselines. Anticipating the acrobatics of modern players, one nineteenth-century outfielder ran back and climbed a fence to catch a long fly. This field also was used for football, so the best nines soon moved to a site on First Avenue near 14th Street, close to the Southern Railroad tracks. A plank fence and 600-seat grandstand were erected, but many kranks watched from the slag pile of the Alice Furnace beyond the outfield. The facility became known as "Slag Pile Park," and one team was called the "Slag Pilers."

Slag Pile Park was the home of Birmingham's 1885 charter entry in the Southern League. There was no club the following year, but as SL teams disbanded in 1887 the Birmingham "Babies" were birthed to finish the season. The 1888 Birmingham "Maroons" won the pennant behind first-sacker Tom Lynch (.331). There was not enough support for the Maroons to defend their title in 1889, but when the SL again faltered Birmingham fielded another mid-season entry.

The Southern League did not operate the next two years, but when the circuit reorganized in 1892 the Birmingham "Grays" won the second half and compiled the season's best record. In 1893 the Birmingham "Pets" disbanded in early June, probably because of the new nickname, and the city did not field an SL team for the next two seasons. In 1896 Birmingham tried the SL again with the "Rustlers," and the "Reds" attempted play during the abortive 1898 season. There was no interest in organizing a team in 1899, which proved to be the last year of the old Southern League.

But when the Southern Association was organized in 1901, the Birmingham "Barons" were charter members. Birmingham had a population of only a few thousand during the 1880s, but the booming industrial city soared past 100,000 early in the twentieth century, and the Barons would play in every season of the SA. The Barons brought Birmingham its first SA pennant in 1906, behind the league's best three-man rotation: Kaiser Wilhelm (22–13, including the first perfect game in SA history), Ginger Clark (22–14, the second year in a row he had won 22 games), and Rip Reagan (20–8). The next season Wilhelm led the league in victories (23–14), hurled five iron-man doubleheaders (9–1), and established all-time SA records with 11 shutouts and 56 consecutive scoreless innings. The 1907 batting champ was first baseman Buttermilk Meek (.340), and two years later outfielder Bill McGilvray (.291) became the only SA batter to win the title with less than a .300 average.

In February 1910, millionaire industrialist Rick Woodward

purchased the Barons from J. W. McQueen and immediately began to erect a new ballpark at West Second Avenue and East 18th Street. Rickwood Field was built at a cost of $75,000 along the same configuration as Pittsburgh's Forbes Field, which had opened in 1909 as the big leaguers' first concrete-and-steel stadium (Neil Park in Columbus, Ohio, became the minors' first concrete-and-steel facility in 1905). Bleachers curved around the right field foul line, which was only 334 feet from the plate; but the left field line was 405 feet away, and center field stretched 470 feet from the batter's box. (The fences eventually were moved in, and the big hand-operated scoreboard in left was replaced by a computerized scoreboard in 1981.) Rickwood Field opened on August 18, 1910, and 10,000 fans watched the Barons defeat Montgomery, 2–1. Southpaw Harry Coveleskie arrived at mid-season and hurled 21 victories before the year ended.

In 1912 Rickwood flew a pennant as the Barons showcased outfielder Jim Johnston, who stole 81 bases — one of six consecutive theft titles a Baron claimed from 1908 through 1913. In 1913 Birmingham fans enjoyed the superb pitching of southpaw Harry Coveleskie (28–9) and righthander Bill Prough (23–6), and the next year Curley Brown (21–7) and E. Hardgrove (20–9) led the Barons to another flag.

Birmingham continued to feature standout pitchers during this era: future Hall of Famer Burleigh Grimes in 1915 (17–13) and 1916 (20–11); Carmen "Specs" Hill in 1917 (26–12); John Morrison (26–12) and Charles Glazner (24–10) in 1920; Eddie "Satchelfoot" Wells in 1927 (13–1) and 1928 (25–7); and Dick Ludolph (21–8) and Bob Hasty (22–11) in 1929. Another stalwart of this period was second baseman Stuffy Stewart, who played for the Barons (with time out for several big league stints) from 1920 through 1929, managing the club in 1923 and 1924. Stewart was a five-time SA stolen base champ (1921, 1922, 1924, 1925 and 1928) while setting the all-time league record for thefts (370).

An even more familiar fixture in Birmingham was Carleton Molesworth. At the age of 19, in 1895, Molesworth pitched in four games for Washington (0–3), and soon switched to the out-field. After the Southern Association was organized he played a few seasons for Montgomery, winning the batting title in 1905 (.312). The next year he signed with Birmingham, remaining one of the top hitters in the SA for five seasons (.302 in 1908 and

A Birmingham club of the 1920s.
— Courtesy Birmingham Barons

.300 in 1910). In 1909, after a last-place finish the previous year, he replaced Harry Vaughn as manager. He was a playing manager for three seasons, but he quit the outfield after his hitting tailed off in 1911 (.243). Molesworth produced pennants in 1912 and 1914, and managed the Barons into the 1922 season, suffering only two losing records. His 13½ consecutive seasons as Birmingham's pilot set an all-time SA record, since Larry Gilbert's 15 years as New Orleans manager was interrupted by a season in the front office.

Johnny Dobbs managed the Barons from 1925 through 1929. In 1927 his Barons established an all-time SA mark with 19 consecutive victories, then he led the club to back-to-back pennants the next two seasons. The 1928 Barons, sparked by batting champ Babe Bigelow (.395) won the first half of the schedule and swept Memphis in four straight games before bowing to Houston in Birmingham's first Dixie Series. In 1929 the Barons won an outright pennant race, then beat Dallas for the first of six Dixie Series triumphs.

Johnny Dobbs moved to Atlanta the next year, and he was succeeded by Clyde Milan, who guided the Barons to the 1931 pennant behind Jimmy Waldrop (20–5), Bob Hasty (21–13) and Ray Caldwell (19–7). The opening game of the Dixie Series against Houston was termed "the best game ever played in Birmingham." Over 20,000 fans jammed Rickwood to watch 43-year-old Ray Caldwell face Texas League MVP Dizzy Dean (26–10, 303 K, 1.53 ERA), the only pitcher ever to post a Triple Crown throughout the minors. Barons' second baseman Billy Bancroft, who had been a great football star in Birmingham, doubled home the only run of the game as the veteran Caldwell outdueled Diz, 1–0. Houston rebounded to take the next three games as Dean threw a shutout, but the Barons rallied to win the last three contests and the Series.

In 1936 the Barons finished third but won the playoffs before dropping the Dixie Series to Tulsa, Birmingham's second — and last — series loss. Two years later lights were installed at Rickwood, but a decade would pass before another flag would fly over the old stadium. In the meantime fans could enjoy such performers as Ed Heusser in 1942 (22–6) and batting-RBI champ Tom Neill in 1946 (.374, 116 R, 124 RBI).

The 1948 Barons, powered by first baseman Walt Dropo (.359, 14 HR, 102 RBI) and outfielders Tom O'Brien (.359, 19 HR, 131 R, 137 RBI) and George Wilson (.335, 27 HR, 102 RBI), finished third, but won the playoffs, then defeated Fort Worth in the Dixie Series. In 1951, with George Wilson (.325, 29 HR, 112 RBI) joined in the outfield by young, speedy Jimmy Piersall (.346), the Barons finished second, then roared through the playoffs with eight consecutive victories before beating Houston for another Dixie Series triumph.

Manager Cal Ermer guided Birmingham to first place in 1958. A fine pitching staff was led by Bill Harrington (20–7) and strikeout champ Joe Grzenda (16–7, 189 K), while punch was provided by outfielder Bob Thorpe (.324 with 23 homers). The Barons won the playoffs and the Dixie Series, this time over Corpus Christi. The Barons carved out the best record again the next year, winning the first half of a split season behind outfielder George Alusik (.309) and second baseman Steve Boros (.305 with a league-leading 23 stolen bases), but losing the playoffs to Mobile. The 1960 batting champ, Stan Palys (.370, 28 HR, 116 RBI), and ERA leader Ron Nischwitz (14–7, 2.31) led the Barons to the playoff finals. The next season — which proved to be the

SA's last — the struggling league played a straight pennant race, and the Barons finished a close second behind Palys (.333) and victory-complete game-percentage leader Howard Koplitz (23–3 with a no-hitter).

There was no pro ball at Rickwood in 1962 and 1963, but when the Southern League opened play in 1964 the Barons were charter members. Birmingham finished second by one game, hosted the All-Star contest, and led the SL in attendance. But that attendance figure was just 95,000, and when the Barons dropped into the cellar in 1965 only 28,000 fans came out to Rickwood. Birmingham again dropped out of professional baseball.

In 1967 the colorful owner of the Kansas City A's, Charlie O. Finley, installed the Birmingham Athletics at Rickwood. Finley had once lived in Birmingham, and he stocked his SL A's with promising young players. ERA and percentage leader George Lauzerique (13–4, 2.30) twirled a seven-inning perfect game at the age of 19, while former SA strikeout champ Joe Grzenda now provided standout relief (6–0 with a 1.20 ERA in 52 appearances). Rollie Fingers showed flashes of future stardom (6–5 and a 2.21 ERA). The offense was led by a trio of All-Stars: outfielders Reggie Jackson (.293 with 17 homers and a league-leading 17 triples) and Stan Wojcik (.296, one point off the batting title), and first baseman Joe Rudi (.288 with 13 homers). The talented Athletics won the pennant and, in the first — and last — Dixie Series since the Barons' 1958 victory, beat Albuquerque in postseason play.

In 1969 the efforts of home run champ Bob Brooks (.292, 23 HR, 100 RBI) and ERA leader La Don Boyd (13–5, 2.19) brought Birmingham into second place. During the Dixie Association experiment of 1971, Birmingham played in the Central Division but had the worst record of all 14 teams. Back in the Southern League in 1972, Birmingham finished in the cellar for three consecutive years, and in 1973 and 1974 season attendance was only a little more than 20,000. There was another losing record in 1975, and Birmingham again dropped out of Organized Baseball.

In 1981 the Montgomery Rebels, SL affiliates of the Detroit Tigers, moved to Birmingham. The SALLY had expanded to 10 teams, and the new Barons were members of the Western Division. All-Star first baseman Mike Laga (.289 with 31 homers) led the SL in total bases, while outfielder Ken Baker won the 1982 batting title (.342). The 1983 Barons roared to the best record in the league, winning the Western Division and downing Jacksonville in the playoffs. The champions, managed by Roy Majtyka, led the SL in hitting and logged 57 of their 91 victories at Rickwood. The offensive leaders were outfielder Stan Younger (.309), first baseman Greg Norman (.300) and third-sacker George Foussianes (.270 with 22 homers), while the pitching staff featured victory leader Don Heinkel (19–6), ERA titlist Roger Mason (7–4, 2.06), percentage leader Keith Comstock (12–3), and lefthanded starter Colin Ward (10–3).

The next five years brought losing records to Birmingham, although outfielder Bruce Fields was the 1985 batting titlist (.323) and outfielder-DH Ron Rollin was the 1987 home run champ (.244, 39 HR, 106 RBI). Rollin helped produce a Cinderella story with the 1987 Barons. Birmingham won the first half in the West, but plummeted to the cellar during the second half of the schedule. Despite only a 68–75 composite record, the Barons swept Huntsville in three straight to claim another Western Division crown, then took three of four from Charlotte in the finals.

It was a fitting finish to the final season at Rickwood. In 1988 the Barons moved into "The Met," Hoover Metropolitan Stadium,

Birmingham slugger Mike Yastrzemski (Carl's son) in action.
— Courtesy Birmingham Barons

a magnificent $14 million facility erected south of Birmingham at Hoover. A standing-room-only crowd of 13,279 jammed the 10,000-seat Met for the opening game. A year later the Barons again won the Western Division and the finals, over Huntsville and Greenville respctively. Manager Ken Berry utilized the talents of All-Star third baseman Robin Ventura (.278) and a deep pitching staff: southpaws Wayne Edwards (10–4), Wedsel Groom (13–8) and Gardner Hall (12–8), and righthander Antonio Menendez (10–4).

The next year Ken Berry's Barons won the second half in the West with the league's best offense, spearheaded by first baseman Frank Thomas (.323 with 18 homers) and RBI champ Matt Stark (.309, 14 HR, 109 RBI). The Barons lost the division playoff to Memphis, but bounced back in 1991 to defeat Knoxville for another Western Division crown. The Barons lost the finals to Orlando, but fans enjoyed the pitching of All-Star southpaw Wilson Alvarez (10–6 with a 1.83 ERA and 165 Ks in 152 IP) and righthander Bo Kennedy (10–3, 2.32 ERA). In 1993 the Barons carved out the best record in the league behind strikeout champ Scott Ruffcorn (9–4 with 141 Ks in 135 IP), stolen base titlist Brandon Wilson (.270, 43 SB), All-Star outfielder Jerry Wolak (.305), and hard-hitting third basemen Olmedo Saenz (.347) and Ron Coomer (.324). The 1993 Barons claimed another Western Division crown with a three-game sweep over Nashville, then defeated Knoxville, three games to one, for the SL championship. Terry Francona was named Manager of the Year.

Since 1980 the Southern League has headquartered in Birmingham. In that year Jimmy Bragan, a former SA player and SL manager who made his home in Birmingham, assumed the SL presidency, and the league office currently is located in the suburb of Trussville.

Year	Record	Pcg.	Finish
1964	80–60	.571	Second
1965	54–85	.388	Eighth
1967	84–55	.604	First
1968	66–74	.471	Fourth
1969	78–62	.557	Second
1970	73–65	.529	Third
1971	48–93	.340	Sixth
1972	49–90	.353	Eighth
1973	50–88	.362	Eighth
1974	54–81	.400	Eighth

1975	65–69	.485	Fifth
1981	71–70	.504	Fifth
1982	69–74	.483	Seventh
1983	91–54	.628	First (won Western Division and finals)
1984	66–81	.449	Ninth
1985	57–86	.399	Tenth
1986	70–73	.490	Eighth
1987	68–75	.476	Seventh (won Western Division and finals)
1988	62–82	.431	Ninth
1989	88–55	.615	First (won Western Division and finals)
1990	77–67	.535	Fourth (lost opener)
1991	77–66	.538	Second (won Western Division, lost finals)
1992	68–74	.479	Sixth
1993	78–64	.549	First (won Western Division and finals)

Carolina
(Mudcats)

In the summer of 1991, at a former North Carolina tobacco farm, a scene was repeated that seemed scripted from the popular baseball film *Field of Dreams*. Headlights stretched for miles as automobiles filled with fans and curiosity seekers drove slowly toward the real field of dreams, Five County Stadium. Raleigh businessman Steve Bryant had nurtured boyhood dreams of becoming a big league player, and as an adult he determined to bring professional baseball to his home area. In 1988 he purchased the Class A Greensboro Hornets and the Columbus Astros of the SL. Bryant changed the Columbus nickname and logo to "Mudcats," triggering a highly remarkable Mudcat Mania that would transfer to North Carolina for the 1991 season.

The move of the Mudcats to the Raleigh area was complicated by the proximity of the Class A Durham Bulls. By 1991 minor league territorial rights extended for 35 miles from an existing franchise, but Bryant purchased a 55-acre ballpark site for $650,000 at a location north of Zebulon — and just the proper distance from Durham. Although Zebulon had a population of only 3,100, there are more than one million people at Raleigh and other nearby communities. Support for the Mudcats became evident when Five County Stadium could not be completed in time for the beginning of the season. The Mudcats would play

The 1992 Carolina Mudcats.

— Courtesy Carolina Mudcats

until July at old Fleming Stadium in Wilson, 24 miles east of Zebulon. On opening night a standing-room-only crowd armed with umbrellas defied the rain, and during the next few months Fleming Stadium averaged over 4,000 per game.

The gates at Fleming Stadium opened on July 3, with larger crowds (3,000 fans were turned away on opening night) and parades of auto headlights. Dirt from the cinematic field of dreams was sprinkled over the infield at Five County Stadium. When Pittsburgh, Carolina's big league affiliate, played an exhibition with the minor leaguers, Pirates' star Barry Bonds bought more than $2,000 worth of Mudcat merchandise for his friends.

The first Mudcat manager was former minor league pitcher Marc Bombard, and he aided in the remarkable development of Tim Wakefield, a one-time position-player who displayed a dancing knuckleball. The young righthander pitched the opening game and went on to post an impressive record (15–8 with a league-leading 8 complete games) for a losing team. No other hurler could win in double figures, but righty Dennis Tafoya provided solid relief (1.99 ERA in 40 appearances). Infielder Kevin Young paced the team in hitting (.342 in 75 games) and switch-hitter Terry Crowley led the Mudcats in seven offensive categories, including hits, runs, homers and RBIs (.264, 60 R, 7 HR, 45 RBI). But team hitting was weak overall (.242) and the Mudcats finished last in home runs with only 39.

In 1992 the Mudcats dropped to last place (56–92), but attendance rose from 217,000 to 263,000; the league attendance title was lost to Birmingham by fewer than 200 fans. Team hitting (.243) once more was weak, and again the Mudcats finished last in homers with 55. Outfielder Scott Bullett provided solid hitting (.270) throughout the season, and Dennis Tafoya returned to steady the bullpen (.311 ERA in 41 G). The next season brought the first winning record and league-leading attendance (328,207). The fans who flocked to Mudcat games enjoyed the play of first-sacker Rich Audie (.289 with 18 homers), shortstop Tony Womack (.304) and outfielder Javier Ortiz (.339 during a limited stay), and the franchise planned even more excitement, promotions and stadium improvements for 1994.

Year	Record	Pcg.	Finish
1991	66–76	.465	Eighth
1992	59–92	.361	Tenth
1993	74–67	.525	Third

Charlotte
(Hornets, Orioles, Knights)

Charlotte's first season in Organized Baseball was a mixture of success and failure. One of six charter members of the Class C North Carolina League, Charlotte roared to a 39–8 record behind batting champ Buck Weaver (not the Buck Weaver of Black Sox notoriety). But attendance and financing were inadequate, and Charlotte withdrew from the league on July 9, 1902. The next day Wilmington also withdrew, then the league disbanded two days later, declaring Charlotte champion of the abbreviated season.

In 1905 Charlotte helped organize the Virginia-North Carolina League, a four-team Class D Circuit which operated only one season. Three years later Charlotte helped form another Class D loop, the Carolina Association, which became the North Carolina State League in 1913. Charlotte played in this circuit from 1908 until 1917, when play halted in May because of wartime conditions. The club won the 1916 pennant and produced three batting champs: Al Humphrey in 1909 (.296), F. P. Wofford in 1911 (.392), and Harry Weiser in 1914 (.333).

Charlotte joined the Class C SALLY in 1919, winning the championship in 1923, the year the league was elevated to Class B status. Clarence Mitchell won the 1920 hitting title (.320), and Ernest Padgett was the 1922 batting champ (.333). Also in 1922, outfielder Ben Paschal led the SALLY in runs, hits, triples, homers and RBIs, despite playing in only 98 games (.326, 19 3B, 18 HR, 114 RBI, 131 R), then repeated as run, home run, and RBI leader the next year (.351, 26 HR, 122 RBI, 147 R).

The Depression caused the SALLY to suspend operations after the 1930 season, but Charlotte moved to the Class C Piedmont League and won the pennant in 1931 and 1932. The 1931 club (100–37) dominated the Piedmont behind Frank Packard, who led the league in batting, runs, hits, homers and RBIs (.366, 21 HR, 123 RBI, 145 R); Charlotte finished with a 13½-game lead over second-place Raleigh, then beat Raleigh in the playoffs. But Charlotte sagged to the cellar in 1935, and did not play in 1936. Charlotte rejoined the Piedmont League in 1937, however, and played through the 1942 season. Robert Estalella was the 1937 batting and home run champ (.349 with 33 homers), then sparked Charlotte to the 1938 playoff title by leading the Piedmont in batting, homers, runs, and RBIs (.378, 38 HR, 123 RBI, 134 R).

During these years Charlotte played at old Hayman Park, a cozy wooden ballpark with left field just 286 feet down the line, right field 309 feet away, and center 410 feet from the plate. Charlotte had become part of the Washington farm system, and by 1940 Senators' owner Clark Griffith had decided to build a new ballpark at a site he had acquired at 400 Magnolia Avenue. In 1941 the Hornets moved into their new home, $40,000 Clark Griffith Park. There was a good lighting system, the wooden grandstand seated 4,000, including 600 reserved seats, and bleachers accommodated another 1,500. But after two seasons, Clark Griffith Park stood empty, because the Hornets did not play during the last three years of World War II.

In 1946 Charlotte helped form the Class B Tri-State League, then won the new circuit's first pennant and playoff. Charlotte repeated as playoff champs the next year, then in 1951 finished first (100–40), 15 games ahead of second-place Asheville, as Francisco Campos won the batting crown (.368). The next year Bruce Barnes was the hitting champ (.370), sparking Charlotte to the 1952 playoff title. Charlotte won another playoff championship the following season, then moved up to the Class A SALLY for 1954. Charlotte won the SALLY playoffs in 1957, and rose to Double-A with the league in 1963.

The Charlotte Hornets thus became part of the Southern League, finishing fourth during the inaugural season of 1964. The Hornets were fifth in 1965, then sixth in 1966. By this time a favorite of Charlotte fans was righthander Garland Shifflett, who spent six seasons, 1963–68, in a Hornet uniform. In 1963 he led the league in relief appearances (8–4 in 59 G), then became a starter-reliever in 1964 (7–7) and 1965 (10–8). Shifflett returned to the bullpen, again leading the league in appearances in 1966 (9–8 and 1.98 ERA in 63 G), 1967 (12–7 and a 1.45 ERA in 69 G), and 1968 (12–6 in 77 G).

Another fan favorite of even longer tenure in Charlotte was Minnie Mendoza, who played 10 seasons for the Hornets: 1960–61, 1963–68, and 1971–72. Through the years Mendoza played second, third, short and outfield, twice leading the SL in hits, banging out the most doubles in 1968 (.303, 35 2B), and winning batting crowns in 1967 (.297) and 1971 (.316).

In 1969 Charlotte won the SL pennant and led the nearest team in attendance by almost 100,000 (146,141 total). Right-hander Bill Zepp paced the league in victories (15–3 with 2.34 ERA), while reliever Robert Gebhard provided brilliant bullpen work (13–3 with a 1.23 ERA and a league-leading 19 saves in 50 games). The next year outfielder Steve Brye was the batting champ (.307), and third baseman Dan Monzon led the league in hits (.288).

During the 1971 Dixie Association season, Charlotte won the six-team Eastern Division and posted the best record (92–50) of all 14 association clubs. Managed by Harry Warner, the Hornets defeated Asheville in the opening series of the playoffs, then won the finals with a three-game sweep over the Arkansas Travelers. Minnie Mendoza had his best season (.316), southpaw Dick Rusteck led the SL in ERA and victories (17–8, 2.40), and starter-reliever Greg Jaycox was formidable from the other side of the mound (15–5).

The next year Danny Vossler was the ERA champ (10–8, 2.11 in 43 G), while fellow righthander Bill Campbell was the strikeout king (13–10 with 204 Ks). But the big baseball news of 1972 in Charlotte was the decision of the parent Minnesota Twins to place a Class A club alongside the Double-A Hornets in Clark Griffith Park. When the SL Hornets were on the road, the Charlotte Twins would host a Western Carolinas League opponent. But the strategy of daily games at Griffith Park did not work. In 1972 the Hornets drew nearly 70,000 fans, but in 1972 the Hornets attracted fewer then 31,000, while the Twins pulled in a miniscule attendance of 12,835. Minnesota moved their Class A club to Geneva of the New York-Pennsylvania League and transferred their SL franchise to Orlando.

Charlotte was without pro baseball for three seasons. Clark Griffith tried unsuccessfully to sell his old ballpark to various businesses, and in 1974 he announced his intentions to demolish Griffith Park. But the next year Jim Crockett, a prominent Charlotte businessman and sportsman, purchased the facility for $87,000, renaming it Crockett Park. Baltimore moved its SL franchise from Asheville to Charlotte, and Crockett's sister, Frances, an experienced businesswoman, became GM of the Charlotte Orioles.

The 1976 O's made the SL playoffs behind future Baltimore star Eddie Murray (.298), All-Star infielders Blake Doyle (.299) and Martin Parrill (.274), and righthander Dave Ford (17–7), who led the SL in victories, strikeouts, innings, complete games and shutouts. The next year the O's finished at the bottom of the Eastern Division, despite the efforts of batting champ Mark Corey (.310), home run leader Tom Chism (.298 with 17 homers), ERA titlist Sammy Stewart (9–6, 2.08), and victory leader Bryn Smith (15–11). Following another season in the Eastern cellar, the O's made the 1979 playoffs, although, as in 1976, Charlotte was defeated in the opening round.

In 1980 manager Jimmy Williams again led the O's to the playoffs, executing a three-game sweep over Savannah for the Eastern Division crown, then defeating Memphis to claim the SL championship. The offense was led by future Baltimore standout Cal Ripken, Jr. (.276 with 25 homers) and All-Star outfielder Drungo Hazewood (.261 with 28 homers), while the best pitchers were righthander Dan Ramirez (16–8) and reliever Russ Pensiero (9–4 in 40 G).

The 1981 O's failed to make the playoffs, despite strong performances from second baseman Vic Rodriguez (.306), catcher Willie Royster (.265 with 31 homers), and veteran righthander

Don Welchel (13–7). There were losing records the next two seasons, although shortstop Jesus Alfaro was a 1982 All-Star (.301), and came back strong the next year (.286 with 19 homers). Second-sacker Vic Rodriguez played well in 1982 (.291 in 47 G), then led the SL in hits in 1983 (.298), while outfielder Larry Sheets tied for the 1983 home run title (.288 with 25 homers).

Charlotte won another SL championship in 1984, even though the O's barely made the playoffs. The O's finished the first half at the bottom of the Eastern Division, but rallied to tie Orlando for the second-half lead. In a one-game playoff, Charlotte beat Orlando, 4–3, for the right to play Greenville for the division title. The O's downed Greenville, three games to one, then swept Knoxville in three games for the pennant. Right-hander Ken Dixon led the SL in strikeouts, victories, innings and complete games (16–8, 211 Ks, 20 CG in 29 starts), and reliever Nat Snell posted the most saves (9–4 with 19 saves in 52 G).

A few weeks before the start of the 1985 season, Crockett Park was ravaged by fire following a high school game. But makeshift seating was put together, and the O's continued to play in the shell of their old ballpark. Charlotte repeated as Eastern Division champs, defeating Columbus in the playoff opener before dropping the finals to Huntsville, three games to two. Right-hander John Habyan (13–5) was named to the All-Star Team, while first baseman Kevon Torve (.290 with 15 homers) and second-sacker Ricky Jones (.280 with 22 homers) helped the O's lead the SL in team home runs. The next year Charlotte slipped to a losing record, despite the play of first baseman Chris Padget (.324, 22 HR, 96 RBI), DH-third baseman Tom Dodd (.323, 28 HR, 100 RBI), All-Star second baseman Billy Ripken, and ERA champ Eric Bell (9–6, 3.05).

Tom Dodd returned in 1987 to lead the SL in RBIs (.289, 37 HR, 127 RBI) and win the MVP award. Other heavy hitters included second-sacker Pete Stanicek (.315), outfielders Matt Cimo (.308 with 18 homers) and Sherwin Cijntje (.304), and first baseman Dave Falcone (.293, 14 HR, 92 RBI), and the O's led the league in team batting (.272). Charlotte beat Jacksonville for another Eastern Division crown, but lost the finals to Birmingham.

Charlotte failed to return to the playoffs for the next four seasons. Nevertheless, outfielder Butch Davis was the 1988 batting champ (.301), and the next year Shawn Boskie was the strikeout king (11–8, 164 Ks), while reliever Laddie Renfroe turned in an incredible performance by leading the SL in victories, games, and games finished (19–7, 78 G, 58 GF).

By this time momentous changes were occurring within Charlotte's professional franchise. After the 1987 season Frances Crockett sold the club to Charlotte businessman George Shinn, who announced his intention to pursue a Triple-A franchise. Shinn signed Roman Gabriel, the former NFL quarterback who had been a high school baseball star in North Carolina, to take charge of baseball operations. The team nickname was changed to "Knights," and the longtime affiliation with Baltimore was ended in 1989 as the Knights became a Cubs' farm club.

A new stadium was essential, and Shinn acquired a building site on the outskirts of the city, at Rock Hill in York County, *South* Carolina. Knights Castle was planned to be a 10,000-seat, $12 million, state-of-the-art facility that could be expanded into a 70,000-seat stadium for NFL football. While Knights Castle was under construction during the 1989 season, the Knights played in a temporary park in the future parking lot, with an attendance of 157,720. Knights Castle opened in 1990, and attendance for a losing team jumped to 271,502, the most of any SL team. In 1991

Knights Castle, a 10,000-seat state-of-the-art stadium, opened in 1990.

attendance rose to 313,791, the largest of any Double-A club, and at mid-season Charlotte was awarded a Triple-A expansion franchise for the 1993 season.

The 1991 Knights showcased home run and RBI champ Elvin Paulino (.257, 24 HR, 81 RBI), hit leader Fernando Ramsey (.276, 37 SB), and All-Star shortstop Alex Arias (.275, 23 SB). In 1992, Charlotte's final SL season, Greenville (100–43) dominated the Eastern Division. Charlotte had the second-best record in the East (70–73), and was permitted to challenge the Braves in the playoff opener. But Greenville swept the Knights before defeating Chattanooga in the finals. Knights Castle was the site of the 1992 Double-A All-Star Game, and the season attendance was 338,047 — again the largest of any Double-A club and a fitting sendoff for the 1993 International League.

Year	Record	Pcg.	Finish
1964	73–67	.521	Fourth
1965	72–68	.514	Fifth
1966	64–74	.464	Sixth
1967	75–65	.536	Fourth
1968	72–68	.514	Third
1969	81–59	.579	First
1970	66–73	.475	Sixth
1971	92–50	.648	First
1972	70–70	.500	Fifth
1976	74–66	.529	Third (lost opener)
1977	69–71	.493	Fifth
1978	66–78	.458	Eighth
1979	73–69	.514	Fifth (lost opener)
1980	72–72	.500	Fifth (won Eastern Division and finals)
1981	74–69	.517	Fourth
1982	66–77	.462	Ninth
1983	69–77	.473	Sixth
1984	75–72	.510	Fourth (won Eastern Division and finals)
1985	78–65	.545	Third (won Eastern Division, lost finals)
1986	71–73	.493	Sixth
1987	85–60	.586	Second (won Eastern Division, lost finals)
1988	69–75	.479	Seventh
1989	70–73	.490	Sixth
1990	65–79	.451	Ninth
1991	74–70	.514	Fifth
1992	70–73	.490	Fifth (lost opener)

Chattanooga
(Lookouts)

Chattanooga's first impressive baseball club was backed by the Roane Iron Company, downing other local nines and the best teams from Nashville, Knoxville, and Mobile. The Chattanooga Roanes played on a vacant lot at the corner of Douglas and Vine, and big league clubs stopped off to practice there during spring training trips.

Chattanooga helped form the Southern League in 1885, playing at Stanton Field until 1905. The 1892 SL flag flew over Stanton Field, and on July 3, 1894, arc lights were rigged at the ballpark and one of the first night games was staged as an experiment (Chattanooga won, 9–0).

In 1901 Chattanooga became a charter member of the Southern Association, providing the first league president, Captain John B. Nicklin, who also had served as SL club president from 1893 through 1895. Mims Hightower was club president in 1901 and 1902, but after consecutive last-place finishes he sold the franchise to Montgomery.

Late in the 1905 season Shreveport, on an SA road trip, finished its schedule in Chattanooga because of a yellow fever epidemic in Louisiana. In 1909 O. B. Andrews bought a SALLY franchise for Chattanooga, and a contest among fans produced the nickname "Lookouts." The Lookouts claimed the SALLY championship, playing home games at Chamberlain Field, then went on to win the first unofficial Dixie Series, downing Atlanta of the SA in seven games.

After the season, Andrews paid $12,000 for Little Rock's SA franchise. He then built Andrews Field at Third and O'Neal streets, the site where Engel Stadium would be erected two decades later. Chattanooga fan support was solid, even though the SA Lookouts posted almost twice as many losing seasons as winning records. But in 1913 southpaw Harry "The Giant Killer" Coveleskie rewarded Lookout fans by leading the SA in victories (28–9) and twirling a 1–0 no-hitter over Montgomery. Two years later the Lookouts rang up seven consecutive shutouts, setting a league record from September 9 through 14. Righthander George Cunningham hurled three of the shutouts, en route to leading the SA in victories, winning percentage, and strikeouts (24–12 with 167 Ks), while adding a no-hitter against Birmingham for good measure.

Following the 1929 season Clark Griffith purchased Chattanooga as a farm club for his Washington Senators. Griffith sent a former Washington pitcher (and batboy), Joe Engel, to run the Lookouts, and the colorful Engel would prove to be a promotional genius as well as an outstanding judge of baseball talent. His first assignment was to supervise construction of a 12,000-seat ballpark which would be called "Engel Stadium," and which would be the site of the imaginative promotions of the "Barnum of Baseball."

In 1932 Engel engineered Chattanooga's first SA pennant, carrying a protest over postponed games all the way to the commmmissioner of baseball, Judge Kenesaw Mountain Landis, and edging Memphis by a fraction of a percentage point. The manager was Bert Niehoff, who already had produced two SA champions. The Lookouts led the league in hitting (.310), behind third-sacker Cecil Travis (.362), center fielder Joe Bonowitz (.350), and right fielder Johnny Gill (.344 with 120 RBIs). Most of the starting and relieving was done by ERA champ Clyde Barfoot (21–10, 2.76 ERA in 46 games), Alex McColl (21–9, 41 G), Leon Pettit (18–8, 48 G), and Duster Mails (17–9 in 47 G).

The next season Gill led the SA in RBIs (.325, 110 RBI), and outfielder Fred Sington won the 1936 batting title (.384). In 1939 outfielder Bill Nicholson played in only 105 games before being sold for $35,000 to the Cubs, but he still led the SA in homers (.334, 23 HR). Rookie manager Kiki Cuyler took up the slack with stolen base champ Stan Benjamin (.323, 43 SB) and victory leaders Dick Bass (19–10) and Dick Lanahan (19–11), and the Lookouts put on a late surge which brought another flag to Chattanooga.

There were no pennants during the 1940s, but hitting crowns were won by Mike Dejan (.370) in 1940, Rene Monteagudo (.370) in 1944, and Gil Coan (.372) in 1945, who also led the league in homers (16) and stolen bases (37), and who repeated as stolen base champ in 1947 (.340, 42 SB). Lefthander Bill Kennedy was the ERA titlist in 1942, (2.43) and the victory leader in 1947 (20–11).

Manager Cal Ermer guided the Lookouts to another flag in

1952. The pitching staff featured victory leader Al Sima (24–9), Sonny Dixon (19–14) and Jim Pearce (12–5), and the best hitters were second baseman Ellis Clary (.311), outfielder Ernie Oravetz (.306), and first-sacker Roy Hawes (.276, 20 HR, 93 RBI). Other stars of the 1950s included 1956 batting champ Stan Roseboro (.340) and future Hall of Famer Harmon Killebrew, who led the SA in homers (.279, 29 HR, 101 RBI) and assists by a third baseman in 1957, and who made a final minor league appearance the next year (.308 in 86 G). Jim Lemon blasted four homers in one game in 1955, and in 1959 Jim Kaat fanned 19 batters in a single game.

Following the 1959 season, the Washington Senators ended their 30-year affiliation with Chattanooga, but the resourceful Joe Engel remained at the helm of the Lookouts and arranged a working agreement with the Phillies. In 1961 Chattanooga, winners of only three previous Southern Association pennants, claimed the final SA flag by a margin of one game over Birmingham. Manager Frank Lucchesi showcased third-sacker Wayne Graham (.331), who led the league in at-bats, hits, total bases and doubles, outfielder-first baseman Gerald Reimer (.323), and righthander John Boozer (19–9, with a league-leading 4 shutouts).

When the SA folded Chattanooga missed the 1962 season, but in 1963 Engel and the Phillies placed a club in the SALLY, as the historic Class A league elevated to AA status. The next year the AA circuit became the Southern League, but losing seasons in 1963–1964–1965 cost Chattanooga its fan support (57,116–40,331–25,707) and franchise.

Joe Engel died in 1969, and his stadium, largely unused, began to deteriorate. But in 1976 Woodrow Reid and the Oakland Athletics placed another Southern League team in Chattanooga at renovated Engel Stadium. Over 8,300 fans attended the first Lookout game in a decade, and the club went on to make the playoffs (70–68, with a defeat in the playoff opener). During the next 11 seasons there was only one winning record (in 1979), but Lookout fans could cheer numerous individual performances. The 1979 club was led by batting champ Joltin' Joe Charboneau (.352). Other hitting crowns were claimed by Chris Bando in 1980 (.349), Kevin Rhomberg in 1981 (.367), Ivan Calderon in 1983 (.311), Brick Smith in 1986 (.344), Dave Myers in 1987 (.328), Adam Casillas in 1990 (.336), and Scott Pose in 1992 (.342). Sto-

Chattanooga's Engel Stadium, built in 1930 and beautifully renovated 60 years later.

len base kings included Derek Bryant in 1976 (.302 with 42 SB), Jeff Cox in 1977 (68), Kevin Rhomberg in 1981 (.366 with 74 SB), and Donell Nixon who set the all-time SL record in 1984 (102).

The Lookouts of 1988, managed by Tom Runnels and featuring victory and ERA leader Chris Hammond (16–5, 1.72), made the playoffs, won the Western Division, then swept Greenville, winners in the East, in three games. It was Chattanooga's first championship in 27 years, but in 1992 the Lookouts roared to another Western Division title before being edged by Greenville in the finals, three games to two. Offensive punch was provided by batting champ Scott Pose (.342), who also led the SL in hits, runs, and on-base percentage, and home run leader Tom Costo (.241 with 28 homers). The pitching staff featured the SL's top reliever, Jerry Spradlin (1.38 ERA with 38 saves and 53 GF in 59 G), victory leader Mike Anderson (13–7), another right-handed starter, Robert Ayala (12–6), and reliever Rodney Imes (7–2 in 45 G).

The 1993 Lookouts put up another winning record with strong pitching and hitting. Righthanded reliever Chris Bushing led the SL in saves and appearances (6–1 with 29 saves in 61 G);

Mike Ferry (13–8) was the victory co-leader; Chris Hook (12–8) was another solid righthanded starter; and righty Jeff Pierce also provided impressive relief (22 saves in 46 G). The offense featured switch-hitting DH Mark Merchant (.301), first baseman Jamie Dismuke (.306, 20 HR, 91 RBI), and outfielder Keith Gordon (.291).

Chattanooga's SL affiliations following the agreement with Oakland included the Cleveland Indians (1978–82), Seattle Mariners (1983–86), and Cincinnati Reds (1987–present). Richard Holtzman purchased the Lookouts in 1987 and engineered a $2 million renovation of Engel Stadium, completed in 1990. Two years later turf was installed because of frequent wet field postponements, and today the historic ballpark offers a nostalgic but streamlined setting for the national pastime. "Our only goal," pledges the energetic Holtzman, "is good family entertainment."

Year	Record	Pcg.	Finish
1964	65–74	.468	Sixth
1965	60–80	.429	Seventh
1976	70–68	.507	Fourth (lost opener)
1977	61–75	.449	Sixth
1978	63–80	.441	Tenth
1979	75–69	.521	Fourth
1980	61–83	.424	Ninth
1981	67–75	.472	Seventh
1982	63–80	.441	Tenth
1983	68–75	.476	Fifth
1984	68–81	.439	Tenth
1985	66–77	.462	Eighth
1986	64–78	.451	Tenth
1987	68–75	.476	Sixth
1988	81–62	.566	Second (won Western Division and finals)
1989	58–81	.417	Ninth
1990	66–78	.458	Eighth
1991	73–71	.507	Sixth
1992	90–53	.629	Second (won Western Division, lost finals)
1993	72–69	.511	Fourth

Columbus
(Confederate Yankees, White Sox, Astros, Mudcats)

The Columbus Babies played in the Southern League in 1896, then the Columbus River Snipes became charter members of the Georgia State League in 1906, although the Class D circuit played only half a season, and did not resume operations for several years. In 1909 the Columbus Foxes (the manager was first baseman Jim Fox) joined the Class C SALLY and played until 1917. Righthander Roy Radabaugh starred for the Foxes in 1909 (25-9), 1910 (22-15), and 1911 (27-6). The Foxes won back-to-back pennants in 1910 and 1911, and added another championship in 1915. Phil Redding was the 1914 strikeout champ (16-12, 184 Ks), then led the SALLY in victories and winning percentage (19-6) the next year, while third baseman Hardin Herndon claimed consecutive stolen base crowns in 1915 (.324, 38 SB) and 1916 (.303, 59 SB). Columbus dropped out of the SALLY during the wartime season of 1917, and did not field another pro team for a decade.

When Columbus prepared to play in a reorganized Class B Southeastern League in 1926, there was a local squabble as to whether newly-completed Memorial Stadium was suitable for baseball. T. E. Golden, a prominent Columbus businessman and a backer of the earlier Foxes, arranged for a site beside the Chattahoochee River, and contractor Charlie Frank Williams built Golden Park in two weeks. The Foxes won the 1926 pennant and playoff, and played in the Southeastern through the 1930 season, when Depression conditions caused the league to halt operations. The Southeastern tried again in 1932, and Columbus was one of six clubs, but the league folded on May 23.

The SALLY reorganized in 1936, and the Columbus Red Birds joined up as part of the extensive farm system of the St. Louis Cardinals. Stocked with talented Cardinal farm hands— ERA champ Joe Sims (14-7, 2.44), southpaw Spud Krist (20-9), run, hit and walk leader Jim Gruzdis (.330, 147 R, 108 W), RBI king Stan Tutaj (.329, 129 RBI), triples leader Enos Slaughter (.325, 20 3B, 118 RBI), and All-Star catcher Francis Healy (.316)

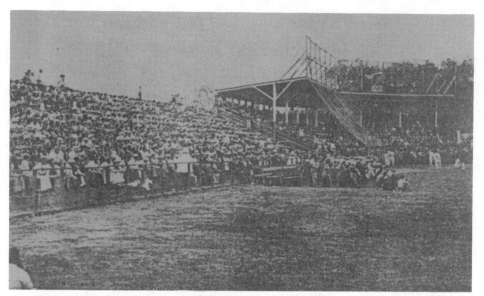

The first game held at the original Golden Park was on April 26, 1926, the opening day of the Southeastern League, when Columbus played the Montgomery Lions.

— the Red Birds won the 1936 pennant and playoff. Columbus finished first again the next year, featuring Joe Sims for part of the season (7–3, 1.33 ERA), hit leader Dave Smith (.337), RBI champ Herb Bremer (.305, 20 HR, 101 RBI), and stolen base king Cecil Garriott (.295, 30 SB), who repeated as theft titlist in 1938 (.320, 57 SB). The 1938 RBI champ was first baseman Bill Prout (.354, 110 RBI).

The Red Birds once more finished first in 1939, then won the playoffs the next season. Southpaw Bill Seinsoth won the ERA crown for the 1939 pennant-winners (17–10, 2.41), Rollie VanSlate was the strikeout champ (17–12, 170 Ks), and young first baseman Walt Alston helped trigger the offense (.323). The 1940 playoff titlists showcased batting champ Hooper Triplett (.369, 133 R, 105 RBI), RBI king Ray Sanders (.349, 108 R, 152 RBI), run leader Eddie Knoblauch (.345, 135 R), and strikeout champ Freddie Martin (17–12, 208 Ks). Knoblauch repeated as run leader in 1941 (.336, 114 R), but after the next season there was no more baseball in Golden Park for the duration of the war.

The SALLY resumed play in 1946, and the Columbus Cardinals promptly recorded back-to-back first-place finishes. In 1951 catcher Lou Kahn won the batting title (.351) and wooden Golden Park was rebuilt in concrete and steel. The Cardinals dropped into the cellar in 1954, and after a next-to-last finish the following season, St. Louis severed the two-decades-long affiliation with Columbus.

The Columbus Foxes made it to the 1956 finals behind batting and run titlist Len Green (.318, 92 R, 93 RBI). Columbus dropped out of the SALLY in 1958, tried to come back as a Pirate affiliate in 1959, but the club was transferred to Gastonia on July 6.

The new Southern League beckoned in 1964, and Columbus entered Double-A ball as the Confederate Yankees. The New York farm club finished seventh, but the next year the Confederate Yankees edged Asheville for the pennant by a fraction of a percentage point (.572 to .571). First baseman Roy White led the SL in runs and hits (.300, 19 HR, 103 R), righty Tom Shafer put in a scintillating half-season (10–2), and Columbus posted the league's best attendance (72,732). In 1966, however, the Confederate Yankees dropped to seventh place, attendance plummeted (48,847), and Columbus relinquished its SL franchise.

After two seasons without professional baseball, Columbus backers obtained Evansville's SL franchise, which was the Double-A affiliate of the Chicago White Sox. But the Columbus White Sox suffered a losing record and the league's poorest attendance (23,714). Columbus changed parent clubs, to the Houston Astros, and manager Jimmie Williams led the Columbus Astros to the 1970 pennant. Righthander Ken Forsch was the victory co-leader (13–8, 2.05 ERA), Walt Harris (11–9, 2.02 ERA) and Mike Flanagan (11–5, 2.58 ERA) also pitched effectively, and the offense was sparked by first baseman John Dolinsek (.296).

During the 1971 Dixie Association arrangement, the Columbus Astros finished last in the six-team Eastern Division. The next season the SL was back up to eight teams, and the Astros played in the Western Division. In 1973 Columbus was transferred to the Eastern Division, as All-Star outfielder Jayson Moxey led the SL in triples (.301, 13 3B), fireballer Doug Konieczny was the strikeout king (12–12 with 222 Ks in 213 IP), lefthander Russ Rothermel won the ERA crown (9–9, 1.81), and outfielder Al Leaver claimed the stolen base title (.248, 54 SB). Despite a losing record, Columbus led the SL in attendance (90,017), and repeated the feat with even greater totals (106,462) while finishing last in the East in 1974. A third consecutive attendance title came in 1975 (74,797), as Astros fans enjoyed the performances of strikeout champ Joe Sambito (12–9, 140 Ks) and ERA titlist Don Larson (7–8, 2.18).

The 1976 Astros finished in the SL cellar, improved only one notch in the next season, and suffered another losing record in 1978. But in 1979 the Astros roared to the best record in the 10-team SL and swept Charlotte for the Eastern Division crown, before losing the finals to Nashville. Columbus led the league in team fielding, hitting, doubles and homers (.277, 223 2B, 138 HR), and posted the second-best staff ERA. Catcher Alan Knicely was the home run champ (.289 with 33 homers), outfielder Danny Heep led the SL in hits and total bases (.327 with 21 homers), southpaw Del Leatherwood was the victory leader (15–11), and righthander Billy Smith was right behind (14–9). Jim Johnson was voted Manager of the Year.

In 1980 the Astros barely missed the playoffs, despite the play of victory leader Jim MacDonald (17–7) and All-Star infielder John Ray (.324). The next year the Astros showcased ERA champ Mark Ross (8–10, 2.25), RBI leader Larry Ray (.253, 21 HR, 87 RBI), and slick-fielding outfielder Chris Jones (.324, 37 SB, 102 R). Columbus made the 1982 playoffs, but fell to Jacksonville in the opening round. In 1983 future Houston star Glenn Davis tied for the home run title (.299, 25 HR, 85 RBI).

The 1985 Astros won the first half, but lost the division playoff to Charlotte. Righthanded starter Don August (14–8) and reliever Richard Bombard (7–3 in a league-leading 52 G) headed a staff that posted the SL's best ERA. The offense was built around third-sacker Charles Jackson (.310), first baseman Glenn Carpenter (.302), outfielder Anthony Walker (.294), and outfielder-infielder Jim Sherman (.279, 20 HR, 90 RBI).

The next year the Astros finished the first half with the worst record in the league, but rebounded to the second-half lead. Columbus then beat Jacksonville, three games to one, for the Eastern Division crown, and defeated Huntsville, three games to one, to win the 1986 SL championship. Larry Ray returned to provide power (.275, 25 HR, 108 RBI), and there was more punch from third baseman Ken Caminiti (.300), catcher Jeff Datz (.325 in 59

Since 1926 baseball in Columbus has been played at the site beside the Chattahoochee River, and today Golden Park is the home of the RedStixx.

G), and outfielder Mike Fuentes (.303), Joe Mikulik (.301) and Gerald Young (.280).

In 1987 Caminiti finished second in the hitting race by three points (.325), while Carlo Colombino was third in the 1988 batting race (.285) and replaced Caminiti as the All-Star third baseman. After the 1988 season the Columbus club was purchased by Steve Bryant, a Raleigh businessman whose goal was to bring Double-A baseball to his home area. Bryant changed the Columbus nickname from Astros to Mudcats, a scavenger catfish that was not duplicated anywhere else in professional sports. On opening night in Golden Park, in 1989, concessionaires sold out the entire *season's* supply of caps, and other souvenirs with the Mudcat logo proved equally marketable.

The 1989 Mudcats featured All-Star righthander Darryl Kile (11–6), and outfielder Eric Anthony (.300 with 28 homers), who won the home run crown and was selected Most Valuable Player. In 1990 first baseman Luis Gonzalez tied for the home run title (.265, 24 HR, 89 RBI).

Steve Bryant moved the Mudcats to North Carolina for the 1991 season, but Columbus found a home in the Class A SALLY as a Cleveland affiliate. After one season as the Columbus Indians, the club adopted another distinctive nickname, the RedStixx. At home in handsome and historic Golden Park, and under the resourceful leadership of personable GM John Dittrich, the RedStixx offer fans a model example of professional baseball.

Year	Record	Pcg.	Finish
1964	65–74	.468	Eighth
1965	79–59	.572	First
1966	63–76	.453	Seventh
1969	65–75	.464	Fourth
1970	78–59	.569	First
1971	51–91	.359	Sixth
1972	59–80	.424	Seventh
1973	69–70	.496	Sixth
1974	65–73	.471	Sixth
1975	70–64	.522	Fourth
1976	58–80	.420	Eighth
1977	60–77	.438	Seventh
1078	70–73	.490	Sixth
1979	84–59	.587	First (won Eastern Division, lost finals)
1980	76–68	.528	Fourth
1981	63–78	.447	Ninth
1982	74–69	.517	Third (lost opener)
1983	64–79	.448	Seventh
1984	69–71	.493	Sixth
1985	79–65	.549	Second (lost opener)
1986	70–70	.500	Fifth (won Eastern Division and finals)
1987	67–76	.469	Eighth
1988	69–74	.483	Sixth
1989	71–72	.497	Fifth
1990	67–77	.465	Seventh

Evansville
(White Sox, Esox)

"Evansville is blazing a trail out of minor league difficulties and showing the way to the baseball world. There is nothing else approaching it in the minor league world."

This proclamation was made in 1915 by Louis Heilbrenner, president of the Class B Central League. Heilbrenner was referring to Bosse Field, regarded as the first municipally-owned stadium in the history of organized baseball. Bosse Field was built at a cost of $100,000 by the Evansville school board and named for Mayor Benjamin Bosse, who had helped design and implement construction of the park.

The 8,000-seat stadium was located just north of the downtown area in Garvin Park. Intended as an all-sports facility, Bosse Field hosted a capacity crowd for the opening baseball game of 1915, then that night accommodated another 1,500 fans who watched a wrestling match under improvised lighting. The covered grandstand and outfield fences were built of brick, and there has never been a ball hit over the 477-foot center field fence (in 1951 an interior wire fence reduced the home run distances). President Heilbrenner's prediction eventually would prove true, as professional franchises at both the major and minor league levels regularly expect their stadiums to be provided by municipal, county, and state funding.

Playing in wooden Louisiana Street Park, the Evansville Evas participated in the Three-I League in 1902, then moved to the Central League the next season. In 1908 Evansville won the Central League pennant, behind batting champ Charles French (.339) and victory leader Charles Wacker (27–8). Evansville's club folded during the 1911 season, but the city participated in the Class D Kitty League in 1912, then returned to the Central League in 1913. There was another Central League flag in 1915, the year Bosse Field opened.

Like most minor league cities, Evansville was out of baseball in 1918, but came back in 1919 with a revived Three-I League. Evansville claimed the Three-I pennant in 1930, then moved back to the Central League in 1932 and promptly won another flag. Depression conditions forced Evansville to give up pro ball after the 1932 season. In 1938 Evansville returned to the Three-I League and won the pennant, then won again in 1941. The Three-I League halted operations for three years during World War II, but Evansville and the Three-I League bounced back strongly after the war. Evansville won playoff titles in 1946 and 1948, and claimed Three-I pennants in 1949, 1952, 1954, 1956, and 1957. Despite consistent success on the field, however, Evansville succumbed to the minor league problems of the 1950s and dropped out of baseball following the 1957 championship season.

Through the years Bosse Field had showcased many fine play-

Bosse Field opened in 1915, and hosted SL baseball from 1966 through 1968. The hit movie A League of Their Own *was filmed at Bosse.*

ers. In 1941 20-year-old Warren Spahn led the Three-I League in victories, winning percentage, and ERA (19–6. 1.82). Another 20-year-old future Hall of Famer, first baseman Hank Greenberg, led the 1931 Three-I League in doubles, games played, putouts and assists (.318 with 41 2Bs). Outfielder Chuck Klein began his Hall of Fame career with Evansville in 1927 (.327), while noted curveballer Tommy Bridges led the Three-I League in strikeouts before being called up to Detroit in 1930. Another Hall of Famer, outfielder Edd Roush, spent his first two seasons at the old Louisiana Street Park in 1912 (.284) and 1913 (.317).

After Evansville pulled out of the Three-I League, eight years passed before professional baseball returned to Bosse Field. In 1966, when three cities dropped out of the Southern League and three cities moved into the circuit, Evansville replaced Lynchburg as the SL farm club of the White Sox. The Evansville White Sox, or Esox, finished third with a losing record, 20 games out of first, but posted the league's best attendance (69,697). The best Esox of 1966 were righthander Francisco Carlos (15–8) and infielder Lorenzo Fernandez (.302).

Evansville again finished third in 1967 and again led the SL in attendance (54,020). Outfielder-first baseman Gary Johnson was the doubles leader (.280 with 29 2B), righthander Dan Murphy provided outstanding relief (10–2 with a 1.97 ERA in 52 G), and southpaw starter-reliever Dan Lazar missed the ERA title by a fraction of a percentage point (9–8, 2.30).

The next year Evansville sagged to the SL cellar. Although the Esox rapped out the best team average of 1968, that figure was modest (.249), and the club hit the fewest home runs of the year (56). Outfielder-first baseman Ossie Blanco was Evansville's most effective player (.289). Attendance dropped badly (35,027), and after the season the White Sox shifted their affiliation to Columbus.

One year later, however, the American Association expanded from six to eight teams, and a community-owned franchise brought Triple-A ball to Bosse Field, which was leased for one dollar per year. For the next 15 seasons Evansville would be one of the smallest cities in Triple-A, but the Triplets won championships in 1972, 1975 and 1979. In 1983, however, Louisville of the American Association became the first minor league team to break one million in attendance, and other AA clubs upgraded their crowds accordingly. But Evansville barely drew 100,000 in 1984, and during the season the board of directors sold the franchise to Larry Schmittou, who took the AA club to Nashville and moved his Southern League franchise to Huntsville.

Bosse Field became the home of the University of Evansville Aces in 1985, and two years later the old stadium served as a host facility for the United States-Japan exhibition series. Picturesque Bosse Field was used in the filming of the popular movie about women's baseball, *A League of Their Own,* and many Evansville residents were offended by the actress-singer Madonna. Year in and year out the Aces boast an excellent college team, but local fans still harbor hopes that one day a professional franchise will return to Evansville.

Year	Record	Pcg.	Finish
1966	68–72	.486	Third
1967	76–63	.547	Third
1968	55–84	.396	Sixth

Greenville
(Braves)

"Greenville was a capital base ball town long before its present growth had been attained. It is one of the Southern Carolina cities in which the game has been better understood . . . ." This complimentary passage, occasioned by a Greenville SALLY pennant, appeared in the 1927 *Reach Guide*, and aptly described a community that had been baseball crazy since the nineteenth century.

Amateur nines first played in the front lot of the Female College and at other vacant lots around Greenville. In the 1890s there were paid players in the Tin Pan League, which included teams from Greenville, Spartanburg, Charlotte, and other communities. Admission was 25 cents to a small grandstand off West Street (later changed to Hampton), where Central Baptist Church would be built. Other playing sites were on Memminger Street and at Furman Field, on Furman University property off Augusta Street. For decades excellent baseball was played by millworkers in the textile league.

The 1907 the Greenville Edistoes helped form the Class D South Carolina League, playing at Furman Park. The next year the Greenville Spinners became part of another new Class D League, the Carolina Association. The first batting champ was a young Greenville outfielder, Joseph Jefferson Jackson (.346), who was called "Shoeless Joe" because he had played barefooted for the nearby Brandon Mill textile league team. The Spinners won the 1910 pennant, but the Carolina Association folded two years later.

The Spinners joined the SALLY League when it was reorganized in 1919. In 1923 third baseman Zinn Beck won the batting title (.370) with teammate George Rhinehardt a fraction of a point behind, and the next season Rhinehardt became the only hitter in SALLY history to bat over .400 (.404, with a league-leading 32 steals).

Greenville won back-to-back SALLY pennants in 1926 and 1927. Righthander Wilcy Moore led the 1926 SALLY in victories and winning percentage (30–4) and set an all-time record with 17 consecutive wins, before going on to a brilliant rookie season with the famous 1927 New York Yankees. Infielder Bill Rhiel won the 1926 batting title (.386), while teammate Russell Scarritt (.377) set all-time SALLY marks for hits (243), runs (150), total bases (375) and at-bats (645). The 1927 champs were led by home run-RBI champ Mule Shirley (.331, 32 HR, 128 RBI), player-manager Frank Walker (.335), and victory leader Billy Bayne (26–10).

Outfielder Tilly Walker was the 1928 home run champ (.344 with 33 homers), while slugging young outfielder Murray "Red" Howell won back-to-back RBI crowns in 1929 (.341, 21 HR, 135 RBI) and 1930 (.340, 25 HR, 147 RBI, and a league-leading 123 runs and 193 hits). The 1930 Spinners won the pennant behind Howell, victory and percentage leader Huey Harmon (25–9), home run champ Jim Hudgens (.305, 39 HR, 114 RBI), doubles leader George Rhinehardt (.353 with 42 2B), player-manager Joe Schepner (.312), righthander Frank Pearce (22–13), and out-fielder Dixie Walker (.401 in 73 games), who was promoted to the International League before qualifying for the batting title.

The SALLY halted operations after the 1930 season. Green-ville fielded one of four teams in the Class D Palmetto League for 1931, but the circuit folded in July. Greenville fans had to weather the remainder of the Depression with textile mill teams, but in 1938 Joe Cambria put together another club for the SALLY, which had been reorganized two years earlier and which was expanding from six teams to eight. The Spinners were the first team to play in Meadowbrook Park, a lighted, $25,000 stadium that sometimes was called Cambria Park.

Outfielder-third baseman Doug Dean, who started the sea-son with Savannah, won the 1938 batting crown (.385), and the next year shortstop Hal Quick led the SALLY in hits and RBIs (.338, 189 H, 106 RBI). The SALLY did not operate for three years during World War II, but in 1946 the Spinners returned to Meadowbrook Park. In 1947 player-manager Frenchy Bordagaray (.342 in 48 games) hit and spat on umpire Dallas Blackiston in a July 14 game at Augusta, and he was fined $50 and suspended for 60 days (Pepper Martin took over as field general).

The 1948 Spinners finished third, then beat Macon and Col-umbia for the playoff title. The next season the Spinners again finished third and made it to the finals behind strikeout king Ray Moore (11–12, 229 Ks in 204 IP) and stolen base champ Maynard DeWitt (.298, 48 SB). But a losing season in 1950 resulted in the lowest attendance in the league, and Greenville dropped out of the Class A SALLY and joined the Class B Tri-State League. The Spinners did not participate in 1953, then rejoined the Tri-State League for the final two seasons of its existence.

In 1961 Meadowbrook Park, which had undergone major repairs following a 1948 fire, was renovated, a $7,500 scoreboard was placed in the outfield, and Greenville rejoined the SALLY. Lefthander Nick Wilhite was the 1961 ERA and strikeout champ (16–9, 1.80, 161 K), and righthander Camilio Extevis led the 1962 SALLY in victories and complete games (18–9 with 23 CG in 25 GS). But in 1963, when the SALLY moved up to Class AA, Greenville stayed in Class A with the Western Carolinas League. The Greenville Braves won the 1963 playoffs, and the 1970 Greenvile Red Sox ran away with the pennant. In 1966 the Greenville Mets showcased 19-year-old Nolan Ryan, who led the league in victories, percentage, and — of course — strikeouts (17–2 with 272 Ks in just 183 innings).

On Valentine's Day 1972, Meadowbrook Park was severely damaged by fire. There was a $42,000 fire insurance policy, but the city allotted only $2,000 for stadium repairs. Makeshift seating was provided, but merely 11,481 fans came out to the shell of Meadowbrook — nicknamed the "Alamo." A section of the left field wall was blown down, and when Greenville played Spartanburg in the playoffs, Verner Ross, club owner since 1962, staged his home games in Spartanburg "because I couldn't make any money here." He moved his franchise at the end of the season, and Greenville would not rejoin Organized Baseball for 12 years.

In 1984 Atlanta moved their Southern League farm club from Savannah to Greenville, and the Greenville Braves promptly posted the best record in the 10-team SL. Doc Estes (.341) won the batting crown, fellow outfielder Michael Cole (.305, 105 R, 110 W) led the league in runs and walks, and righthander David Clay provided superb relief (10–3, 1.80 ERA in 51 appearances).

At Greenville Municipal Stadium fans viewed future Atlanta stars such as Tom Glavine (11–6 in 1986) and Ron Gant (.247 in 1987 as a second baseman). In 1988 the Braves again compiled the best record in the league, downing Jacksonville for the Eastern Division crown before losing the playoff finals to Chattanooga. Second-sacker Mark Lemke (.270, 30 2B, 16 HR) led the SL in

Greenville Municipal Stadium.

hits, total bases and at-bats, and outfielder Barry Jones (.284 with 16 homers) added another strong bat.

In 1989 Buddy Bailey, the 1988 Manager of the Year, again led Greenville to the Eastern Division title before falling in the playoff finals. Two years later the Braves once more put up the league's best record, finishing 10½ games ahead of second-place Birmingham before being tripped up by Orlando in the playoff opener (many of the best players already had been promoted). The MVP was first baseman Ryan Klesko (.291), the Outstanding Pitcher was righthanded reliever Mark Wohlers (0.57 ERA and 21 saves in 28 appearances), outfielder Keith Mitchell performed powerfully in half a season (.327, 19 HR, 47 RBI in 60 G), victory leader Napoleon Robinson (16–6, 2.27 ERA) and Turk Wendell (11–3, 2.56 ERA) provided excellent starting pitching, and Chris Chambliss was voted Manager of the Year.

The 1992 Braves proved to be one of the finest teams in recent minor league history. Managed by Grady Little, the Braves were 50–20 at home and 50–23 on the road, becoming the first SL team ever to win 100 games and the first minor league club to reach 100 victories since Peninsula of the Carolina League in 1980. Blue-chip prospect Chipper Jones put in a brilliant half-

The 1991 Greenville Braves were guided to the playoffs by former big league star Chris Chambliss (standing, far left). Standouts included All-Star outfielder Keith Mitchell (front, far left – .327), victory leader Napoleon Robinson (middle, second from left – 16–6), percentage leader Turk Wendell (middle, third from left – 11–3), MVP Ryan Klesko (standing, third from left – .291), and Outstanding Pitcher Mark Wohlers (standing, fourth from left – 0.57 ERA in 28 G).

— Courtesy Greenville Braves

season at shortstop (.346, 17 2B, 11 3B, 9 HR in 67 G), catcher Javy Lopez (.321) was named Player of the Year, and outfielder Milton Nieves (.283) and righthander Nate Minchey (13–6) were voted to the All-Star Team. Greenville led the SL in team fielding, ERA, hitting and home runs. The Braves were shut out just six times in 143 games, while the pitching staff blanked the opposition 24 times. Greenville was 9–2 in extra-inning games and 27–13 in one-run contests. The Braves swept Charlotte in the playoff opener, then outlasted Chattanooga in the finals to cap a magnificent season.

Greenville continued to roll in 1993, finishing atop the East in the first half of the season. Key players were righty Mike Hostetler (8–5 in 19 starts), relievers Dale Polley (8–1 in 42 G) and Carlos Reyes (8–1, 2.06 ERA in 33 G), third baseman Ed Giovanola (.281), and outfielder Pedro Swann (.306). In the opening playoff game, Mike Hostetler twirled a no-hitter over Knoxville, beating the SL's top offensive club, 2–0, while recording the only postseason no-hitter in Southern League history. But Knoxville rallied to win the Eastern Division, three games to two, ending Greenville's season.

Year	Record	Pcg.	Finish
1984	80–61	.567	First (lost opener)
1985	70–74	.486	Seventh
1986	73–71	.507	Fourth
1987	70–74	.486	Fifth
1988	87–57	.604	First (won Eastern Division, lost finals)
1989	70–69	.504	Fourth (won Eastern Division, lost finals)
1990	57–87	.396	Tenth
1991	88–56	.611	First (lost opener)
1992	100–43	.699	First (won Eastern Division and finals)
1993	75–67	.528	Second (lost opener)

Huntsville
(Stars)

Until Huntsville joined the Southern League in 1985, the northern Alabama community had little experience in professional baseball. In 1911 Huntsville was enlisted in the year-old Southeastern League, finishing fifth in the six-team Class D circuit. The next year Huntsville had another losing record, and at mid-season the club transferred to Talladega. Huntsville tried again in 1930, joining the Class D Georgia-Alabama League. But after a last-place finish Huntsville dropped out of Organized Baseball for more than half a century.

Following the 1984 season, Larry Schmittou succeeded in moving his Nashville Sounds from the Double-A Southern Legaue to the Triple-A American Association. But Schmittou wanted to maintain his SL franchise, and negotiations with Huntsville resulted in the construction of a stadium and the birth of the Southern League Stars.

By the 1980s Huntsville, home of a NASA Space Center, enjoyed the highest per capita income of any city in Alabama. On September 3, 1984, the City Council voted to construct a multi-purpose facility on the old airport grounds. Named after a five-term mayor, Joe W. Davis Stadium was built in 32 weeks and boasted VIP boxes and a seating capacity of 10,260.

Former big league All-Star Don Mincher became the first general manager and immediately created a positive impact for professional baseball in Huntsville (the popular Mincher still serves the Stars as PR director and radio analyst). An affiliate was secured with the Oakland Athletics, who supplied a talented pool of players. Powerful young outfielder Jose Canseco only played 58 games before earning promotion to Triple-A, but performed so impressively (.318, 25 HR, 80 RBI) that he was voted MVP. All-Star first baseman Rob Nelson also supplied power (.232, 32 HR, 98 RBI), and manager Brad Fischer guided the Stars to the Western Division title and victory over Charlotte, three games to two, for the SL championship. Huntsville also led the league with a total attendance of more than 300,000.

The next year Fischer again led the Stars to the Western Division crown before falling to Columbus in the finals. MVP Terry Steinbach was the RBI king (.325, 24 HR, 132 RBI), first-sacker Jose Tolentino led the league in hits (.315, 16 HR, 105 RBI), second baseman Gary Jones was the run leader (.311, 116 R), Brian Guinn (.283) was named All-Star shortstop, and the pitching staff was paced by southpaw Greg Cadaret (12–5) and righty Kirk McDonald (12–5). The Stars led the SL in team hitting (.289),

Joe W. Davis Stadium opened in 1985 as the home of the Huntsville Stars.

posted the best record of the season, and again totaled the highest attendance with over 263,000 paid admissions.

In 1987 Huntsville repeated as attendance leader (256,000) as Fischer put the Stars in the playoffs for the third consecutive season. The Stars lost the playoff opener but infielder Joe Xavier led the league in doubles and sacrifices (.301, 37 2B), and shortstop Walt Weiss (.285) earned All-Star recognition before a late-season callup. The Stars dropped to the cellar the next year, but rebounded to the playoffs in 1989. Although Huntsville was defeated in the opening round, Jeff Newman directed the Stars to the second-best record of the season and was voted Manager of the Year. Righthander Ray Young (13–6) and saves leader Joe Klink (26 saves in 57 appearances) formed the core of the pitching staff, while the offense centered around All-Star outfielder Dann Howitt (.281, 26 HR, 111 RBI).

Newman guided Huntsville to the third-best record of 1990, but the Stars missed the playoffs. Shortstop Scott Brosius led the league in hits, doubles and total bases (.296, 39 2B, 23 HR), righthander Dan Eskew was the percentage leader (14–3), and reliever Steve Chitren recorded the most saves (27 saves and a 1.68 ERA in 48 G).

In 1991 Joe W. Davis Stadium was the site of the first Double-A All-Star Game. The 1991 Stars plummeted to the cellar, but vaulted back into the playoffs in 1992. Manager Casey Parsons led Huntsville to the third-best record of the season, but the Stars were swept in the playoff opener by Chattanooga. At the second annual Double-A All-Star Game at Charlotte's Knights Castle, Huntsville first-sacker Marcos Armas won the Star of Stars Award as the game's MVP. Armas (.283, 17 HR, 84 RBI) also was named to the SL All-Star Team, along with infielder Darryl Vice (.295) and outfielder Scott Lydy (.305). Righthander Patrick Bronswell was a victory co-leader (13–7), Jeff Bittinger was effective for half a season (10–5 in 17 GF), and strong relief was provided by Todd Revenig (1.70 ERA and 33 saves in 53 G) and fellow righty David Latter (8–1 as a long reliever in 47 G). The 1993 batting champ was first baseman Jim Bowie (.333, 14 HR, 101 RBI), who also won the title with Jacksonville in 1991. Other crowd-pleasing players included All-Star catcher George Williams (.299), southpaw Scott Baker (10–4), and fireballing righthander Steve Karsay (8–4 with 122 Ks in 118 IP).

The 1992 Huntsville Stars made the playoffs behind ace reliever Todd Revenig (front, far right – 1.70 ERA and 33 saves in 58 G), All-Star Game MVP Marcos Armas (standing, fifth from right –.283), and victory co-leader Bronswell Patrick (standing, third from right – 13-7).

Year	Record	Pcg.	Finish
1985	78–66	.542	Fourth (won Western Division and finals)
1986	78–63	.553	First (won Western Division, lost finals)
1987	74–70	.514	Third (lost opener)
1988	59–85	.410	Tenth
1989	82–61	.573	Second (lost opener)
1990	79–65	.549	Third
1991	61–83	.424	Tenth
1992	83–61	.563	Third (lost opener)
1993	71–70	.504	Sixth

Jacksonville
(Suns, Mets, Expos)

In 1892 Jacksonville participated in the only nineteenth-century season of the Florida State League, then became a charter member of the SALLY in 1904. The Jacksonville Jays won the 1908 pennant by 12 games, leading the league in team hitting and fielding and featuring percentage leader C. V. Sitton (17-5). The Jays became the Tarpons in 1911, and the next year the Tarpons brought another SALLY championship to Jacksonville. The Tarpons pulled out of the SALLY in 1917, and Jacksonville did not reappear in the league for two decades.

The Jacksonville Scouts rejoined the Class C Florida State League in 1921, but finished in last place. The team nickname was changed to Indians for 1922, but Jacksonville stayed in the cellar, then once more dropped out of professional baseball. In 1926 the Jacksonville Tars helped revive the Class B Southeastern League, winning the 1927 pennant behind victory and percentage leader Ben Cantwell (25–4), and showcasing the 1928 batting champ, minor league great Moose Clabaugh (.366). The Tars played at 1701 Myrtle Avenue in a wooden ballpark known at different times as Barnes' Field, Douglas Field, Durkee Field, and Red Cap Stadium. The Depression put the Southeastern out of business after the 1930 season; the league tried again in 1932, but folded on May 23.

The SALLY reorganized for 1936, and the Jacksonville Tars won the first half of a split schedule before falling to Columbus in the finals. The Tars were led by Henry Bazner (20–7) and Roy "Goat" Walker (20–8), who won again in 1937 (19–13) and 1938 (21–7). The 1938 batting champ was Hugh Todd (.384). The SALLY halted operations for the duration of the war after the 1942 season, but the league and the Tars resumed play in 1946. In 1951 manager Ben Geraghty guided the Tars to the finals, as southpaw Vince DiLorenzo led the SALLY in victories (22–8).

During the 1953 season the SALLY brought integrated baseball to the South, and the Jacksonville Braves led the way with MVP second baseman Hank Aaron, who paced the league in batting, RBIs, doubles, runs, hits, putouts and assists (.362, 22 HR, 115 R, 125 RBI), outfielder Horace Garner (.305), and shortstop Felix Mantilla (.278). Other talent included outfielder Jim Frey (.317), first-sacker Joe Andrews (.311), strikeout and victory leader Larry Lassalle (19–5, 185 Ks), and co-victory leader Ray Ditmar (19–11). Manager Ben Geraghty stabilized the team in the face of racial difficulties, and the Braves finished first, then came within one victory of winning the playoffs.

Geraghty produced another first-place club the next year, again winning the opening round of playoffs and again losing the finals in the seventh game. Horace Garner (.323) and Joe Andrews (.296) returned, while other stars were RBI champ

Clarence Riddle (.318, 28 HR, 112 RBI) and pitching Triple Crown winner Humberto Robinson (23–8, 243 Ks, 2.41 ERA). Geraghty, batting champ Wes Covington (.326), and Horace Garner (.294 with 18 homers) led the Braves into the playoffs again in 1955. That year the Braves moved into Jacksonville Baseball Park, a 10,264-seat stadium boasting a handsome brick outfield wall.

The following season Geraghty's Braves took it all, finishing first by eight games, then winning the playoff opener and finals without a loss. Fireballing lefthander Juan Pizarro performed brilliantly (23–6, 1.77 ERA, and 318 Ks in 274 IP), while third baseman Ed Barbarito was the home run and RBI king (.310, 27 HR, 99 RBI). In 1958 ERA champ Ross Carter (17–7, 2.19) led the Braves to the playoff finals.

Despite a last-place finish and miserable attendance (25,156) in 1961, Jacksonville jumped to the Triple-A International League for 1962 as Sam W. Wolfson, former president of the SALLY, secured Havana's IL franchise. With Ben Geraghty back at the helm and a roster headed by batting and stolen base champ Vic Davalillo (.346 with 24 thefts) and MVP shortstop Tony Martinez (.287), the Jacksonville Suns marched to the IL pennant and to

Sam W. Wolfson Park, home of the Jacksonville Suns.

the last game of the playoff finals. Attendance increased almost tenfold (229,579).

The next year the Suns plunged to the cellar of the 10-team IL, then roared back to first place in 1964. The first-to-last-to-first pattern of 1962–63–64 is unique in International League history. The 1968 Suns finished fourth, but won the playoff opener over the first-place Toledo Mud Hens, then executed a four-game sweep over Columbus in the finals. But attendance was disappointing in 1967 and 1968, and the parent Mets moved their IL franchise to Tidewater for 1969.

After one season without a team, in 1970 Jacksonville resurrected the Suns as a Southern League expansion club. The first SL Suns finished in the second division, but southpaw Dave Hartman won the ERA crown (9–10, 2.01) and outfielder-first baseman Jim Covington was the home run champ (.254 with 21 homers). In 1971 the Suns affiliated with Cleveland, then changed to Kansas City a year later. Manager Billy Gardner guided the 1973 Suns to the Eastern Division title, but Jacksonville lost the championship playoff with Montgomery, three games to one. Gardner again led the Suns to the Eastern crown in 1974, although there was another disappointing loss in the SL playoff, this time to Knoxville, three games to two. The Suns were last in team hitting (.238), but a good pitching staff was headed by left-handed reliever Norman Angelini (9–7 in a league-leading 56 G) and righthander starter Al Autry (10–5).

In 1977 the Suns finished last in the first half, then rebounded to the second-half lead. Jacksonville beat Savannah for the Eastern Division championship before dropping the finals to Montgomery. First baseman-DH Ron Johnson (.270, 23 HR, 104 RBI, and 40 2B) set the all-time SL record for doubles in 1980. Onix Concepcion (.322) was the 1980 All-Star shortstop, and catcher Don Slaught was impressive (.335) in 1981. The Suns posted the best record of 1982 under manager Gene Lamont, finishing first in the East in both halves. Second-place Columbus was allowed to play Jacksonville in the playoff opener, but the Suns won, three games to one, before losing the finals to Nashville by the same margin. Outfielder Dave Leeper led the offense (.293), and he hit for the same average in 1983 (.293 in 36 G).

Gene Lamont took the Suns back to the finals in 1983. Righthander Mark Gubicza won the strikeout crown (14–12 , 146 Ks) and John Morris was an All-Star outfielder (.288, 23 HR, 92 RBI). The Suns finished atop the East for the division crown, but lost the championship finals to Birmingham, three games to one. In 1984 first baseman Andres Galarraga was voted MVP (.289, 27 HR, 87 RBI), and righthander Mark Williams claimed the ERA title (5–6, 2.49)

The Suns became a Montreal affiliate in 1984, and the next year the club was compelled to adopt the Expos team nickname. The 1986 Expos won the first half in the East, but lost the division playoff to Columbus. Reliever Kevin Price led the league in appearances (8–6 with 20 saves in 60 G), while the offense was charged by switch hitter John Daughtery (.317), second baseman Armando Moreno (.311), and All-Star outfielder Alonzo Powell (.301). The next year manager Tommy Thompson again brought the Expos to the divisional playoff, winning the second half with the best record of 1987 before losing to Charlotte, three games to two. Slugging outfielders Mike Berger (.293, 22 HR, 93 RBI) and Larry Walker (.287, 26 HR, 87 RBI) were named to the All-Star Team. Pitching titles were monopolized by the Jacksonville staff: Brian Holman was the ERA champ (14–5, 2.50), *reliever* John Trautwein was the victory leader (15–4 in 56 G), tall lefthander Randy Johnson was the strikeout king (11–8 with 163 Ks in 140 IP), and reliever Kevin Price led the SL in saves and games finished (9–4 with 19 saves and 45 GF in 57 G).

The next two years were losing seasons, but in 1990 the Expos finished atop the East in the second half before falling to Orlando in the division playoff. Outfielder Terrel Hansen led the league in home runs (.260 with 24 homers), Greg Colbrunn (.301) was the All-star catcher, southpaw Brian Barnes was the strikeout champ (13–7 with 213 Ks in 201 IP), and reliever Jeff Carter won the ERA crown (8–3, 1.84 in 52 G).

In 1991 Jacksonville changed affiliations, from Montreal to Seattle, and the team nickname again became the Suns. The Suns missed the playoffs, but first baseman Jim Bowie won the batting title (.310) and catcher Jim Campanis was named to the All-Star Team. The 1992 Suns showcased All-Star baseman Brian Turang, stolen base champ Ellerton Maynard (.283 with 38 thefts), Jim Bowie (.286 in 80 G), and strikeout leader Jim Converse (.12–7 with 157 Ks in 159 IP). Second baseman Ruben Santana (.301, 21 HR, 84 RBI) made the 1993 All-Star Team, and more than

250,000 fans turned out to watch a last-place club. The 1994 schedule will mark Jacksonville's 25th consecutive season in the Southern League, the most of any SL city.

Year	Record	Pcg.	Finish
1970	67–70	.480	Fifth
1971	63–77	.450	Fourth
1972	59–80	.424	Seventh
1973	76–60	.559	Second (lost finals)
1974	78–60	.565	First (lost finals)
1975	59–79	.428	Eighth
1976	66–72	.478	Sixth
1977	72–66	.522	Fourth (won Eastern Division, lost finals)
1978	73–69	.544	Third
1979	69–72	.489	Sixth
1980	63–81	.438	Eighth
1981	65–77	.458	Eighth
1982	83–61	.576	First (won Eastern Division, lost finals)
1983	77–68	.531	Fourth (won Eastern Division, lost finals)
1984	76–69	.524	Third
1985	73–70	.510	Fifth
1986	75–68	.524	Second (lost opener)
1987	85–59	.590	First (lost opener)
1988	69–73	.486	Fifth (lost opener)
1989	68–76	.472	Seventh
1990	84–60	.583	Second (lost opener)
1991	74–69	.517	Fourth
1992	68–75	.476	Seventh
1993	59–81	.421	Tenth

Knoxville
(Smokies, White Sox,
Knox Sox, Blue Jays, K-Jays)

"In 1865 I started the first baseball team in the South," reminisced Knoxville insurance man S. B. Dow in 1921. Perhaps not the entire South, but certainly in Knoxville. Dow met with interested players at Cooper's Billiard Rooms. Dow was elected captain of the "Knoxvilles," and the team removed trash and cut cockleburs at a large open field near the edge of town, where high banks around the field provided natural bleachers. At the opening game a band played, businessmen shut down their stores, and the natural bleachers overflowed with kranks. Dow used an extra long bat to pole the ball, and the Knoxvilles walloped numerous home runs in their games.

In May 1878 the East Tennessee University "Reds" hosted a Knoxville nine on the college campus. The Reds won, 8–4, but when classes ended in June, the two squads merged into "The Original Knoxville Reds," a crack outfit that took on all comers until the mid-1880s.

The first pros were organized in 1894 by Frank Moffett, who played left field. The Knoxville Reds played at Baldwin Park off Dale Avenue; admission to the wooden grandstand was 75 cents, or 50 cents for bleacher seats, and once the park was jammed with a crowd of 3,000. Moffett brought in name teams, and paid his best players $100 per month. The Knoxville Indians helped organize the Southeastern League, which operated in 1896 and 1897.

After the turn of the century, Knoxville participated in three outlaw leagues. In 1902 Frank Moffett put together another squad of Reds and helped form the Appalachian League with Bristol, Greenville and Johnson City. The "Appy" played four days a week. Knoxville participated in the Tennessee-Alabama League in 1904, a loop in which young Ty Cobb previewed his talents. The next season Knoxville entered the Tennessee-Alabama-Georgia League —the "TAG."

In July 1909 Charleston's SALLY club collapsed and was transferred to Knoxville, where the Appalachians played at a diamond at Chilhowee Park. That season Knoxville staged a night game, when the Chicago Cherokees brought their own lights and a supply of whitewashed baseballs (Knoxville made seven errors and lost, 5–2). In 1910 the Appalachians won the first pennant of the Class D Southeastern League. The catcher was Bill Meyer, who had played at Knoxville High School and who would eventually become a notable manager; when he died in 1957 Knoxville's stadium was renamed in his honor.

With Frank Moffett as manager, the Knoxville Reds spent 1911 through 1914 in the Class D Appalachian League. The Reds finished second the first three years, with Frank Davis winning the strikeout title in 1911 and the percentage crown in 1912 (13–3), and Elmer Lawrence leading the league in victories and percentage in 1913 (24–7). The Appalachian League folded early in the 1914 season, and Knoxville did not field another pro team until 1921.

The Appalachian League reorganized in 1921. Owned by Frank Moffett, the Knoxville Pioneers played at wooden Caswell Park, located off Magnolia Avenue on Jessamine Street. The Pioneers won back-to-back pennants in 1923 and 1924, as R. E. Leach was the 1923 victory and percentage leader (17–4) and Art Ruble won the 1924 batting championship (.350).

In 1925 the SALLY expanded from six to eight clubs, and the Knoxville Smokies moved up to the Class B league. The Smokies finished last in 1925 and next-to-last in 1926, positions that would become so familiar in future seasons that fans would chant, "S.O.S. — Same Old Smokies!" But in 1927 the Smokies finished third behind batting and home run champ Bill Barrett (.360, 39 HR, 100 RBI) and Gerald Myers (23–11, and 26–11 in 1926), while Oscar Felber (.366) kept the hitting title in Knoxville in 1928.

The 1929 Smokies finished first in the SALLY and won the championship playoff behind pitching duo John Walker (25–9) and L. Bates (23–11), run leader Elwood Smith (.322, 119 R), shortstop Boob McNair (.391 in 91 G), and outfielder Frank Waddey (.354 in 90 G). Despite success on the field, Depression conditions kept the Smokies from returning for 1930. During the 1931 season, however, Mobile of the Southern Association experienced similar difficulties, and the franchise was transferred to Knoxville.

City councilman W. N. Smithson persuaded the council to raze antique Caswell Park and build a new facility, which was named Smithson Stadium. In 1953 the 22-year-old wooden ballpark burned and was replaced at a cost of $500,000 by 6,700-seat Knoxville Municipal Stadium. Four years later, the Jessamine Street ballpark was renamed Bill Meyer Stadium.

The Smokies would play in the Southern Asssociation until 1944. But Knoxville was a perennial second-division team, finishing in the cellar in 1932, 1935, 1937 (42–111), 1938, 1940, 1941 and 1942. Hardcore fans enjoyed the performance of 1933 batting champ Frank Waddey (.361), and of home run titlists Earl Webb in 1936 (.348, 20 HR, 102 RBI), Tom Haley in 1938 (.284 with 24 homers), Dutch Meyer in 1940 (.333 with 22 homers), and Cecil Dunn in 1943 (.295 with 19 homers). By mid-season of 1944, however, owner Bob Allen had given up, and on July 4 the team transferred to Mobile. The move was made during the night, and Knoxville fans who came to the ballpark the next day knew nothing about the loss of their team until the players failed to appear.

In 1946 the Smokies returned as part of the Class B Tri-State League. Outfielder Bob Churchill blasted his way to the 1948 batting crown (.406 with a league-leading 28 triples), and the Smokies reached the playoffs in 1946 and 1950. In 1953 Knoxville moved into the Mountain States League, for what proved to be the final season of the Class D circuit. Jim Tugerson won 29 of the team's 70 victories and fanned a league-leading 286 batters, and the Smokies triumphed in the Shaughnessy Playoffs. The Tri-State League welcomed Knoxville back the next year, and the Smokies promptly won another Shaughnessy championship.

The Tri-State League folded a year later, but on June 18, 1956, Montgomery's Class A SALLY club was moved to Knoxville. In 1957 the Smokies made the playoffs, and the next season there was standout pitching from victory and percentage leader Jerry Walker (18–4) and strikeout king Chuck Estrada (15–11, 181 Ks). The 1959 Smokies, managed by former big leaguer Johnny Pesky and sparked by ERA and percentage titlist Jim Proctor (15–5, 2.19), finished in first place, although the team was defeated in the playoff opener. The Smokies made it to the finals the following year behind batting champ Purnal Goldy (.342, 20 HR, 106 RBI), RBI titlist Leo Smith (.301, 16 HR, 111 RBI), and run and triples leader Dick McAuliffe (.301, 21 3B, 109 R). Fireballer Leo Marentette was the 1962 strikeout champ (14–11, 205 Ks), as the Smokies reached the playoff finals.

Knoxville moved up to Double-A with the SALLY in 1963, and the next year the Smokies became charter members of the newly named Southern League. In 1965 outfielder Gerry Reimer (.310) won the hitting crown, while righthanders Tom Frondorf (16–7) and Milt Osteen (16–9) led the SL in victories. The 1966 Smokies finished last, despite the efforts of batting champ John Fenderson (.324), run and hit leader Sam Thompson (.307, 22 SB, 114 R), and RBI titlist Bob Robertson (.287, 32 HR, 99 RBI). The Smokies stayed in the cellar the next year, with a meager attendance of only 21,390. The Cincinnati farm club was moved to Asheville for 1968, and Knoxville dropped out of Organized Baseball.

During the 1971 season the SL and the Texas League could field only seven teams each, combining in an awkward arrangement called the Dixie Association. In 1972 the Texas League acquired an eighth team, while Knoxville joined the SL as a White Sox affiliate. During the eight seasons of this affiliation, the SL team would be called the Knoxville White Sox or the Knox Sox. Manager Joe Sparks guided the Sox to second place in the Western Division with an offensive attack led by future big league infielder Bucky Dent (.296). The next year righthander Joe Henderson (17–4) led the SL in victories and winning percentage.

The 1974 Knox Sox won the Western Division, then beat Jacksonville, three games to two, for the SL championship. Outfielder Nyls Nyman led the league in hitting, runs, hits and triples (.325), righthander Leo Williams (13–9) headed the pitching staff, offense was added by second-sacker Manny Estrada (.297) and All-Star first baseman Mike Squires (.287), and Jim Napier was voted Manager of the Year. In 1975 Mike Squires (.304) again was named All-Star first baseman, and in 1976 outfielder Larry Foster (.311) was the batting champ.

The Knox Sox enjoyed a triumphant season in 1978. Tony LaRussa and Joe Jones shared managerial duties, guiding Knoxville to the best record in the 10-team SL. The Knox Sox led the

Knoxville's Bill Meyer Stadium was built in 1931, then rebuilt after a 1953 fire.

league in team hitting, doubles and triples, won both halves to secure the division title, then beat Savannah in the finals, two games to one. Outfielder Joe Gates won the batting title and scored the most runs (.332, 85 R), while Mark Naehring (.302) was named All-Star third baseman. Naehring (.294) was back on the All-Star Team the next year.

In 1980 Knoxville began a long affiliation with Toronto, assuming the Blue Jays nickname, but often being called the K-Jays. The 1982 K-Jays won the first half in the West, but lost the division championship to Nashville. Tim Thompson (.282 with 18 homers) was the All-Star first baseman, third-sacker Jeff Reynolds (.242 with 20 homers) also made the All-Star Team, and righthanded reliever Tom Lukish led the SL in appearances (54) and saves (20).

Knoxville returned to the playoffs in 1984, winning the first half before falling into last place during the second half. Manager John McLaren rallied the K-Jays and beat Nashville, three games to one, to claim the division title, then fell to Charlotte in the finals. Second baseman Mike Sharperson (.304) led the offense and was named to the All-Star Team. The next year McLaren guided the K-Jays to the second-half lead behind southpaw Steve Davis (17–6, 2.45), who led the SL in wins and ERA and was voted Pitcher of the Year. Knoxville lost the division crown to Huntsville, three games to one.

In 1986 Knoxville again won the second half, behind home run champ Glenallen Hill (.279, 31 HR, 96 RBI) and the league's stingiest pitching. Once more the K-Jays faltered in the division playoff, losing to Charlotte, three games to two. The 1987 K-Jays failed to make the playoffs, but slugging outfielder Geronimo Berroa pounded his way onto the All-Star Team (.287, 36 HR, 108 RBI), and fellow outfielder Bernie Tatis led the league in runs (.279, 101 R). Catcher Francisco Cabrera (.284 with 20 homers) and strikeout king Alex Sanchez (12–5 with 166 Ks in 149 IP) made the 1988 All-Star Team, while fellow righty Steve Cummings (14–11) set the all-time SL record for starts (33). The 1991 K-Jays won the second half after a weak start, but lost the division title to Birmingham. The next year the K-Jays boasted All-Star outfielder Juan DeLarosa (.329) and All-Star DH Nigel Wilson (.274 with 26 homers).

For 1993 it was decided to return to the traditional nickname,

The 1992 Knoxville Blue Jays featured All-Star outfielder Juan DeLarosa (middle, fifth from right – .329) and All-Star DH Nigel Wilson (standing, far left – .274 with 26 homers).

— Courtesy Knoxville Blue Jays

and the Smokies rebounded from a weak start to lead the East in the second half. MVP catcher Carlos Delgado was the home run and RBI champ (.303, 25 HR, 102 RBI), southpaw Huck Flener was the victory co-leader (13–6), and All-Star shortstop Alex Gonzalez was the run co-titlist (.289, 38 SB, 93 R). The SL's top offense also was charged by first baseman Tim Hyers (.306), hustling second-sacker Joey Lis (.290), and outfielders Shawn Green (.283) and Don Sheppard (.281). The Smokies defeated Greenville, three games to two, for the Eastern Division championship, before falling to Birmingham in the finals.

Year	Record	Pcg.	Finish
1964	67–73	.479	Fifth
1965	73–66	.525	Fourth
1966	61–75	.449	Eighth
1967	47–91	.341	Sixth
1972	76–64	.543	Fourth
1973	70–69	.504	Fifth
1974	72–63	.533	Third (won finals)
1975	63–75	.457	Sixth
1976	61–77	.442	Seventh
1977	50–87	.365	Eighth
1978	88–56	.611	First (won Western Division and finals)
1979	65–76	.461	Seventh

1980	57–87	.396	Tenth
1981	63–80	.441	Tenth
1982	73–71	.507	Fifth
1983	64–82	.438	Eighth
1984	70–75	.483	Eighth (won Western Division, lost finals)
1985	79–64	.552	First (lost opener)
1986	74–70	.514	Third (lost opener)
1987	68–76	.472	Eighth
1988	75–69	.521	Fourth
1989	67–76	.469	Eighth
1990	67–77	.465	Seventh
1991	67–77	.465	Eighth (lost opener)
1992	56–88	.389	Ninth
1993	71–71	.500	Eighth (won Eastern Division, lost finals)

Lynchburg
(White Sox)

A hotbed of amateur baseball, Lynchburg boasted more than 100 nines by 1886, the Hill City's centennial anniversary. The Lynchburg Base Ball Association sold stock at $10 per share and organized a professional team, which was outfitted in silver-gray uniforms with maroon trim. Hill City Park was built near the fairgrounds on Park Avenue, between Orchard and Forest streets. There was a grandstand, but the original outfield fence was so low that kranks could watch the games without buying a ticket.

In 1906 Lynchburg became a charter member of the Class C Virginia League, winning the first pennant behind victory leader Walter Moser (24–8). Succeeding years brought one losing record after another, however, and last-place Lynchburg folded during the 1912 season. Lynchburg re-enlisted for the 1917 season, but the Virginia League disbanded on May 16.

More than two decades passed without pro ball in the Hill City. In 1936 the Fair Association was liquidated, and the city paid $30,000 for the 28-acre fairgrounds property. The City Council planned to build an all-sports stadium, but Councilman Edley Craighill suggested that the dirt from the excavation of the football field be used as a seating base for adjoining football and baseball stadiums. The WPA provided labor and equipment and spent more than $100,000, while the city spent over $189,000.

The baseball field had 5,000 seats, including 2,500 under the roofed grandstand.

Lynchburg rejoined the four-team Class D Virginia League in 1939, and won the pennant the next year. In 1941 the circuit added two teams and moved back up to Class C, but ceased operations for the duration of the war after the 1942 season. New City Stadium did not go unused, however, as Lynchburg transferred to the Class B Piedmont League, one of the few minor circuits which continued play during the war. Lynchburg finished first in 1944 and won the playoffs. Another pennant came in 1948, as big Steve Bilko led the Piedmont League in batting, doubles and homers (.333 with 20 HR). The next year Lynchburg again won the pennant, as well as the playoffs. But after the 1955 season the Piedmont League disbanded, and Lynchburg spent the next three years without a pro team.

In 1959 Lynchburg joined the Class D Appalachian League, finished last in the standings and attendance, and again dropped out of Organized Baseball. Late in the 1962 season, however, first-place Savannah of the Class A SALLY League experienced racial difficulties and moved the remaining home games to Lynchburg's City Stadium. Lynchburg remained in the SALLY as a White Sox affiliate when the circuit moved up to Double-A, reaching the 1963 finals.

The SALLY became the Southern League in 1964, and Lynchburg won the first SL pennant. Manager George Noga commanded the services of the league's best pitching staff, featuring righthander Jose Lizondro (15–9) and ERA, victory, percentage, innings and complete game leader Manly "Shot" Johnston (20–7, 2.46), who also blasted three home runs in one game as the team's best pinch hitter (.292 with 7 HR in 78 G). The offense was triggered by home run, hit, total base and run leader Dick Kenworthy (.312, 29 HR, 97 RBI), first baseman Grover Jones (.299) and second-sacker Lorenzo Fernandez (.287). There were to be no playoffs, and Lynchburg edged Birmingham for the first-place flag by a one-game margin.

The next year, under manager Gordon Maltzberger, Lynchburg slipped to third place. Lorenzo Fernandez was back at second base (.260), and Jose Lizondro returned to the pitching staff for part of the season (10–3). Francisco Carlos, a starter in 1964 (11–11), also returned to the 1965 staff (10–14). Other 1965 starters were Fred Klages (13–10) and Bob Lasko (12–9). The best hitters were catcher Duane Josephson (.300) and outfielder Bill Voss (.284 with 18 homers).

For 1966 the White Sox moved their Double-A SL franchise to Evansville, while placing Lynchburg in the Class A Carolina League. In 1970 Lynchburg became a Minnesota affiliate, and in 1973 the Lynchburg Twins won the Carolina League pennant. There was another change of affiliation in 1975, to the Texas Rangers, and another the next year, to the New York Mets. The Lynchburg Mets finished first in 1977, and won the playoffs in 1978. The Lynchburg Mets finished first and won the 1983 playoffs behind brilliant performances from pitching Triple Crown winner Dwight Gooden (19–4, 2.50 ERA and 300 Ks in 191 IP) and batting, runs, triples, and stolen base champ Lenny Dykstra (.358, 132 R, 14 3B, 105 SB).

In 1984 Lynchburg repeated as first place and playoff winners, and in 1985 the Mets finished first for the third consecutive year. Lynchburg became a Boston farm club in 1988, and the Lynchburg Red Sox reached the playoff finals in 1991 and 1992 and finished first in the latter season.

Year	Record	Pcg.	Finish
1964	81–59	.579	First
1965	75–64	.540	Third

Macon
(Peaches)

The first baseball diamond in Macon was Mulberry Park, laid out at the foot of Mulberry Street on the Central City side of Fifth. A trolley line passed just beside the park, and by the 1880s there was a roofed grandstand and a plank fence. Macon became a charter member of the Southern League, playing SL ball in Mulberry Park in 1885 and 1886, with season tickets selling for $12.50.

Macon did not field another Southern League team until 1892, when Daisy Park was built from the old hippodrome at Central City Park. Named after Mayor S. B. "Daisy" Price, the ballpark soon was called Central City Park. The semi-circular grandstand seated 4,000; grandstand tickets cost 25 cents and bleacher seats were 15 cents, or 25 cents for two. Central City Park hosted Southern League visitors in 1892, 1893 and 1894, and was the home of other professional teams until destroyed by fire in 1926.

In 1904 Macon was a founding member of the South Atlantic League, and the Peaches won the first two SALLY pennants. The 1904 champs were led by victory and strikeout king Brindle Bayne (30–13, 288 Ks), while the 1905 Peaches featured victory leader Rob Spade (25–8), percentage titlist S. D. Loucks (16–3), and run and stolen base champ Paul Sentell (.315, 50 SB), who lost the batting crown to young Ty Cobb. Player-manager W. A. Smith enjoyed his best season at the plate in 1905 (.285). But no more championships followed, and a last-place Macon club dropped out early in the 1917 season.

Macon permanently rejoined the SALLY in 1923, after Charleston surrendered its club on June 5. In 1930 Macon finally claimed another SALLY pennant, behind the pitching of ERA champ Phil Gallivan (20–8, 2.61) and the hitting of outfielders Parham (.352) and Cohen (.335). But the Depression caused the SALLY to halt operations after the 1930 season, and the league did not reorganize until 1936. By this time Macon played at Luther Williams Field, a concrete stadium built on the site of old Central City Park.

The 1941 pennant was brought to Macon by a fine team, which included ERA and percentage titlist Frank Marino (19–1, 2.16), batting and RBI champ Cy Block (.357 with 112 RBIs), victory leader Stan West (23–7), shortstop Eddie Stanky (.315), outfielder Edgar Hartness (.314), stolen base king Cecil Garriott (.283 with 26 thefts), and righthander Foster Thornton (18–12). After the war Macon finished first and won the 1949 playoffs behind righthanders Robert Spicer (20–6) and Jim Atchley (20–7), then finished first and repeated as playoff winners the next year. The 1950 champs boasted RBI king Lewis Davis (.305, 14 HR, 119 RBI), victory leader Stan Karpinski (26–12), fellow righthander Fred Woolpert (19–8), southpaw Bill Seinsoth (18–11), and run and hit leader Gus Gregory (.295, 116 R).

Macon bounced back from a cellar finish in 1957 to win the 1958 playoffs. But Macon dropped back into the cellar in 1959 and 1960, then dropped out of Organized Baseball. In 1962 Macon returned to the SALLY, and the next year the league advanced to Double-A. Manager Dave Bristol led his Cincinnati farmhands to the best record of 1963.

Macon continued the Cincinnati affiliation in 1964, the inaugural season of the renamed Southern League. With fiery Red Davis at the helm, the Peaches finished third behind batting champ Len Boemer (.329 with a league-leading 32 doubles), RBI leader Lee May (.303, 25 HR, 110 RBI), outfielder Gerald Reimer (.309 with 21 homers), and strikeout king Dave Galligan (17–8, 168 Ks).

But the Reds moved their Double-A farm club to Knoxville, which was only 260 miles from Cincinnati down I-75, 300 miles closer than Macon. Montgomery replaced Macon in the SL lineup for 1965. The next year, however, three cities left the SL, and Macon returned to the league as a Philadelphia affiliate. Former big leaguer Andy Seminick was the manager, but the Peaches finished third with a losing record. Southpaw Bill Edgerton led the league in victories and winning percentage (17–4), while outfielder Richard Barry was the doubles leader (.291 with 20 2B).

The SL shrunk to six teams for 1967, and Macon became a Pittsburgh farm club. The Peaches struggled to stay out of the

Entrance to Macon's Luther Williams Field.

cellar, finally finishing fifth. Don Osborne opened the season as a temporary manager, and was replaced on May 10 by Frank Oceak. The best players were All-Star catcher Carl Taylor (.293) and infielder Robert Oliver (.285, 17 HR, 80 RBI). But the Peaches brought only 30,000 fans into Luther Williams Field, and Macon dropped out of baseball for the next 12 seasons.

When the SALLY reorganized as a Class A circuit in 1980, the Macon Peaches enlisted as a co-op team. The Peaches affiliated with Detroit the next year, and with St. Louis in 1983. The Cardinals provided a spectacular player, speedy outfielder Vince Coleman, who won the 1983 batting title (.350) and stole an incredible total of 145 bases in just 113 games. But Macon switched to the Pirates the next year, an affiliation that lasted through the 1987 season. Macon again dropped out of pro ball, but returned to the SALLY in 1991 as an Atlanta farm club.

Year	Record	Pcg.	Finish
1964	75–65	.536	Third
1966	67–73	.479	Fourth
1967	55–85	.393	Fifth

Memphis
(Chicks)

The first professional club in Memphis was the 1877 Red Stockings. Playing home games at Central Park, the Red Stockings won 25 of 31 League Alliance contests before disbanding in July because of "poor press coverage." Amateur baseball dominated the next several seasons, with the Eckfords, the Memphis Blues, the Olympic Parks (who played, of course, at Olympic Park), and the Riversides (who featured a one-armed pitcher named Jimmy Carr—a forerunner of Pete Gray in the 1940s).

Late in 1884 Vic Smith of the Eckfords called a meeting in Charlie Gallina's saloon on Beale Avenue to organize another professional team. Enthusiasts in Nashville formed a similar club, and by the next spring six other cities provided teams which rounded out the original Southern League. The Memphis "Leaguers" used Olympic Park (at the current site of the Memphis Area Transit Authority Bus Terminal) as their home field.

The Leaguers were a losing aggregation, and during the season General Sam Carnes bought the club for $1,200. The 1886 Leaguers showcased pitcher Eddie Knouff, who struck out 390 hitters while winning 24 of the team's 44 victories. The next season first baseman Wally Andrews produced the highest batting average in the history of the Southern League (.413 with 135 runs and 194 hits in 97 G).

In 1888 the club acquired gray uniforms and changed the team name to "Grays." The Grays became the "Giants" a few years later, but also were sometimes called the "Lambs" and, quizzically, the "Fever Germs." The 1894 Giants brought Memphis its only Southern League pennant, but after one more year the club disbanded, missing the last three SL seasons.

But when the Southern Association was organized in 1901 the Memphis "Egyptians" were charter members. SA games were played at Red Elm Park, a 3,000-seat facility built in 1896 and bounded by Edgeway and Dunlap streets and Jefferson and Madison avenues. Although the right field fence was just 301 feet down the foul line, and dead center was a mere 366 feet away, left field was a distant 424 feet down the line.

Memphis won back-to-back pennants in 1903 and 1904. In 1906 righthanded spitballer Glenn Leibhardt set the all-time SALLY record for victories (35–11, with 45 CG in 46 GS), going 9–1 in five iron-man doubleheader performances. Also in 1906, during a pre-season exhibition with the Philadelphia Athletics, the A's eccentric southpaw, Rube Waddell, was being hit by the bush leaguers with one out in the ninth. He ordered all of his teammates except the catcher and one infielder back to the dugout, then struck out the last two batters.

The team was labeled the "Turtles" in 1907 when a turtleback diamond was built up at Red Elm Park. This uninspiring nickname was changed to "Chickasaws" or "Chicks" in 1915 by club president John D. Martin, who emphasized the geographical proximity of the Chickasaw tribe and recalled the undefeated "Chicks" amateur club of college players of 1897. At the end of the 1914 season, the SA team was sold by Frank Coleman to Russell Gardner, who brought in Martin to run the club (Martin would go on to serve as Southern Association president from 1919 through 1938). In 1915 Gardner more than doubled the seating capacity of his ballpark to 6,500. He also changed the name of the facility to Russwood Park, emphasizing the rustic look of the wooden grandstand but undoubtedly influenced by the first four letters of his own name.

In 1921 Russwood Park was expanded to accommodate 11,000 fans, and in that same year the Chicks set an SA record with 104 victories. The pennant-winners were led by RBI champ Polly McLarry (.352, 120 R, 135 RBI), victory leader Oscar Tuero (27–8), outfielders Red Camp (.345), Don Brown (.331) and Gus Williams (.326), Paul Zahniser (22–12) and Otto Merz (19–8). Three years later the Chicks brought the 1924 flag to Memphis behind legendary manager Johnny Dobbs (who engineered another 104-victory season), RBI-doubles-triple-hits champ Roy Carlyle (.368, 233 H, 47 2B, 20 3B, 122 RBI), percentage leader Otto Merz (20–6), and southpaw Cy Warmoth (20–11).

Third baseman-outfielder Tommy Taylor was the batting and RBI leader in 1926 (.383, 129 R, 135 RBI). Memphis native Doc Prothro was appointed player-manager in 1928 and led the Chicks to split-season titles that year and in 1933, and to a pennant in 1930. Prothro departed after the 1934 season, but returned as manager and part-owner in 1942. The 1934 Chicks won the flag with a high-octane hitting attack fueled by batting champ Joe Hutcheson (.380, 29 HR, 113 RBI), outfielder Frank Waddey (.344), and longtime Memphis stars Tex Jeanes (.336, 111 R, 119 RBI) and Frank Brazill (.333, 17 HR, 117 RBI).

Brazill came to Memphis in 1929, played every position except pitcher and catcher, and posted successive averages of .343, .333, .308, .322 and .317, before dipping to .237 during the early part of 1934. Tex Jeanes spent part of five seasons during the 1920s in the big leagues, but played with Birmingham from 1924 through 1926 (.347 in 1925). After trying to pitch for the Giants in 1927, Tex spent the latter part of the season with Memphis (.328), and he was the Chicks' center fielder for the next four years, hitting .373, .344, .336 and .298. Another Memphis regular of this era was Andy Reese, who set the all-time SA record for hits (1,641) and doubles (320) while wearing a Chicks uniform. He first played at Russwood in 1926 (.307), then went up to the Giants for the next four seasons. He returned to Memphis in 1931 and, like Frank Brazill, Tex hit well in each of the remaining years of the 1930s: .341, .336, .324, .281 (with 108 RBIs, the most of 1934), .322, .285, .305, .333 and .322.

In 1932 righthander "Boom-Boom" Beck, who pitched in 13 leagues during a 27-year career, led the SA in victories, percentage and strikeouts (27–6, .818, 139 Ks). Night baseball came to Russwood in 1936. The next year right fielder Coaker Triplett won the hitting title (.356), while big Ted Kluszewski was the batting champ in 1947 (.377). During World War II one-armed Pete Gray came to Memphis and captivated the baseball world. The fleet outfielder played well in 1943 (.289), then had an MVP season in 1944 (.333 with a league-leading 68 steals) and went on to spend the final wartime season with the St. Louis Browns.

With future Hall of Famer Luke Appling at the helm in 1952, Memphis beat New Orleans in a single game to determine the fourth-place playoff team. Then the Chicks stunned first-place Chattanooga with a four-game sweep, defeated Mobile in the finals for the first Memphis playoff title in 12 tries, and capped the season with a Dixie Series triumph over Shreveport (Memphis had lost the postseason classic in 1921, 1924 and 1930). The next year Appling brought Memphis its first pennant finish since 1930, although the Chicks faltered in the playoff opener.

In 1955 Memphis again was battling for first place when player-manager Jack Cassini was severely beaned. The Chicago White Sox, parent club of the Chicks, sent Ted Lyons to take over the club. Lyons, who had just been named to the Hall of Fame as a White Sox pitcher, took the Chicks into Birmingham, trailing the Barons by five and a half games. The Chicks staged a miraculous finish, beating the Barons in eight straight games, including three consecutive one-run decisions in Birmingham. Once again the first-place Chicks were eliminated in the playoff opener. Outfielder Don Nicholas stole an incredible 84 bases for the 1952 champs, while outfielder Ed White led the attack for the pennant-winners both in 1953 (.330) and in 1955 (.342, 17 HR, 107 RBI).

On Easter Sunday, April 17, 1960, the Chicago White Sox and Cleveland Indians played an exhibition game at Russwood. That night the historic old stadium was engulfed in flames that destroyed 16 nearby businesses and badly damaged two hospitals. The Chicks had to shift their opening series to the road while readying Hodges Field, a high school stadium, for professional baseball. But it was only 204 feet down the right field foul line at Hodges, and despite a 40-foot-high screen there were 11 home runs in the home opener against Birmingham. Such homers soon were designated ground rule doubles, but Hodges Field generally was unsatisfactory. The Chicks shifted to another city park, Tobey Park, and even played five "home" games at Golden Park in Columbus, Georgia. Total attendance was less than 49,000, and with no ballpark available the Memphis Chicks disbanded after the 1960 season, just one year before the Southern Association folded.

During this period the Texas League managed to continue operations with only six teams. When the Texas League finally expanded back to eight clubs, Memphis was awarded one of the extra franchises. The Memphis Blues played at new Blues' Stadium at the State Fairgrounds. In 1969 the Blues won the Eastern Division and swept Western Division champion Amarillo to claim the Texas League crown. The next year Memphis repeated as Eastern Division champs but lost the playoffs to the Albuquerque Dodgers. In 1971 Memphis played in the Central Division of the Dixie Association, then returned to the Texas League after the one-year experiment. In 1973 Memphis again won the Eastern Division and beat San Antonio for another Texas League championship.

Dr. Bernard Krauss had purchased the Blues a few years earlier, hoping to bring major league ball to Memphis. After the 1973 season Dr. Krauss acquired an International League franchise, elevating the Blues to Triple-A status. The 1974 Blues won the Southern Division with the best record in the IL, but lost in postseason play to Rochester. After a losing season in 1975 produced only 75,000 fans, Dr. Krauss was forced to sell the club. The Blues made another IL playoff appearance in 1976, but club debts rose to $400,000, and the franchise was returned to the league.

One year later, Avron Fogelman placed a Double-A team named the Memphis Chicks in the Southern League. Blues' Stadium was renamed Tim McCarver Stadium, after the Memphis native who sold peanuts at Russwood, played for the Chicks in 1960, and went on to become a standout big league catcher. (McCarver was deeply appreciative but commented that, "I'm just glad they didn't want to name it Tim McCarver *Memorial* Stadium.") Pete Gray was present to throw out the first ball of 1978. "We expected a couple of thousands fans to attend the first Memphis Chicks game of the new era," reminisced Fogelman, "and ended up with over 10,000!" Seating capacity was only 6,900, but the outfield was roped off and everyone was admitted. Fogelman was determined to expand the stadium to 10,000, and succeeded within two years.

Memphis fans in 1978 were treated to an MVP performance by home run champ Eddie Gates (.315 with 25 homers). The next year DH Dave Hostetler (.270, 20 HR, 114 RBI) led the SL in RBIs as Memphis defeated Montgomery in a one-game playoff to determine the Western Division winner in the first half. The Chicks lost the division championship to Nashville, but came back to win the Western Division in 1980 before falling to Charlotte in the playoff finals. The best players were stolen base champ Anthony Johnson (.299 with 60 steals), who also starred for the '79 Chicks (.292), and All-Star outfielder Pat Rooney (.280, 28 HR, 102 RBI), who pounded 15 home runs in July.

In 1980 the Chicks made the playoffs for the third year in a row behind percentage leader Bob Tenenini (10–2), reliever Tom Gorman (12–9 in 52 appearances), All-Star shortstop Bryan Little (.293), and infielder-DH Jerry Fry (.303 with 24 homers). The Chicks lost the divisional playoff to Memphis, then did not make another postseason appearance for seven years. But in 1982 outfielder Michael Fuentes (.267, 37 HR, 115 RBI) was the home run and RBI champ, and in 1986 the greatest attraction since Pete Gray came to town: football star Bo Jackson spent his first several weeks in professional baseball wearing a Chicks uniform (.277 in 53 games).

Outfielder-first baseman Matt Winters won the 1988 home run and RBI titles (.275, 25 HR, 91 RBI) and was named Most Valuable Player. Winters led the Chicks to first place in the West during the second half, but Chattanooga won the divisional playoff. In 1990, however, Memphis beat Birmingham for a Western Division title, then claimed its first SL championship by downing Orlando in the finals, three games to two. Manager Jeff Cox employed the talents of MVP first baseman Jeff Conine (.320, 15 HR, 95 RBI), All-Star third-sacker Sean Berry (.292), versatile infielder Stewart Cole (.308), All-Star outfielder Bobby Moore (.303), and righthanded starter-reliever Hector Wagner (12–4 with a 2.03 ERA in 40 games).

The 1993 Double-A All-Star Game was held in Memphis. Opposing celebrity managers aligned Larry King for the National

The 1990 SL championship trophy, displayed in the office of the Memphis Chicks, which overlooks right field at Tim McCarver Stadium.

Leaguers against Bob Costas for the American Leaguers; King and Costas were in uniform, and King's squad won, 12–7. David Hersh, majority owner of the Chicks, chose the All-Star pre-game luncheon to announce that Costas had joined his ownership group, alongside such other celebrities as Ron Howard, Maury Povich and Tim McCarver. The 1993 Chicks featured outfielder Adam Casillas (.304) and Les Norman (.291 with 17 homers), righthander Mike Fyhrie (11–4), third baseman Joe Randa (.295), and first-sacker Joe Vitiello (.288). Despite a ninth-place finish, these players put on enough of a show to maintain the Chicks' customary strong attendance (230,000).

Year	Record	Pcg.	Finish
1978	71–73	.493	Fifth

1979	82–62	.569	Third (lost opener)
1980	83–61	.576	Second (won Western Division, lost finals)
1981	77–66	.538	Third (lost opener)
1982	70–74	.486	Sixth
1983	61–85	.418	Tenth
1984	71–75	.486	Seventh
1985	65–79	.451	Ninth
1986	69–75	.479	Ninth
1987	72–71	.503	Fourth
1988	79–64	.552	Third (lost opener)
1989	59–84	.413	Tenth
1990	73–61	.507	Fifth (won Western Division and finals)
1991	61–83	.424	Ninth
1992	71–73	.493	Fourth
1993	63–77	.450	Ninth

Mobile
(Athletics, White Sox)

In 1887 Mobile was one of six cities which fielded teams for the third season of the Southern League. The Swamp Angels tottered to a 5–19 start, however, then dropped out of the league. Mobile returned for the 1889 season as the Bears, but the SL was shaky and disbanded in mid-summer. Mobile became a Southern League regular during the 1890s, playing as the Bluebirds in 1894 and as the Blackbirds in 1892, 1898, and 1899.

During the 1905 season, Natchez of the Class D Cotton States League moved its franchise to Mobile in July. Mobile won the Cotton States pennant the next two years, then joined the Southern Association in 1908. Usually a second-division team, Mobile bottomed out in 1917 (34–117), finishing 62½ games off the pace. But in 1922 the Bears finally won a Southern Association pennant and dumped powerful Fort Worth in the Dixie Series, starring catcher John Schulte (.357) and hurlers Oscar Fuhr (22–14), Charles Fulton (20–14) and Dutch Henry (19–4). The next year Fuhr again was a standout (23–14), Tommy Long was the victory leader (27–7), Emil Huhn won the batting crown (.345), and Denny Williams was the run and hit titlist (.333, 129 R, 212 H), but Mobile finished second.

In 1930 the Bears finished last (40–112), and the club was sold to Robert Allen, who moved the franchise to Knoxville.

The 1922 Mobile Bears, champions of the Southern Association.
— Courtesy Erik Overbey Collection
University of South Alabama Archives

Mobile played in the Class B Southeastern League in 1932, but the circuit folded on May 23. The Southeastern League reorganized in 1937, and the Mobile Skippers played until wartime conditions halted operations after the 1942 season. The Skippers won the Shaughnessy playoffs in 1939, then finished first and again claimed the playoff title in 1941.

The Bears once more became a part of the Southern Association in 1944, when Knoxville's club was transferred to Mobile on July 4. The following year the Bears won the playoffs behind catcher Harry Chozen (.353), righthander Bill Thomas (20–12), first-sacker John Douglas (.328), outfielder-first baseman Ted Mueller (.324), shortstop Bill White (.324) and outfielder George Shuba (.320, 114 R, 103 RBI).

In 1947 Mobile finished first by half a game, then again won the playoffs. Outfielder Cal Abrams led the SA in runs and walks (.324, 134 R, 124 W), lanky Chuck Connors played first, outfielder George Shuba returned to pace the Bears in homers and RBIs (.288, 21 HR, 108 RBI), and ERA champ Bob Hall (18–8, 2.80) headed a deep pitching staff. Cal Abrams starred again the next year (.337, 120 R, 154 W), and in 1949 George Shuba (.328 with 28 homers) led the Bears to the playoff finals.

The Bears were finalists again in 1952, then won the 1955 playoffs and recorded a Dixie Series triumph over Shreveport.

The '55 champs boasted ERA titlist Ralph Mauriello (18–8, 2.76) and RBI leader Jim Gentile (.290, 28 HR, 109 RBI). The next year the Bears again made the playoffs behind the ERA champ, Bill Dailey (15–8, 3.18), and the RBI king, Gordy Coleman (.316, 27 HR, 118 RBI).

In 1958 manager Mel McGaha guided Mobile to the playoff finals, and the following season McGaha's Bears won the play-offs. Gordy Coleman recorded a Triple Crown (.353, 30 HR, 110 RBI), Bear veteran John Waters led the SA in runs (.301, 103 R), and second baseman Ken Kuhn added a strong bat to the lineup (.305). Bill Dailey, who pitched for the Bears for five seasons, won another ERA crown (11–5, 2.41), while Wynn Hawkins (14–9, 2.55) and southpaws Walt Seward (9–4, 2.88) and Carl Mathias (17–9 with a league-leading 183 Ks) rounded out the top four SA hurlers in the ERA race.

The Southern Association was disbanded after the 1961 sea-son, and Mobile's 11,000-seat Hartwell Field — also known as League Park and Monroe Park — fell into disuse. But Birmingham dropped out of the new Southern League following the 1965 sea-son, and the Athletics moved their SL affiliation to Mobile. John McNamara managed the Mobile Athletics to the 1966 pennant, finishing nine and a half games ahead of second-place Asheville and 20 or more games in front of the rest of the league. Right-hander Blue Moon Odom was impressive in 19 starts (12–5), fu-ture Oakland manager Tony LaRussa was a promising second baseman (.294 in 51 G), southpaw Bill Edgerton led the SL in victories and winning percentage (17–4), and third-sacker Sal Bando (.277) began to develop the skills of a future big leaguer.

Mobile's inaugural season in the SL had produced a champi-onship, but A's owner Charlie Finley moved his Double-A club back to Birmingham, where McNamara promptly won another pennant. Despite delivering the second-best attendance of 1966 (53,000 at a time when most minor league totals were modest), Mobile again was without baseball. In 1970, however, the South-ern League expanded to eight teams, and Mobile rejoined the circuit as a White Sox farm club.

Tom Saffell was named manager of the Mobile White Sox, but the team was weak and Larry Sherry finished the season at the helm. Sherry doubled up as a reliever (3–4 with a 2.45 ERA in 26 G), and lefthander John Bauer also provided solid relief (3–2 in 43 G). Southpaw Mike Baldwin was effective as a starter for part of the season (5–3, 1.96), and so was righty Eddie Smith (5–6, 1.83) and lefty Jim Magnuson (5–5, 1.94). The only strong hitter was outfielder Ossie Blanco (.299 in 54 G), as the Sox finished next-to-last in team hitting (.225) and last in home runs (a meager 40). Mobile also was next-to-last in the standings and in attendance (35,775), and the White Sox moved their affiliation to Asheville for 1971. Mobile has been out of Organized Baseball since 1970, but in recent years there have been increasing efforts to secure another SL franchise and revive the Bears. Although it will be necessary to finance and construct a new stadium, Mobile is the frontrunner city to become the permanent home of the SL Nashville Xpress in 1995.

Year	Record	Pcg.	Finish
1966	88–52	.629	First
1970	59–78	.431	Seventh

Montgomery
(Rebels)

Montgomery participated in the old Southern League during the 1890s: as the Lambs (1892), Colts (1893), Grays (1895–96), and Senators (1898–99). Chattanooga's Southern Association club became the Montgomery Black Sox in 1903, and player-manager Lew Whistler led the SA in home runs (.305 with 18 homers). The Black Sox nickname was cast aside in favor of Senators for 1904, but the team sank to the cellar. The 1905 Senators, however, rose to second place behind batting champ Carleton Molesworth (.312). The team was renamed the Climbers in 1909, the Billikens in 1911, and the Rebels in 1912. There was another runner-up finish in 1911, as second baseman Del Pratt led the SA in hitting and runs (.316, 96 R) and outfielder Pete Daley was the co-leader in runs scored (.306, 96 R). But after a dismal last-place season in 1914, (54–100), Montgomery dropped out of Organized Baseball.

The Montgomery Rebels tried the SALLY in 1916, but the club folded on June 21. Montgomery did not field another team for a decade, when the Lions joined the Class B Southeastern

League in 1926. Batting champ John Kloza (.380) led the Lions to a second-half title, although Montgomery lost the playoff series. In 1928 the Lions again won the second half, then went on to down Pensacola in the championship series.

The Southeastern League disbanded after the 1930 season, but tried again in 1932. The circuit folded on May 23, with the Montgomery Capitals in the cellar. The Southeastern League reorganized in 1937, this time with the Montgomery Bombers in the cellar. After another last-place finish in 1938, the Bombers changed their name to Rebels. The 1942 Rebels charged to the pennant, finishing first by 12 1/2 games, then beating Anniston and Jackson to win the playoffs. The Southeastern then halted operations for the duration of the war, but on July 9, 1943, Chattanooga's Southern Association club transferred to Montgomery.

Montgomery sat out the 1944 and 1945 seasons, then the Rebels became part of the revamped Southeastern League in 1946. The Rebels made the 1946 playoffs, but lost the opening round. In the 1947 playoffs the Rebels beat first-place Jackson, four games to three, then outlasted second-place Gadsden, also four games to three, to win the finals. In 1948 the Rebels finished first by nine and a half games, then defeated Anniston and Jackson to claim back-to-back playoff titles.

For decades professional baseball in Montgomery had been played at the Cramton Bowl, a stadium just south of Madison Avenue that also was heavily utilized for football. In 1949 the Rebels moved across Madison Avenue to Paterson Field, a 6,000-seat ballpark with a symmetrical outfield (330 feet down the lines and 380 feet from home to center), a covered grandstand, and generous parking.

Montgomery reached the 1950 playoffs but fell to first-place Pensacola in the opener. When the Southeastern League disbanded permanently after the season, the Rebels moved up to the Class A SALLY. Montgomery took first place and won the 1951 playoffs behind home run champ Dick Greco (.310, 33 HR, 103 RBI), RBI king William Johnson (.274, 12 HR, 107 RBI), run and walk leader Banks McDowell (.299, 121 R, 148 W), and outfielder Len Morrison (.310, 16 HR, 104 RBI).

In 1952 Greco led the SALLY in homers and RBIs (.298, 24 HR, 135 RBI), and Morrison also returned (.308, 23 HR, 116

RBI) to power the renamed Montgomery Grays to another play-off crown. Charlie Metro managed both championship clubs, but the Metro magic vanished in 1953 as the Grays dropped into the cellar. Montgomery reverted to the Rebels nickname the next year, and the 1955 Rebels reached the playoff finals behind hit leader George Toepfer (.321) and fleet outfielder Albie Pearson (.305 with a league-leading 132 walks).

Mired in last place in 1956, Montgomery's club moved to Knoxville on June 18. On July 14, however, the last-place Little Rock team of the Southern Association was transferred to Montgomery for the remainder of the season. In 1957 the Montgomery Rebels joined the Class D Alabama-Florida League, posting the best record in the six-team circuit. The Rebels finished first again in 1959, plunged to the cellar the next year, and wound up last in 1962, the league's final season.

Montgomery had no team for three years, but in 1965 the Rebels became part of the Southern League as a Detroit affiliate. Southpaw Fred Fisher (14-6) was the percentage titlist, and in 1966 righthander George Korince won the strikeout crown (9-8 with 183 Ks in 182 IP). The 1967 Rebels rose to second place behind victory and strikeout leader Dick Drago (15-10, 134 Ks) and RBI champ Barry Morgan (.257, 12 HR, 87 RBI). Frank Carswell was voted Manager of the Year, and in 1968 he again brought the Rebels in second, including a 16-game winning streak. Montgomery had the SL's best pitching staff, featuring righthanders James Brown (14-9), Ronnie Chandler (12-8), and George Korince, who returned to win another strikeout crown (13-7, 146 Ks). The offense was led by home run champ Wayne Redmond (.260 with 26 homers), repeat RBI titlist Barry Morgan (.273, 18 HR, 91 RBI), and run leader Paul Pavelko (.254, 93 R).

On July 1, 1969, first-sacker George Kalafatis (.254 with 21 homers) blasted four home runs in one game. There was a scintillating pennant race in 1970, as Montgomery (79-60, .568) lost the flag to Columbus (78-59, .569) by an eyelash. Once again the Rebels boasted the league's best pitching staff: righthander Chip Swanson (12-5), who fired the only perfect game in SL history on August 14 against Savannah; percentage titlist Lerrin LaGrow (11-4); strikeout and victory leader Bill Gilbreth (12-11, 192 Ks); and fellow southpaw James Foor (10-6). During the 1971 Dixie

Built in 1949, Paterson Field hosted SL baseball in Montgomery from 1965 through 1980, and was the home of championship clubs in 1972, 1973, 1975, 1976 and 1977.

Association season, Montgomery played in the six-team Eastern Division, finishing in the middle of the pack.

Manager Fred Hatfield guided Montgomery to the Western Division crown in 1972, then led the Rebels to a three-game sweep over Asheville for the SL championship. The offense was built around All-Star outfielder Marvin Lane (.312) and Robert Robinson (.249, 28 HR, 94 RBI), first-sacker Joe Staton (.289) and All-Star catcher Gene Lamont (.273). The SL's stingiest mound corps featured southpaw Dan Bootchack (12–6) and right-handers Danny Fife (14–7) and Steve Grilli (11–3).

In 1973 Hatfield improved on the previous year's success, repeating as Western Division champ with the best record in the SL, and beating Jacksonville in the playoffs, three games to one. There were three key returnees: All-Star first baseman Joe Staton (.282), and hurlers Steve Grilli (12–7) and Chip Swanson (10–4). Swanson twirled six shutouts, an all-time SL record that was matched in 1980 by Rebel southpaw George Cappuzello. Right-hander David Lemanczyk pitched four games late in the season (3–1), including an August 4 no-hitter over Asheville.

Under field general Les Moss, the 1975 Rebels won the Western Division, then swept Orlando in three games to claim another SL championship. Ebullient righthander Mark Fidrych had his final tuneup (2–0 in 7 G) before taking Detroit by storm. Southpaw Bob Sykes (14–10) was the mainstay of the pitching staff, while the offense was sparked by two All-Stars, outfielder John Valle (.283 with 23 homers) and third-sacker Philip Manlowski (.283).

The next year, under a changed format, Les Moss guided the Rebels to the second-half lead with the top record in the SL, then beat Chattanooga for another Western Division crown. In the finals the Rebels once again defeated Orlando for a second consecutive pennant. The league's best offense was triggered by first baseman-outfielder Tim Corcoran (.309), All-Star shortstop Glenn Gulliver (.277 in 51 G), and outfielder Dan Gonzales (.292). The pitching staff featured all-time SL ERA champ Dave Rozema (12–4, 1.57) and percentage leader Dennis DeBarr (11–2 in 43 appearances).

The Rebels were even better in 1977. All-Star second baseman Lou Whitaker was the run titlist (.280, 38 SB, 81 R), All-Star shortstop Alan Trammel was the triples leader (.291, 19 3B, 78 R) lefthander Gary Christenson led the league in winning percentage (13–4), and new field general Ed Brinkman was named Manager of the Year. For the second season in a row the Rebels ran up the league's best mark, winning both halves in the West and being awarded the division title with a 24½-game lead over second-place Chattanooga. Montgomery beat Eastern Division winner Jacksonville, two games to none, to claim an unprecedented third consecutive championship. The Rebels had won the Southern League crown in five of the last six seasons.

The Rebels finally tailed off the next year, then dropped to the Western cellar in 1979, despite the play of All-Star infielder Manny Castillo (.307 in 74 G). The 1980 Rebels featured All-Star DH Eddie Gates (.280, 25 HR, 91 RBI) and righthander Larry Pashnick (13–4). But there was another losing season, and attendance was unimpressive (91,168) compared with Nashville (575,676), Memphis (322,037), and four other clubs over 100,000. Detroit moved its SL operation to Birmingham, and Montgomery has not fielded another professional team. But Paterson Field is handsomely maintained and hosts the NCAA Division II World Series, and perhaps one day the pros will return to Montgomery.

Year	Record	Pcg.	Finish
1965	63–74	.460	Sixth
1966	66–72	.478	Fifth

1967	80–58	.580	Second
1968	80–57	.584	Second
1969	62–73	.459	Fifth
1970	79–60	.568	Second
1971	73–69	.514	Third
1972	78–61	.561	Third
1973	80–58	.580	First
1974	61–76	.445	Seventh
1975	73–61	.545	Second
1976	81–56	.591	First
1977	86–51	.628	First
1978	67–77	.465	Seventh
1979	62–81	.434	Eighth
1980	68–76	.472	Sixth

Nashville
(Sounds, Xpress)

Baseball was introduced to Nashville in 1862 by soldiers of the Union Army of occupation. There were spirited amateur games and enthusiastic crowds, which led to the support of various semi-pro and professional clubs. Baseball, along with other recreational activities, centered around the Sulphur Spring Bottom north of the state capital. A low-lying area featuring a sulphur spring and salt lick, the Bottom became a trading, watering and picnic spot in the earliest pioneer times, and during the 1860s it was natural to lay out baseball grounds. In September 1867 the "Nashville and Phoenix Base Ball Clubs" played a three-game series to determine the county champion, arousing great interest and controversy because of the "marked unfairness and partiality on the part of the Umpire."

In 1885 Cap Anson brought his Chicago White Stockings to Nashville for three weeks of spring training at the Sulphur Spring Bottom. Part of the regimen, of course, called for the players to "take the waters." Thus energized, the White Stockings charged to the National League pennant with a .776 winning percentage (87–25).

That same year was the inaugural season of the Southern League, and Nashville first baseman Leonard Sowders (.309) won the first SL batting title. The Nashville Americans returned for another year of SL play in 1886, the Blues participated in 1887, the Tigers represented the city in 1893–94, and the Seraphs tried for an elusive pennant in 1895. Nashville could not win an SL flag, and dropped out of the league after the 1895 season.

When the Southern Association was formed in 1901, Newt Fisher of Nashville was a primary organizer, and he managed the Volunteers to the first two SA pennants. Pitcher-outfielder Hugh Hill led the Vols to the 1902 flag with the highest batting average in SA history (.416) and the best record on the pitching staff (21–11). The right fielder on both championship teams was Doc Wiseman, who played for the Vols from 1901 through 1911. He usually hit in the .250s, but he was so adept at traversing the hilly right field at Athletic Park that he was nicknamed "Goat."

During Wiseman's tenure as a Vol, the poetic sportswriter Grantland Rice renamed Sulphur Spring Bottom the Sulphur *Dell*, because it offered easier rhymes. The new name stuck, and soon another pennant flew over Sulphur Dell as the 1916 Vols won behind manager-shortstop Roy Ellam and righthander Shotgun Rogers (24–12 with a perfect game).

There was not another championship for more than two decades, but the Volunteers entertained Nashville fans with awesome hitting displays. Vol hitters collected a record 18 SA batting championships, including five straight during 1951–55 and nine out of 11 during 1948–58. The only three batters in SA history to hit .400 were Vols: Hill in 1902 (.416), left fielder Phil Weintraub in 1934 (.401), and first baseman Les Fleming (.414) in 1941. Legendary minor league hitter Moose Clabaugh won back-to-back titles in 1931 (.378) and 1932 (.382).

In 1926 the diamond and grandstand at Sulphur Dell were switched from the northeast corner of the block to the southwest, producing an even hillier and shorter (262 feet) right field. Left-handed sluggers took such advantage of the short porch that pitchers called the ballpark "Suffer Hell."

In 1930 first baseman Jim Poole set new SA marks for homers and RBIs (.364, 50 HR, 167 RBI), while teammate Jay Partridge was close behind (.361, 40 HR, 127 RBI). A 30-foot screen was added to the 16-foot fence in right, but lefthanded power hitters continued to compile eye-popping numbers: outfielder "Double" Joe Dwyer (.383, 65 2B, 117 RBI), who set the all-time SA record for doubles in 1936; outfielders Charles Workman (.353, 52 HR,

182 RBI), who broke Poole's 1930 records, and Charlie Gilbert (.362, 42 HR, 155 RBI) in 1948; catcher Carl Sawatski (.360, 45 HR, 153 RBI), outfielder Babe Barna (.341, 42 HR, 138 RBI), and first baseman Tookie Gilbert (.334, 33 HR, 122 RBI) in 1949; first baseman Jack Harshman (.251, 47 HR, 141 RBI) in 1951. Most spectacular of all was outfielder Bob Lennon (.345, 64 HR, 161 RBI), who won a Triple Crown in 1954 and set the all-time SA home run mark (42 of his homers sailed over The Fence).

The father of heavy-hitting Charlie and Tookie Gilbert was Larry Gilbert, a former SA batting champ who had managed New Orleans to five SA pennants in 15 seasons. He moved to Nashville in 1939 and managed the Vols for 10 years, producing first-place finishes in 1940, 1943, 1944 and 1948, six straight playoff titles in 1939–1940–1941–1942–1943–1944, and Dixie Series championships in 1940–1941–1942. Another Gilbert-built team, the 1949 Vols, finished first, won the playoffs, and took another Dixie Series.

All of the power hitting in the Sulphur Dell seemed to inspire power pitching: 16 Nashville hurlers, more than from any other team, won SA strikeout titles. Other standout pitching performances were turned in by Boots Poffenberger in 1940 (26–9), Garman Mallory in 1949 (20–4), Bob Schultz in 1950 (25–6), and former lefthanded slugger turned lefthanded pitcher Jack Harshman in 1953 (23–7, and .315 with 12 homers as a hitter). Despite these and other mound heroics, in the long history of the Southern Association, no pitcher who called "Suffer Hell" home ever managed to win an ERA title.

After the SA folded in 1961, Sulphur Dell was empty for one season. When the SALLY went up to Class AA in 1963, Nashville fielded a team, but the Vols finished last and attendance was poor. The Vols disbanded, Sulphur Dell was razed, and today the historic site is used for parking.

But the city's baseball tradition was too strong to die, and in 1978 Nashville joined the Southern League as an expansion franchise. The energetic and innovative Larry Schmittou brought professional baseball back to Nashville at a time when the home of country-western music was reaching new heights as an entertainment haven. Schmittou consciously identified his team, the "Sounds," with the city's entertainment scene, and C & W stars such as Larry Gatlin; Jerry Reed, Conway Twitty and Richard

Sterben (bass singer of the Oak Ridge Boys) became Sounds stockholders. Prior to a 1989 game the author watched the Oak Ridge Boys photograph an album cover with the ballpark as a backdrop. Fans were able to visit with the singers and take photos, and during pregame ceremonies the Oaks stood at home plate to sing the national anthem. Indeed, through the years "The Star Spangled Banner" has been delivered by the Oaks, Larry Gatlin, the Statler Brothers, Lee Greenwood, Loretta Lynn, Charlie McCoy, Boots Randolph, Charlie Pride, Lynn Anderson, Tiny Tim, and a host of other stars. From 1978 through 1984 Schmittou made the Nashville Sounds the Southern League's most glamorous and successful franchise.

Herschel Greer Stadium was built south of downtown at the foot of St. Cloud Hill in Fort Negley Park (Fort Negley atop the hill was a key point in Nashville's Civil War fortifications). In each of Nashville's seven SL seasons, Herschel Greer Stadium hosted the circuit's leading attendance. Although there was little to cheer about on the field in 1978 (strikeout leader Jay Howell fanned 173 hitters in 166 innings, but the Sounds finished a weak ninth), 380,000 fans turned out, more than double the total of the second-highest attendance. Over the next six years the Sounds made the playoffs each season, winning three division championships and two playoff titles, and finishing first twice. For four straight seasons, 1979–1982, attendance soared past the half-million mark.

The 1979 Sounds beat Memphis for the Western Division title, then defeated Columbus for the SL championship. Outfielder Paul Householder (.283, 20 HR, 95 RBI) led the league in fielding, Duane Walker (.303) led the SL with 15 triples, Scott Brown was the ERA champ (9–2, 2.40), and righthanded reliever Geoffrey Combe was the save leader (54 G, 27 SV, 2.07 ERA).

In 1980 Nashville changed affiliations from the Reds to the Yankees, and manager Stump Merrill guided the Sounds to back-to-back first-place finishes. The 1980 Sounds lost the opening round of playoffs, but showcased home run-RBI king Steve Balboni (.301, 34 HR, 122 RBI), ERA champ Andy McGaffigan (15–5, 2.38), and All-Stars Buck Showalter (.324) and Pat Tabler (.296). The next year Nashville won another Western Division title behind first-sacker Don Mattingly (.316), fleet outfielder Willie McGee (.322), run leader Thad Wilborn (.295, 106 RBI),

Herschel Greer Stadium, with the hilltop in the background where the ruins of Fort Negley are located. The Nashville Sounds played SL baseball here from 1978 through 1984, leading the league in attendance in each season. The 18,000-seat stadium welcomed SL crowds for the Nashville Xpress in 1993 and 1994.

and strikeout-complete game champ Jim Werly (13–11, 193 K, 18 CG in 28 GS).

Success continued in 1982 as the Sounds defeated Knoxville for a second consecutive Western Division crown, then beat Jacksonville to claim another SL championship. Buck Showalter was back in Nashville for another strong season (.294), outfielder Brian Dayett provided power (.280, 34 HR, 96 RBI), Stefan Wever led the SL in victories, ERA and strikeouts (16–6, 191 K, 2.78), and fellow righthander Clay Christianson was the victory co-leader (16–8). The next two years saw the Sounds fall in the opening round of playoffs, although fans enjoyed the play of right-hander Tim Burke (12–4) in 1983, and of 1984 home run champ Dan Pasqua (.243, 33 RH, 91 RBI).

In 1984 Larry Schmittou purchased the Evansville Triplets of the American Association, and in 1985 moved the Triple-A franchise to Nashville. Nashville's SL franchise was placed in Huntsville, but the Southern League later would make a unique reappearance at Herschel Greer Stadium.

Nashville became a solid member of the American Association, winning an Eastern Division crown in 1990 and continuing to enjoy excellent attendance. In 1993, when Charlotte moved up from the Southern League to Triple-A and a proposed transfer to New Orleans was blocked shortly before the season began, the SL suddenly had a homeless franchise.

With typical daring, Schmittou offered Herschel Greer Stadium for the 1993 season. The Nashville Xpress would schedule SL home games during Sounds road trips, offering pro ball on a daily basis to local fans. Schmittou reasoned that the additional expense of running the stadium every day would total about $500,000, requiring an overall attendance of 600,000 to 650,000 to break even. The Double-A Xpress drew almost 179,000, while the Triple-A Sounds enjoyed crowds adding up to nearly 439,000, bringing Nashville's total 1993 attendance to more than 617,000. The Xpress, a Minnesota farm club, enjoyed a winning record behind run leader Rich Becker (.287, 93 R), Pitcher of the Year Oscar Munoz (11–4), and second baseman Brian Raabe (.286). The Xpress won the first half in the West, but fell to the eventual SL champions, Birmingham, in the playoff opener. Schmittou was satisfied, and it was decided to keep the Xpress in Nashville for 1994 while the search for a permanent home for the SL club continued.

Year	Record	Pcg.	Finish
1978	64–77	.454	Ninth
1979	83–61	.576	Second (won Western Division and finals)
1980	97–46	.678	First (lost opener)
1981	81–62	.566	First (won Western Division, lost finals)
1982	77–67	.535	Second (won Western Division and finals)
1983	88–58	.603	Second (lost opener)
1984	74–73	.503	Fifth (lost opener)
1993	72–70	.507	Fifth (lost opener)

Orlando
(Twins, O-Twins, Sun Rays)

In 1919 the Orlando Caps originated professional baseball in the central Florida city by becoming charter members of the Class D Florida State League. The circuit moved up to Class C for 1921–24, reverted to Class D in 1925–28, 1936–41 and 1946–62, then advanced to Class A status in 1963. Orlando participated in the Florida State League during each of these seasons and for 10 more years, until joining the Southern League in 1973. The city also placed a team in the Florida East Coast League in 1942, when the Florida State League did not operate, but the Class D circuit folded on May 14, with Orlando atop the standings. Through the Florida State years the team nickname changed to Tigers (1921), Bulldogs (1922–24), Colts (1926–28), Gulls (1937), Senators (1938–42, 1946–54), C. B.'s (1955), Sertomas (1956), Flyers (1957–58), Dodgers (1959–61), and Twins or O-Twins (1963–72).

In December 1920 Joe Tinker, a future Hall of Famer ("Tinker-to-Evers-to-Chance"), took over the Orlando club as owner-manager. He immediately won a pennant, and the wooden ballpark, built in 1914, was named Tinker Field in his honor. A popular site for big league spring training, Tinker Field was rebuilt and expanded for $50,000 in 1923. In 1940 the WPA allocated $85,000 to construct a football stadium—the current Citrus Bowl—just east of the ballpark, and another $30,000 was provided to renovate Tinker Field. A concrete grandstand cost $310,000 in 1963, and new lights added another $67,000. The Washington Senators made Tinker Field their spring training site in 1936, a practice continued when the franchise became the Minnesota Twins in 1961, and 500 seats from Washington's Griffith Stadium were placed atop the new grandstand at Tinker Field.

During the pregame of a spring training exhibition contest at Tinker Field between the Senators and Athletics, Clark Griffith and Connie Mack staged a race on the basepaths. The two legendary baseball men were in their eighties, but Griffith started at first and Mack at third, then headed for home. The venerable

Architect's drawing of Orlando's proposed new football stadium, which was built by the WPA in 1940 and which today is the much larger Citrus Bowl. Tinker Field may be seen to the right, or west.

gentlemen arrived at the plate simultaneously in a pre-planned tie to please the crowd.

The Orlando Bulldogs won the 1923 pennant behind batting and home run champ Al Green (.382 with 14 homers). The Orlando Senators claimed the 1940 playoff title with a four-game sweep over Sanford. In 1946, when the Florida State League reorganized after the war, the Senators won the pennant and the playoffs, a triumph only slightly tainted when catcher Ike Seone was suspended for the rest of the season after assaulting an umpire during a July game.

The 1948 Senators took the flag behind Charles Heinbaugh, who led the league in batting, hits, and runs (.338, 182 H, 129 R). Batting champ Bruce Barnes (.372) led the Senators to another pennant in 1950, and the next year Gene Oravetz was the hitting and run leader (.364, 122 R). Orlando won back-to-back pennants in 1954 and 1955, then fell into the cellar for the next two seasons. Losing teams continued to play at Tinker Field, and following meager attendance (13,554) in 1961, Orlando dropped out of the league.

The Orlando Twins returned to the Class A Florida State League for 1963. In 1967 the O-Twins won the Eastern Division, but lost the championship playoff to St. Petersburg. The next year manager Ralph Rowe again led the O-Twins to a division title, and this time Orlando won the playoffs. In 1969 Harry Warner, who had managed the O-Twins from 1963 through 1965, guided the O-Twins to a third consecutive division crown, before dropping the finals to Miami. Early Wynn managed the O-Twins in 1972, the same year the old pitcher was named to the Hall of Fame.

The next season the O-Twins, again under the tutelage of Harry Warner, joined the Southern League. Outfielder Ed Palat (.285 with 20 homers) made the All-Star Team, but Orlando had a losing record in its inaugural SL season. In 1974 the O-Twins enjoyed a winning record under home run and RBI champ Bob Gorinski (.278, 23 HR, 10 RBI), homer co-leader Mike Poepping (.262, 23 HR, 75 RBI), and walk titlist Jack Maloof (.300, 105 W).

Maloof returned in 1975 and again led the SL in walks (.317, 105 W), DH-first baseman Jim Obradovich was the home run and RBI king (.229, 27 HR, 74 RBI), while righthanders Bob Maneely (14–8) and Mike Seberger (13–7) paced the pitching staff. Orlando won the Eastern Division with the best record in the SL, but lost the championship playoff to Montgomery. Dick Phillips was voted Manager of the Year.

In 1976 Jim Obradovich was back to lead the league again in homers and RBIs, as well as runs and walks (.265, 21 HR, 68 RBI, 84 R, 113 W). Manager Dick Phillips also returned to guide the O-Twins to the second-half title in the East. Orlando beat Charlotte to win another division crown, but again lost to Montgomery in the finals. The next year the O-Twins posted the best record in the East, but did not win either half and missed the playoffs.

Although the 1978 Twins won the first half in the East, Savannah prevailed in the division playoff. Righthander Tom Sheehan was the SL victory leader (17–8), while a fine offense was sparked by DH-first baseman Frank Estes (.323), first-sacker Jesus Vega (.297 in 73 G), and All-Star outfielder Tom Sain (.293).

The star of 1981 was MVP catcher Tim Laudner, who blasted his way to the all-time Southern League home run record (.284, 42 HR, 104 RBI). The O-Twins led the SL in homers (167) behind

Laudner, All-Star third baseman Gary Gaetti (.270, 30 HR, 93 RBI), All-Star outfielder Randy Bush (.290, 22 HR, 94 RBI), and outfielder-first baseman Scott Ullger (.269, 29 HR, 87 RBI). Manager of the Year Tom Kelly used this high-powered attack to win the SL championship, beating Savannah for the Eastern Division crown, then downing Nashville, three games to one, in the finals.

In 1984 DH-third baseman Stan Holmes (.280, 25 HR, 101 RBI) won the RBI title, while southpaw Bryan Oelkers (16–11) was the victory co-leader. The next year DH-first baseman Mark Funderburk was the home run and RBI champ (.283, 34 HR, 116 RBI), while run and hit leader Alexis Marte (.320, 117 R), outfielder Mark Davidson (.302, 25 HR, 106 RBI) and shortstop Bob Ralston (.301) contributed to the SL's most productive offense. In 1986 the attack was triggered by first baseman Gene Larkin (.321, 15 HR, 104 RBI), third-sacker Jeff Trout (.321), and second baseman Doug Palmer (.317).

Orlando adopted the nickname Sun Rays in 1989, and celebrated by making the playoffs for the first time since 1981. The Sun Rays fell to Greenville in the divisional playoffs, but shortstop Scott Leius (.303) won the batting title, righthander reliever Pete Delkus claimed the ERA crown (1.87 in 76 G), first baseman Paul Sorrento was the RBI champ (.255, 27 HR, 112 RBI), and southpaw Mark Guthrie logged a superb half-season (8–3 with 103 Ks in 96 IP and a 1.97 ERA).

Manager Ron Gardenhire again led the Sun Rays to the playoffs the next year. Lefthanders Dennis Neagle (12–3), Doug Simons (15–12), and Brian Barnes (13–7 with 213 Ks in 201 IP) headed a strong pitching staff; Simons was the victory titlist and Barnes led the SL in strikeouts and innings. The Sun Rays beat Jacksonville, three games to one, to win the Eastern Division, before falling to Memphis in the finals, three games to two.

In 1991 former Orlando slugger Scott Ullger guided the Sun Rays to the SL championship. Orlando finished in the Eastern cellar during the first half, then began a pennant drive behind ERA titlist Pat Mahomes (8–5, 1.78 with 136 Ks in 116 IP), strikeout champ Mike Trombley (12–7, 175 Ks) and All-Star third baseman Cheo Garcia (.282). The Sun Rays swept Greenville to cop a second consecutive Eastern Division crown, then beat Birmingham in the finals, three games to one.

In 1993 the long Orlando affiliation with the Twins (and

Palm trees grace Orlando's Tinker Field.

Senators) ended, but the Sun Rays became a Cubs farm club. Baseball continued to be attractive in The City Beautiful as attendance at Tinker Field exceeded 217,000.

Year	Record	Pcg.	Finish
1973	65–70	.481	Seventh
1974	73–61	.545	Second
1975	81–75	.587	First (lost finals)
1976	75–64	.540	Second (won Eastern Division, lost finals)
1977	76–61	.555	Second
1978	82–61	.573	Second (lost opener)
1979	60–81	.426	Ninth
1980	65–78	.455	Seventh
1981	79–63	.556	Second (won Eastern Division and finals)
1982	74–70	.514	Fourth
1983	62–83	.429	Ninth
1984	79–65	.549	Second
1985	72–71	.503	Sixth
1986	70–73	.490	Eighth
1987	61–82	.427	Tenth
1988	66–75	.468	Eighth
1989	79–65	.549	Third (lost opener)

1990	85–59	.590	Third (lost opener)
1991	77–67	.535	Third (won Eastern Division, lost finals)
1992	60–82	.423	Eighth
1993	71–70	.504	Seventh

Savannah
(Senators, Indians, Braves)

During the Civil War, Union troops occupied a hulking brick fortification outside Savannah, Fort Pulaski, where the soldiers played the first baseball games in the city's history. Amateur baseball thrived, and in 1893 the Savannah Electrics joined the Southern League. The next season Savannah's second — and last — SL club was called the Modocs, a forerunner of the "Indian" nickname that would become Savannah's favorite for professional baseball.

Savannah's DeSoto Hotel was the site for an organizational meeting on November 24, 1903, that launched the SALLY League. The Savannah Pathfinders (soon renamed Indians) played at Bolton Street Park, and Andy Oyler won the first SALLY batting crown (.301). In 1906 the Savannah Indians claimed their initial SALLY pennant behind batting champ Ed Sabrie (.290) and percentage leader Walt Deaver (18–4).

Outfielder Shoeless Joe Jackson (.358) won the 1909 batting crown, while the Indians moved to a new wooden stadium, Athletic Park. In 1913 batting champ Coalyard Mike Handiboe (.314) and victory leader Dick Robertson (28–8) helped produce another pennant, and the next year Handiboe was the run leader (.305, 79 R) as the second-place Indians won the SALLY playoffs. But the Indians plunged into the cellar in 1915, then dropped out of Organized Baseball for more than a decade.

In 1926 Savannah joined a reorganized Class B Southeastern League, but three years later the Indians withdrew before the end of the 1928 schedule. Not until 1936, when the SALLY reorganized after an absence of five years, did the Indians resurface, playing in Municipal Stadium. Two seasons later Savannah edged Macon by half a game for the 1938 pennant, as John Pezzullo led the SALLY in victories and strikeouts (26–9, 218 Ks). The Indians again finished first in 1940, the same year a hurricane wrecked the wooden grandstand at Municipal Stadium. The WPA rebuilt Municipal Stadium (later renamed Grayson Stadium) into an impressive facility that also accommodated football contests.

The Indians, along with the rest of the SALLY, went on hiatus during the wartime seasons of 1943–1944–1945. Savannah and the SALLY went back into action in 1946, and the next year the Indians won the playoffs. The key player of 1947 was lanky lefthander Lou Brissie, a war hero who overcame severe leg injuries to win a pitcher's Triple Crown (23–5, 1.91 ERA, 278 Ks). The 1952 batting champ was Tom Hamilton (.343), and in 1953 the Indians helped bring integration to the SALLY by signing third baseman Izzy Israel and outfielder Junior Reedy.

Right fielder Al Pinkston won the 1954 hitting crown (.360) and sparked Savannah to another playoff championship. The 1957 batting champ was Tom St. John (.326), who was the hit leader in 1959 (.283), the same season that home run and RBI king Cliff Cook set the all-time Savannah record for homers (.255, 32 HR, 100 RBI). Savannah won the playoff title in 1960, but the parent Pirates decided not to return for the next season. The next year the White Sox placed a team in Savannah, and the SavSox finished first in the 1962 SALLY. Racial difficulties

Savannah's 1940 SALLY pennant-winners featured second baseman Connie Ryan (middle, second from left – .316), righthander Ed Nowak (middle, third from right – 19–7), outfielder Jack Barnes (middle, second from right – .333), catcher Herb Crompton (middle, far right – .339), and righthander Peter Stein (standing, far right – 18–9).

prompted the White Sox to transfer the last few games of the schedule to Lynchburg, and Savannah did not return to Organized Baseball for five years.

Following the 1967 season the six-team Southern League lost two clubs. Joe Buzas, a former infielder who had become a highly resourceful minor league owner, arranged an affiliation with Washington and placed a Double-A team in Savannah. The Savannah Senators finished next-to-last in 1968 and last in 1969, but in 1970 Cleveland arranged an affiliation, which allowed Savannah to use the traditional "Indians" nickname.

For 1971 Atlanta moved their Double-A franchise from Shreveport of the Texas League to Savannah, and the Savannah Braves played in the Eastern Division of the Dixie Association arrangement. The next year the Southern League was up to eight teams. Savannah was placed in the Eastern Division, and manager Clint Courtney guided the Braves to the second-best record of 1972 and the leading season attendance (78,000) in the SL. But the Braves finished one game behind division-winner Asheville and missed the playoffs, despite the efforts of an All-Star infield: first baseman Jack Pierce (.292, 23 HR, 103 RBI), second-sacker Manny Ruiz (.270), and third baseman and stolen base champ Rod Gilbreath (.277 with 45 thefts).

In 1973 Savannah again finished second in the East, as All-Star outfielder Greg Foreman led the league in walks (.259, 27 HR, 114 W). The next season lefthanded *reliever* Mike Beard won the ERA title (2.40 in 47 G), while southpaw Domingo Figueroa was the leader in wins and percentage (15–4). Dale Murphy was voted All-Star catcher in 1976 (.267), but soon he was converted to the outfield, and he would go on to win back-to-back MVP awards with the Atlanta Braves.

The 1977 Savannah Braves won the first half in the East, but lost the division playoff to Jacksonville. Bruce Benedict was the All-Star catcher (.273), another future Atlanta regular, Glenn Hubbard, held down second base, and first-sacker Jerry Keller led the SL in RBIs and homers (.253, 17 HR, 86 RBI). In 1978 the Braves won the second half, then beat Orlando in the playoff opener for the Eastern Division championship, before losing the finals to Knoxville. Righthander Roger Alexander was the ERA champ (10–6, 1.84) and James Wessinger (.279) was named All-Star shortstop.

Although Savannah dropped to the cellar in 1980, the Braves were second-half leaders in 1981, before losing the division play-off to Charlotte. Righthander Steve Bedrosian led the SL in strikeouts, innings, and starts (14–10 with 161 Ks in 203 IP). The next year the Braves again lost the division playoff after winning the second half. Righthander Craig McMurtry was the victory leader (15–11), Albert Hall was an All-Star outfielder (.308), and third baseman Brook Jacoby (.292) honed the skills he would soon employ in the big leagues.

In 1983 Savannah won the first half but dropped the division playoff to Jacksonville. The Braves featured stolen base king Michael Cole (.285 with 75 thefts), RBI champ Miguel Sosa (.245, 17 HR, 93 RBI), outfielders Milt Thompson (.303) and Frank Estes (.303), and DH-first baseman Glen Bockhorn (.287 with 20 homers). Despite carving out the best record in the East, however, Savannah's attendance was the lowest (66,000) in the 10-team SL, and Atlanta decided to move its Double-A club to Greenville.

When St. Louis shifted its Class A SALLY franchise from Macon to Savannah, the Savannah Cardinals reached the 1984 playoffs. With the SALLY expanded to 12 teams, the Cardinals

The baseball grandstand at Savannah's Grayson Stadium.

won the Southern Division in 1990 before losing the finals to Charleston. In 1993, still hosting the 14-team SALLY in nostalgic Grayson Stadium, the Cardinals registered the season's best record, then won the playoffs to cap a memorable season.

Year	Record	Pcg.	Finish
1968	57–79	.419	Fifth
1969	59–76	.437	Sixth
1970	71–67	.514	Fourth
1971	57–84	.404	Fifth
1972	80–59	.576	Second
1973	71–68	.511	Third
1974	73–65	.529	Fourth
1975	70–64	.522	Fourth
1976	69–71	.493	Fifth
1977	77–63	.550	Third (lost opener)
1978	72–72	.500	Fourth (won Eastern Division, lost finals)
1979	60–83	.420	Tenth
1980	77–67	.535	Third (lost opener)
1981	70–70	.500	Sixth (lost opener)
1982	69–75	.479	Eighth
1983	81–64	.559	Third (lost opener)

League Records

Old Southern League Records, 1885–1899

ANNUAL STANDINGS

1885		
Atlanta	60–31	.659
Augusta	68–36	.653
Macon	58–48	.547
Columbus	42–39	.518
Nashville	55–37	.507
Memphis	38–54	.413
Chattanooga	30–59	.337
Birmingham	17–64	.210

1886		
Atlanta	64–28	.695
Savannah	56–33	.629
Nashville	46–43	.517
Memphis	44–46	.488
Charleston	41–50	.450
Augusta	21–31	.404
Macon	32–59	.351
Chattanooga	20–34	.270

1887		
New Orleans	75–40	.652
Charleston	65–41	.613
Memphis	64–52	.551
Nashville	34–30	.531
Birmingham	20–61	.246
Mobile	5–19	.208
Savannah	7–27	.205

1888		
Birmingham	32–19	.627
Memphis	26–24	.520
New Orleans	25–32	.438
Charleston	20–28	.416

1889		
New Orleans	43–7	.860
Charleston	22–14	.611
Atlanta	19–25	.479
Memphis	12–24	.333
Mobile	6–17	.261
Birmingham	4–17	.190

1892		
Birmingham	73–50	.593
Mobile	66–57	.537
New Orleans	66–57	.537
Montgomery	66–58	.532
Chattanooga	63–57	.525
Atlanta	58–65	.472
Macon	51–69	.425
Memphis	46–76	.377
1893		
Charleston	51–32	.614
Macon	54–38	.587
Atlanta	55–39	.585
Memphis	53–38	.581
Savannah	53–38	.581
Augusta	51–39	.567
Chattanooga	48–45	.516
New Orleans	40–51	.439
Mobile	38–53	.417
Montgomery	38–57	.400
Birmingham	25–39	.391
Nashville	33–60	.355
Pensacola	9–19	.321
1894		
Memphis	39–17	.702
Mobile	38–19	.655
Charleston	33–22	.600
Savannah	30–26	.536
New Orleans	28–33	.468
Nashville	24–33	.414
Atlanta	21–37	.362
Macon	15–41	.268
1895		
Atlanta	70–37	.654
Nashville	69–38	.645
Evansville	66–38	.635
Memphis	32–37	.464
Mobile	37–63	.455
Montgomery	40–70	.364
1896		
New Orleans	68–31	.686
Montgomery	60–36	.625
Atlanta	36–36	.500
Mobile	39–56	.410
Birmingham	26–41	.388
Columbus	34–63	.350
1899		
Mobile	24–10	.600
Shreveport	20–21	.488
New Orleans	20–22	.476
Dallas	17–22	.430
Montgomery	4–9	.308

BATTING CHAMPS – OLD SOUTHERN LEAGUE

1885	Leonard Sowders, Nash.	.309
1886	John Cline, Atlanta	.353
1887	Wally Andrews, Memphis	.413
1888	John Sneed, New O.	.354
1892	Weddige, Macon	.329
1893	Charles Frank, Memphis	.390
1895	Lew Whistler, Chatt and Mobile	.404
1896	Darby Knowles, Atlanta	.358

STOLEN BASE CHAMPS – OLD SOUTHERN LEAGUE

1885	Dennis Mack, Macon	91
1886	Blondy Purcell, Atlanta	72
1887	Charles Campau, Sav. and New O.	115
1888	Moose Werden, New O.	49
1896	Abner Powell, New O.	60

Southern Association Records, 1901–1961

ANNUAL STANDINGS

1901

Nashville	80–40	.634
Little Rock	76–45	.628
Memphis	68–55	.610
New Orleans	68–55	.584
Shreveport	55–66	.455
Chattanooga	45–73	.391
Birmingham	45–70	.390
Selma	37–78	.322

1902

Nashville	80–40	.667
Little Rock	77–45	.611
New Orleans	72–47	.605
Atlanta	55–63	.456
Chattanooga	50–68	.424
Shreveport	48–72	.400
Birmingham	39–80	.327

1903

Memphis	73–51	.589
Little Rock	71–50	.587
Shreveport	68–58	.539
Atlanta	62–60	.508
Nashville	60–64	.484
Birmingham	59–64	.480
Montgomery	53–67	.442
New Orleans	46–78	.370

1904

Memphis	81–54	.600
Atlanta	78–57	.578
New Orleans	79–58	.577
Birmingham	73–64	.533
Nashville	72–67	.518
Little Rock	61–74	.452
Shreveport	55–81	.404
Montgomery	44–88	.333

1905

New Orleans	84–45	.651
Montgomery	73–54	.575
Atlanta	71–61	.542
Shreveport	69–60	.535
Birmingham	70–61	.534
Memphis	69–62	.527
Nashville	47–88	.348
Little Rock	37–90	.291

1906

Birmingham	86–46	.652
Memphis	79–55	.590
Atlanta	80–56	.588
New Orleans	75–61	.551
Shreveport	70–66	.515
Montgomery	64–65	.496
Nashville	45–92	.328
New York	40–98	.290

1907

Atlanta	78–54	.591
Memphis	74–57	.565
New Orleans	68–66	.507
Little Rock	66–66	.500
Birmingham	61–71	.474
Shreveport	62–70	.470
Montgomery	62–71	.466
Nashville	59–78	.431

1908

Nashville	75–56	.573
New Orleans	76–57	.571
Memphis	73–62	.540
Montgomery	68–65	.511
Mobile	67–67	.500
Atlanta	63–72	.467
Little Rock	62–76	.449
Birmingham	53–82	.333

1909

Atlanta	87–49	.640
Nashville	82–55	.594
Montgomery	76–60	.559
New Orleans	73–64	.533
Mobile	64–77	.454
Birmingham	60–79	.429
Little Rock	59–80	.424
Memphis	51–88	.367

1910

New Orleans	87–53	.621
Birmingham	79–61	.564
Atlanta	75–63	.543
Chattanooga	66–71	.482
Nashville	64–76	.457
Mobile	63–75	.457
Memphis	62–76	.449
Montgomery	59–80	.421

1911

New Orleans	78–54	.591
Montgomery	77–58	.570
Birmingham	76–62	.551
Nashville	69–64	.519
Chattanooga	67–71	.486
Memphis	62–71	.466
Mobile	57–76	.429
Atlanta	54–84	.391

1912

Birmingham	85–51	.625
Mobile	79–58	.576
New Orleans	71–64	.526
Nashville	67–70	.489
Memphis	68–71	.489
Montgomery	64–75	.460
Chattanooga	59–75	.440
Atlanta	54–83	.394

1913

Atlanta	81–56	.591
Mobile	81–57	.587
Birmingham	74–64	.536
Chattanooga	70–64	.526
Montgomery	68–69	.496
Memphis	64–74	.463
Nashville	62–76	.446
New Orleans	45–85	.346

1914

Birmingham	88–62	.587
Mobile	88–67	.562
New Orleans	80–65	.552
Atlanta	78–66	.542
Nashville	77–72	.517
Chattanooga	73–78	.483
Memphis	61–78	.412
Montgomery	54–100	.351

1915

New Orleans	91–63	.591
Birmingham	86–67	.562
Memphis	81–73	.526
Nashville	75–78	.490
Atlanta	74–79	.483
Chattanooga	73–78	.476
Mobile	68–86	.441
Little Rock	65–87	.427

1916

Nashville	84–54	.609
New Orleans	73–61	.544
Birmingham	69–62	.526
Little Rock	70–65	.518
Atlanta	70–67	.511
Memphis	68–70	.493
Chattanooga	65–74	.467
Mobile	45–91	.331

1917

Atlanta	98–56	.637
New Orleans	89–61	.593
Birmingham	87–66	.569
Memphis	81–73	.527
Nashville	77–73	.513
Chattanooga	76–74	.507
Little Rock	64–86	.427
Mobile	34–117	.220

1918

New Orleans	49–21	.700
Little Rock	41–28	.594
Mobile	35–32	.522
Birmingham	33–31	.516
Chattanooga	35–34	.507
Memphis	32–28	.457
Nashville	30–40	.429
Atlanta	18–49	.269

1919

Atlanta	85–53	.616
Little Rock	74–56	.569
New Orleans	74–61	.548
Mobile	67–69	.493
Memphis	66–73	.475
Chattanooga	65–73	.471
Birmingham	59–77	.434
Nashville	55–83	.399

1920

Little Rock	88–59	.599
New Orleans	86–62	.581
Atlanta	85–62	.578
Birmingham	85–69	.552
Memphis	72–77	.484
Mobile	68–86	.441
Nashville	65–89	.422
Chattanooga	53–98	.351

1921

Memphis	104–49	.679
New Orleans	97–57	.630
Birmingham	90–63	.558
Little Rock	74–77	.490
Atlanta	73–78	.483
Nashville	62–90	.409
Mobile	58–94	.382
Chattanooga	52–102	.338

1922

Mobile	97–55	.638
Memphis	94–58	.618
New Orleans	89–64	.582
Little Rock	86–67	.562
Birmingham	74–80	.481
Chattanooga	59–93	.388
Nashville	56–96	.368
Atlanta	55–97	.362

1923

Memphis	104–49	.680
Atlanta	99–54	.647
New Orleans	93–60	.647
Nashville	93–60	.510
Mobile	68–84	.447
Chattanooga	63–89	.414
Birmingham	54–98	.356
Little Rock	51–101	.336

1924

New Orleans	89–57	.610
Mobile	88–66	.571
Memphis	76–70	.521
Atlanta	78–73	.516
Birmingham	75–74	.503
Nashville	75–77	.493
Chattanooga	63–83	.417
Little Rock	53–92	.365

1925

Atlanta	87–67	.565
New Orleans	85–68	.556
Nashville	81–72	.529
Memphis	80–73	.523
Mobile	73–78	.483
Chattanooga	71–82	.464
Birmingham	67–85	.441
Little Rock	67–86	.438

1926

New Orleans	101–53	.656
Memphis	95–57	.625
Birmingham	87–61	.588
Nashville	83–68	.550
Atlanta	75–76	.497
Chattanooga	55–94	.369
Mobile	56–96	.368
Little Rock	51–98	.342

1927

New Orleans	96–57	.627
Birmingham	91–63	.591
Memphis	89–64	.582
Nashville	84–69	.549
Atlanta	70–81	.484
Mobile	67–87	.435
Chattanooga	59–94	.386
Little Rock	56–97	.366

1928

Birmingham	99–54	.647
Memphis	97–55	.638
New Orleans	73–74	.497
Mobile	74–76	.493
Little Rock	72–82	.468
Chattanooga	67–85	.441
Atlanta	66–87	.431
Nashville	59–94	.386

1929

Birmingham	93–60	.608
Nashville	90–63	.588
New Orleans	89–64	.582
Memphis	88–66	.571
Atlanta	78–75	.510
Little Rock	63–91	.409
Mobile	57–95	.375
Chattanooga	55–99	.357

	1930			**1935**	
Memphis	98–55	.641	Atlanta	91–60	.605
New Orleans	91–61	.599	New Orleans	86–67	.562
Birmingham	85–68	.556	Memphis	84–70	.545
Atlanta	84–69	.549	Nashville	82–69	.543
Little Rock	81–73	.526	Chattanooga	75–75	.500
Chattanooga	67–87	.435	Little Rock	75–78	.490
Nashville	66–87	.431	Birmingham	59–95	.385
Mobile	40–112	.263	Knoxville	57–95	.375
	1931			**1936**	
Birmingham	97–55	.638	Atlanta	94–59	.614
Little Rock	87–66	.569	Nashville	86–65	.570
Memphis	84–69	.549	Birmingham	82–70	.539
Chattanooga	79–74	.516	New Orleans	81–71	.533
New Orleans	78–75	.510	Little Rock	77–76	.503
Atlanta	78–76	.506	Knoxville	63–87	.420
Knoxville	57–94	.377	Chattanooga	64–89	.418
Nashville	51–102	.333	Memphis	60–90	.400
	1932			**1937**	
Chattanooga	98–51	.658	Little Rock	97–55	.595
Memphis	101–53	.656	Memphis	88–64	.579
Little Rock	77–75	.507	New Orleans	84–66	.560
Nashville	75–78	.490	Nashville	80–73	.523
Birmingham	68–83	.450	Birmingham	75–76	.497
New Orleans	66–84	.440	Chattanooga	56–95	.371
Atlanta	62–90	.408	Knoxville	42–111	.274
Knoxville	60–93	.392		**1938**	
	1933		Atlanta	91–62	.595
Memphis	95–58	.621	Nashville	84–66	.560
New Orleans*	88–65	.575	New Orleans	79–70	.530
Nashville	75–69	.521	Memphis	77–75	.507
Birmingham	76–75	.533	Little Rock	75–76	.497
Chattanooga	74–77	.423	Birmingham	73–79	.480
Knoxville	68–82	.453	Chattanooga	66–85	.437
Atlanta	62–86	.419	Knoxville	59–91	.393
Little Rock	62–90	.408		**1939**	
	1934		Chattanooga	85–65	.567
New Orleans	94–60	.610	Memphis	84–67	.556
Nashville	87–65	.579	Nashville	85–68	.555
Memphis	79–72	.523	Atlanta	83–67	.553
Chattanooga	78–75	.509	Knoxville	79–73	.520
Atlanta	77–74	.509	Little Rock	68–83	.450
Knoxville	73–80	.477	Birmingham	64–89	.418
Birmingham	64–90	.416	New Orleans	57–93	.380
Little Rock	59–95	.383			

1940			**1945**		
Nashville	101–47	.682	Atlanta	94–46	.671
Atlanta	93–58	.616	Chattanooga	85–55	.607
Memphis	79–72	.523	Mobile	74–85	.532
Chattanooga	73–79	.480	New Orleans	73–67	.521
New Orleans	71–80	.470	Memphis	68–72	.486
Birmingham	70–81	.464	Birmingham	58–82	.414
Little Rock	59–90	.396	Nashville	55–84	.396
Knoxville	57–96	.373	Little Rock	52–88	.371

1941			**1946**		
Atlanta	99–55	.643	Atlanta	96–58	.623
Nashville	83–70	.542	Memphis	90–63	.588
New Orleans	78–75	.510	Chattanooga	79–73	.520
Chattanooga	78–76	.506	New Orleans	75–77	.493
Birmingham	73–79	.480	Nashville	75–78	.490
Little Rock	71–82	.464	Mobile	75–78	.490
Memphis	69–85	.448	Birmingham	68–84	.447
Knoxville	62–91	.405	Little Rock	52–99	.344

1942			**1947**		
Little Rock	87–59	.596	Mobile	94–59	.614
Nashville	85–66	.563	New Orleans	93–59	.612
Birmingham	79–73	.520	Nashville	80–73	.523
New Orleans	77–73	.513	Chattanooga	79–75	.513
Atlanta	76–78	.494	Atlanta	73–78	.483
Memphis	72–80	.474	Birmingham	73–80	.477
Chattanooga	66–86	.434	Memphis	69–85	.448
Knoxville	61–88	.409	Little Rock	51–103	.331

1943			**1948**		
Nashville	83–55	.601	Nashville	95–58	.621
New Orleans	78–58	.573	Memphis	92–61	.601
Little Rock	78–62	.557	Birmingham	84–69	.549
Montgomery	69–70	.496	Mobile	75–75	.500
Knoxville	65–71	.478	New Orleans	70–83	.458
Birmingham	63–76	.453	Atlanta	69–85	.448
Atlanta	60–79	.432	Little Rock	67–83	.447
Memphis	56–81	.409	Chattanooga	58–96	.377

1944			**1949**		
Atlanta	86–53	.619	Nashville	95–57	.625
Memphis	84–55	.609	Birmingham	91–62	.595
Nashville	79–61	.564	Mobile	82–69	.543
Little Rock	66–72	.478	New Orleans	77–75	.507
Birmingham	64–75	.460	Atlanta	71–82	.464
Mobile	63–74	.459	Little Rock	69–85	.448
Chattanooga	57–83	.409	Memphis	65–88	.425
New Orleans	57–83	.409	Chattanooga	60–92	.395

	1950			**1955**	
Atlanta	92–69	.609	Memphis	90–63	.588
Birmingham	87–62	.584	Birmingham	88–65	.575
Nashville	86–64	.573	Chattanooga	80–74	.519
Memphis	81–70	.536	Mobile	79–75	.513
New Orleans	71–79	.473	Nashville	77–74	.510
Mobile	70–79	.470	New Orleans	76–75	.503
Chattanooga	59–89	.399	Atlanta	70–84	.455
Little Rock	52–96	.351	Little Rock	52–102	.338

	1951			**1956**	
Little Rock	93–60	.608	Atlanta	89–65	.578
Birmingham	83–71	.539	Memphis	82–72	.532
Mobile	80–74	.519	Mobile	82–73	.529
Memphis	79–75	.513	Birmingham	81–74	.523
Nashville	78–76	.506	New Orleans	79–75	.513
Atlanta	76–78	.494	Chattanooga	76–78	.494
New Orleans	64–90	.418	Nashville	75–79	.487
Chattanooga	62–91	.405	Montgomery	53–101	.344

	1952			**1957**	
Chattanooga	86–66	.566	Atlanta	87–67	.565
Atlanta	82–72	.532	Memphis	86–67	.562
Mobile	80–73	.523	Nashville	83–69	.546
Memphis	81–74	.522	Chattanooga	83–70	.542
New Orleans	80–75	.516	Mobile	75–78	.490
Nashville	73–79	.480	Birmingham	74–79	.484
Little Rock	68–85	.444	Little Rock	64–88	.421
Birmingham	64–90	.416	New Orleans	60–94	.390

	1953			**1958**	
Memphis	87–67	.565	Birmingham	91–62	.595
Nashville	85–69	.552	Mobile	84–68	.553
Atlanta	84–70	.545	Atlanta	84–70	.545
Birmingham	78–76	.506	Chattanooga	77–76	.503
New Orleans	76–78	.494	Nashville	76–78	.494
Chattanooga	73–81	.474	Little Rock	74–80	.481
Mobile	66–87	.431	Memphis	69–84	.451
Little Rock	66–87	.431	New Orleans	57–94	.377

	1954			**1959**	
Atlanta	94–60	.610	Birmingham	92–61	.601
New Orleans	92–62	.597	Mobile	89–63	.586
Birmingham	81–70	.536	Nashville	84–64	.568
Memphis	80–74	.519	Memphis	76–77	.497
Chattanooga	75–76	.497	Shreveport	75–79	.487
Little Rock	64–90	.416	New Orleans	68–81	.456
Nashville	64–90	.416	Chattanooga	67–86	.438
Mobile	63–91	.409	Atlanta	56–96	.368

1960			1961		
Atlanta	87–67	.565	Chattanooga	90–62	.592
Shreveport	86–67	.562	Birmingham	89–63	.586
Little Rock	82–69	.543	Little Rock	80–73	.523
Birmingham	83–70	.542	Atlanta	77–74	.510
Mobile	79–72	.523	Macon	75–79	.487
Nashville	71–82	.464	Nashville	69–83	.454
Memphis	59–87	.404	Shreveport	69–84	.451
Chattanooga	60–93	.392	Mobile	61–92	.399

SOUTHERN ASSOCIATION PLAYOFF RESULTS

1928 Birmingham defeated Memphis 4 games to 0.

1933 New Orleans defeated Memphis 3 games to 2.

1934 New Orleans defeated Nashville 3 games to 2.

1935 Atlanta defeated Nashville 3 games to 0. New Orleans defeated Memphis 3 games to 0. **FINALS:** Atlanta defeated New Orleans 3 games to 0.

1936 Birmingham defeated Nashville 3 games to 2. New Orleans defeated Atlanta 3 games to 2. **FINALS:** Birmingham defeated New Orleans 3 games to 0 with 1 tie.

1937 Atlanta defeated Memphis 3 games to 1. Little Rock defeated Atlanta 3 games to 2. **FINALS:** Little Rock defeated Atlanta 4 games to 3.

1938 Atlanta defeated Memphis 3 games to 2. Nashville defeated New Orleans 3 games to 2. **FINALS:** Atlanta defeated Nashville 4 games to 1 with 1 tie.

1939 Atlanta defeated Chattanooga 3 games to 0. Nashville defeated Memphis 3 games to 0. **FINALS:** Nashville defeated Atlanta 4 games to 3.

1940 Nashville defeated Chattanooga 3 games to 0. Atlanta defeated Memphis 3 games to 2. **FINALS:** Nashville defeated Atlanta 4 games to 2.

1941 Nashville defeated New Orleans 3 games to 1. Atlanta defeated Chattanooga 3 games to 1. **FINALS:** Nashville defeated Atlanta 4 games to 3.

1942 Nashville defeated Birmingham 3 games to 1. Little Rock defeated New Orleans 3 games to 1. **FINALS:** Nashville defeated Little Rock 4 games to 0.

1943 Nashville defeated New Orleans 4 games to 1.

1944 Nashville defeated Memphis 4 games to 3.

1945 New Orleans defeated Atlanta 4 games to 1. Mobile defeated Chattanooga 4 games to 2. **FINALS:** Mobile defeated New Orleans 4 games to 1.

1946 Atlanta defeated New Orleans 4 games to 3. Memphis defeated Chattanooga 4 games to 2. **FINALS:** Atlanta defeated Memphis 4 games to 3.

1947 Mobile defeated Chattanooga 4 games to 0. Nashville defeated New Orleans 4 games to 1. **FINALS:** Mobile defeated Nashville 4 games to 3.

1948 Nashville defeated Mobile 4 games to 3. Birmingham defeated Memphis 4 games to 2. **FINALS:** Birmingham defeated Nashville 4 games to 2.

1949 Nashville defeated New Orleans 4 games to 2. Mobile defeated Birmingham 4 games to 1. **FINALS:** Nashville defeated Mobile 4 games to 2.

1950 Atlanta defeated Memphis 4 games to 0. Nashville defeated Birmingham 4 games to 1. **FINALS:** Nashville defeated Atlanta 4 games to 1.

1951 Little Rock defeated Memphis 4 games to 2. Birmingham defeated Mobile 4 games to 0. **FINALS:** Birmingham defeated Little Rock 4 games to 0.

1952 Memphis defeated New Orleans in a single game to determine fourth place. Memphis defeated Chattanooga 4 games to 0. Mobile defeated Atlanta 4 games to 2. **FINALS:** Memphis defeated Mobile 4 games to 2 with 1 tie.

1953 Birmingham defeated Memphis 4 games to 1. Nashville defeated Atlanta 4 games to 2. **FINALS:** Nashville defeated Birmingham 4 games to 1.

1954 Atlanta defeated Memphis 4 games to 2. New Orleans defeated Birmingham 4 games to 2. **FINALS:** Atlanta defeated New Orleans 4 games to 1.

1955 Mobile defeated Memphis 4 games to 3. Birmingham defeated Chattanooga 4 games to 2. **FINALS:** Mobile defeated Birmingham 4 games to 2.

1956 Mobile defeated Birmingham in a single game for third place. Atlanta defeated Birmingham 4 games to 0. Memphis defeated Mobile 4 games to 3. **FINALS:** Atlanta defeated Memphis 4 games to 3.

1957 Atlanta defeated Chattanooga 4 games to 2. Nashville defeated Memphis 4 games to 2. **FINALS:** Atlanta defeated Nashville 4 games to 0.

1958 Birmingham defeated Chattanooga 4 games to 1. Mobile defeated Atlanta 4 games to 0. **FINALS:** Birmingham defeated Mobile 4 games to 1.

1959 Mobile defeated Birmingham 4 games to 1.

1960 Birmingham defeated Atlanta 3 games to 2. Little Rock defeated Shreveport 3 games to 1. **FINALS:** Little Rock defeated Birmingham 3 games to 2.

DIXIE SERIES RESULTS

Southern Association teams listed first; winner in CAPS; record in parentheses.

1920 Little Rock v. FORT WORTH (2-4-1)

1921 Memphis v. FORT WORTH (2-4)

1922 MOBILE v. Fort Worth (4-2-1)

1923 New Orleans v. FORT WORTH (2-4-1)

1924 Memphis v. FORT WORTH (3-4-1)

1925 Atlanta v. FORT WORTH (2-4)

1926 New Orleans v. DALLAS (2-4-1)

1927 New Orleans v. WICHITA FALLS (0-4)

1928 Birmingham v. HOUSTON (2-4)

1929 BIRMINGHAM v. Dallas (4-2)

1930 Memphis v. FORT WORTH (1-4)

1931 BIRMINGHAM v. Houston (4-2)

1932 CHATTANOOGA v. Beaumont (4-1)

1933 NEW ORLEANS v. San Antonio (4-2)

1934 NEW ORLEANS v. Galveston (4-2)

1935 Atlanta v. OKLAHOMA CITY (2-4)

1936 Birmingham v. TULSA (0-4)

1937 Little Rock v. FORT WORTH (1-4)

1938 ATLANTA v. Beaumont (4-0-1)

1939 Nashville v. FORT WORTH (3-4)

1940 NASHVILLE v. Houston (4-1)

1941 NASHVILLE v. Dallas (4-0)

1942 NASHVILLE v. Shreveport (4-2)

1943-45 No series.

1946 Atlanta v. DALLAS (0-4)

1947 Mobile v. HOUSTON (2-4)

1948 BIRMINGHAM v. Fort Worth (4-1)

1949 NASHVILLE v. Tulsa (4-3)

1950 Nashville v. SAN ANTONIO (3-4)

1951 BIRMINGHAM v. Houston (4-2)

1952 MEMPHIS v. Shreveport (4-2)

1953 Nashville v. DALLAS (2-4)

1954 ATLANTA v. Houston (4–3)	1958 BIRMINGHAM v. Corpus Christi
1955 MOBILE v. Shreveport (4–0)	(4–2)
1956 Atlanta v. HOUSTON (2–4)	1959–66 No series.
1957 Atlanta v. HOUSTON (2–4)	1967 BIRMINGHAM v. Albuquerque
	(4–2)

PRESIDENTS OF THE SOUTHERN LEAGUE

1901	Reed Kent, W. J. Boles,	1919–38	Judge J. D. Martin
	J. B. Nicklin	1938–42	Major Trammell Scott
1902	J. B. Nicklin	1943–46	William G. Evans
1903–15	Judge W. B. Kavanaugh	1947–60	Charles A. Hurth
1915–18	Robert H. Baugh	1960–61	Hal Totten

SA BATTING CHAMPIONS

1901	Jack Hulseman, Spt.	.392	1932	Moose Clabaugh, Nash.	.382
1902	Hugh Hill, Nash.	.416	1933	Frank Waddey, Knox.	.361
1903	James Smith, NO–Spt.	.354	1934	Phil Weintraub, Nash.	.401
1904	John Gilbert, LR	.327	1935	Doug Taitt, Nash.	.355
1905	Carl Molesworth, Mtgy.	.312	1936	Fred Sington, Chatt.	.384
1906	Sid Smith, Atl.	.326	1937	Coaker Triplett, Mem.	.356
1907	Buttermilk Meek, Birm.	.340	1938	Johnny Hill, Atl.	.338
1908	Tris Speaker, LR	.350	1939	Bert Haas, Nash.	.365
1909	Bill Mc Gilvray, Birm.	.291	1940	Mike Dejan, Chatt.–Birm.	.371
1910	Jos Jackson, NO	.354	1941	Les Fleming, Nash.	.414
1911	Derrill Pratt, Mtgy.	.316	1942	Charles English, Nash.	.341
1912	Harry Welchonce, Atl.	.325	1943	Ed Sauer, Nash.	.368
1913	Harry Welchonce, Atl.	.338	1944	Rene Monteagudo, Chatt.	.370
1914	Moose McCormick, Chatt.	.332	1945	Gil Coan, Chatt.	.372
1915	Elmer Miller, Mob.	.326	1946	Tom Neill, Birm.	.374
1916	Bill Jacovson, LR	.346	1947	Ted Kluszewski, Mem.	.377
1917	Sam Hyatt, Chatt.	.334	1948	Smokey Burgess, Nash.	.386
1918	Ira Flagstead, Chatt.	.334	1949	Bob Borkowski, Nash.	.376
1919	Larry Gilbert, NO	.349	1950	Pat Haggerty, LR	.346
1920	Harry Harper, LR	.354	1951	Herb Barna, Nash.	.358
1921	Ike Boone, NO	.389	1952	Rance Pless, Nash.	.364
1922	Cutch Schleibner, LR	.354	1953	Bill Taylor, Nash.	.350
1923	Emil Huhn, Mob.	.345	1954	Bob Lennon, Nash.	.345
1924	Carlyle Smith, Atl.	.385	1955	Charles Williams, Nash.	.368
1925	Wilbur Good, Atl.	.379	1956	Stan Roseboro, Chatt.	.340
1926	Tommy Taylor, Mem.	.383	1957	Stan Palys, Nash.	.359
1927	Wilbur Davis, NO	.376	1958	Jim Fridley, Nash.	.348
1928	Elliot Bigelow, Birm.	.395	1959	Gordon Coleman, Mob.	.353
1929	Art Weis, Birm.	.345	1960	Stan Palys, Birm.	.370
1930	Joe Hutcheson, Mem.	.380	1961	Don Saner, LR	.349
1931	Moose Clabaugh, Nash.	.378			

HOME RUN CHAMPIONS

1913	Dee Robertson, Mob.	11	1937	Willie Duke, Nash.	19
1914	Bill Jacobson, Chatt.	15	1938	Bud Hafey, Knox.	24
1915	Fred Thomas, NO	11	1939	Wm. Nicholson, Chatt.	23
1916	Mon Harris, Chatt.	9	1940	Augie Dugas, Nash.	22
1917	Fred Bratchi, Mem.	14		L. D. Meyer, Knox.	22
1919	Tex McDonald, Nash.	8	1941	Les Burge, Atl.	38
1920	Bing Miller, LR	14	1942	Charles Workman, Nash.	29
1921	Dutch Bernsen, Birm.	22	1943	Cecil Dunn, Knox.	19
1922	Red Camp, Mem.	12	1944	Cecil Dunn, Mob.-Chatt.	14
	Joe Connolly. LR	12	1945	Gil Coan, Chatt.	16
	John Shulte, Mob.	12	1946	Ted Pawelek, Nash.	15
1923	Dan Clark, Brim.-Atl.	19	1947	Al Flair, NO	24
1924	John Anderson, Chatt.	26	1948	Charles Workman, Nash.	52
1925	Nick Cullop, Atl.	30	1949	Carl Sawatski, Nash.	45
1926	Yam Yaryan, Birm.	20	1950	Bill Wilson, Mem.	36
1927	Babe Bigelow, Birm.	19	1951	John Harshman, Nash.	47
1928	Dan Taylor, Mem.	20	1952	Frank Thomas, NO	35
1929	Jim Poole, Atl.-Nash.	33	1953	Bill Wilson, Mem.	34
1930	Jim Poole, Nash.	50		Ralph Atkins, LR	34
1931	Moose Clabaugh, Nash.	23	1954	Bob Lennon, Nash.	64
1932	Stan Keyes, Nash.	35	1955	Bob Hazle, Nash.	29
1933	Joe Hutsheson, Mem.	18	1956	John Powers, NO	39
1934	Henry Oana, Atl.	17	1957	Harmon Killebrew, Chatt.	29
1935	Poco Taitt, Nash.	17	1958	Kent Hadley, LR	34
1936	Poco Taitt, Nash.	20	1959	Gordon Coleman, Mob.	30
	Earl Webb, Knox.	20	1960	Jim McManus, Spt.	32
			1961	Bill Gabler, Macon	30

RBI LEADERS

1921	Paul McLarry, Mem.	135	1944	Lindsay Deal, LR-Nash.	124
1924	Roy Carlyle, Mem.	122	1945	Ted Cieslak, Atl.	120
1925	Chick Tolson, Nash.	143	1946	Tom Neill, Birm.	124
1926	Tommy Taylor, Mem.	135	1947	Al Flair, NO	128
1927	Babe Bigelow, Birm.	143	1948	Charles Workman, Nash.	182
1928	Mule Shirley, Birm.	133	1949	Carl Sawatski, Nash.	153
1929	Jim Poole, Atl.-Nash.	127	1950	Bill Wilson, Mem.	125
1930	Jim Poole, Nash.	167	1951	Walt Moryn, Mob.	148
1931	Babe Bigelow, Chatt.	125	1952	Frank Thomas, NO	131
1932	Andy Reese, Mem.	121	1953	Dick Sinovic, Atl.	126
1933	John Gill, Chatt.	110	1954	Bob Lennon, Nash.	161
	Eddie Rose, NO	110	1955	Jim Lemon, Mob. 109	
1934	Henry Oana, Atl.	102		Jim Gentile, Chatt. 109	
1935	Gee Gee Gleeson, NO	105	1956	Gordon Coleman, Mob.	118
1936	Poco Taitt, Nash.	132	1957	Jesse Levan, Chatt.	114
1937	Eddie Rose, NO-Atl.	112	1958	Charles Coles, Nash.	107
1938	M. VanRobays, Knox.	110	1959	Gordon Coleman, Mob.	110
1939	Norman Young, Knox.	137	1960	Leo Posada, Spt.	108
1940	Robert Boken, Nash.	118	1961	Stan Palys, Birm.	114
	Augie Dugas, Nash.	118			
	Willard Marshall, Atl.	118			

SA STOLEN BASE LEADERS

1901	Johnny Gilbert, LR	56	1932	Andy Reese, Mem.	33
1903	James Smith, NO–Spt.	48	1933	Lance Richbourg, Nash.	30
1904	Joe Rickert, NO	77	1934	Walter French, LR	34
1905	Snapper Kennedy, Spt.	57	1935	Red Nonnenkamp, LR	36
1906	Robert Byrne, Spt.	46		Stormy Weatherly, NO	36
1907	Neal Ball, Mtgy.	50	1936	Ollie Marquardt, Mem.	28
	Dode Paskert, Atl.	50	1937	Louis Bush, Mem.	32
1908	Tom Downey, Birm.	42	1938	Paul Campbell, LR	41
1909	Henline, Birm.	43	1939	Stan Benjamin, Chatt.	43
1910	Bill McGilvray, Birm.	44	1940	Tony Lupien, LR	26
1911	Art Phelan, Birm.	57	1941	Calvin Chapman, Chatt.	21
1912	John Johnston, Birm.	81	1942	Charlie Brewster, Nash.	29
1913	Bobby Messenger, Birm.	67	1943	Hank Sauer, Nash.	30
1914	Leo Callahan, Nash.	54	1944	Pete Gray, Mem.	68
1915	Fred Thomas, NO	53	1945	Gil Coan, Chatt.	37
1916	Buzzy Wares, LR	42	1946	Pete Laysen, NO	33
1917	Dick Kauffman, Nash.	57	1947	Gil Coan, Chatt.	42
1918	Dinty Barbare, NO	25	1948	Wayne Blackburn, LR	36
1919	Larry Gilbert, NO	42	1949	David Williams, Atl.	27
1920	Dixie Carroll, Mem.	54	1950	Forrest Jacobs, Mobile	22
1921	Stuffy Stewart, Birm.	66	1951	Russell Rose, Mobile	31
1922	Stuffy Stewart, Birm.	47	1952	Don Nicholas, Mem.	84
1923	Kiki Cuyler, Nash.	68	1953	Brandon Davis, NO	36
1924	Stuffy Stewart, Birm.	67	1954	Len Johnston, Mem.	39
1925	Stuffy Stewart, Birm.	53	1955	Luis Aparicio, Mem.	48
1926	Ed Lewis, Chatt.	37	1956	John Waters, Mobile	20
1927	Dan Taylor, Mem.	37	1957	Don Nicholas, Nash.	16
1928	Stuffy Stewart, Birm.	61	1958	John Reed, NO	22
1929	Wally Dashiell, Chatt.	50	1959	Steve Boros, Birm.	23
1930	Guy Sturdy, Birm.	33	1960	Gene Wallace, Atl.	14
1931	Walter French, LR	51	1961	Bob Saverine, LR	41

SA .400 HITTERS

1902	.416	Hugh Hill, Nash.	1934	.401	Phil Weintraub, Nash.
1941	.414	Les Fleming, Nash.			

SA PITCHERS — MOST VICTORIES —

1901	Sample, Spt.–Nash.	25	1910	Otto Hess, NO	25
1902	Larry Stewart, NO–Spt.	23	1911	Otto Hess, NO	23
1903	Red Fisher, Nash.	24	1912	Al Demaree, Mobile	24
1904	Frank Smith, Atl.	31	1913	Harry Coveleskie, Chatt.	28
1905	Ginger Clark, Birm.	22	1914	Curley Brown, Birm.	21
1906	Glenn Leibhardt, Mem.	35	1915	Geo. Cunningham, Chatt.	24
1907	Irvin Wilhelm, Birm.	23	1916	Dickey Kerr, Mem.	24
1908	Ralph Savidge, Mem.	20		Tom Rogers, Nash.	24
1909	Hub Perdue, Nash.	23		Scott Perry, Atl.	24

1917	Carmen Hill, Birm.	26	1939	Ed Heusser, Mem.	19
1918	Hub Perdue, NO	12		Dick Bass, Chatt.	19
1919	Rube Robinson, LR	23		Dick Lanahan, Chatt.	19
1920	Roy Walker, NO	26	1940	Boots Poffenberger, Nash.	26
	John Morrison, Birm.	26	1941	Ed Heusser, Atl.	20
	Rube Robinson, LR	26		Frank Veverka, Mem.	20
	Tom Sheehan, Atl.	26		Red Barrett, Birm.	20
1921	Oscar Tuero, Mem.	27	1942	Bill Seinsoth, NO	24
1922	Rube Robinson, LR	26	1943	Jess Danna, NO	22
1923	Tommy Long, Mobile	27	1944	Ellis Kinder, Mem.	19
1924	Ray Francis, Atl.	24	1945	Lew Carpenter, Atl.	22
1925	Joe Martina, NO	23	1946	Mickey McGowen, Atl.	22
1926	Lute Roy, NO	24	1947	Bill Kennedy, Chatt.	20
1927	Joe Martina, NO	23	1948	Norman Brown, Atl.	22
1928	Eddie Wells, Birm.	25	1949	Garmen, Mallory, Nash.	20
1929	Climax Blethen, Atl.	22	1950	Robert Schultz, Nash.	25
	Benny Frey, Nash.	22	1951	Frank Biscan, Mem.	16
	Harry Kelley, Mem.	22		Al Yaylian, LR	16
1930	Billy Bayne, Chatt.	21		Bob McCall, LR	16
1931	Fred Johnson, NO	21		Bobo Newsom, Birm.	16
	Bob Hasty, Birm.	21		Tom Lakos, Mobile	16
1932	Walter Beck, Mem.	27	1952	Al Sima, Chatt.	24
1933	Fred Johnson, NO	21	1953	Jack Harshman, Nash.	23
	Clay Touchstone, Brim.	21	1954	Leo Cristante, Atl.	24
	Harry Kelley, Mem.	21	1955	Ralph Mauriello, Mobile	18
1934	Harry Kelley, Mem.–Atl.	23	1956	Al Papai, Memphis	20
1935	Al Milnar, NO	24	1957	Bob Kelly, Nash.	24
	Tiny Chaplin, Nash.	24	1958	Bill Harrington, Birm.	20
1936	Byron Speece, Nash.	22		Bob Hartman, Atl.	20
1937	Byron Humphries, NO	20		Jim O'Toole, Nash.	20
1938	Tom Sunkel, Atl.	21	1959	Don Bradey, NO	19
	Bill Crouch, Nash.	21	1960	Pete Richert, Atl.	19
	Red Evans, NO	21	1961	Howard Koplitz, Birm.	23

SA PITCHERS — WINNING PERCENTAGE —

1901	Allemang, LR	21–4	.833
1902	Bill Damman. Mem.	18–5	.782
1903	Whoa Bill Fisher, Nash.	24–11	.686
1904	Frank Smith, Atl.	31–10	.786
1905	Ted Breitenstein, NO	21–5	.777
1906	Tom Hughes, Atl.	25–5	.833
1907	Roy Castleton, Atl.	17–8	.680
1908	Ted Breitenstein, NO	17–6	.739
1909	Oliver Jones, Atl.	20–7	.740
1910	Otto Hess, NO	25–9	.735
1911	Otto Hess, NO	23–8	.777
1912	Al Demaree, Mob.	24–10	.706
1913	Bill Prough, Birm.	23–6	.793

1914	Curley Brown, Brim.	21–7	.750
1915	George Cunningham, Chatt.	24–12	.667
1916	Rube Robinson, LR	11–1	.917
1917	Dick Robertson, NO	21–8	.724
1918	Dick Robertson, NO	10–1	.909
1919	Tom Sheehan, Atl.	17–3	.850
1920	Chief Yellowhorse, LR	21–7	.750
1921	Tom Phillips, NO	25–7	.781
1922	Roy Walker, NO	12–1	.923
1923	Tommy Long, Mobile	27–7	.750
1924	Dutch Henry, NO	10–2	.833
1925	Joe Martina, NO	23–13	.639
1926	Earl Hilton, NO	16–3	.842
1927	Eddie Wells, Birm.	13–1	.929
1928	Lute Roy, Birm.	19–5	.792
1929	Dick Ludolph, Birm.	21–8	.724
1930	Shepherd, Memphis	12–4	.775
1931	Jimmy Walkup, Birm.	20–5	.800
1932	Walter Beck, Memphis	27–6	.818
1933	Fred Johnson, NO	21–9	.700
1934	Fred Johnson, NO	20–5	.800
1935	Al Milnar, NO	24–5	.828
1936	Dutch Leonard, Atl.	13–3	.813
1937	Byron Humphries, NO	20–7	.741
1938	Tom Sunkel, Atl.	21–5	.808
1939	Ed Heusser, Mem.	19–7	.731
1940	Boots Poffenberger, Nash.	26–9	.743
1941	Russ Meers, Nash.	16–5	.762
1942	George Dockins, NO	14–5	.737
1943	Bill Stewart, Nash.	18–5	.783
1944	Boyd Tepler, LR	12–2	.857
1945	Lew Carpenter, Atl.	22–2	.917
1946	Les Willis, Mem.	18–7	.720
1947	Walker Cress, NO	15–5	.750
1948	Roman Brunswick, Mem.	12–0	1.000
1949	Garmen Mallory, Nash.	20–4	.833
1950	Robert Shultze, Nash.	25–6	.807
1951	Don Carlsen, NO	11–3	.786
1952	Al Sima, Chatt.	24–9	.727
1953	Jack Harshman, Nash.	23–7	.767
1954	Leo Cristante, Atl.	24–7	.774
1955	Richard, Strahs, Mem.	10–2	.833
1956	Les Phillips, NO	11–4	.733
1957	Don Minnick, Chatt.	17–6	.739
1958	Bill Harrington, Birm.	20–7	.741
1959	Steve Kraly, Nash.	10–3	.769
	Robert Milliken, Mem.	10–3	.769
1960	Jim Maloney, Nash.	14–5	.737
1961	Howard Koplitz, Birm.	23–3	.885

SA PITCHERS — MOST STRIKEOUTS —

1913	Elmer Brown, Mnty.	156	1938	Tom Sunkel, Atl.	178
1914	Roy Walker, NO	200	1939	Alpha Brazle, LR	122
1915	Geo. Cunningham, Chatt.	167	1940	Ace Adams, Nash.	122
1916	Roy Walker, NO	173	1941	Russ Meers, Nash.	161
1917	Roy Walker, NO	231	1942	Geo. Jeffcoat, Nash.	146
1918	Bill Bailey, NO	55	1943	Weldon West, Mem.	134
1919	Claude Jonnard, LR	134	1944	Boyd Tepler, Nash.	147
1920	Roy Walker, NO	237	1945	Al Treichel, LR	207
1921	Claude Jonnard, LR	234	1946	Bob McCall, Nash.	179
1922	Cy Warmoth, Nash.–LR	170	1947	Ben Wade, Nash.	145
1923	Joe Martina, NO	149	1948	John Perkovich, Mem.	153
1924	Cy Warmoth, Mem.	133	1949	Bill MacDonald, NO	137
1925	Geo. Pipgras, Atl.–Nash.	141	1950	Marv Rotblatt, Mem.	203
1926	Guy Morton, Mem.	110	1951	Dick Littlefield, Mem.	195
1927	Joe Martina, NO	103	1952	Al Worthington, Nash.	152
	Oscar Fuhr, Nash.	103	1953	Jim Constable, Nash.	183
1928	Eddie Wells, Birm.	129	1954	Joe Margoneri, Nash.	184
1929	Bill Hughes, LR	90	1955	Eugene Host, LR	184
1930	Billy Bayne. Chatt.	112	1956	Bob Kelly, Nash.	180
1931	Bobo Newsom, LR	152	1957	George Brunet, LR	235
1932	Walter Beck, Mem.	139	1958	Jim O'Toole, Nash.	189
1933	Jackie Reid, Nash.	135		Joe Grzenda, Birm.	189
1934	Steamboat Struss, LR	148	1959	Carl Mathias, Mob.	183
1935	Al Milnar, NO	140	1960	Pete Richert, Atl.	251
1936	Jinx Poindexter, LR	144	1961	Bo Belinsky, LR	182

SA PITCHERS — LOWEST EARNED RUN AVERAGE —

1919	Hub Perdue, NO	1.56	1939	Herman Besse, Mem.	2.48
1921	Claude Jonnard, LR	2.31	1940	Crip Polli, Chatt.	3.00
1922	Rube Robinson, LR	2.01	1941	Emile Lochbaum, Atl.	2.74
1923	Dan McGraw, Mem.	2.29	1942	Bill Kennedy, Chatt.	2.43
1924	Pug Cavet, NO	2.66	1943	Ed Lopat, LR	3.05
1925	Rube Robinson, LR	2.73	1944	Howard Fox, Birm.	2.71
1926	Hod Lisenbee, Mem.	2.48	1945	Lew Carpenter, Atl.	1.82
1927	Dave Danforth, NO	2.25	1946	Bill Ayers, Atl.	1.95
1928	Harry Kelley, Mem.	2.38	1947	Bob Hall, Mobile	2.80
1929	Leo Moon, LR	2.85	1948	Mike Palm, Birm.	2.20
1930	Leo Moon, LR	2.98	1949	Jim Suchecki, Birm.	2.77
1931	Bill Bean, NO	2.82	1950	Marv Rotblatt, Mem.	2.67
1932	Clyde Barfoot, Chatt.	2.76	1951	Frank Bisean, Mem.	2,55
1933	Fred Johnson, NO	3.03	1952	Wade Browning, Mob.	2.90
1934	Al Milnar, NO	2.61	1953	Art Fowler, Atl.	3.03
1935	Harry Kelley, Mem.–Atl.	2.50	1954	Nelson King, NO	2.25
1936	Luther Thomas, Atl.	2.82	1955	Ralph Mauriello, Mob.	2.76
1937	Hugh Casey, Birm.	2.55	1956	Bill Dailey, Mobile	3.18
1938	Tom Sunkel, Atl.	2.33	1957	Hy Cohen, Memphis	2.72

| 1958 | Bob Davis, LR | 2.17 | 1960 | Ron Nischwitz, Birm. | 2.31 |
| 1959 | Bill Dailey, Mobile | 2.41 | 1961 | Jack Smith, Atl. | 2.09 |

SA PITCHERS – 30-GAME WINNERS

| 1906 | 35–11 | Glenn Leibhardt, Mem. |
| 1904 | 31–10 | Frank Smith, Atl. |

SA LIFETIME RECORDS

BEST LIFETIME HITTING RECORDS

Years	Harry Knaupp	12
	Doc Wiseman	12
Games	Fred Graff	1,523
Average	Babe Bigelow	.359
At–Bats	Andy Reese	5,205
Runs	Eddie Rose	858
Hits	Andy Reese	1,641
Doubles	Andy Reese	320
Triples	Tommy Taylor	120
Home Runs	Joe Hutcheson	107
RBIs	Eddie Rose	866
	Andy Reese	865
Stolen Bases	Stuffy Stewart	370

BEST LIFETIME PITCHING RECORDS

Years	Harry Kelley	13
	Rube Robinson	13
Games	Harry Kelley	515
Innings	Rube Robinson	3,128
Victories	Rube Robinson	208
	Harry Kelley	206
Losses	Rube Robinson	169
Strikeouts	Roy Walker	1,213

SA SEASON RECORDS

BEST INDIVIDUAL BATTING RECORDS

Average	Hugh Hill (Nashville, 1902)	.416
Games	Roy Ellam (Birmingham, 1915)	161
At–Bats	Gene Paulette (Nashville, 1915)	685
Runs	Charles Gilbert (Nashville, 1948)	178
Hits	Wilbur Good (Atlanta, 1925)	236
Doubles	Joe Dwyer (Nashville, 1936)	65
Triples	Ike Boone (New Orleans, 1921)	27
	Elliott Bigelow (Chattanooga, 1925)	27
	Danny Taylor (Memphis, 1927)	27
Home Runs	Bob Lennon (Nashville, 1954)	64
Extra Base Hits	Bob Lennon (Nashville, 1954)	
	33 2Bs, 6 3Bs, 64 HRs	103
RBIs	Charles Workman (Nashville, 1948)	182
Stolen Bases	Don Nicholas (Memphis, 1952)	84
Walks	Charles Gilbert (Nashville, 1948)	155
Strikeouts	Elwood Grantham (Nashville, 1948)	133
HBP	Barney Munch (Atlanta, 1917)	22
Hitting Streak (Games)	Harry Bates (Nashville, 1925)	46

BEST INDIVIDUAL PITCHING RECORDS

Games	Jerry Lock (Memphis, 1960)	74
Complete Games	Glenn Leibhardt (Memphis, 1906)	45
Victories	Glenn Leibhardt (Memphis, 1906)	35
Losses	Ray Roberts (Mobile, 1921)	27
Winning Pcg.	Roman Brunswick (Memphis, 1948, 12–0)	1.000
Lowest ERA	Hub Perdue (New Orleans, 1919)	1.56
Most Innings	Tom Sheehan (Atlanta, 1920)	375
Consecutive Wins	Al Milnar (New Orleans, 1935)	17
Shutouts	Irvin Wilhelm (Birmingham, 1907)	11
Strikeouts	Pete Richert (Atlanta, 1960)	251
Walks	Richard Weik (Chattanooga, 1948)	173

SOUTHERN ASSOCIATION CENTURY CLUB

Winners			Losers		
1921	Memphis	104–49	1917	Mobile	34–117
1923	Memphis	104–49	1930	Mobile	40–112
1926	New Orleans	101–53	1937	Knoxville	42–111
1932	Memphis	101–53	1947	Little Rock	51–103
1940	Nashville	101–47	1931	Nashville	51–102
			1921	Chattanooga	52–102
			1955	Little Rock	52–102
			1923	Little Rock	51–101
			1956	Mobile	53–101
			1914	Montgomery	54–100

SALLY Records Through 1963

ANNUAL STANDINGS

1904			1906		
Macon	67–45	.598	Savannah	72–41	.637
Savannah	63–48	.567	Augusta	70–45	.609
Charleston	59–50	.541	Macon	58–53	.523
Jacksonville	58–57	.504	Columbia	52–59	.469
Columbia	47–62	.431	Charleston	48–61	.440
Augusta	41–73	.360	Jacksonville	36–77	.318

1905			1907		
Macon	75–45	.625	Charleston	75–46	.620
Savannah	71–56	.559	Jacksonville	68–51	.571
Jacksonville	68–59	.535	Macon	68–54	.557
Augusta	57–71	.445	Augusta	59–61	.492
Charleston	53–70	.431	Savannah	56–63	.471
Columbia	52–75	.409	Columbia	36–87	.293

1908

Jacksonville	77–34	.694
Savannah	64–45	.587
Augusta	51–59	.464
Columbia	46–58	.442
Macon	48–68	.412
Charleston	44–66	.400

1909

Chattanooga	77–36	.681
Columbus	72–49	.595
Augusta	64–49	.561
Savannah	60–61	.496
Chtn–Knox	52–60	.464
Macon	49–68	.419
Jacksonville	47–66	.416
Columbia	42–76	.356

1910

Columbus	70–49	.588
Macon	68–50	.576
Savannah	61–58	.513
Jacksonville	60–58	.508
Augusta	51–68	.429
Columbia	46–72	.385

1911

Columbia	82–49	.639
Columbus	86–50	.632
Albany	82–53	.609
Macon	72–62	.537
Jacksonville	56–79	.415
Savannah	56–81	.409
Augusta–SAL	52–71	.423
Charleston	41–84	.328

1912

Jacksonville	70–41	.631
Savannah	66–50	.569
Columbus	61–51	.545
Albany	52–62	.456
Macon	51–62	.451
Columbia	41–75	.353

1913

Savannah	78–38	.672
Columbus	60–55	.522
Jacksonville	60–58	.509

Macon	55–60	.478
Charleston	48–68	.414
Albany	46–68	.404

1914

Charleston	78–46	.629
Savannah	72–50	.590
Albany	64–57	.529
Columbia	60–66	.476
Jacksonville	58–64	.475
Columbus	55–67	.451
Macon	52–68	.433
Sugusta	52–73	.416

1915

Columbus	52–36	.591
Charleston	51–36	.587
Macon	48–39	.552
Columbia	44–42	.512
Albnay	41–45	.477
Augusta	41–45	.477
Jacksonville	35–51	.407
Savannah	34–52	.395

1916

Columbia	73–50	.594
Charleston	69–55	.556
Augusta	68–55	.553
Columbus	65–62	.512
Jacksonville	57–65	.467
Macon	55–67	.451
Montgomery	42–47	.472
Albnay	30–47	.389

1917

Charleston	47–23	.671
Columbia	43–28	.606
Jacksonville	33–35	.485
Augusta	27–41	.397
Columbus	8–19	.296
Macon	7–19	.269

1919

Columbia	55–39	.585
Charlotte	55–41	.573
Greenville	52–45	.536
Charleston	49–48	.505
Augusta	45–52	.464
Spartanburg	33–64	.344

1920

Columbia	76–44	.633
Greenville	72–55	.567
Spartanburg	56–65	.463
Charlotte	58–68	.460
Augusta	55–68	.447
Charleston	54–71	.432

1921

Columbia	95–53	.642
Charleston	83–54	.562
Augusta	78–68	.534
Greenville	71–76	.483
Spartanburg	61–68	.415
Charlotte	52–93	.359

1922

Charleston	80–48	.625
Charlotte	73–59	.533
Columbia	71–60	.541
Spartanburg	63–68	.481
Augusta	54–76	.415
Greenville	50–82	.379

1923

Charlotte	89–56	.614
Macon	82–58	.586
Greenville	77–65	.538
Augusta	73–62	.533
Spartanburg	74–66	.528
Col'bia–Gast	44–86	.338

1924

Augusta	74–47	.612
Charlotte	73–48	.604
Spartanburg	61–60	.508
Greenville	59–60	.496
Asheville	56–62	.470
Macon	37–82	.311

1925

Spartanburg	80–49	.621
Charlotte	79–50	.613
Macon	69–58	.543
Augusta	69–59	.539
Asheville	66–63	.512
Greenville	60–68	.469
Columbia	47–82	.364
Knoxville	44–85	.341

1926

Greenville	98–50	.662
Asheville	80–66	.547
Augusta	80–67	.544
Charlotte	77–72	.517
Spartanburg	74–74	.500
Macon	71–74	.489
Knoxville	68–79	.463
Columbia	40–106	.274

1927

Greenville	92–56	.622
Spartanburg	81–67	.547
Knoxville	79–68	.537
Asheville	76–73	.510
Macon	76–73	.510
Chalotte	72–78	.480
Columbia	65–81	.445
Augusta	52–97	.349

1928

Asheville	97–49	.664
Macon	80–68	.541
Augusta	75–69	.521
Spartanburg	73–72	.503
Knoxville	73–75	.493
Columbia	67–78	.462
Charlotte	60–86	.411
Greenville	60–88	.405

1929

Knoxville	85–61	.582
Ashville	84–62	.575
Charlotte	79–67	.541
Greenville	71–73	.486
Macon	69–79	.466
Augusta	68–78	.466
Columbia	68–79	.463
Spartanburg	59–84	.413

1930

Macon	87–52	.612
Greenville	85–57	.598
Asheville	79–61	.564
Augusta	68–70	.493
Charlotte	61–72	.459
Columbia	39–101	.279

1936		
Columbus	97–53	.647
Jacksonville	88–57	.607
Macon	87–64	.576
Savannah	64–84	.432
Augusta	56–94	.373
Columbia	55–95	.367

1937		
Columbus	79–59	.572
Macon	77–59	.566
Savannah	78–60	.566
Jacksonville	65–73	.471
Augusta	62–78	.448
Columbia	52–84	.382

1938		
Savannah	81–60	.574
Macon	81–61	.570
Columbia	74–66	.529
Augusta	74–66	.529
Jacksonville	70–69	.504
Columbus	70–70	.500
Spartanburg	54–82	.397
Greenville	53–83	.390

1939		
Columbus	83–55	.601
Augusta	83–56	.597
Savannah	80–59	.576
Macon	71–64	.526
Greenville	64–76	.457
Jacksonville	63–75	.457
Columbia	58–81	.417
Spartanburg	51–87	.370

1940		
Savannah	94–56	.627
Columbus	88–63	.583
Macon	84–67	.556
Greenville	77–72	.517
Augusta	77–73	.513
Columbia	74–77	.490
Jacksonville	64–88	.421
Charleston	44–106	.293

1941		
Macon	90–50	.643
Columbia	89–51	.636
Columbus	68–69	.496
Augusta	64–74	.464
Jacksonville	63–75	.457
Charleston	61–76	.445
Greenville	60–77	.438
Savannah	57–80	.416

1946		
Columbus	79–60	.568
Columbia	79–61	.564
Greenville	76–62	.551
Augusta	76–73	.547
Charleston	65–75	.464
Jacksonville	65–75	.464
Macon	61–79	.436
Savannah	55–81	.404

1947		
Columbus	88–65	.575
Savannah	85–66	.563
Charleston	83–69	.546
Augusta	81–69	.540
Greenville	77–77	.500
Macon	70–82	.461
Jacksonville	66–87	.431
Columbia	59–94	.386

1948		
Charleston	87–65	.572
Macon	86–69	.558
Greenville	84–69	.549
Columbia	79–72	.523
Jacksonville	78–75	.510
Columvus	65–83	.439
Augusta	64–87	.424
Savannah	63–87	.420

1949		
Macon	96–58	.623
Savannah	84–68	.553
Greenville	82–72	.532
Columbus	80–73	.523
Jacksonville	73–81	.474
Augusta	69–83	.454
Charleston	68–83	.450
Columbia	59–93	.388

1950

Macon	90–63	.588
Columbia	83–70	.542
Savannah	83–70	.542
Charleston	79–72	.523
Columbus	78–73	.517
Greenville	68–85	.444
Augusta	66–87	.431
Jacksonville	63–90	.412

1951

Montgomery	85–55	.607
Jacksonville	79–58	.577
Macon	75–63	.543
Charleston	75–65	.536
Columbus	68–71	.489
Savannah	64–74	.464
Augusta	62–76	.449
Columbia	46–92	.333

1952

Columbia	100–54	.649
Columbus	87–67	.565
Montgomery	86–68	.558
Macon	83–71	.539
Charleston	78–75	.510
Savannah	74–79	.484
Jacksonville	69–85	.448
Augusta	38–116	.247

1953

Jacksonville	93–44	.679
Columbia	92–48	.657
Columbus	67–70	.489
Savannah	68–73	.482
Macon	67–74	.475
Augusta	65–74	.468
Charleston	55–84	.396
Montgomery	50–90	.357

1954

Jacksonville	83–57	.593
Savannah	80–60	.571
Macon	78–61	.561
Coumbia	77–62	.554
Montgomery	68–72	.486
Charlotte	62–77	.446
Augusta	58–82	.414
Columbus	51–86	.372

1955

Columbia	89–51	.636
Jacksonville	79–61	.564
Augusta	76–64	.543
Montgomery	75–64	.540
Macon	67–73	.479
Savannah	61–79	.436
Columbus	58–81	.417
Charlotte	54–86	.386

1956

Jacksonville	87–53	.621
Charlotte	79–61	.564
Columbus	79–61	.564
Augusta	74–66	.529
Macon	64–76	.457
Columbia	64–76	.457
Savannah	60–80	.429
Knoxville	53–87	.379

1957

Augusta	98–56	.636
Charlotte	86–67	.562
Savannah	81–72	.529
Knoxville	81–73	.526
Columbus	81–73	.526
Jacksonville	76–78	.494
Columbia	59–95	.383
Macon	53–101	.344

1958

Augusta	77–63	.550
Jacksonville	76–64	.543
Macon	70–70	.500
Charlotte	69–71	.497
Knoxville	67–73	.479
Savannah	61–79	.436

1959

Knoxville	78–62	.557
Charlotte	75–65	.536
Charleston	71–69	.507
Col's–Gastonia	70–69	.504
Asheville	70–70	.500
Savannah	76–73	.479
Jacksonville	65–75	.464
Macon	63–76	.453

1960				**1962**		
Columbia	83–56	.597		Savannah	92–47	.662
Charlotte	79–61	.564		Knoxville	86–54	.614
Savannah	78–61	.561		Macon	80–59	.576
Knoxville	71–67	.514		Asheville	70–70	.500
Jacksonville	70–69	.504		Greenville	65–75	.464
Asheville	62–77	.446		Augusta	75–83	.407
Charleston	59–80	.424		Ports–Norfolk	55–85	.393
Macon	54–85	.388		Charlotte	54–86	.386

1961				**1963**		
Asheville	87–50	.635		Macon	81–59	.579
Knoxville	75–64	.540		Asheville	79–61	.564
Greenville	72–66	.522		Lynchburg	79–61	.564
Columbia	70–65	.519		Augusta	75–63	.543
Charleston	70–68	.507		Knoxville	71–68	.511
Ports–Norfolk	66–72	.478		Chattanooga	62–78	.443
Charlotte	61–79	.436		Charlotte	58–82	.414
Jacksonville	51–88	.367		Nashville	53–86	.381

SALLY PLAYOFFS

1909 Chattanooga defeated Augusta 4 games to 3.

1911 Columbus defeated Columbia 4 games to 2.

1912 Jacksonville defeated Columbus 4 games to 1.

1914 Savannah defeated Albany 4 games to 2.

1915 Columbus defeated Macon 4 games to 1 with 2 ties.

1916 Augusta defeated Columbia 4 games to 0.

1917 Columbia defeated Charleston 4 games to 2.

1923 Charlotte defeated Macon 4 games to 1.

1929 Knoxville defeated Asheville.

1930 Greenville defeated Macon 4 games to 2.

1936 Columbus defeated Jacksonville 4 games to 2.

1937 Savannah defeated Columbus 3 games to 0. Macon defeated Jacksonville 3 games to 2. **FINALS:** Savannah defeated Macon 3 games to 1.

1938 Savannah defeated Columbia 4 games to 3. Macon defeated Augusta 4 games to 2. **FINALS:** Macon defeated Savannah 4 games to 3.

1939 Augusta defeated Macon 4 games to 3. Savannah defeated Columbus 4 games to 3. **FINALS:** Augusta defeated Savannah 4 games to 0.

1940 Columbus defeated Greenville 4 games to 0. Macon defeated Savannah 4 games to 2. **FINALS:** Columbus defeated Macon 4 games to 2.

1941 Columbia defeated Macon 4 games to 2.

1942 Augusta defeated Columbus 4 games to 1. Columbia defeated Greenville 4 games to 2. **FINALS:** Augusta defeated Columbia 4 games to 0.

1947 Augusta defeated Columbus 4 games to 2. Savannah defeated Charleston 4 games to 3. **FINALS:** Savannah defeated Augusta 4 games to 1.

1948 Columbia defeated Charleston 4 games to 3. Greenville defeated Macon 4 games to 3. **FINALS:** Greenville defeated Columbia 4 games to 1.

1949 Macon defeated Columbus 4 games to 3. Greenville defeated Savannah 4 games to 3. **FINALS:** Macon defeated Greenville 4 games to 1.

1950 Macon defeated Charleston 3 games to 2. Columbia defeated Savannah 3 games to 2. **FINALS:** Macon defeated Columbia 4 games to 0.

1951 Montgomery defeated Charleston 3 games to 2. Jacksonville defeated Macon 3 games to 2. **FINALS:** Montgomery defeated Jacksonville 4 games to 0.

1952 Macon defeated Columbia 3 games to 0. Montgomery defeated Columbus 3 games to 2. **FINALS:** Montgomery defeated Macon 4 games to 2.

1953 Jacksonville defeated Savannah 3 games to 1. Columbia defeated Columbus 3 games to 0. **FINALS:** Columbia defeated Jacksonville 4 games to 3.

1954 Jacksonville defeated Columbia 3 games to 1. Savannah defeated Macon 3 games to 0. **FINALS:** Savannah defeated Jacksonville 4 games to 3.

1955 Augusta defeated Columbia 1 game to 0. Montgomery defeated Jacksonville 1 game to 0. **FINALS:** Augusta defeated Montgomery 2 games to 1.

1956 Jacksonville defeated Charlotte 1 game to 0. Columbus defeated Augusta 1 game to 0. **FINALS:** Jacksonville defeated Columbus 2 games to 0.

1957 Augusta defeated Savannah 2 games to 0. Charlotte defeated Knoxville 2 games to 0. **FINALS:** Charlotte defeated Augusta 2 games to 1.

1958 Macon defeated Augusta 1 game to 0. Jacksonville defeated Charlotte 1 game to 0. **FINALS:** Macon defeated Jacksonville 2 games to 0.

1959 Charleston defeated Knoxville 3 games to 2. Gastonia defeated Charlotte 3 games to 2. **FINALS:** Gastonia defeated Charleston 3 games to 0.

1960 Savannah defeated Columbia 3 games to 1. Knoxville defeated Charlotte 3 games to 1. **FINALS:** Savannah defeated Knoxville 3 games to 0.

1961 Macon defeated Savannah 3 games to 0. Knoxville defeated Asheville 3 games to 1. **FINALS:** Savannah defeated Knoxville 3 games to 0.

1962 Macon defeated Savannah 3 games to 0. Knoxville defeated Asheville 3 games to 1. **FINALS:** Macon defeated Knoxville 3 games to 1.

SALLY PRESIDENTS

1904–08	Charles W. Boyer	1946–51	Earl Blue
1909–11	W. R. Joyner	1952–53	Dick Butler
1912–17	N. P. Corish	1954–56	Bill Terry
1919–23	W. H. Walsh	1957	Sam W. Wolfson
1924–30	W. G. Bramham	1958–63	Sam C. Smith, Jr.
1936–41	Dr. E. M. Wilder		

SALLY BATTING CHAMPIONS

1904	Andrew Oyler, Sav.	.301	1915	C. M. Chauncey, Mac.	.359
1905	Ty Cobb, Augusta	.326	1916	Harry Purce, Jax	.316
1906	Ed Sabrie, Savannah	.290	1917	Harry Camp, Chtn.	.357
1907	Tom Raftery, Mac.	.301	1919	Walter Johnson, Cbia.	.362
1908	Wilbur Murdock, Mac.	.302	1920	C. H. Marshall, Char.	.320
1909	Joe Jackson, Sav.	.358	1921	Goose Goslin, Cbia.	.390
1910	Juan Viola, Aug.	.305	1922	Ernest Pedgett, Char.	.333
1911	Scotty Alcock, Alb.	.333	1923	Zinn Beck Grnv.	.370
1912	Hayden Herndon, Alb.	.324	1924	Geo. Rhinehardt, Grnv.	.404
1913	Al Handiboe, Sav.	.314	1925	Everett Bankston, Cbia.	.388
1914	George Stinson, Macon	.322	1926	William Rhiel, Grnv.	.386

1927	Tom Angley, Macon	.362		1950	Peter Kraus, Chtn.	.323
1928	Oscar Felber, Knox.	.366		1951	Louis Kahn, Cbus.	.351
1929	Stanley Keyes, Ash,	.377		1952	Tom Hamilton, Sav.	.325
1930	Hal Sullivan, Asheville	.374		1953	Hank Aaron, Jax	.362
1936	William Prout, Mac.	.342		1954	Al Pinkston, Sav.	.360
1937	Jack Bolling, Mac.	.343		1955	Wes Covington, Jax	.326
1938	Doug Dean, Sav.-Grnv.	.385		1956	Leonard Green, Cbus.	.318
1939	Hugh Todd, Jax	.384		1957	Tom John, Sav.	.326
1940	Hooper Triplett, Cbus.	.369		1958	George Alusik, Aug.	.325
1941	Seymour Block, Macon	.357		1959	Nathan Dickerson, Ash.	.362
1942	Henry Bradford, Jax	.342		1960	Purnal Goldy, Knox.	.342
1946	Ted Kluzsewski, Cbia.	.352		1961	Teo Acosta, Cbia.	.343
1947	Ralph Brown, Aug.	.357		1962	Elmo Plaskett, Ash.	.350
1948	Harold Summers, Aug.	.331		1963	Marvin Staehle, Nash.	.337
1949	William Lutes, Jax	.313				

SALLY HOME RUN CHAMPIONS

1904	Miller, Cbia.-Aug.-Sav.	5		1942	Henry Bradford, Jax	13
1912	Walton Cruise, Mac.	8		1946	Robert Erps, Cbus.	16
1919	Ab Wingo, Grnv.	11		1947	Lloyd Lowe, Cbus.	19
1920	McMillian, Greenville	14			Wm. Hockenbury, Sav.	19
1921	August Felix, Chtn.	19		1948	Harold Summers, Aug.	28
1922	Ben Paschal, Char.	18		1949	Ray Cash, Macon	19
1923	Ben Paschal, Char.	26		1950	James Dickey, Cbus.	20
1924	Clarence McCrone, Ash.	28		1951	Richard Greco, Mtgy.	33
1925	Pete Daniels, Grnv.	29		1952	Richard Greco, Mtgy.	24
1926	Randolph Moore, Grnv.	35		1953	Tom Giordano, Sav.	24
1927	William Barrett, Knox.	39		1954	Clarence Riddle, Jax	28
	Ernest Shirley, Grnv.	39			James Dickey, Mac.	28
1928	Clarence Walker, Grnv.	33		1955	Wiley Wms., Sav,-Jax	28
1929	Frank Welch, Grnv.	29		1956	Ed Barbarito, Jax	27
1930	James Hudgens Grnv.	39		1957	Jacques Monette, Knox.-Jax	25
1936	Dee Moore, Macon	18		1958	Carl Warwick, Macon	22
1937	Nick Etten, Sav.	21		1959	Clifford Cook, Sav.	32
1938	Dan Pavlovic, Mac.-			1960	Donn Clendenon, Sav.	28
	Spar.-Sav.	17		1961	Gary Rushing, Ash.	25
1939	Dan Pavlovic, Sav.	19		1962	Dick Means, Char.-Ash.	36
1940	Beverly Ferrell, Grnv.	21		1963	Jim Hicks, Mac.-Lyn.	21
1941	James Walsh, Jax	17			Fred Loesekam, Lyn.	21
	Clyde Vollmer, Cbia.	17				

SALLY RBI LEADERS

1920	Everett Bankston, Grnv.	86		1926	Randolph Moore, Grnv.	134
1921	Goose Goslin, Cbia.	131		1927	Ernest Shirley, Grnv.	128
1922	Ben Paschal, Char.	114		1928	David Davis, Aug.	125
1923	Ben Paschal, Char.	122		1929	Murray Howell, Grnv.	135
1924	Charles Tolson, Char.	111		1930	Murray Howell, Grnv.	147
1925	R. J. Ducotte, Char.	124		1936	Stanley Tutja, Cbus.	129

1937	Herbert Bremer, Cbus.	101	1953	Hank Aaron, Jax	125
1938	Leon Prout, Cbus.	110	1954	Clarence Riddle, Jax	112
1939	Harold Quick, Grnv.	106	1955	William Thompson, Cbia.	94
1940	Ray Sanders, Cbus.	152		Larry Osborne, Aug.	94
1941	Seymour Block, Mac.	112	1956	Ed Barbarito, Jax	99
1942	Henry Bradford, Jax	107	1957	Ray Barber, Knox.	97
	Hugh Todd, Jax	107	1958	George Alusik, Aug.	88
1946	Roy Broome, Cbus.	99		Harry Warner, Char.	88
1947	Walt Schuerbaum, Aug.	118	1959	Cliff Cook, Sav.	100
1948	Harold Summers, Aug.	115	1960	Leo Smith, Knox.	111
1949	Roy Peterson, Macon	100	1961	Gary Rushing, Ash.	99
1950	Lewis Davis, Macon	119	1962	Grover Jones, Sav.	101
1951	William Johnson, Mtgy.	107	1963	Jim Hicks, Mac.-Lyn.	82
1952	Richard Greco, Mtgy.	135			

SALLY STOLEN BASE LEADERS

1905	Paul Sentelle, Mac.	50	1937	Cecil Garriott, Cbus.	30
1906	King, Savannah	55	1938	Cecil Garriott, Cbus.	57
1907	Tom Raftery, Chtn.	80	1939	James Adlam, Aug.	30
1908	Pelkey, Savannah	59	1940	Cecil Garriott, Macon	40
1909	John Bierkotte, Jax-Aug.	56	1941	Cecil Garriott, Macon	26
1910	Lee, Macon	42	1942	Leon Treadway, Sav.	27
1911	Forbes Alcock, Alb.	66	1946	Roy Hartsfield, Chtn.	18
1912	George Whitted, Jax	44	1947	Eddie Pullen, Cbus.	52
1913	Walter Keating, Cubs.	52	1948	Lloyd Merriman, Cbia.	44
1914	Tom McMillian, Chtn.	46	1949	Maynard DeWitt, Grnv.	48
1915	Hardin Herndon, Cbus.	38	1950	Edwin Rider, Aug.	27
1916	Hardin Herndon, Cbus.	59	1951	Richard Smith, Chtn.	28
1917	Guy Dunning, Cbia.	34	1952	Ross Passineau, Chtn.	38
1919	Warren Butts, Char.	49	1953	Everett Joyner, Cbus.	19
1920	Flash Archdeacon, Char.	44		Don Murrow, Mtgy.	19
1921	Arthur Trefry, Aug.	6	1954	Jack Mitchell, Aug.	22
1922	Kiki Cuyler, Chtn.	35	1955	Sam Drake, Macon	24
1923	McCue, Cbia.-Gast.	25	1956	Dan Morejohn, Sav.	18
1924	Geo. Rhinehardt, Grnv.	32	1957	Angelo Dagres, Knox.	31
1925	Harold Anderson, Ash.	31	1958	Mike Napoli, Macon	29
1926	Sanders, Charlotte	42	1959	Willard Fox, Macon	29
1927	Charles Fullis, Mac.	41	1960	Hiraldo Ruiz, Cbia.	55
1928	Ben Chapman, Ash.	30	1961	Teo Acosta, Cbia.	40
1929	Edcallier, Ash.-Macon	36	1962	Ruthford Salmon, Knox.	25
1930	H. Snyder, Macon	40	1963	Teo Acosta, Macon	21

SALLY .400 HITTERS

1924   Geo. Rhinehardt, Grnv.   .404

SALLY PITCHERS — MOST VICTORIES —

1904	Brindle Bayne. Mac.	30	1939	Ed Wissman, Cbus.	21
1905	Robert Spade, Mac.	25		Leo Twardy, Aug.	21
1906	Nap Rucker, Aug.	27	1940	James Davis, Aug.	23
1907	Bugs Raymond, Chtn.	35	1941	Stanley West, Macon	23
1908	P. Sitton, Augusta	19	1942	Mack Stewart, Chtn.	24
	Ed Welsher, Columbia	19	1946	Richard Starr, Aug.	19
1909	Roy Radabaugh, Cbus.	25	1947	Lou Brissie, Sav.	23
1910	Sam Weems, Macon	25	1948	Frank Smith, Cbia.	21
1911	Phil Douglas, Macon	28	1949	Al Burch, Sav.	20
1912	Albert Schultz, Sav.	25		Robert Spicer, Macon	20
1913	Dick Robertson, Sav.	28		James Atchley, Macon	20
1914	Wiley, Albany	24		John Fasholz, Cbus.	20
1915	Phil Redding, Cbia.	19	1950	Stan Karpinski, Macon	20
1916	Reid Zellars, Macon	22	1951	Vince DiLorenzo, Jax	20
1917	John Meador, Chtn.	13	1952	Barney Martin, Cbia.	23
1919	Rube Eldridge, Charlotte	20	1953	Larry Lassalle, Jax	19
1920	Jessie Doyle, Grnv.	25	1954	Humberto Robinson, Jax	23
1921	Lee Johnson, Columbia	24	1955	Charley Rabe, Cbia.	21
1922	Charles Brown, Charlotte	21	1956	Juan Pizarro, Jax	23
1923	Lee Bolt, Charlotte	20	1957	Freddy Olivo, Jax	16
1924	Charles Fulton, Aug.	24		Angel Oliva, Char.	16
1925	Jack Killeen, Spar.	27		Matt Saban, Char.	16
1926	Wiley Moore, Grnv.	30	1958	Jerry Walker, Knox.	18
1927	Bill Bayne, Grnv.	26	1959	Byron Taylor, Ash.	18
1928	Bill Harris, Ash.	25	1960	Ken Hunt, Cbia.	16
1929	Jim Walker, Knox	25	1961	Byron Taylor, Char.	17
1930	Huey Harmon, Grnv.	25	1962	Camilo Estevis, Grnv.	18
1936	Arthur Evans, Macon	21	1963	Troy Giles, Ash.	18
1937	Arthur Evans, Macon	23		Fred Talbot, Lyn.	18
1938	John Pezullo, Sav.	26			

SALLY PITCHERS — WINNING PERCENTAGE —

1904	Conrad Welch, Sav.	24–10	.706
1905	Bob Spade, Macon	25–8	.758
1906	Walt Deaver, Savannah	18–4	.716
1907	Bugs Raymond, Chtn.	35–11	.716
1908	Veddor Sitton, Jax	17–5	.773
1909	Prince Gaskill, Chatt.	21–4	.808
1910	Rufus Nolley, Sav.	19–3	.864
1911	Roy Radaugh, Cbus.	27–6	.818
1912	Henry Weldel, Columbus	15–5	.750
1913	Dick Robertson, Sav.	28–8	.778
1914	Walter Smallwood, Sav.	17–6	.739
1915	Dolf Redding, Cbus.	19–6	.760
1916	James, Columbia	15–5	.750
1917	John Meador, Chtn.	13–2	.876

1919	Jesse Doyle, Grnv.	18–6	.750
1920	Larry Cheney, Cbia.	23–6	.793
1921	Ray Jordan, Cbia.	21–2	.913
1922	Charles Brown, Char.	21–8	.724
1923	Yeargin, Greenville	18–9	.667
1924	Charles Fulton, Aug.	24–8	.750
1925	Clarence Blethen, Macon	16–5	.762
1926	Wiley Moore, Grnv.	30–4	.882
1927	Clarence Hodge, Spar.	16–5	.762
1928	William Harris, Ash.	25–9	.735
1929	John Walker, Knox.	25–9	.735
1930	Huey Harmon, Grnv.	25–9	.735
1936	Henry Bazner, Jax	20–7	.741
1937	Arthur Evans, Macon	23–8	.742
1938	John Pezzullo, Sav.	26–9	.743
1939	Ed Wissmann, Cbus.	21–9	.700
1940	Robert Chipman, Sav.	17–5	.773
1941	Frank Marino, Macon	19–1	.950
1942	Adrian Zabala, Jax	16–5	.762
1946	Herman Wehmier, Cbia.	17–6	.739
1947	Tom Poholsky, Cbus.	16–3	.842
1948	Don Osborn, Macon	17–3	.850
1949	Alfred Burch, Sav.	20–6	.769
1950	George Dries, Cbia.	14–5	.737
1951	Vince DiLorenzo, Jax	22–8	.733
1952	Dennis Reeder, Cbus.	20–6	.769
1953	Larry Lassalle, Jax	19–5	.792
1954	Ralph Birkofer, Cbia.	14–3	.824
1955	Charley Rabe, Cbia.	21–7	.750
1956	Evilio Hernandez, Char.	18–4	.818
1957	Ronald Rozman, Aug.	15–1	.938
1958	Jerry Walker, Knox.	18–4	.818
1959	James Proctor, Knox.	15–5	.750
1960	Kenneth Hunt, Cbia.	16–6	.727
1961	James Hardison, Ash.	16–2	.889
1962	Marvin Fodor, Macon	15–4	.789
1963	Fred Talbot, Lyn.	18–6	.750

SALLY SEASON RECORDS
BEST INDIVIDUAL SEASON BATTING RECORDS

Average	George Rhinehardt (Greenville, 1924)	.404
Games	Donald LeJohn (Macon, 1957)	157
At–Bats	Russell Scarritt (Greenville, 1926)	645
Runs	Russell Scarritt (Greenvile, 1926)	150
Hits	Russell Scarritt (Greenville, 1926)	243
Doubles	Robert Winters (Columbia, 1939)	58
Triples	Dusty Cooke (Asheville, 1928)	30

Home Runs	William Barrett (Knoxville, 1927)	39
	Ernest Shirley (Greenville, 1927)	39
	James Hudgens (Greenville, 1930)	39
Total Bases	Russell Scarritt (Greenville, 1926)	375
RBIs	Raymond Sanders (Columbus, 1940)	152
Stolen Bases	Tom Raftery (Charleston, 1922)	80
Walks	Banks McDowell (Montgomery, 1951)	148
Strikeouts	Robert Thomson (Columbus, 1950)	163
HBP	Ernest Vache (Charleston, 1922)	26
Hitting Streak (Games)	Alfred Pinkston (Savannah, 1954)	36

SALLY PITCHERS – LOWEST EARNED RUN AVERAGE –

1920	Leo Townsend, Chtn.	2.65	1946	Richard Starr, Aug.	2.07
1921	Roy Jordan, Cbia.	2.10	1947	Lou Brissie, Sav.	1.91
1922	Godfrey Brogan, Chtn.	2.90	1948	Alfred Boresh, Cbia.	2.13
1923	Rufus Clarke, Aug.	2.90	1949	Sanford Silverstein, Sav.	2.10
1924	Charles Fulton, Aug.	3.07	1950	Morris Savransky, Cbia.	2.35
1925	Harry Smythe, Aug.	2.83	1951	Stan West, Macon	2.31
1926	Rainey, Ash.–Augusta	2.84	1952	George Dries, Chtn.	1.92
1927	Billy Bayne, Grnv.	2.87	1953	Harold Valentine, Cbia.	2.11
1928	Joe Heving, Ash.	2.46	1954	Humberto Robinson, Jax	2.41
1929	Dick Niehaus, Spar.	2.80	1955	Charley Rabe, Cbia.	2.01
1930	Phil Gallivan, Macon	2.94	1956	John Tsitouris, Aug.	1.51
1936	Joe Sims, Cbus.	2.44	1957	Ron Rozman, Aug.	1.64
1937	Clarence Blethenm Sav.	2.29	1958	Ross Carter, Jax	2.19
1938	Jake Baker, Macon	1.97	1959	James Proctor, Aug.	2.19
1939	William Seinsoth, Cbus.	2.41	1960	Charley Rabe, Cbia.	2.39
1940	Witt Guise, Cbia.	2.16	1961	Nick Willhite, Grnv.	1.80
1941	Frank Marino, Macon	2.16	1962	Richard Lines, Ash.	2.11
1942	Jake Levy, Macon	1.85	1963	Tom Richards, Lyn.	2.22

30-GAME WINNERS

1907	35–11	Bugs Raymond, Chtn.
1926	30–4	Wilcy Moore, Grnv.
1904	30–13	Brindle Bayne, Macon

SALLY PITCHERS   – MOST STRIKEOUTS –

1904	Brindle Bayne, Macon	228	1915	Dana Fillingim, Chtn.	129
1905	Harry Kane, Sav.	228	1916	Reidzellars, Macon	237
1907	Bugs Raymond, Chtn.	335	1917	Berlyn Horne, Jax	93
1908	Clarke, Macon	203	1919	J. D. Thompson, Grnv.	128
1909	Wagner, Cbia.–Augusta	202	1920	Larry Cheney, Cbia.	183
1912	Albert Schultz, Sav.	315	1921	Willard Davis, Aug.	174
1913	Dick Robertson, Sav.	235	1922	George Pipgras, Chtn.	175
1914	Dolf Redding, Cbus.	184	1923	Lee Bolt, Char.	133

1924	Alex Gibson, Ash.	140	1948	Ed Burtschey, Sav.	178
1925	James Lyle, Ash.	131	1949	Ray Moore, Grnv.	129
1926	Ormand, Greenville	160	1950	Robert Graber, Chtn.	205
1927	John Walker, Spar.	139	1951	Harry Byrd, Sav.	180
1928	Norcum Raunch, Macon	147	1952	Barney Martin, Cbia.	174
	Leroy Mehaffey, Cbia.	147	1953	Larry Lassalle, Jax	185
1929	John Allen, Ash.	173	1954	Humberto Robinson, Jax	243
1930	James Mooney, Char.	185	1955	Charley Rabe, Cbia.	219
1936	Ralph Braun, Jax	172	1956	Juan Pizarro, Jax	318
1937	Lakey Harkrader, Cbia.	133	1957	William Smith, Cbus.	196
1938	John Pezzullo, Sav.	218	1958	Chuck Estrada, Knox.	181
1939	Holland VanSlate, Cbus.	170	1959	Ray Daviault, Macon	169
1940	Fred Martin, Cbus.	208	1960	Ken Hunt, Cbia.	221
1941	Lee Anthony, Jax	202	1961	Nick Willhite, Grnv.	161
1942	William Ayers, Sav.	143	1962	Leo Marentette, Knox.	205
1946	Richard Starr, Aug.	233	1963	Troy Giles, Ash.	159
1947	Lou Birssie, Sav.	278			

SALLY INDIVIDUAL SEASON PITCHING RECORDS

Games	Willie Powell (Knoxville, 1958)	70
Complete Games	Irvin Stein (Charleston, 1941)	29
Victories	Bugs Raymond (Charleston, 1907)	35
Losses	Dick Robertson (Savannah, 1911)	26
Winning Pcg.	Frank Marino (Macon, 1941, 19–1)	.950
Lowest ERA	John Tsitouris (Augusta, 1956)	1.51
Most Innings	Reid Zellars (Macon, 1916)	376
Consecutive Wins	Wiley Moore (Greenville, 1926)	17
Shutouts	Harry Kane (Savannah, 1906)	9
Strikeouts	Bugs Raymond (Charleston, 1907)	335
Walks	George Burpo (Columbia, 1947)	203

SALLY CENTURY CLUB

	Winner			**Losers**	
1952	Columbia	100–54	1940	Charleston	44–106
			1930	Columbia	39–101
			1957	Macon	53–101

Southern League Records, 1964–1993

ANNUAL STANDINGS

1964

Lynchburg	81–59	.579
Birmingham	80–60	.571
Macon	75–65	.536
Charlotte	73–67	.521
Knoxville	67–73	.479
Chattanooga	65–74	.468
Columbus	65–74	.468
Asheville	52–86	.377

1965

Columbus	79–59	.572
Asheville	80–60	.571
Lynchburg	75–64	.540
Knoxville	73–66	.525
Charlotte	72–68	.514
Montgomery	63–74	.460
Chattanooga	60–80	.429
Birmingham	54–85	.388

1966

Mobile	88–52	.629
Asheville	78–61	.561
Evansville	68–72	.486
Macon	67–73	.479
Montgomery	66–72	.478
Charlotte	64–74	.464
Columbus	63–76	.453
Knoxville	61–75	.449

1967

Birmingham	84–55	.604
Montgomery	80–58	.580
Evansville	76–63	.547
Charlotte	75–65	.536
Macon	55–85	.393
Knoxville	47–91	.341

1968

Asheville	86–54	.614
Montgomery	80–57	.584
Charlotte	72–68	.514
Birmingham	66–74	.471
Savannah	57–79	.419
Evansville	55–84	.396

1969

Charlotte	81–59	.579
Birmingham	78–62	.557
Asheville	69–69	.500
Columbus	65–75	.464
Montgomery	62–73	.459
Savannah	59–76	.437

1970

Columbus	78–59	.569
Montgomery	79–60	.568
Birmingham	73–65	.529
Savannah	71–67	.514
Jacksonville	67–70	.489
Charlotte	66–73	.475
Mobile	59–78	.431
Asheville	59–80	.424

1971

Charlotte	92–50	.648
Asheville	90–51	.638
Montgomery	73–69	.514
Jacksonville	63–77	.450
Savannah	57–84	.404
Columbus	51–91	.359
Birmingham	48–93	.340

1972

EASTERN DIVISION

Asheville	81–58	.583
Savannah	80–59	.576
Charlotte	70–70	.500
Jacksonville	64–75	.460

WESTERN DIVISION

Montgomery	78–61	.561
Knoxville	76–64	.543
Columbus	59–80	.424
Birmingham	49–90	.353

1973

EASTERN DIVISION

Jacksonville	76–60	.559
Savannah	71–68	.511
Columbus	69–70	.496
Orlando	65–70	.481

WESTERN DIVISION			WESTERN DIVISION		
Montgomery	80–58	.580	Montgomery	86–51	.628
Asheville	71–69	.507	Chattanooga	61–75	.449
Knoxville	70–69	.504	Columbus	60–77	.438
Birmingham	50–88	.362	Knoxville	50–87	.365

1974

EASTERN DIVISION		
Jacksonville	78–60	.565
Orlando	73–61	.545
Savannah	73–65	.529
Columbus	65–73	.471
WESTERN DIVISION		
Knoxville	72–63	.533
Asheville	70–67	.511
Montgomery	61–76	.445
Birmingham	54–81	.400

1975

EASTERN DIVISION		
Orlando	81–57	.587
Savannah	70–64	.522
Columbus	70–64	.522
Jacksonville	59–79	.428
WESTERN DIVISION		
Montgomery	73–61	.545
Birmingham	65–69	.485
Knoxville	63–75	.457
Asheville	63–75	.457

1976

EASTERN DIVISION		
Orlando	75–64	.540
Charlotte	74–66	.529
Savannah	69–71	.493
Jacksonville	66–72	.478
WESTERN DIVISION		
Montgomery	81–56	.591
Chattanooga	70–68	.507
Knoxville	61–77	.442
Columbus	58–80	.420

1977

EASTERN DIVISION		
Orlando	76–61	.555
Savannah	77–63	.550
Jacksonville	72–66	.522
Charlotte	69–71	.493

1978

EASTERN DIVISION		
Orlando	82–61	.573
Jacksonville	73–69	.544
Savannah	72–72	.500
Columbus	70–73	.490
Charlotte	66–78	.458
WESTERN DIVISION		
Knoxville	88–56	.611
Memphis	71–73	.493
Montgomery	67–66	.465
Nashville	64–77	.454
Chattanooga	63–80	.441

1979

EASTERN DIVISION		
Columbus	84–59	.587
Charlotte	73–69	.514
Jacksonville	69–72	.489
Orlando	60–81	.426
Savannah	60–83	.420
WESTERN DIVISION		
Nashville	83–61	.576
Memphis	82–62	.569
Chattanooga	75–69	.521
Knoxville	65–76	.461
Montgomery	62–81	.434

1980

EASTERN DIVISION		
Savannah	77–67	.535
Columbus	76–68	.528
Charlotte	72–72	.500
Orlando	65–78	.455
Jacksonville	63–81	.438
WESTERN DIVISION		
Nashville	97–46	.678
Memphis	83–61	.576
Montgomery	68–76	.472
Chattanooga	61–83	.424
Knoxville	57–87	.396

1981

EASTERN DIVISION

Orlando	79–63	.556
Charlotte	74–69	.517
Savannah	70–70	.500
Jacksonville	65–77	.458
Columbus	63–78	.447

WESTERN DIVISION

Nashville	81–62	.566
Memphis	77–66	.538
Birmingham	71–70	.504
Chattanooga	67–75	.472
Knoxville	63–80	.441

1982

EASTERN DIVISION

Jacksonville	83–61	.576
Columbus	74–69	.517
Orlando	74–70	.514
Savannah	69–75	.479
Charlotte	66–77	.462

WESTERN DIVISION

Nashville	77–67	.535
Knoxville	73–71	.507
Memphis	70–74	.486
Birmingham	69–74	.483
Chattanooga	63–80	.441

1983

EASTERN DIVISION

Savannah	81–64	.559
Jacksonville	77–68	.531
Charlotte	69–77	.473
Columbus	64–79	.448
Orlando	62–83	.428

WESTERN DIVISION

Birmingham	91–54	.628
Nashville	88–58	.603
Chattanooga	68–75	.476
Knoxville	64–82	.438
Memphis	61–85	.418

1984

EASTERN DIVISION

Greenville	80–61	.567
Orlando	79–65	.549
Jacksonville	76–69	.524
Charlotte	75–72	.510
Columbus	69–71	.493

WESTERN DIVISION

Nashville	74–73	.503
Memphis	71–75	.486
Knoxville	70–75	.483
Birmingham	66–81	.449
Chattanooga	68–81	.439

1985

EASTERN DIVISION

Columbus	79–65	.549
Charlotte	78–65	.545
Jacksonville	73–70	.510
Orlando	72–71	.503
Greenville	70–74	.486

WESTERN DIVISION

Knoxville	79–64	.553
Huntsville	78–66	.542
Chattanooga	66–77	.462
Memphis	65–79	.451
Birmingham	57–86	.399

1986

EASTERN DIVISION

Jacksonville	75–68	.524
Greenville	73–71	.507
Columbus	70–70	.500
Charlotte	71–73	.493
Orlando	70–73	.490

WESTERN DIVISION

Huntsville	78–63	.553
Knoxville	74–70	.514
Birmingham	70–73	.490
Memphis	69–75	.479
Chattanooga	64–78	.451

1987

EASTERN DIVISION

Jacksonville	85–59	.590
Charlotte	85–60	.586
Greenville	70–74	.486
Columbus	67–76	.469
Orlando	61–82	.427

WESTERN DIVISION

Huntsville	74–70	.514
Memphis	72–71	.503
Chattanooga	68–75	.476
Birmingham	68–75	.476
Knoxville	68–76	.472

1988		
EASTERN DIVISION		
Greenville	87–57	.604
Jacksonville	69–73	.486
Columbus	69–74	.483
Charlotte	69–75	.479
Orlando	66–75	.468
WESTERN DIVISION		
Chattanooga	81–62	.566
Memphis	79–64	.552
Knoxville	75–69	.521
Birmingham	62–82	.431
Huntsville	59–85	.410

1989		
EASTERN DIVISION		
Orlando	79–65	,549
Greenville	70–69	.504
Columbus	71–72	.497
Charlotte	70–73	.490
Jacksonville	68–76	.472
WESTERN DIVISION		
Birmingham	88–55	.615
Huntsville	82–61	.573
Knoxville	67–76	.469
Chattanooga	58–81	.417
Memphis	59–84	.413

1990		
EASTERN DIVISION		
Orlando	85–59	.590
Jacksonville	84–60	.583
Columbus	67–66	.465
Charlotte	65–79	.451
Greenville	57–87	.396
WESTERN DIVISION		
Huntsville	79–65	.549
Birmingham	77–67	.535
Memphis	73–61	.507
Knoxville	66–77	.465
Chattanooga	66–78	.458

1991		
EASTERN DIVISION		
Greenville	88–56	.611
Orlando	77–67	.535
Jacksonville	74–69	.517
Charlotte	74–70	.514
Carolina	66–76	.465
WESTERN DIVISION		
Birmingham	77–66	.538
Chattanooga	73–71	.507
Knoxville	67–66	.465
Memphis	61–83	.424
Huntsville	61–83	.424

1992		
EASTERN DIVISION		
Greenville	100–42	.699
Charlotte	70–73	.490
Jacksonville	68–75	.476
Orlando	60–82	.423
Carolina	59–92	.361
WESTERN DIVISION		
Chattanooga	90–53	.629
Huntsville	81–63	.563
Memphis	71–73	.493
Birmingham	68–74	.479
Knoxville	56–88	.389

1993		
EASTERN DIVISION		
Greenville	75–67	.528
Carolina	74–67	.525
Orlando	71–70	.504
Knoxville	71–71	.500
Jacksonville	59–81	.421
WESTERN DIVISION		
Birmingham	78–64	.549
Chattanooga	72–69	.511
Nashville	72–70	.507
Huntsville	71–70	.504
Memphis	63–77	.450

PLAYOFF RESULTS

1972	Montgomery defeated Asheville 3 games to 0.
1973	Montgomery defeated Jacksonville 3 games to 1.
1974	Knoxville defeated Jacksonville 3 games to 2.
1975	Montgomery defeated Orlando 3 games to 0.

1976 Orlando defeated Charlotte 1 game to 0. Montgomery defeated Chattanooga 1 games to 0. **FINALS:** Montgomery defeated Orlando 3 games to 0.

1977 Jacksonville defeated Savannah 2 games to 1. **FINALS:** Montgomery defeated Jacksonville 2 games to 0.

1978 Savannah defeated Orlando 2 games to 0. **FINALS:** Knoxville defeated Savannah 2 games to 1.

1979 Columbus defeated Charlotte 2 games to 0. Nashville defeated Memphis 2 games to 1. **FINALS:** Nashville defeated Columbus 3 games to 1.

1980 Charlotte defeated Savannah 3 games to 0. Memphis defeated Nashville 3 games to 1. **FINALS:** Charlotte defeated Memphis 3 games to 1.

1981 Orlando defeated Savannah 3 games to 1. Nashville defeated Memphis 3 games to 0. **FINALS:** Orlando defeated Nashville 3 games to 1.

1982 Jacksonville defeated Columbus 3 games to 1. Nashville defeated Knoxville 3 games to 1. **FINALS:** Nashville defeated Jacksonville 3 games to 1.

1983 Jacksonville defeated Savannah 3 games to 1. Birmingham defeated Nashville 3 games to 2. **FINALS:** Birmingham defeated Jacksonville 3 games to 1.

1984 Charlotte defeated Greenville 3 games to 1. Knoxville defeated Nashville 3 games to 1. **FINALS:** Charlotte defeated Knoxville 3 games to 0.

1985 Charlotte defeated Columbus 3 games to 1. Huntsville defeated Knoxville 3 games to 1. **FINALS:** Huntsville defeated Charlotte 3 games to 2.

1986 Columbus defeated Jacksonville 3 games to 1. Huntsville defeated Knoxville 3 games to 1. **FINALS:** Columbus defeated Huntsville 3 games to 1.

1987 Birmingham defeated Huntsville 3 games to 0. Charlotte defeated Jacksonville 3 games to 2. **FINALS:** Birmingham defeated Charlotte 3 games to 1.

1988 Chattanooga defeated Memphis 3 games to 1. Greenville defeated Jacksonville 3 games to 2. **FINALS:** Chattanooga defeated Greenville 3 games to 0.

1989 Birmingham defeated Huntsville 3 games to 1. Greenville defeated Orlando 3 games to 1. **FINALS:** Birmingham defeated Greenville 3 games to 0.

1990 Memphis defeated Birmingham 3 games to 1. Orlando defeated Jacksonville 3 games to 1. **FINALS:** Memphis defeated Orlando 3 games to 2.

1991 Birmingham defeated Knoxville 3 games to 0. Orlando defeated Greenville 3 games to 0. **FINALS:** Orlando defeated Birmingham 3 games to 1.

1992 Greenville defeated Charlotte 3 games to 0. Chattanooga defeated Huntsville 3 games to 1. **FINALS:** Greenville defeated Chattanooga 3 games to 2.

1993 Birmingham defeated Nashville 3 games to 0. Knoxville defeated Greenville 3 games to 2. **FINALS:** Birmingham defeated Knoxville 3 games to 1.

PRESIDENTS OF THE SOUTHERN LEAGUE

1964–71	Sam Smith
1971–78	Billy Hitchcock
1979–94	Jimmy Bragan

SL BATTING CHAMPIONS

1964	Len Boehmer, Macon	.329	1979	Joe Charboneau, Chatt.	.352
1965	Gerald Reimer, Knox.	.310	1980	Chris Bando, Chatt.	.349
1966	John Fenderson, Knox.	.324	1981	Kevin Rhomberg, Chatt.	.366
1967	Minnie Mendoza, Char.	.297	1982	Ken Baker, Birm.	.342
1968	Arlie Burge, Ash.	.317	1983	Ivan Calderson, Chatt.	.311
1969	Donnie Anderson, Ash.	.324	1984	Frank Estes, Grnv.	.341
1970	Steve Brye, Char.	.307	1985	Bruce Fields, Birm.	.323
1971	Minnie Mendoza, Char.	.316	1986	Brick Smith, Chatt.	.344
1972	Mike Reinbach, Ash.	.346	1987	David Myers, Chatt.	.328
1973	Bob Andrews, Ash.	.309	1988	Butch Davis, Char.	.301
1974	Nyls Nyman, Knox.	.325	1989	Scott Leius, Orl.	.303
1975	Charles Heil, Ash.	.322	1990	Adam Casillas, Chatt.	.336
1976	Larry Foster, Knox.	.311	1991	James Bowie, Jax	.310
1977	Mark Corey, Char.	.310	1992	Scott Pose, Chatt.	.342
1978	Joe Gates, Knox.	.332	1993	Jim Bowie, Hunt.	.333

SL HOME RUN CHAMPIONS

1964	Dick Kenworthy, Lyn.	29	1978	Eddie Gates, Mem.	25
1965	Orlando McFarlane, Ash.	22	1979	Alan Knicely, Cbus.	33
1966	Bob Robertson, Ash.	32	1980	Steve Balboni, Nash.	34
1967	Rogelio Alvarez, Ev.	19	1981	Tim Launder, Orl.	42
	Craig Nettles, Char.	19	1982	Michael Fuentes, Mem.	37
1968	Wayne Redmon, Mtgy.	26	1983	Glenn Davis, Cbus.	25
1969	Robert Brooks, Birm.	23		Larry Sheets, Char.	25
1970	James Covington, Jax	21	1984	Dan Pasqua, Nash.	33
1971	Ken Hottman, Ash.	37	1985	Mark Funderburk, Orl.	34
1972	Mike Reinbach, Ash.	30	1986	Glenallen Hill, Knox.	31
1973	Terry Clapp, Ash.	35	1987	Rondal Rollin, Birm.	39
1974	Bob Gorinski, Orl.	23	1988	Matt Winters, Mem.	25
	Mike Poepping, Orl.	23	1989	Eric Anthony, Cbus.	28
1975	Jim Obradovich, Orl.	27	1990	Terrell Hansen, Jax	24
1976	Jim Obradovich, Orl.	21		Luis Gonzales, Cbus.	24
1977	Tom Chism, Char.	17	1991	Elvin Paulino, Char.	24
	Alfredo Javier, Cbus.	17	1992	Tim Costo, Chatt.	28
	Charles Keller, Sav.	17	1993	Carlos Delgado, Knox.	25

SL RBI LEADERS

1964	Lee May, Macon	110	1968	Barry Morgan, Mtgy.	91
1965	Charles Leonard, Ash.	78	1969	Donnie Anderson, Ash.	100
1966	Bob Robertson, Ash.	99	1970	James Clark, Birm.	73
1967	Barry Morgan, Mtgy.	87		Reggie Sanders, Birm.	73

1971	Ken Hottman, Ash.	116	1983	Miguel Sosa, Sav.	93
1972	Mike Reinbach, Ash.	109	1984	Stan Holmes, Orl.	101
1973	Terry Clapp, Ash.	98	1985	Mark Funderburk, Orl.	116
1974	Bob Gorinski, Orl.	100	1986	Terry Steinbach, Hunt.	132
1975	Jim Obradovich, Orl.	74	1987	Tom Dodd, Char.	127
1976	Jim Obradovich, Orl.	68	1988	Matt Winters, Mem.	91
1977	Charles Keller, Sav.	86	1989	Paul Sorrento, Orl.	112
1978	Sal Rende, Chatt.	87	1990	Matt Stark, Birm.	109
1979	Dave Hostetler, Mem.	114	1991	Elvin Paulino, Char.	81
1980	Steve Balboni, Nash.	122	1992	Scott Cepicky, Birm.	87
1981	Larry Ray, Cbus.	107	1993	Carlos Delgado, Knox.	102
1982	Mike Fuentes, Mem.	115			

SL STOLEN BASE LEADERS

1964	George Spriggs, Ash.	33	1979	LaMart Harris, Jax	68
1965	Wayne Comer, Mtgy.	31	1980	Anthony Johnson, Mem.	60
1966	Sam Thompson, Knox.	60	1981	Kevin Rhomberg, Chatt.	74
1967	Angel Bravo, Evans.	24	1982	Milt Thompson, Sav.	68
1968	Allan Lewis, Birm.	37	1983	Mike Cole, Sav.	75
1969	Tom Simon, Sav.	24	1984	Donell Nixon, Chatt.	102
1970	Hagan Anderson, Mtgy.	24	1985	Alex Marte, Orl.	64
1971	John Gamble, Mtgy.	38	1986	Gerald Young, Cbus.	54
1972	Rod Gilbreath, Sav.	45	1987	Bernie Tatis, Knox.	55
1973	Alberto Leaver, Cbus.	54	1988	Jeff Huson, Jax	56
1974	Kenzie Davis, Jax	38	1989	Charles Penigar, Birm.	64
1975	Sheldon Mallory, Jax	42	1990	Paul Rodgers, Knox.	41
1976	Derek Bryant, Chatt.	42	1991	Shawn Gilbert, Orl.	43
	Roger Cador, Sav.	42	1992	Ellerton Maynard, Jax	38
1977	Jeff Cox, Chatt.	68	1993	Brandon Wilson, Birm.	43
1978	LaMart Harris, Mem.	45			

SL PITCHERS — MOST VICTORIES —

1964	Manly Johnston, Lyn.	20	1976	David Ford, Mem.	17
1965	Tom Frondorf, Knox.	16	1977	Bryn Smith, Mem.	15
	Milt Osteen, Knox.	16	1978	Terry Sheehan, Orl.	17
1966	Bill Edgerton, Mob.	17	1979	Del Leatherwood, Cbus.	15
1967	Dick Drago, Mtgy.	15	1980	James MacDonald, Cbus.	17
1968	Grover Powell, Ash.	16	1981	Craig McMurtry, Sav.	15
1969	Bill Zepp, Char.	15	1982	Clay Christiansen, Nash.	16
1970	Ken Forsch, Cbus.	13		Stefan Wever, Nash.	16
1971	Jim MacDonnell, Ash.	17	1983	Don Heinkel, Birm.	19
	Dick Rusteck, Char.	17	1984	Bryan Oelkers, Orl.	16
1972	Paul Mitchell, Ash.	16		Ken Dixon, Char.	16
1973	Joe Henderson, Knox.	17	1985	Steven Davis, Knox.	17
1974	Domingo Figueroa, Sav.	15	1986	Anthony Kelley, Cbus.	14
1975	Ken Kravec, Knox.	14	1987	John Trautwein, Jax	15
	Bob Maneely, Orl.	14	1988	Chris Hammond, Chatt.	16
	Bob Sykes, Mtgy.	14	1989	Laddie Renfroe, Char.	19

1990	Doug Simons, Orl.	15		Pat Bronswell, Hunt.	13
1991	Napoleon Robinson, Grnv.	16		Steve Trachsel, Char.	13
1992	Mike Anderson, Chatt.	13	1993	Huck Flener, Knox.	13
	Nathan Minchey, Grnv.	13		Mike Ferry, Chatt.	13

SL PITCHERS — WINNING PERCENTAGE —

1964	Manley Johnston, Lyn.	20–7	.741
1965	Fred Fisher, Mtgy.	14–6	.700
1966	Bill Edgerton, Mobile	17–5	.810
1967	George Lazerique, Birm.	13–4	.765
1968	Jose Paredos, Char.	12–3	.800
1969	John Gregory, Mtgy.	11–2	.846
1970	Lerrin LaGrow, Mtgy.	11–4	.733
1971	Dennis O'Toole, Ash.	13–3	.813
1973	Joe Henderson, Knox.	17–4	.810
1974	Domingo Figueroa, Sav.	15–4	.789
1975	Jack Kucek, Knox.	10–4	.714
1976	Dennis DeBarr, Mtgy.	11–2	.846
1977	Gary Christenson, Mtgy.	13–4	.765
1978	Terry Sheehan, Orl.	17–8	.680
1979	Gregory Hughes, Nash.	11–4	.733
1980	Larry Pashnick, Mtgy.	13–4	.765
1981	Bob Tenenini, Mem.	10–2	.833
	Pete Filson, Nash.	10–2	.833
1982	Mark Brown, Char.	8–2	.800
1983	Keith Comstock, Birm.	12–3	.800
	Tom Waddell, Sav.	8–2	.800
1984	Les Strode, Mem.	9–2	.818
1985	Mike Skinner, Char.	11–1	.917
1986	Mike Campbell, Chatt.	9–1	.900
1987	Jeff Bettendorf, Birm.	9–1	.900
1989	Lee Upshaw, Grnv.	8–2	.800
1990	Dan Eskew, Hunt.	14–3	.824
1991	Turk Wendell, Grnv.	11–3	.786
1992	Andy Nezelek, Grnv.	9–2	.818
1993	Oscar Munoz, Nash.	11–4	.733

SL PITCHERS — MOST STRIKEOUTS —

1964	David Galligan, Mac.	168	1973	Doug Konieczny, Cbus.	222
1965	Luke Walker, Ash.	197	1974	Mike Stanton, Cbus.	146
1966	George Korince, Mtgy.	183	1975	Joe Sambito, Cbus.	140
1967	Dick Drago, Mtgy.	134	1976	David Ford, Char.	121
1968	George Korince, Mtgy.	146	1977	Matt Keough, Chatt.	153
1969	Paul Coleman, Mtgy.	153	1978	Jay Howell, Nash.	173
1970	Bill Gilbreth, Mtgy.	192	1979	Robert Veselic, Orl.	151
1971	Chris Floethe, Birm.	225	1980	Steve Bedrosian, Sav.	161
1972	Bill Campbell, Char.	204	1981	Jamie Werly, Nash.	193

1982	Stefan Wever, Nash.	191	1988	Alex Sanchez, Knox.	166
1983	Mark Gubieza, Jax	146	1989	Shawn Boskie, Char.	164
1984	Ken Dixon, Char.	211	1990	Brian Barnes, Jax	213
1985	Scott Bankhead, Mem.	128	1991	Mike Trombley, Orl.	175
	John Hoover, Char.	128	1992	James Converse, Jax	157
1986	Terry Taylor, Chatt.	164	1993	Scott Ruffcorn, Birm.	141
1987	Randy Johnson, Jax	163			

SL PITCHERS — LOWEST EARNED RUN AVERAGE —

1964	Manley Johnston, Lyn.	2.46	1979	Scott Brown, Nash.	2.40
1965	Luke Walker, Ash.	2.26	1980	Andy McGaffigan, Nash.	2.38
1966	Dave Roberts, Ash.	2.61	1981	Mark Ross, Cbus.	2.25
1967	George Lauzerique, Birm.	2.29	1982	Stefan Wever, Nash.	2.78
	Dan Lazar, Evan.	2.29	1983	Roger Mason, Birm.	2.08
1968	Grover Powell, Ash.	2.54	1984	Mark Williams, Jax	2.49
1969	LaDon Boyd, Birm.	2.19	1985	Steve Davis, Knox.	2.45
1970	David Hartman, Jax	2.01	1986	Eric Bell, Char.	3.05
1971	Dick Rusteck, Char.	2.40	1987	Brian Holman, Jax	2.50
1972	Danny Vossler, Char.	2.11	1988	Chris Hammond, Chatt.	1.72
1973	Russ Rothermel, Cbus.	1.81	1989	Pete Delkus, Orl.	1.87
1974	Mike Beard, Sav.	2.40	1990	Jeff Carter, Jax	1.84
1975	Don Larson, Cbus.	2.18	1991	Pat Mahomes, Orl.	1.78
1976	Dave Rozema, Mtgy.	1.57	1992	Larry Thomas, Birm.	1.94
1977	Sam Stewart, Char.	2.08	1993	James Baldwin, Birm.	2.25
1978	Roger Alexander, Sav.	1.84			

SL MOST VALUABLE PLAYERS

1972	Mike Reinbach, OF, Ash.	1983	John Morris, OF, Jax
1973	Jayson Moxey, OF, Cbus.	1984	Andres Galarraga, 1B, Jax
1974	Nyls Nyman, 1B, Knox.	1985	Jose Canseco, OF, Hunt.
1975	Mike Squires, 1B, Knox.	1986	Terry Steinbach, C, Hunt.
1976	Larry Foster, OF, Knox.	1987	Tom Dodd, DH, Char.
1977	Alan Trammell, SS, Knox.	1988	Matt Winters, OF, Mem.
1978	Eddie Gates, 2B, Mem.	1989	Eric Anthony, OF, Cbus.
1979	Dan Heep, OF, Cbus.	1990	Jeff Conine, 1B, Mem.
	Alan Knicely, C, Cbus.	1991	Ryan Klesko, 1B, Grnv.
1980	Steve Balboni, 1B, Nash.	1992	Javy Lopez, C, Grnv.
1981	Tim Laudner, C, Orl.	1993	Carlos Delgado, C, Knox.
1982	Brian, Dayett, OF-3B, Nash.		

SL SEASON RECORDS
BEST INDIVIDUAL BATTING RECORDS

Average	Kevin Rhomberg (Chattanooga, 1981)	.366
Games	Doug Baker (Birmingham, 1983)	146
	Jesus Alfaro (Charlotte, 1984)	146
At-Bats	Stan Younger (Birmingham, 1981)	588
Runs	Mike Reinbach (Asheville, 1972)	123

Hits	Kevin Rhomberg (Chattanooga, 1981)	187
Doubles	Ron Johnson (Jacksonville, 1980)	40
Triples	Alan Trammel (Montgmoery, 1977)	19
Home Runs	Tim Laudner (Orlando, 1981)	42
Extra Base Hits	Geronimo Berroa (Knoxville, 1987)	
	33 2Bs, 3 3Bs, 36 HRs	72
RBIs	Terry Steinbach (Huntsville, 1986)	132
Stolen Bases	Donell Nixon (Chattanooga, 1984)	102
Walks	Gary Jones (Huntsville, 1986)	128
Strikeouts	Rondal Rollin (Birmingham, 1987)	218
HBP	Rusty Crockett (Charlotte, 1990)	32
Hitting Streak (Games)	Greg Tubbs (Greenville, 1987)	33

BEST INDIVIDUAL PITCHING RECORDS

Games	Laddie Renfro (Charlotte, 1989)	78
Complete Games	Ken Dixon (Charlotte, 1984)	20
Victories	Manley Johnston (Lynchburg, 1964)	20
Losses	Kent Bottenfield (Jacksonville, 1989)	17
Winning Pcg.	Mike Skinner (Charlotte, 1985, 11–1)	.917
Lowest ERA	David Rozema (Montgomery, 1976)	1.57
Most Innings	Ken Dixon (Charlotte, 1984)	240
Consecutive Wins	Bill Edgerton (Mobile, 1966)	12
	Bill Zepp (Charlotte, 1969)	12
Shutouts	Charles Swanson (Montgomery, 1973)	6
	George Cappuzzello (Montgomery, 1980)	6
Strikeouts	Chris Floethe (Birmingham, 1971)	225
Walks	Scott Elam (Knoxville, 1982)	146

SOUTHERN LEAGUE CENTURY CLUB
1981   Greenville   100–43

SOUTHERN HALL OF FAMERS

Members of the Hall of Fame who have played, managed or umpired in the Original Southern League (OSL), the Southern Association (SA), or the Sally (SALLY), or the modern Southern League (SL).

Hank Aaron (Jacksonville, SALLY, 1953)
Walt Alston (Columbus, SALLY, 1939)
Luis Aparicio (Memphis, SA, 1955)
Luke Appling (Atlanta, SA, 1930; mgr. — Memphis, SA, 1951–53, 1959)
Chief Bender (Mgr. — Savannah, SALLY, 1946)
Fred Clarke (Montgomery, OSL, 1983–94)
Ty Cobb (Augusta, SALLY, 1904–5)
Kiki Cuyler (Charleston, SALLY, 1922; Nashville, SA, 1923; mgr. — Chattanooga, SA, 1939–41; Atlanta, SA, 1945–48)
Bill Dickey (Little Rock, SA 1925–26, 1928, player-mgr. — 1947)
Bob Gibson (Columbus, SALLY, 1957)

Goose Goslin (Columbia, SALLY, 1920–21)
Burleigh Grimes (Chattanooga, SA, 1913–14; Birmingham, SA, 1914–16)
Rogers Hornsby (Chattanooga, SA, 1939)
Waite Hoyt (Memphis, SA, 1917; Nashville, SA, 1918)
Cal Hubbard (Umpire — SALLY, 1930)
Joe Jackson (Savannah, SALLY, 1909; New Orleans, SA, 1910)
Travis Jackson (Little Rock, SA, 1921–22)
Fergie Jenkins (Chattanooga, SL, 1964)
Harmon Killibrew (Charlotte, SALLY, 1956; Chattanooga, SA, 1957–58)
Bob Lemon (New Orleans, SA, 1939)
Al Lopez (Macon, SALLY, 1928; Atlanta, SA, 1929)
Eddie Mathews (Atlanta, SA, 1950–51)
Joe McGinnity (Montgomery, OSL, 1893)
Kid Nichols (Memphis, OSL, 1888)
Frank Robinson (Columbia, SALLY, 1954–55)
Joe Sewell (New Orleans, SA, 1920)
Enos Slaughter (Columbus, SALLY, 1936)
Tris Speaker (Little Rock, SA, 1908)
Willie Stargell (Asheville, SALLY, 1961)
Casey Stengel (Montgomery, SA, 1912)
Pie Traynor (Birmingham, SA, 1921)
Dazzy Vance (Memphis, SA, 1917–18)
Lloyd Waner (Columbia, SALLY, 1926)
Hoyt Wilhelm (Jacksonville, SALLY, 1948–49; pitching coach — Nashville, SL, 1982–84)

Bibliography

Guides

The library of the Baseball Hall of Fame in Cooperstown supplied photocopied sections from the annual baseball guides which provide information essential to a project of this nature. In chronological order, the guides studied were :

Spalding's Official Base Ball Guide (1885–1886, 1889, 1905–1906, 1924–1940).
Reach's American Association Base Ball Guide (1887–1888).
Reach's Official Base Ball Guide (1892–1896).
Reach's Official American League Guide (1904).
The Reach Official American League Guide (1907–1923).
Official Baseball Record Book (1941).
Baseball Guide and Record Book (1942–1961).
Official Baseball Guide (1962–1992).

Books

Aaron, Henry, with Lonnie Wheeler. *I Had a Hammer, The Hank Aaron Story*. New York: HarperPaperbacks, 1991.

Alexander, Charles C. *Ty Cobb*. New York: Oxford University Press, 1985.

Allen, Maury. *You Could Look It Up, The Life of Casey Stengel*. New York: Times Books, 1979.

Bacon, Eve. *Orlando, A Centennial History*. 2 Vols. Chuluota, Florida: The Mickler House, Publishers, 1975.

Bailey, Jim. *Arkansas Travelers, 79 Years of Baseball*. Little Rock: Arkansas Travelers Baseball Club, Inc., [1980].

Barnes, Frank. *The Greenville Story*. n. p., 1956.

Benson, Michael. *Ballparks of North America. A Comprehensive Historical Reference of Baseball Grounds, Yards and Stadiums, 1845 to Present*. Jefferson, North Carolina: McFarland & Company, Inc., 1989.

Carter, Craig, ed. *Daguerreotypes*. 8th Edition. St. Louis: The Sporting News Publishing Co., 1990.

Cobb, Ty, with Al Stump. *My Life In Baseball, The True Record*. Lincoln: University of Nebraska Press, 1961.

Constitution of the Southern League of Professional Baseball Clubs. 1992.

Creamer, Robert W. *Stengel, His Life and Times*. New York: Dell Publishing Co., Inc., 1984.

Darby, Cecil, ed. *The South Atlantic League DOPE BOOK for 1948.* N. p.: South Atlantic League Dope Book, 1948.
———. *The South Atlantic League DOPE BOOK for 1949.* N. p., 1949.
———. *The South Atlantic League DOPE BOOK for 1951.* N. p., 1951.
Dolson, Frank. *Beating the Bushes, Life in the Minor Leagues.* South Bend, Indiana: Icarus Press, 1982.
Durso, Joseph. *Casey, The Life and Legend of Charles Dillon Stengel.* Englewood Cliffs, New Jersey: Prentice-Hall, Inc., 1967.
Egerton, John. *Nashville, The Faces of Two Centuries, 1780–1980.* Nashville: PlusMedia Incorporated, 1979.
Evans, Billy, ed. *Southern Association Baseball Records From 1901 to 1943 Inclusive.* N. p., 1944.
Fidrych, Mark, and Tom Clark. *No Big Deal.* Philadelphia and New York: J. B. Lippincott Company, 1977.
Fifty Years with the Chicks, 1901–1950. N. p., 1951.
Filichia, Peter. *Professional Baseball Franchises.* New York: Facts On File, Inc., 1993.
Finch, Robert L., L. H. Addington, and Ben Morgan, eds. *The Story of Minor League Baseball.* Columbus, Ohio: The Stoneman Press, 1953.
Flynt, Wayne. *Montgomery, An Illustrated History.* Woodland Hills, California: Windsor Publications, Inc., 1980.
Friddle, Linda, *Famous Greenville Firsts.* Greenville, S.C.: The Metropolitan Arts Council, 1986.
Friend, J. P. *Cotton States League, Golden Anniversary, 1902–1951.* N. p., 1951.
———. *Record Makers of the South Atlantic League, 1904–1960.* Blytheville, Ark.: Friend News Service, 1960.
Frommer, Harvey. *Primitive Baseball, The First Quarter-Century of the National Pastime.* New York: Atheneum, 1988.
———. *Shoeless Joe and Ragtime Baseball.* Dallas: Taylor Publishing Company, 1992.
Gammon, Wirt. *Your Chattanooga Lookouts Since 1885.* Chattanooga: Chattanooga Publishing Company, 1955.
Goldstein, Richard. *Spartan Seasons – How Baseball Survived the Second World War.* New York: Macmillan Publishing Co., Inc., 1980.
Guinozzo, John. *Memphis Baseball.* N. p., 1980.
Hagemann, Bob. *Memphis Chicks, 1901–60, 1978.* Memphis: Memphis Chicks, 1978.
Henley, John C., Jr. *This Is Birmingham.* Birmingham, Alabama: Southern University Press, 1960.
A History of Montgomery in Pictures. Montgomery, Alabama: Society of Pioneers of Montgomery, 1978.
Hornsby, Rogers, and Bill Surface. *My War With Baseball.* New York: Coward-McCann, Inc., 1962.
Hurth, Charles A. *Baseball Records, The Southern Association, 1901–1947.* New Orleans: Published by The Southern Association, 1947.
Jackson, Bo, and Dick Schapp. *Bo Knows Bo.* New York: Jove Books, 1990.
James, Bill. *The Bill James Historical Abstract.* New York: Villard Books, 1986.
Johnson, Lloyd, and Miles Wolff, eds. *The Encyclopedia of Minor League Baseball.* Durham, N. C.: Baseball America, Inc., 1993.

Kyle, F. Clason. *Images: A Pictorial History of Columbus, Georgia.* Norfolk/Virginia Beach, Virginia: The Donnings Company/ Publishers, 1986.
Lowry, Philip J. *Green Cathedrals.* Reading, Massachusetts: Addison-Wesley Publishing Co., Inc., 1992.
MacLean, Norman, ed. *Who's Who In Baseball 1989.* New York: Who's Who In Baseball Magazine Co., Inc., 1989.
McMillan, Malcolm C. *Yesterday's Birmingham.* Miami, Florida: E. A. Seemann Publishing, Inc., 1975.
McRaven, Henry. *Nashville, "Athens of the South."* Chapel Hill: Scheer & Jervis, 1949.
Obojski, Robert. *Bush League, A History of Minor League Baseball.* New York: Macmillan Publishing Co., Inc., 1975.
Reichler, Joseph L. *The Baseball Encyclopedia.* New York: Macmillan Publishing Co., Inc., 1979.
Reidenbaugh, Lowell. *Take Me Out to the Ball Park.* St. Louis: The Sporting News Publishing Co., 1983.
Rogosin, Donn. *Invisible Men, Life in Baseball's Negro Leagues.* New York: Atheneum, 1985.
Ryan, Bob. *Wait Till I Make the Show, Baseball in the Minor Leagues.* Boston: Little, Brown and Company, 1974.
Society for American Baseball Research. *Minor League Baseball Stars.* Vol. I. Manhattan, Kansas: Ag Press, Inc., 1984.
Society for American Baseball Research. *Minor League Baseball Stars.* Vol. II. Manhattan, Kansas: Ag Press, Inc., 1985.
Society for American Baseball Research. *Minor League Baseball Stars.* Vol. III. Birmingham: EBSCO Media, 1992.
Somers, Dale A. *The Rise of Sports in New Orleans, 1850–1900.* Baton Rouge: Louisiana State University Press, 1972.
The Southern League of Professional Baseball Clubs, 1973 Press, Radio and T. V. Guide. Opelika, Alabama: Published by The Southern League, 1973.
Southern League Records Book. Chicago: Compiled and edited for the Southern League by the Howe News Bureau, 1973.
Terrell, Bob. *McCormick Field, Home of Reality.* Asheville, N. C.: Bob Terrell Publisher, 1991.
Tomlinson, Gerald. *The Baseball Research Handbook.* Kansas City: Society for American Baseball Research, 1988.
Turkin, Hy, and S. C. Thompson. *The Official Encyclopedia of Baseball.* New York: A. S. Barnes and Company, 1956.

Game Programs

A great deal of information about the backgrounds of specific professional baseball clubs and their ballparks may be found in game programs. Modern game programs frequently are in magazine format and contain historical articles and statistical information. Publications that I found to be of interest and use included:

Asheville Tourists Official Game Program. 1992.
Birmingham Barons Souvenir Program. 1992.

Carolina Mudcats Souvenir Yearbook. 1991, 1992, 1993.
Catch the Rising Huntsville Stars. 1992.
Chattanooga Lookouts Media Guide. 1992.
Columbus RedStixx Souvenir Program. 1993.
First Pitch, Official Magazine of the Charlotte Knights. 1992.
Greenville Braves Official Magazine and Yearbook. 1992.
Heatin' Up the Summer, The Official Yearbook of the Knoxville Blue Jays. 1992.
Huntsvillle Stars Official Souvenir Program. 1989.
Jacksonville Suns Souvenir Program. 1993.
Lynchburg Red Sox Official Souvenir Program. 1990.
Memphis Chicks Official Souvenir Program. 1992.
Nashville Sounds Official Souvenir Program. 1989.
Orlando Cubs Souvenir Program. 1993.
Savannah Cardinals Official Souvenir Program. 1992.

Articles

Kavanaugh, Jack. "Joe Charboneau: Far-Out Phenom." *The Baseball Research Journal* (Vol. 18, 1989), 9–10.
Hendrickson, Robert. "How Pete Gray Defied the Odds." *Baseball Digest* (May 1971), 226–228.
Lamb, David. "A Season in the Minors." *National Geographic* (April 1991), 40–73.
Nightingale, Dave. "The Major Minor League." *The Sporting News* (August 9, 1993), 22–23.
"Southern Bases." Narrated by Ernie Harwell. Atlanta Public Television, 1992.
"Southern Digs In for New Season of AA Ball." *Shreveport Magazine* (April 1961), 20–21.

Newspapers

Atlanta *Constitution* (1962–66)
Baseball America (1991–93)
Charlotte *News* (1985)
Charlotte *Observer* (1932, 1940, 1969, 1974, 1976, 1987)
Chattanooga *News-Free Press* (1962, 1965, 1966, 1972)
Columbus *Ledger-Enquirer* (1989, 1990)
Greenville *News-Piedmont* (1947, 1972, 1976, 1983, 1984)
Macon *Daily Telegraph* (1885, 1886, 1892, 1893, 1898, 1919, 1923)
Memphis *Commercial Appeal* (1935, 1939, 1940, 1941, 1950, 1973, 1974, 1975, 1976, 1977)
Nashville *Banner* (1867, 1967, 1970, 1971, 1978)
Orlando *Morning Sentinel* (1920, 1923, 1932, 1934, 1937, 1940, 1956, 1960, 1963)
Savannah *Morning News* (1938, 1940, 1957, 1960, 1970)

Local Baseball Files

Atlanta-Fulton County Library
Chattanooga-Hamilton County Bicentennial Library
East Tennessee Historical Collections, Knoxville

Greenville County Public Library
Huntsville Public Library
McGee Public Library, Knoxville
Memphis Public Library
Nashville Room, The Public Library of Nashville and Davidson County
Orlando Public Library
Public Library of Charlotte and Mecklenberg County
Savannah Public Library
Shreveport Public Library
W. C. Bradley Memorial Library, Columbus
Washington Memorial Library, Macon

Index